INFAMOUS COMMERCE

Infamous Commerce

Prostitution in Eighteenth-Century British Literature and Culture

LAURA J. ROSENTHAL

Cornell University Press

Ithaca and London

First published 2006 by Cornell University Press

Printed in the United States of America

Library of Congress Cataloging-in-Publication Data

Rosenthal, Laura J. (Laura Jean), 1960–
    Infamous commerce : prostitution in eighteenth-century British literature and culture / Laura J. Rosenthal.
        p.   cm.
    Includes bibliographical references and index.
    ISBN-13: 978-0-8014-4404-3 (cloth : alk. paper)
    ISBN-10: 0-8014-4404-7 (cloth : alk. paper)
    1. English literature—18th century—History and criticism.
2. Prostitution in literature.   3. Prostitution—Great Britain—History—18th century.   I. Title.
    PR448.P73R67   2006
    820.9′3552—dc22   2006001753

Cornell University Press strives to use environmentally responsible suppliers and materials to the fullest extent possible in the publishing of its books. Such materials include vegetable-based, low-VOC inks and acid-free papers that are recycled, totally chlorine-free, or partly composed of nonwood fibers. For further information, visit our website at www.cornellpress.cornell.edu.

Cloth printing   10 9 8 7 6 5 4 3 2 1

This book is dedicated to Russ, Sophie, and Victor
And to my parents, Bernard and Evelyn Rosenthal

Contents

Acknowledgments

My debts accumulated during this project are many. I would like first to thank the press readers Kathy Temple and Jean Marsden, whose combination of attention, rigor, and generosity made this project better than it would have been otherwise. I am also grateful for having been able to work once again with executive editor Bernard Kendler, as well as with acquisitions editor Peter Wissoker. I would like to thank the library personnel at the University of Maryland, Florida State University, the Newberry Library, the Huntington Library, the Folger Shakespeare Library, the Library of Congress, the New York Public Library, the Houghton Library, and the British Library. The opportunity to pursue my research in these libraries and the generosity of these institutions made this project not only possible but often delightful. This project has benefited from indispensable support in the form of research grants from Florida State University, the National Endowment for the Humanities, and the Newberry/British Academy Award for Research in Great Britain. The University of Maryland allowed me crucial release time in the first year of my new position. Many valued colleagues have offered various forms of encouragement, help, and guidance over the duration of this project, including in particular Helen Burke, Jim O'Rourke, Ralph Berry, Rip Lhamon, Vin Carretta, Helen Deutsch, Alison Conway, James Turner, Bob Markley, Paula McDowell, Charlotte Sussman, Tita Chico, Helen Thompson, Barbara Benedict, Greg Clingham, John Stevenson, David Mazella, Mita Choudhury, Kristina Straub, Danny O'Quinn, Ruth Perry, Bill Warner and the late, much-missed Doug Canfield. Special thanks go to Lisa Freeman, who helped me work through the introduction and many other aspects of this project, and to Donna Heiland and Bernard Rosenthal (my father), both of whom read the entire manuscript with care and insight. Jennifer Hobgood proved a tireless and sensitive research assistant in the early stages of this project; Megan Campbell and Michael Lukas contributed their talents in later stages. This work has also benefited greatly from many opportunities for presentation, discussion, and feedback at the Modern Language Association (MLA), the American Society for Eighteenth-Century Studies (ASECS), and the Group for Early Modern Cultural Studies (GEMCS), for which I am grateful. I would also like to thank Felicity Nussbaum for the opportunity to present an early version of chapter 7 at "The Global Eighteenth Century" conference at UCLA, Margaret Ferguson and Nancy Wright for the opportunity to contribute an essay related to this project (on Sally Salisbury) to their volume *Women, Property, and the Letters of the Law in Early Modern England* (Toronto: University of Toronto Press, 2004), and Bucknell University Press for permission to publish a revised version of my essay "Infamous Commerce: Transracial Prostitution in the South Seas and Back" from Laura J. Rosenthal and Mita Choudhury, eds., *Monstrous Dreams of Reason: Body, Self and Other in the Enlightenment* (2002) as chapter 7 here. I am grateful to the New York Public Library for permission to reproduce *The Double Disappointment* (1774) and to the British Museum for permission to reproduce Plate 1 of *A Harlot's Progress* (1732).

My deepest gratitude, however, goes to my family for providing patience, love, support, and pleasing distraction: my husband, Russell Mardon, my daughter, Sophie Miranda Rosenthal, and my son, Victor Joseph Mardon.

INFAMOUS COMMERCE

Introduction

> The Word *Prostitute* does not always mean a W—; but is used
> also, to signify any Person that does any Thing for *Hire*.
>   Tristram Shandy [pseud], *Miss C—y's Cabinet of Curiosities*

Pursued by the businessman-criminal Peachum for his neck, Captain Macheath in *The Beggar's Opera* (1728) takes refuge with his whores. Women seem unable to resist Macheath, and these ladies welcome their patron as warmly as do his lovers Polly and Lucy in other scenes. One, however, stands apart: As she sidles up to the Captain, flirtatiously pulls out his pistols, and draws him toward her by the neck for a kiss, Jenny Diver signals to Peachum and the constables to capture their disarmed quarry. Her betrayal surprises even the other prostitutes, who nevertheless had previously recognized Jenny as different: "though her fellow be never so agreeable," Mrs. Coaxer comments, "she can pick his pocket as coolly as if money were her only pleasure. Now that is a command of the passions uncommon in a woman!"[1] Even in the presence of the dashing Macheath, Jenny Diver possesses the unusual capacity to choose calculated profit over immediate pleasure.

This scene represents two different models of prostitution: a more common one in which women find themselves in the trade because they cannot resist sexual pleasure and sensual luxury (Diana Trapes notes elsewhere that Macheath always dressed his ladies well), and the unusual possibility of a Jenny Diver, who never goes to a tavern with a man "but in view of business." Jenny distinguishes work from recreation: "I have other hours and other sorts of men for my pleasure," she declares (2.4.76–78). While the other prostitutes, like Macheath himself, reveal their passions as their weakness, Jenny's self-control and capacity for delayed gratification align her (even literally) with the dispassionate Peachum, who has his own thieves hanged for the

1

profit. A fellow contractarian, Jenny understands prostitution as commercial exchange rather than sensual indulgence. These two models of prostitution—prostitution as the embrace of pleasure and prostitution as the sacrifice of pleasure to business—appear side by side in this play and indeed in the eighteenth century as a whole. Yet these two models, as I will show, represent not just a clash of values or perceptions, but a point of transition as well.

Generally speaking and allowing for overlap and exceptions, in the eighteenth century we can see a shift in representations from early inscriptions in which prostitutes embody insatiable desire to later configurations in which the economic meaning of the transaction of prostitution becomes increasingly prominent, even to the point that prostitutes appear to embody a new kind of commercial identity that can empower or threaten the individual through self-control, self-sacrifice, and self-division in marketplace exchanges. In the Restoration, writers generally do not represent prostitutes as divided creatures who rationally sell their commodified sexual labor. The assumption tends to be the opposite: Whores constantly seek sexual encounters to fulfill their burning desires and also sometimes manage to wheedle gold out of their cullies. One finds little distinction in the language of the period, in fact, between the meaning of "prostitute" and "whore," words that later distinguish sex workers from sexually desiring and/or available women. By the end of the eighteenth century, however, prostitutes often become so profoundly associated with the sacrifice of some part of the core self to the demands of the marketplace that writers use prostitute figures to engage the conflicting constructions and negotiations of personal identity in Britain's emergent commercial society. Much to the fascination of eighteenth-century writers, prostitution undermined the separation of the public and private spheres at the moment of their inception, for it placed in the marketplace the very thing—sexuality—understood to define the private sphere that in theory provided a haven from business.[2] Prostitution thus exposed the contradictions of the emergent bourgeois culture in the earliest moments of its formation. In different representations, prostitution could evoke both the disturbing and potentially liberating ways in which early capitalist relations were dislodging traditional forms of status and power—disturbing as Jonathan Swift's beautiful nymph going to bed who, as she pulls out her glass eye, false teeth, and cat-pissed plumpers, dissolves into a pile of commodities, but also comically liberating in the figure of Fanny Hill, who trades poverty for comfort through infamous commerce. Writers represented prostitutes as, on the one hand, radical self-owning individuals; on the other hand, the scandal of their commodity tested the boundaries of commodification itself. In the eighteenth century, the figure of the prostitute thus exposes and probes the costs and the benefits of commercial modernity. The prostitute came to suggest, with particular force in this period, the disturbing Mandevillian insight into the compatibility between activities and desires traditionally understood as vicious and the ordinary demands of emergent capitalist relations.

We need, then, to read representations of prostitution in this period not just in the context of infamy but also in the context of commerce. The transformation of Great Britain into a commercial society during the eighteenth century has received considerable attention in recent years.[3] Historians have documented the wide-ranging tensions in this period associated with the fraught transition from a more traditional economy, with its presumed hierarchies, customary rights, and moral constraints, to the gradual separation of economics into its own independent, "rational," nonaffective realm (political economy), scandalously theorized early in the century by Bernard Mandeville. In the eighteenth century, James Thompson argues, "the novel tells one kind of story about early modern value and political economy tells another. . . . Exchange in civil society is supposed to be rational, free from all emotional encumbrance, just as the exchange of vows in courtship is supposed to be free from the taint of monetary coercion."[4] The ideology of early capitalism, then, at least in theory rested on the fragile separation of the financial and the erotic.

In his influential studies of the social, cultural, and political tensions emerging between those with landed wealth and a growing commercial "monied" class that benefited from new and expanded forms of financial circulation in this period, J. G. A. Pocock has suggested that civic humanists embraced neotraditional values as a form of resistance, representing commercial relations not as abstract and logical but as irrational, unpredictable, inherently threatening, and feminine. Prostitutes at first glance provide the perfect civic humanist trope for embodying the marketplace as dangerously passionate and intractably female; the period's literature does not lack figures of this sort. Nevertheless, the wide variety of representations produced in this period offer other possibilities as well. As Srinivas Aravamudan, following Joyce Appleby, has observed, while we ignore Pocock's insights at our peril, his "confinement of commercial discourse and activity to 'a zone of secular irrationality' avoids accounting for the nascent political challenges of capitalism" and fails fully to account for "the extensive retooling of the citizen as consumer throughout the post-Restoration period."[5] Prostitute narratives, I will show, suggest at least as much confrontation of the nascent political (and personal) challenges of capitalism as they do the scapegoating of an irrational, feminized "other." They confront, in various ways, not just the retooling of the citizen as consumer, but the subject cut adrift from traditional structures and who may as a result need to acquire the resources with which to consume. Considerable recent scholarship has productively reconsidered how both the persistence of civic humanism *and* the nascent political challenges of consumer, mercantile, financial, and imperialist capitalism, as well as the early stirrings of its industrial form, shaped literary production, gender identity, and subjectivity in this period;[6] in this context, however, *infamous* commerce has tended to escape historicization.[7] It only makes sense, however, that these shifting economic structures would reshape and draw particular interest to their most explosive combination—the point where the private and the public, the personal and the economic, become disturbingly, undeniably, and intriguingly entangled.

Historically, prostitution took on its modern form during this period, a point that Randolph Trumbach, Tony Henderson, and Judith Walkowitz have demonstrated but defined in different terms.[8] Trumbach argues that prostitution emerged as modern in the eighteenth century when prostitutes became sentimentalized, "reformed," and set apart from other women. Henderson locates this change in the new legal strategies developed from the Restoration to the end of the eighteenth century to police "disorderly" women, noting an increasing tendency for prostitution to be considered as a distinct kind of infraction. Walkowitz, who shows how the nineteenth-century prostitution reform movement had its roots in institutions like the Magdalen Hospital in the eighteenth century, traces a change from an earlier social organization in which women drifted between prostitution and other kinds of employment to a modern construction of prostitutes as diseased "others."[9] But what is "modern" about modern prostitution is not only the way prostitutes become policed, sentimentalized, separated, and reformed, but the way culture represents the transaction of "prostitution" itself. Whatever happened historically between men and women, late seventeenth-century writers do not appear to understand prostitution as a form of labor or as bearing much of a relationship to work (except comically and ironically); they do not tend to see its most immediate significance as economic (or even necessarily represent prostitution as an economic relation at all). These representations certainly—even obsessively—locate prostitution at the heart of a chaotic marketplace and delineate the prostitute's burning desires for sex and money, but neither reformist nor libertine writers (with some interesting exceptions) imagine any troubling tensions between the whore's sexuality and her economic predicament. Eighteenth-century writers, however, become increasingly intrigued by the disturbing intersection of the economic and the personal that prostitution comes to emblematize. While not by any means representing prostitution as legitimate work, writers in this period nevertheless explore the predicament of the prostitute for its economic resonance for (in different ways) emerging middle-class and laboring-class subjectivities. In some ways, prostitutes remained "the other"; in other ways, however, they came to seem more and more like everyone else.

I draw my arguments about this period's representation of prostitution from a wide range of texts produced by an exploding popular print culture, including sermons, reform literature, prostitute biographies, libertine writing, brothel guides, satire, scandal narratives, memoirs, political pamphlets, travel narratives, and pornography.[10] The importance of prostitutes in this period's writing has been previously observed, yet less commonly studied as a topic in its own right. Recent work has shown how prostitution figures prominently in erotic literature and becomes crucial in emerging definitions of female identity;[11] by looking at a wide spectrum of representations, however, I have tried to reconstruct the cultural significance with which contemporaries invested the transaction of prostitution itself, defined in modern terms as the exchange of commodified sexual activity for remuneration. These representations are sometimes, but not necessarily, erotic; they sometimes advance, but other times challenge, emerging gender ideologies. In them, both men and women can function as both buyers and vendors; I have thus sometimes found the analytic separation of sexuality and gender productive.[12] The period's print culture reveals extensive debates over prostitution throughout the century, refers to a networked, publicly visible sex "industry," and describes a new class of "celebrity" prostitutes who traveled independently in elite circles without necessarily securing the patronage of one man in particular. *Infamous Commerce*, however, offers less analysis of historical acts of commercial sex than of its meaning and significance in the print culture of the period. Daniel Defoe, Henry Fielding, Samuel Richardson, and others engaged this cultural discourse in ways that not only helped shape emergent ideological formations of gender, class, labor, and economics but also, I argue, in striking ways held those formations up for scrutiny. Since prostitute figures become virtually ubiquitous in this period's writing, my project is necessarily selective, attempting to balance lesser-known texts with some of the period's canonical works to demonstrate the centrality of this issue and to offer new insight into familiar works. I have tried to capture the range of ways in which this period found meaning in sex work, from the libertine vision, which represents prostitution as a startling anti-Pamelistic form of upward mobility, to the reformist vision, which warns against prostitution as a form of class descent, to multiple points in between.[13] I discuss prostitution throughout as an expression of theatricality; nevertheless, narrative, as the genre that helped to construct modern versions of interiority at least in part through sexuality, has occupied most of my attention here.

A broad cultural understanding based on the variety of representations in the period's print culture reveals the limits of an exclusive focus on female sexuality and female virtue in unpacking the period's rhetoric around and literary interest in prostitution. Eighteenth-century slang provides the first clues: The euphemism for sex work from which I take my title—infamous commerce—suggests the significance for contemporaries of prostitution's economic meaning as well. In less polite circles, "commodity" functioned as slang for female genitalia, a linguistic convergence that invited considerable punning in libertine literature. Female prostitutes were "jades" or "hacks"—literally, horses exhausted by drudgery and by extension anyone who hired him/herself out for remunerative but unengaging, degrading, or unenjoyable work. Male heterosexual prostitutes—"stallions"—could become equine possessions as well.[14] Together these slang terms describe prostitution as a scandalous version of trade and an exhausting form of labor, gendered as feminine but fully imaginable as a male activity as well. At the same time, then, that the construction of prostitution helped produce new categories of gender, class, sexuality, and discipline, in the cultural realm prostitution also acquired another kind of rhetorical and tropological force—one that it has in many ways retained—that uniquely expressed and obliquely confronted the predicament of negotiating identity and survival in the context of commercial modernity and marketplace exchange (in this case, of a commodified service). Jenny Diver, in a play that unabashedly confronts the political significance of emergent capitalist relations, explicitly identifies prostitution as something *other than* the hours and the men reserved for pleasure. She identifies it, in short, as a form of work.

In focusing on prostitution, my project both benefits from and complicates much previous scholarship on women, gender, narrative, and ideology in eighteenth-century studies. While no full-length study of the figure of the prostitute in this period's writing has been undertaken, prostitute figures have attracted attention as negative versions of the virtuous female, as a locus of eroticism, as evidence of textual misogyny, and as central in expressions of imperialist impulses.[15] Most of these analyses read or point to readings of prostitute figures as embodiments of some form of disturbing alterity. Nancy Armstrong, Michael McKeon, and James Thompson have developed compelling theories of the novel in part through the significance of its attention to female sexual virtue: for Armstrong, the virtuous female galvanizes bourgeois ideology; for McKeon, she becomes the locus of honor in progressive ideology, replacing the male honor of aristocratic ideology; for Thompson, she defines the domestic sphere as a private haven from the period's emergent political economy. From these perspectives, prostitution evokes the failure of virtue, the absence of honor, and the violation of the private. James Turner, by contrast, has problematized the moral bifurcation of eighteenth-century texts, demonstrating how prostitutes and virtuous maidens function as eroticized objects in both libertine literature and domestic fiction. Others have pointed to prostitution's symbolic function in economic modernity. Satirists, Laura Brown has argued, use the figure of the woman in general, but often the prostitute in particular, misogynistically to condemn the consumption of exotic luxuries brought by trade. Felicity Nussbaum reveals virtuous British femininity in literature as dependent on sexual, racial, and class "others," including oft-exoticized prostitutes. Like those who associate prostitutes with the violation of domesticity in the novel, however, Turner, Brown, and Nussbaum share a general sense of the whore's posited otherness from the implicitly virtuous, forewarned, stimulated, or exonerated reader.

The degradation, eroticization, exoticization, and condemnation of prostitutes in eighteenth-century literature lies beyond dispute and informs my study. In *Infamous Commerce*, however, I place this observation in tension with another one: that in the eighteenth century, many kinds of texts, from Grub-street whore biographies to major novels by Defoe, Richardson, and Fielding, tell their stories from the perspective of or with some form of empathy for a character faced with a choice between remunerated sexual activity and abject poverty.[16] Further, in both popular culture and more "respectable" literature, the figure who chooses to exchange sexual labor does not necessarily meet with the violent poetic justice that an embodiment of irredeemable otherness might expect. In a range of texts, these characters function, perhaps unexpectedly, as both morally condemned, sexually objectified, and/or exoticized "others," but also as reference points for a range of readers faced with a newly commercialized culture offering new forms of mobility, often without traditional safety nets. Prostitutes represent the fallout of commercial society; they represent the anxious possibility of abandonment to an unforgiving marketplace that threatens the boundaries of personal and national identity. Prostitute figures during the period frequently suggest to readers both an assuring alterity and anxious potential self-recognition in the same breath: This will never be you because you are virtuous and/or male and/or truly British. But is the prostitute, they also inevitably suggest, really the only one who might confront abandonment, the ambiguous boundaries between the public and private, disturbing negotiations of personal identity in the marketplace, and conflicts between a traditional sense of virtue and an unpredictable commercial economy?

This embedded ambivalence distinguishes prostitute figures in the eighteenth century from those that would follow in the nineteenth century. As Amanda Anderson has shown, while Victorian prostitutes also similarly suggest threats to personal identity, they were nevertheless represented as "irredeemably other": "the tendency," reformers avowed, "is all downwards."[17]

Reformers in the eighteenth century, however, felt that prostitutes could actually improve from their abjection, in part because they did not see domesticity as the only alternative. Eighteenth-century reformers were just as likely to see prostitutes as redeemable through legitimate forms of work as through legitimate forms of sexuality. Further, many whore biographies trace a distinct and sometimes spectacular upward rather than a downward tendency: the cherished daughter of a tradesman, Kitty Fisher finds herself surrounded by luxury as a prostitute, moving in the most elite circles. The fictional Fanny Hill begins in poverty and retires to wealth, love, and happiness. Certainly many such figures also meet, like Defoe's Roxana, with a "blast from Heaven" or a more specific punishment; nevertheless, libertine whore biographies typically tell stories of material accumulation rather than (or in addition to) moral decline. The evidence of a broad range of primary sources helps us see that in eighteenth-century culture and narrative, prostitution does not bear simply a negative meaning and that prostitute narratives attracted particular interest for their capacity to explore the self-division and theatricality, but also alienation, believed by philosophers as early as Mandeville to characterize identity in a modern commercial market society.

The emergence of the modern construction of prostitution—what allows the phrase "sex worker" rather than "whore"—depends on the convergence of three eighteenth-century developments: contractarianism, the reconceptualization of gender and the female body, and an increasingly urban culture newly permeated by commercial relations. "Sex work" suggests a contractual agreement, a gendered division of desire that nevertheless becomes constantly undermined by the contractual possibility of reversal, and an identification of social performances, even ones as intimate as sexual contact, as potential commodities. Carole Pateman has argued that the emergence of contractarianism in the eighteenth century did not end patriarchy, but rather rejected the traditional "paternal patriarchy" (the Filmerian rule of the father) in favor of a modern "fraternal patriarchy" that subordinated women not as daughters, but specifically as women, shifting from a top-down hierarchical model to distinctions made on the basis of gender.[18] While I later contest her view of how prostitution functions in this scheme, Pateman's observation of the transition from patriarchal to contract society, which both grants and challenges the female capacity to make contracts on an equal basis, can help us see why prostitution could suggest both the possibilities of power and victimization. From one view, if women really could make contracts in the absence of a top-down patriarchy, then what would stop them from enriching and thus (in a society where money can now overrule traditional subordination in both gender and status) empowering themselves? Reformers, however, constantly warned young women that seemingly sincere males would inevitably fail to honor prostitution contracts, even when they (like Pamela's would-be seducer Mr. B) produced written documents. Such contracts historically were made, but lacked legal enforceability.[19] The lesson of much reform literature, in fact, lies in the unenforceability of sexual contracts for women outside of the state-sanctioned contract of marriage. The first possibility suggests confidence in the empowering possibilities of contract society; the second, the limits of contract itself.

Just as the eighteenth-century's emergent contrarianism demanded a "rational" man of business, so the contractarian model of prostitution demanded the female capacity to endure dispassionate sex. Emergent reconceptualizations of the female body thus become a crucial part of the construction of modern prostitution. Thomas Laqueur has argued that in the early modern period, medical textbooks described only one sex, with the female as an inferior, but similarly desiring, version of the male.[20] By the end of the eighteenth century, however, medical literature described the female body as distinct from the male and thus capable of—even inclined to—experience sexual activity without bodily pleasure. In the Restoration, libertine writers compared prostitution to business as a comic oxymoron, a yoking of opposites: as lascivious creatures of passion, whores would be the last to develop the dispassionate eye for profit and delayed gratification that commercial success demanded. Even when they extracted compensation, they would squander it on stallions and other luxuries. But just as Restoration prostitute figures thus personify excessive desire, so later eighteenth-century prostitute figures could suggest excessive alienation from their bodies and themselves. Prostitution gains nonoxymoronic similarities to "rational" exchange and, as I will show, comes to evoke the broader challenge of enduring unpleasant work or an unpleasant social performance for profit at a time when the construction of social identity itself was undergoing a significant transition. Gradually and unevenly, identity became increasingly dependent on various forms of activity—including labor, self-presentation, manners, accumulation—rather than primarily on birth.[21] Thus the transition in prostitute identity from pure desire to include the possibility of work takes part in, and becomes highly suggestive for, the broader social transition from the equivalence between birth and worth in aristocratic ideology to the bourgeois ideological emphasis on self-construction and self-determination. While Restoration prostitutes feverishly desire and modern stereotypes bifurcate into the passionate whore of pornography and the helpless victim, the eighteenth century nevertheless represented a third possibility of successful, although never uncomplicated, self-division for personal advantage, upward mobility, rescue of a vulnerable dependent, or bare survival.

The widely documented transformation of the categories of gender in the eighteenth century clearly reshaped the meaning of prostitution as well, especially in the separation and gendering, however tenuously or ineffectively, of public and private spheres.[22] But while prostitution has been historically more the work of women than the work of men and while its modern rhetorical force draws from female economic vulnerability as well as constructions of female sexual passivity, "prostitute" and "woman" are overlapping rather than identical categories: not all women were prostitutes and not all prostitutes were women.[23] Certainly the treatment of women as sexual property suggested to several eighteenth-century writers analogies to prostitution—Fielding, for example, calls the proposal to marry Sophia to Blifil "legal prostitution." Nevertheless, as the analogy itself suggests, the culture as a whole vigorously attempted to distinguish prostitute from nonprostitute women. Betsy Thoughtless in Eliza Haywood's novel severely endangers her future just by associating with the disreputable Miss Forward. In some texts, the female prostitute's gender functions as a form of patriarchal displacement: In the new world of commodification, only women will have to exchange their most precious capacities. But as *Tom Jones* and numerous rogue narratives suggest, the eighteenth century fully imagined sex work as a masculine possibility as well. Eighteenth-century prostitute figures even seem to border on an inherently amalgamated gender position of their own, never simply masculine or feminine: Roxana calls herself a "man-woman"; Tom's acceptance of Lady Bellaston's money feminized him. The threat to masculine authority and personal boundaries feminizes men who enter the sexual marketplace; for their part, women negotiating this market must first claim the masculine position of self-ownership. Thus the emergent modern construction of prostitution complicated the reification of gender distinctions even though in some ways it depended on them.

The third historical transformation—the emergence of a commercial society—refers to a range of changes worth specifying. Historians have called attention to the eighteenth century's consumer and financial revolutions: The middle and upper classes gained unprecedented access to a variety of commodities once produced in the home but now available in the marketplace; at the same time, the stock market created profound uncertainties about wealth and value. These historical changes brought intensified moral concerns about both luxury and unpredictability. Not only do prostitutes in many representations consume in excess, spending ill-gotten wealth on silks and baubles, but they also tempt men into irresponsible indulgences as well. The temptation of commercial sex here quintessentially represents the seductions of the new economy and the hazards of the irresponsible desires it provokes. This moralistic vision, however, did not go uncontested: Mandeville and writers who (usually unadmittedly) followed him saw a positive side to desire, even in its most infamous form. Elite prostitutes, several writers observed, became leaders of London fashion, bringing men (and their money) to the city, supporting a high-end clothing industry, and implicitly encouraging other women to keep up with the fashions they set. In this view, prostitution brought prosperity to tradesmen, shopkeepers, merchants, and industrialists. In different texts, then, prostitution can vilify the desire on which commercial culture depends, or it can attempt to compartmentalize this desire into acceptable and infamous forms, or it can collapse those distinctions.

The period's ambivalence toward consumption, however, could not help at least obliquely raising the specter of production, which depended on networks of global trade, colonial exploitation, and slave labor as well as emergent forms of protoindustrial, and then industrial, production at home. In many ways, prostitutes, with their obvious ties to the marketplace, served as disturbing reminders of everything strange and threatening about global commerce: prostitutes wore foreign fashions; they stalked the New Exchange; they haunted coffee houses, with their exotic delicacies; they infiltrated theaters in boxes, the pit, and on stage; they gathered in the pleasure gardens of Vauxhall and the leisure sites of Bath. Eighteenth-century writers associated them, as we will see, with East Indians, West Indians, Catholics, Jews, Muslims, Africans, Italians, the Irish, the French, Scots, Pacific Islanders, "natives" of all kinds, actresses who play these exoticized roles and exoticized versions of the laboring class. Prostitute figures thus in key ways disturbed what Joseph Roach in another context has described as the century's "highly specialized rhetoric of forgetting,"[24] evoking the more anxious possibilities of the consumer revolution and the global reach on which it depended.

As much as prostitute figures commonly evoked the global commercial economy, however, they also pointed to changing systems of production and survival at home: whether prostitutes used their earnings to purchase luxurious silk gowns or bread for their hungry children, they nevertheless gained purchasing power by publicly exchanging sexual labor in the marketplace. Early moralists showed little interest in why women became prostitutes or their economic alternatives; midcentury reformers represented prostitution as a form of idleness rather than work, insisting that under watchful eyes or through newly internalized discipline, streetwalkers could instead be making linen, gloves, artificial flowers, shoes, or lace; they could be winding silk, embroidering waistcoats, printing calicoes, or knitting hose and mittens. Many women who worked as prostitutes, however, also participated in the labor force in other ways as well. Single women in low-paying jobs turned to prostitution during times of unemployment, but also as a supplement to their meager incomes.[25] The intensified literary interest in prostitute figures in the eighteenth century converged with not just emerging bourgeois sexual norms, but with urbanization, enclosure, increasingly limited employment opportunities for women, and a growing dependence on wage labor among many families.[26] Nearly all of this period's prostitute narratives, though clearly in many ways fictionalized, record repeated attempts by their heroines—even the most glamorized ones—to find other ways of making a living. Their general lack of dramatic distinction from other workers must at some level have been clear.[27] As one writer quipped, by going back and forth between service and bawdy houses, such women "neither make good Whores, good Wives, or good Servants."[28] In prostitution, perhaps more than in any other exchange, capitalism's "rhetoric of forgetting" always to some degree fails: while a lump of sugar can disguise its embedded West Indian slave labor and a calico print can forget the painstaking hands of women and children, the whore's commodity can never be separated from the producer.[29] Unlike the rest of the commodity culture that conspired to produce the "highly specialized rhetoric of forgetting," then, prostitute figures inevitably, disturbingly, and intimately linked consumption to production. Their potency as literary figures emerges from their embodiment of excessive consumption and their shocking capacity to awaken memory.

In the first plate of his *Harlot's Progress*, William Hogarth visually captures this complex dynamic by depicting a young girl arriving in London to her fate of prostitution, disease, and death, perhaps tricked, the sewing implements hanging from her waist might suggest, by the possibility of securing another kind of work. Hogarth's depiction had a material foundation: London brothels and streets, Trumbach and Henderson have shown, were populated by women who had come to London seeking employment. Urban prostitution, as contemporaries obsessively observe and historians have confirmed, increased. In the 1690s, contemporaries reported "nightwalking" as a new phenomenon.[30] While preindustrial production took place not only in urban centers but throughout the nation, Hogarth here ties the harlot's progress to urbanization: between 1650 and 1750, London's population rose by 70 percent.[31] Prostitution became associated with the nation's transformation from a rural to a more metropolitan, commercial, and trading economy: to "go upon the town" was to become a whore, a "woman of the town." Hogarth's image, then, links urbanization, mobile labor, and prostitution as part of the same movement, allegorized in *A Harlot's Progress* by the journey from country to city.

While the middle-class admirers of Hogarth certainly must have found some comfort in their smug moral distance from the fallen heroine, it is dif-

William Hogarth, *A Harlot's Progress* (1732), Plate 1 (© Copyright The Trustees of The British Museum).

ficult to imagine that they did not at some level recognize the possibility that they too might some day find themselves in a similarly vulnerable position. In her important study of the "middling sort" in the eighteenth century, whose "complex and conflictual family lives and patterns of sociability" were "heavily marked by the experience of commerce," Margaret Hunt demonstrates the precariousness of solvency in this period.[32] For the middling sort, their very identities "as independent persons," she points out, "were bound up with the translating of work—their own and others'—into money" (209). Remaining in the middle class, Hunt argues, depended on extended networks of family obligation: Couples would borrow capital from relatives to begin a business, and family members ideally came to the assistance of those whose businesses failed. But as the fiction of this period suggests, these networks could themselves fail: Roxana's husband and relatives abandon her; Tom's adoptive father throws him out; Clarissa suffers under her father's curse. These characters all live out the profound middling anxieties of abandonment and its economic consequences: Roxana, Clarissa, and Tom Jones find themselves with their bodies as their primary resource. Clarissa heroically resists prostitution, but Roxana's choice to embrace it also provokes the middle-class anxiety that the women who provided undercompensated or entirely uncompensated domestic labor might begin to imagine alternatives.[33] The commercial revolution brought new uncertainties, but it also brought new opportunities for mobility that we find ambivalently embodied in the figure of the prostitute.

Writers in the eighteenth century turned to prostitute figures, then, not only to condemn the irrational passions raised by commodity culture, erotically to charge their narratives, or to police female sexuality, but perhaps most grippingly to explore the transformation of identity demanded by the social, economic, and the political changes in the period.[34] The eighteenth century's gradual separation of a public, economic sphere from a private, domestic sphere not only gendered these realms and forms of writing associated with them, as James Thompson has shown, but produced an urgency to imagine the possibility, perhaps more commonly experienced than absolute confinement to one or the other, of negotiating between these two spheres.[35] In his confrontation with conflicts between early capitalism and traditional virtue, Mandeville imagines divided, theatrical social performance as the healthiest and most prosperous response. Reviled but repeated, Mandeville described self-division as productive and potentially empowering: A prosperous commercial society demands constant theatricality, a fundamental division between external negotiations and internal desires. Albert O. Hirschman has argued that for eighteenth-century economists in general, "capitalism was supposed to accomplish exactly what was soon to be denounced [by Karl Marx and others] as its worst feature": that is, a self-division that would restrain passionate impulses out of longer term self-interest.[36] Women, Catherine Gallagher has suggested, may sometimes have found this strategy of self-division more readily available or more appealing because they lacked certain rights of individualism and property ownership. Aphra Behn, for example, on occasion exploited accusations against her of prostitution by embracing them as part of her general self-theatricalization.[37] Along these lines but not necessarily "feminist" in their intent, libertine prostitute narratives record glorious transitions from private misery to public triumph that depend on strategic forms of Mandevillian, theatricalized self-division.

Eighteenth-century writers, however, could also represent this self-division as the most tragic form of human alienation possible, giving rise to narratives of extreme pathos around the sacrifice of the most intimate part of the self to the marketplace. This pathetic version of prostitution that emerges later in the century posits sex work as a horrific division brought by the breakdown of traditional bonds, creating a rift between a private identity and a compulsion to mimic enjoyment in an callous public sphere. This version of prostitution, I believe, in some ways melodramatically anticipates Marx's later description of capitalism as systematic alienation, demanding "a break between an individual and his life activity."[38] Eighteenth-century prostitute narratives explore the division between the individual and "life activity" as the result of the brutality of an emergent unforgiving economy bereft of affect and customary obligation: Prostituted women thus, as Ruth Perry observes, "figured the many different kinds of alienation to be found in the new commercial, urban, de-humanized world of the eighteenth century: alienated political service, alienated social relations, capitalized wealth, compromised love."[39] At the same time, however, sometimes the prostitute herself in these narratives can emerge as heroic for her willingness to sacrifice her own self-consistency for the sake of a dependent other. In the nineteenth century, as Judith Walkowitz has observed, the prostitute became "an object of class guilt as well as fear, a powerful symbol of sexual and economic exploitation under industrial capitalism."[40] On the brink of industrial capitalism, the eighteenth century generated narratives that anticipate this class fear and guilt, but that also thoroughly explored both the empowering and tragic possibilities of prostitution as an extreme form of alienation, violently tearing the individual from her (or his) "life activity." While Marx would later excoriate this aspect of capitalism, some eighteenth-century reformers found in repentant Magdalens a productive model for laboring-class subjectivity and subjection.

In eighteenth-century novels, as well as in a broad range of "true" prostitute narratives, travel narratives, periodicals, and reformist texts, then, prostitutes evoke both the "others" on whom the new commercial culture depended for its luxury and the new forms of identity it demanded. I begin in the first chapter by tracing the emergence of the modern construction of prostitution by looking at shifts in representations from the prostitute's desire to her (or his) self-division. Chapter 2 shows how Mandeville's shocking economic theory grew out of his confrontation with the Societies for the Reformation of Manners, which vowed to reclaim the public sphere for legitimate rather than infamous commerce. Chapters 3, 4, 5, and 6 explore different kinds of eighteenth-century "prostitute narratives": Defoe's *Roxana*, popular prostitute biographies from the period, Richardson's *Clarissa*, and Fielding's *Tom Jones*. Popular prostitute biographies, though sometimes sexually and sentimentally exploitative, confront the widespread anxiety of abandonment to the marketplace and explore a range of possible responses to this predicament. Chapters on *Roxana*, *Clarissa*, and *Tom Jones* point to connections between these works and prostitute narratives; each of these novels features characters that become anxious points of identification in exploring the benefits and costs of commercial culture. Defoe explores this tension through Roxana's haunting by the Jew and by her abandonment of her children; Richardson in Clarissa's choice of death over prostitution; and Fielding in Tom's dangerous resemblance to rogues. Attention to the representation of female virtue in eighteenth-century culture has shown the ideological limits of these novels; attention to prostitution, by contrast, opens up different possibilities. My readings may at first appear counterintuitive: Roxana's luxurious life does not come crashing down because she has failed as a mother but because she cannot fully expunge her maternal impulses; Clarissa does not reject sexuality or the body but alienation in Mrs. Sinclair's establishment and her father's; Tom reforms not because the incest scare reveals the dangers of promiscuity but because he realizes that he has become a stallion. It takes a whore rather than a patriarch to ensure his survival. The broader cultural context of popular prostitute narratives and controversies over infamous commerce, however, demand that we read familiar texts differently, abandoning assumptions about the irredeemable otherness of those who alienate sexual labor. In the final chapter I turn outward to show how finding "prostitution" in the South Sea Islands served to normalize the commercial relations that Defoe, Richardson, and Fielding all hold up for scrutiny. The conclusion glances briefly at the polygamy controversy at the end of the century that, I argue, confirms the commodification of sexual labor not as a marginal activity but as central to the self-representation of Great Britain as a commercial nation.

1

A "Cool State of Indifference": Mother Creswell's Academy

Pleasure is a thief to business.
Daniel Defoe, *The Complete English Tradesman*

The most famous literary prostitute of the Restoration—Aphra Behn's Angellica Bianca from *The Rover*—possesses beauty, wit, and nerve, but in the end she does not get what she wants. Angellica looks down from her window with a confidence and power that the other female characters lack; she hangs out her sign and names her own price, but at the end of the play she becomes so outraged by her treatment by the impoverished cavalier Willmore that she holds a gun to his heart. Before the other characters can happily pair off, a dispirited and disarmed Angellica must be escorted off the stage. Behn must expel the courtesan, it seems, in order to move on to the marriages. But in Angellica's mini-tragedy ensconced in the play's larger comic structure, Behn does not, as might her reform-minded contemporaries, represent the prostitute's inevitable fate as disease, poverty, and miserable death. In fact, Angellica lives in wealth and contentment as a courtesan. She faces grief and danger only when, instead of charging men for sex, she turns the tables and compensates Willmore. Pleasure distracts from business, which makes for bad business.

With Angellica Bianca, Behn creates a prostitute character, unlike the self-consciously commodified Jenny Diver, poised between two historical possibilities: a very modern one in which the prostitute exchanges sexual labor in a public, contractarian marketplace, and an older model in which the whore would be the last person in the world to succeed in business because sexual passion, not financial planning, drives her. When Angellica hangs out her picture she confidently evokes the first possibility, but by the end of the play she has reverted to a version of the second, albeit an unusually sympathetic one. As Ruth Mazo Karras has shown, early modern writers in both Europe and England defined prostitutes overwhelmingly by their sexuality, presuming that women prostituted out of sexual desire rather than economic need. In certain times and places bawdy houses were tolerated, although not, Karras argues, out of an understanding of limited economic options for women but as an "outlet" for male sexuality. Authorities viewed prostitutes as extreme embodiments of general female lust.[1] Consistent with Karras's early modern model, Restoration prostitute figures generally display aggressive desire and/or transgressive passion; by the end of the eighteenth century, however, literary prostitutes appeal to reader sympathy on the basis of their *lack* of enjoyment.

Thus the difference between the early modern and the modern construction of the prostitute, this chapter will suggest, lies in this figure's changing relationship to desire, pleasure, the body, economics, and work.[2] Throughout the long eighteenth century, writers describe the prostitute's presumed artifice as theatricality, often in the context of lamenting this feature of the modern world.[3] Nevertheless, Restoration moralists and libertine writers rarely doubt the authenticity of the prostitute's desire; instead, they represent only the most desperate, impoverished, and pathetic whores as failing to enjoy sex, and this usually only as the result of disease, exhaustion, and glutted pleasure. Restoration prostitutes do not necessarily relish each encounter, yet desire—for sexual pleasure, but also for luxury, power, prestige, and wealth—drives their careers and expresses their "true" character. In later constructions, however, prostitute figures often divide themselves between a private "inner" self with a virtuous potential and an exterior, public practice of often highly unpleasant sexual encounters undertaken for compensation.[4] In the Restoration and eighteenth century, prostitute stories facetiously, satirically, ironically, melodramatically, and tragically reflected on the meaning, costs, and benefits of the alienation of some part of the self in the marketplace. But what begins as a comic oxymoron—prostitution as delayed gratification rather than just gratification—becomes during the eighteenth century one of prostitution's central meanings and a widely intriguing figure for a range of commercial experiences.

The Feminist Debate

This chapter distinguishes between constructions of prostitution in the seventeenth century (mostly the second half) and those emerging in the middle of the eighteenth century. Eighteenth-century representations of sex work, while certainly different from those produced today, nevertheless reconfigure key elements from the earlier period in ways that make them recognizably "modern" and relevant to contemporary debates. I begin, then, with a brief discussion of recent feminist analyses of this issue.

Feminist arguments diverge sharply on prostitution, but converge in their definition of sex work as a form of divided selfhood. They disagree, however, as to whether this self-division constitutes one more instance of the alienation of labor in a capitalist marketplace, or whether commercial sex demands so much of the prostitute's being that she loses herself entirely.[5] The debate consistently returns to a few key questions: What exactly do sex workers alienate, labor or themselves? If labor, does it *necessarily* degrade the sex worker? On both sides, feminists condemn forced prostitution and acknowledge the hazards of the sex industry. Advocates of prostitute rights, however, understand prostitution as work that does not inherently differ from other kinds.[6] Even the emotional challenges of sex work, argues Wendy Chapkis, leave prostitution comparable rather than unique, for many forms of work make emotional demands and require affective performances.[7] Anti-prostitution feminists, however, represent prostitution as a devastating form of victimization and tragic self-alienation: Sheila Jeffreys, for example, argues that the prostitute experiences herself as "homeless in her own body": one cannot, she argues, market sexual labor without violating the core of one's being.[8] Citing the historical indivisibility of self and sexuality for women, Carole Pateman concludes that "when a prostitute contracts out use of her body she is thus selling *herself* in a very real sense." Because of this, "for self-protection, a prostitute must distance herself from her sexual use."[9]

Contemporary feminists, then, understand prostitution as a commercial exchange that demands theatrical performance and a certain level of self-division, but disagree as to what the prostitute gives over. Arguments for the prostitute's total self loss, however, seem inconsistent with the continued individuality of prostitutes. In popular rhetoric, this position becomes casually reformulated as "selling the body"; prostitutes, however, normally retain their bodies in such transactions. As prostitute rights advocates point out, representing the prostitute as selling "herself" detracts from recognizing the similarities between prostitution and other forms of labor, which also demand the negotiation of identity in the marketplace.[10] Yet prostitution also holds a unique place in the marketplace: Historically, it has been represented as one of the most troubling kinds of exchange—not just sexually transgressive, but economically transgressive as well. Purchasers of sexual services have been long suspected of abusing financial or patriarchal power; sellers of sexual services have been suspected of abusing capacities designated for exclusively private, noncommercial use. So while prostitution may not be in-

herently different from other forms of labor, it has historically been constructed as an extreme form of commodification that provides a scandalous,
negative version of exchange in implicit contrast to salutary forms, or more
critically as commodification's fallout that reveals the market's potential to
elide the difference between a person and a thing.

   In the modern world, prostitution clearly functions, as Margaret Radin has
argued, as a "contested commodity," comparable to other troubling exchanges such as surrogate motherhood, the sale of human body parts, and
forms of adoption that resemble the purchase of children.[11] Contested commodities, she observes, test the remaining boundaries of the marketplace.
John Locke characterized the rights-bearing subject as one who owns his
own body; nevertheless, three hundred years later the current international
market in body parts troubles many post-Lockean subjects. The boundaries
of the marketplace had even less clarity in the seventeenth and eighteenth
centuries when raising the price of bread could generate clerical debate and
political controversy.[12] Drawing on Radin's insight, then, we can see the feminist conflict over prostitution as not just a disagreement over how best to
challenge the oppression of women but also as an expression of persisting uncertainty about the negotiation of personal identity in commercial society.

   For Radin, sex work calls attention to the "incomplete commodification"
observable even in late capitalism; since the eighteenth century, however,
prostitution has also served as a lightning rod for contestation over commodification itself, as the "obvious" limit to universal commodification and
a trope for the marketplace's ominous incursions into personal identity (even
though, from another point of view, the marketplace *produces* personal identity). Thus even if sex workers do not actually sell themselves or their bodies, the historical formation of female sexuality as the sum of female identity
has constructed prostitution as a figure for the disturbing permeability of
public/private boundaries. Pateman, for example, invokes "universal prostitution" as a dystopic vision of unbounded capitalism; Frank Capra fills Main
Street with prostitutes as shorthand for the ruthless spread of commercialism unabated by George Bailey's resistance in *It's a Wonderful Life*. When
Marx argues, "'prostitution is only a *specific* expression of the *general* prostitution of the *labourer*,'" he clearly uses the presumed obviousness of the sex
worker's alienation (and implicit degradation) as a way of objecting to the
general condition of all workers.[13] This "contested commodity," then, seems
long to have held the power to reveal its disturbing continuities with other
forms of labor and exchange. The explosiveness of prostitution as a political
issue and narrative trope, then, lies not in prostitution's "otherness" but in its
more general implications: as Lynn Sharon Chancer argues, prostitution
"treads into unconsciously threatening waters, remaining marginal and com-

paratively untheorized precisely *because* something about it is so central and meaningful."[14]

"Contested commodities," if sufficiently troubling, bear the potential to challenge commodification itself. For this reason, Radin argues, commercial cultures have attempted to neutralize their disruptive power through "compartmentalization"; that is, the notion that some potential goods and services can be marked as inalienable and preserved from commodification so that other goods and services can circulate unproblematically. Eighteenth-century writers, as we will see in subsequent chapters, commonly turned to this strategy. In the rest of this chapter, however, I want to suggest that prostitution's evocation of the heartlessness of an unbounded marketplace, the exploitation of labor, and an unredeemed commercial dystopia only fully emerges in the early and mid-eighteenth century with the changing meaning of prostitution itself, and that earlier representations make different assumptions. Recent feminist theory continues to debate whether treating a "private" part of the self as an alienable commodity degrades or empowers the prostitute through commercial self-division. In the Restoration, however, this conflict would make limited sense because in most narratives, desire *constitutes* the whore's identity. In the Restoration, the sexually alienated prostitute—the one who takes little pleasure in her work or feels objectified, estranged from herself and from others, the one who sees prostitution as inconsistent with her full identity—appears only rarely and sporadically as a harbinger of emergent possibilities.

"This is the fate of most whores": The Restoration

In *The Rover*, to return briefly to this play, Angellica Bianca's servant Moretta throws up her hands and declares the downfall of her mistress as inevitable: "This is the fate of most whores. Trophies, which from believing fops we win, / Are spoils to those who cozen us again."[15] The charming Willmore not only brings no income, not only accepts *her* money, but also seriously endangers Angellica's affairs with the men who *can* pay. Thus in spite of working for a courtesan, Moretta believes that prostitution hardly ever proves good business because a whore will surely spend any profits on her "stallions," as Angellica does on Willmore. Prostitution consistently fails as a business because whores will always prove incapable of professional distance from their work. As Moretta predicts and her mistress demonstrates, prostitutes are at this time understood to be for the most part incapable, or barely capable, of the sexual distancing that many modern theorists understand prostitution as demanding. Restoration prostitutes remain at home in their sexual bodies. Angellica underprofits because she values her own desire too highly; had she been more interested in alienating her commodified sexual labòr for wealth, she would not have looked twice at Willmore.

While throughout her work Behn explores the tensions for women between desire and economic demand, other less sympathetic writers, not surprisingly, invoke the whore's presumed désire to misogynistic and other political ends. James Turner argues that during this period "whore" was a "fighting word" that suggested "sexual infamy" rather than economic negotiation: "the accusation 'whore' served as a universal indicator of guilt."[16] Women who acquired the whore's reputation became vulnerable to violent attack, either individually (men would slash their faces, as Pinchwife threatens to do to Margery in *The Country Wife*) or collectively, as the riots attacking bawdy houses in this period exemplify. Even the romantic Belville in *The Rover*, Turner points out, suggests breaking Angellica Bianca's windows after Wilmore emerges from her mansion.[17] Prostitution's infamy also functioned politically in attacks on the notorious Stuarts *and* in attacks on their Puritan opponents: satirists on one side mocked the mistresses of Charles II as common whores; on the other side, writers suggested that secretly perverse Puritans visited prostitutes.[18] Restoration poets and satirists consistently represent prostitutes as insatiable in their sexual desires, a point that for Turner contributes to the misogyny of much libertine writing. Other critics, however, have found the Restoration assurance of the whore's desire an intriguing alternative to the female passivity that later representations would demand.[19]

But whether misogynist, liberating, transgressive, or threatening, Restoration texts consistently define prostitutes as women driven toward and indulging in sexual pleasure. Restoration prostitute figures generally do not, as in later sentimental representations, endure sex with a pathetic or professional distance for the sake of the payment. They certainly don't sell "themselves," but they don't even contractually exchange their sexual labor. Any relationship between prostitution and work in these texts, then, generally emerges as satiric or ironic.[20] In these early representations, whores seek pleasure; they often find it with their clients, but when they don't they hire a stallion. They sometimes seek money as well, but in a way consistent with their sensuality, for they also desire luxurious clothing, delicate food, and lavish accommodations. Historically, a woman could be called a "whore" or "prostitute" and even arrested as "disorderly" without any money changing hands. (Currently, remuneration *alone* distinguishes prostitute from nonprostitute sex.) Women in Behn's *Feigned Courtesans* and Eliza Haywood's *Fantomina* disguise themselves as prostitutes to seek erotic opportunities, not payment. Further, while Restoration prostitute stories can certainly seethe with misogyny, they do not generally suggest an intractably gendered or clearly recognized contract. Whores often acquire their money surreptitiously, using seduction as an opportunity for theft; men like Willmore earn money by offering the sexual pleasure a wealthy client may have failed to provide. In contrast with the later understanding of prostitution as a form of self-division, for both whores and stallions in this period's representations, sex with multiple, sometimes-anonymous partners *expresses*, rather than threatens, their core identity.

For reformers, desire and pleasure mark the prostitute's transgression. Few insist on this so starkly as Humphrey Mill, the reformist constable-poet and author of *A Night's Search, Discovering the Nature and Condition of Night-Walkers with Theire Associates*, (1640):

> Widow, maid, or wife,
> If once she does affect a whorish life.
> Then like a Bitch she in her lust will b[u]rne,
> Takes up a rogue, and he must serve the turne.[21]

The whores in Mill's poem do not experience prostitution as full or even partial self-division; rather, once they taste pleasure they must then take to the streets to fill their insatiable and inseparable desires for sex and money. If this transaction alienates anyone, it is the gull, who:

> . . . buyes his sin, and sels himselfe away,
> And now this whore has made this foole her prey. (28)

The whores in Mill always want sex and usually want money, although sometimes their streetwalking does not have a financial goal at all: Mill warns men against the prostitute who with "lust doth burne," who does not "trade for coyne" because "[s]he wants not gold, or any thing beside" (173). According to Mill, some prostitutes even pay men for sex. One such woman meets a man who

> Grew impudent; being taken with her sight,
> Yet feares to speed, because his purse was light.
> When she perceiv'd it, then she gave him gold,
> And what he lov'd, she wisht him to be bold. (178)

Even when prostitutes seek money, they often do so in ways that circumvent straightforward exchange. Mill, for example, points to the danger of prostitutes who wheedle money and gifts out of enthralled admirers. Similarly, a bawd in *The Wandring Whore* recommends that her girls put "their left hand in his Cod-piece, the right hand in his Pocket."[22] The contractarian whore *does* appear in *A Night's Search*, but only briefly as a very low, negative example despised by more successful prostitutes. One prostitute, for example, insists

> I am no market whore, like those that say
> Before they truck, sir, what shall be my pay?
> Such mercenary trulls, that will not trade
> With any man, untill the match be made,
> I even hated: it shall never be sed
> (By any blade) that I am basely bred. (94)

A pimp in *The Wandring Whore* speaks with similar contempt of "those poor lazy, idle whores who F— for necessity, not pleasure, and have scarce a *tufft* of *hair* amongst them all to *cover their Cunnyes*" (no. 4, p. 10). The dispassionate, contractarian whore exists as only the most despised possibility in the illicit community, according to both reformers and libertines. As another prostitute in Mill declares, "I trade in love, the price I never make; / What men doe give, that I may freely take" (48). While Mill clearly sees money as part of the prostitute's pleasure, he, like the libertine writers, understands all but the most despised prostitutes as fully engaged in rather than estranged from their sexual encounters. For Mill, their pleasure to a large extent defines their transgression.

Libertine writers, unsurprisingly, took full advantage of the whore's presumed desire. In *The Wandring Whore*, the bawd Magdelena asks Julietta if she will "be free to be a whore under me." "I am unwilling," replies Julietta, "to be a whore under you, but under an able and sufficient man, I am, and ever was willing" (8). Julietta works for both money *and* enjoyment: Magdalena observes that Julietta, returning from a client, looks "very merry"; "surely you have been well payd, and pleased with your recreation" (11). The anonymous author of *The Character of a Town-Miss* insists that one man rarely satisfies a whore; she must always have "a *French Merchant* to supply her with *Dildo's;* or in default of those, she makes her Gallants Purse maintain two able *Stallions* (that she loves better than him) for performance of points wherein he is *Defective*."[23] Even in *The Insinuating Bawd and the Repenting Harlot*, in which a reformed prostitute bitterly attacks the bawd who initiated her into the trade, the penitent complains that the temptation of sexual pleasure rather than financial gain ruined her reputation. She describes the bawd as "One who by long Experience knew the way/To raise Desires would Tender Youth betray."[24] The bawd becomes a seductress of potential prostitutes, praying on female passion rather than financial predicament.

The London-Bawd, a fictionalized account of a prostitute turned bawd, represents prostitution not as a form of labor or even as a predictably gendered contract, but instead as a series of opportunities for the fulfillment of both male and female desires. The London bawd "[e]ntertains all Comers, and not only find 'em *Beds*, but *Bed-fellows* too, of that Sex which shall be most agreeable to them; which is a Conveniency a Man may go to twenty Honest Houses and not meet with."[25] Not only does she offer a choice of sexual services to male clients, but she also makes arrangements for female clients. In one anecdote we learn "How a Young Woman, by the help of an Old Bawd, Enjoy'd her Lover, and Deceiv'd her Husband" (18). Next the bawd finds a good keeping for a whore, but when the whore's "Paramour cou'd not come to her, by reason of Business, she then sent to the Bawd, who provided her a Stallion to supply his place, which she paid for doing her Drudgery with his Mony" (41). Another episode, in fact, describes a discreet bawdy house designed especially for women whose husbands fail to satisfy them. Each woman must pay an entrance fee and hire an artist to draw her picture, which the bawd then displays in the dining room. After this initial charge, the bawd will then bring men to her, "[w]hereby she not only satisfied her Lustful Desires, but was supplied with Mony likewise, without robbing of her Husband of his Coin, though she wrong'd him more nearly another way" (73). In one anecdote, a suspecting husband visits in disguise and later confronts his wife. Rather than destroying their marriage, however, this incident brings the couple to a better understanding, for he comes to recognize her desire and she comes to recognize his sexual potential, which he had not exhibited at home. As in Wycherley's *Country Wife*, the straying wife suggests the sexual inadequacy of the husband. But while the possibility of Margery's infidelity stirs Pinchwife to threats of violence, the husband in *The London Bawd* admits that he had been slacking off and dedicates himself to improvement. In the end, then, the narrative counts his inadequacy as the greater violation than her prostitution. Sexual desire motivated the wife; the money she earned was extra.

Thus in some popular narratives, just as men use bawds to procure women, so women use bawds to procure men. Similarly, while the words *whore* and *prostitute* consistently referred to females (but do not yet refer to a consistently recognized difference between sexually active women and sex workers), a range of texts in this period suggest ways in which "wandring" males not only associate with but also come to resemble "wandring" whores. These narratives often differentiate the consequences of whoring for women from those for men; nevertheless, they represent the position of sexual opportunist as fully available to both genders. Richard Head and Francis Kirkman's *The English Rogue* (1665–1671) explores one version of the masculine possibility at length. As James Turner points out, the rogue's very name—Meriton Latroon—suggests a paradox of the elite (merit) and the low (latrine).[26] We could also read the name "Meriton," however, as a masculinization of the word "meretrix," a traditional slang term for prostitute and thus a possibility supported by the rogue's self-support through paid sex and frequent association with female prostitutes.[27] This English rogue lives out a comic version of Oroonoko's tragic indignities in Aphra Behn's better-known novel: he too endures exile, betrayal, poverty, slavery, and travel to the far corners of the globe; both this one and Behn's narrative record how mercantile and colonial capitalism sets bodies in motion. Displaced from his native Ireland during the uprising of 1641, Latroon arrives in England with his mother, his only relative to survive this rebellion.[28] But while high romance gives shape to the story of the tragic royal slave and his wife, sexual commerce organizes the experience of the English rogue. After running away from home, a brief stint living with a band of gypsies, and a desperate existence as a beggar, Meriton meets a merchant who likes him, cleans him up, and takes him on as an apprentice. Latroon, however, lacks the patience for legitimate business, and the rest of the first volume describes a continuous flow of money and sex in which the rogue accumulates neither wealth nor a stable relationship. When he runs out of money, he works as a "stallion," pleasing women for coin or privileges. Usually, though, he quickly spends this money on sex with other women: this endless cycle of "getting and spending" repeats itself throughout the narrative.

The English Rogue underscores the hero's feminization through this process when a prostitute in a brothel tricks him out of his clothes, so he puts on hers. He does not adopt women's dress, at least initially, for any other reason than poverty: the whore had taken his clothes and money but left her own dress, and so he decides to function as a woman until he can acquire male attire. He soon, however, finds other advantages: a man notices him and buys him dinner. He also finds a job as a maid, but this quickly leads to exhausting sexual demands not by men, but by women: "I came at length to be very much beloved in general. It was the custom almost every night for the young Gentlewomen to run skittishly up and down into one anothers Chambers; and I was so pestered with them, that they would not let me sleep" (1:97). While some of these women, having seen through his female impersonation, seek him out for heterosexual pleasure, others do not realize his true sex when they get into bed with him. Thus the rogue becomes both sexually and economically liminal, functioning as whoremonger, whore, stallion, and "lesbian" lover. In *The English Rogue*, the position of prostitute belongs to anyone with this relentless wandering desire and who may have nothing to leverage but sexual service. Like female prostitutes in the Restoration, the rogue seeks and relishes sexual experiences, and money can move in either direction. But also like them, he does not necessarily enjoy every encounter. He seduces a rich widow, but eventually "begun to be tyr'd with her too frequent invitations to venereal sports: the more I endeavoured to satisfie her, the more insatiate she was." He leaves, but "not without sufficient recompence for my service."[29]

The rogue thus resembles the female prostitutes in Restoration libertine literature: He wheedles money from the opposite sex, exhausts himself in sexual labor, and spends his excess cash on more sex; his desire seems nearly insatiable, he indulges in luxuries, and he rides the wheel of fortune, moving from place to place, partner to partner. He even impersonates a female prostitute. *The English Rogue*, then, suggests the ways in which dispossession and resulting mobility feminize its hero. But even though Meriton Latroon engages in the same survival strategies and expressions of desire as female prostitutes, the narrative resists the potential collapse of gender difference through this feminization by offering horrific images of female abjection through prostitution. At one point he meets a bawd:

This Tun of Flesh resembled an Elephant for the bigness of her waste; . . . A Nose she had (which with all wonder be it spoken) so long, as that it was a fit resemblance of the Elephants Proboscis or Trunk. . . . Her Teeth were faln out.

Looking into her mouth,

Me thought I saw Hell gaping to devour me; and within that bottomless Concave, I could discern infinite numbers of Souls whose damnation she was accessary to; and coming somewhat too near her, I imagined her breath was bitumenous and smelt of Brimston. (1:83)

The rogue seems to rebound from each of his adventures, however exhausting; overuse, though, wears women down and turns them into mere commodities:

In the faces of the common Traders, by diligent search, you may find some raggs of overworn Beauty, like old Cloaths in Brokers windows, to make you believe, that there are better Wares within; Yet he that trades with them, is like to have a bad bargain, for she can sell him nothing but the Pox, or Repentance. As for their upper parts, they are the Shops of Cupid, and their lower parts are his Warehouse. (4:211)

The English Rogue, though in some ways eliding differences between its hero and female prostitutes, displaces onto female bodies the physical calamities of prostitution: disease, filth, poverty, decay, and abjection. Prostitution turns female bodies into "loathsome stinking Carreon."

As in many late seventeenth-century narratives, desire rather than estrangement characterizes prostitution in *The English Rogue*; nevertheless, the text describes the misery of excessive whoring through tropes of commodification. The souls in the gaping cavern of the bawd's mouth may have belonged to men whom she tempted into sin, but they also must have belonged to women whose sexual labor she exploited. The bawd has grown into a "tun" of flesh, fattened by her profits at the expense of these now-suffering souls.[30] She has consumed so greedily that she can no longer even move. As the "overworn" whores continue in their trade, they evoke less and less of the sexual and more and more of the economic. These "common Traders" become less like humans and more like objects; their upper parts become "shops of Cupid," their lower parts his "Warehouse": they embody commerce. Time has "bankrupted" their value, and now they resemble rotten slabs of meat. The sexual marketplace has drained the life out of them, and they serve as haunting reminders of its capacity to turn a person into a thing. The male body, at least for the moment, remains protected from this fate.

Passions and Interests

The English Rogue, then, describes the terror of commercial absorption through female bodies; the rogue himself, however, displaced and dispossessed by colonial conflicts, often finds himself in the same predicament—and even the same outfit—as the prostitute. Further, the rogue proves no better at business than Behn's Angellica Bianca, for he also spends his profits on his pleasures. For both reformist writers like Mill and roguish writers like Head and Kirkman, prostitutes serve as transgressive figures of endless and reckless desire for money, pleasure, sex, and luxury; they flout the emergent bourgeois values of careful accumulation and delayed gratification. Even though their individualism and mobility align them with the emergent commercial economy, they nevertheless lack the detachment and foresight to invest, accumulate, or think carefully about the economic consequences of their actions. The whores and rogues in Mill, Head, and Kirkman may be crafty and greedy, but their roguishness/whorishness—their *excessive* desire—prevents them from making the most of their opportunities. Commercial society demands desire; at the same time, the most successful traders need something more.

Had he studied whore and rogue narratives as part of capitalism's early self-representation, Albert O. Hirschman might have concluded that they represent exactly the kind of passions that defenders of capitalism believed the new system could regulate—or, more accurately, could counterbalance with other passions.[31] Marx, as Hirschman points out, argued that capitalism repressed the full human personality. But, Hirschman responds, in the early modern era this is precisely what it was supposed to do, as a broad range of philosophers saw the full human personality as dangerous. Throughout his work, Marx contemplated capitalism's fallout through the problem of *alienation*— meaning both the market exchange of a commodity (including labor) and implicitly its resulting fragmentation or dehumanization.[32] While most prostitutes (and impoverished, feminized men who act like prostitutes) in these narratives passionately act on immediate desire, a few publications in this period reflect on the possibilities of contractarianism and distance in sexual commerce. They begin to imagine, in other words, that even in whoring there might be a balance between passions and interests that can be achieved only through a carefully controlled self-division.

The possibility of the dispassionate commodification of sexual labor, in either degrading or empowering forms, appears alongside descriptions of the whore's intractable passion not because such narratives are more "realistic" or because sex work is inherently and transhistorically the most unpleasant form of labor, but because in the late seventeenth century the assumption was the opposite. In this context, to imagine prostitution as work or a business comically yokes opposites, providing an opportunity to reflect on, parody, work through, and advance the idea of dispassionate contractual exchange itself. We see sparks of this tension in *The Crafty Whore* (1658), a dialogue "between two Subtle Bawds" (Thais and Antonia) revealing their "crafty devices."[33] Though ultimately repentant, Thais and Antonia discuss how prostitution has served as a double opportunity for "profit and pleasure" (27). As Thais points out,

> what Woman is so affectionate, as to be satisfied with one Man. Surely it would require the strength of Atlas shoulders, and Hercules his back, to stand to so hard a taske, as the satisfying of the amorous emotions of a lustfull Woman. (39–40)

Given the extreme lasciviousness that Thais claims, it seems unimaginable that any other interest could counterbalance this passion. She proudly offers, however, an anecdote about her own heroic self-control at the beginning of her career. A man courted her to purchase her presumed virginity, a high-priced commodity in the sex trade. Impersonating a virgin, she had to resist sex with him to keep up both the deception and her price.[34] When alone, he "offered to my view a thousand female alluring gestures (which I must confesse the truth had almost overcome my craft and seeming chastity)" (13–14). Despite both his temptations and violent advances, Thais heroically subordinates her passions to her interests. Antonia expresses her incredulity at this feat: "had I been in thy case, I should have even *melted* at his discourse and gestures" (15). Thais sympathizes with her friend's desire, but boasts how she wisely "preferd profit before that momentary delight" (15). While the lover at first grows furious, Thais's strategy eventually pays off. Rather than pursuing sex and money with the same reckless abandon, Thais carefully balances her passion for one against her passion for the other.

The *Whore's Rhetorick* (1683) perhaps most thoroughly explores the possibility of prostitution as the commodification of dispassionate sexual labor in this period. Catherine Gallagher uses *The Whore's Rhetorick* to demonstrate how the prostitute quintessentially embodies the alienation necessary to achieve eventual wholeness and even empowerment in a marketplace economy.[35] The text, however, achieves this by depending on the reader's initial assumption of prostitution as passionate indulgence and satirically proposing the potential novelty, absurdity, and paradox of the sexually unresponsive or self-controlled whore. *The Whore's Rhetorick* features the education of a new girl (Dorothea) into the trade, a standard situation in early pornography. But while Fanny Hill would later submit herself to a *sexual* education, the bawd Mother Creswell assumes that potential prostitutes most urgently needed another kind of knowledge:

> As Trade and Traders increase, so must industry and ingenuity: and there are at this day, such a great plenty of Whores, that to live well, and to continue in that state, it is necessary to understand more than what is vulgar and common.[36]

Sex is vulgar and common. What a whore must *learn* to understand is money: "you must pretend a contempt of money," but at the same time "your avarice must be insatiable" (40). While *The Whore's Rhetorick* ostensibly aims to warn men against savvy whores, it assumes that women begin guilty of desire but innocent of trade. Mother Creswell thus explicitly proposes to form Dorothea in a self-consciously *new* model consistent with the demands of a new economy. The time will eventually come for leisure and comfort, she explains, "when you are cloyed with pleasure, and grown weary of venereal pastimes." She will then be able to retire "like a Usurer, who is grown old and tired with cheating, who has quit both Exchange and Coffee-House on the score of business," but only after "you have suffered sufficient drudgery" (32–33).[37] Mother Creswell distinguishes for Dorothea the difference between the professional and the amateur; unlike the interlocutors in *The Wandring Whore*, however, she reserves her contempt for the latter. She declares that she will confine her remarks for the benefit of those in the trade, as opposed to "the married Women, Widow, or superficial Maid; who do not obey the dictates of interest, but prostitute themselves meerly to gratify their libidinous appetites" (41).

Mother Creswell's hope to create this new, professional whore satirizes the emergent commercial culture by insisting that the prostitute can become like any other commercial agent, thus suggesting the ways that other commercial agents resemble prostitutes. Prostitution thus emerges as an extreme form of normal business rather than simply a sign of unrestrained passion. The whore must "be at least as dexterous in the vending her goods, as the Habberdasher at putting off his small-ware" (38). Prostitutes enter a volatile unpredictable marketplace, but, the bawd points out, "there is incertainty in all traffick" and the best tradesmen learn to take risks (49). In sexual as well as other trades, money erases the distinction between the gentleman and the mechanic; "let men be divided in your Books under the names of Rich, Poor, Liberal, and Niggardly," for "money removes all stench, from the meanest action, by vertue of its purging quality" (50–51). In her treatment of her bawd, the prostitute must imitate the "discreet Merchant" who motivates his ship's captain by allowing him a small portion of the cargo rather than a monthly stipend (81). The smartest prostitutes reinvest in their own value: "nothing advances a Whores credit and reputation more than these external appearances of pomp and grandeur" (110). Yet this is not because an expensive dress makes her more beautiful, but rather because, in Mother Creswell's view, desire is mimetic: "as in other Trades, they that are richest, are ever thought to be furnished with the best Commodities, have most Customers, and sell their Wares at the dearest rates" (110–111). The young whore must recognize that "commodities" (pun surely intended) do not gain value through any intrinsic merit or usefulness, but through the way they announce desirability. Like any fashionable merchant, the whore must "Frenchify" her "Commodities" (114); she must charge regularly or "discredit her government." Dorothea must in particular emulate lawyers, "well stored with Bar-impudence, not to be run down, by dint of sense nor force of Argument." Like a lawyer, she must patiently suffer all

scurrilous abuse, so the Libertines Purse be sufficient to atone the miscarriage: I would have her likewise give her Client a fine story for his Money, as the Lawyers serves his; and lastly let her be sure to hate a poor Lover, as much as the Lawyer does a *pauper* Client. (72)

Dorothea, however, despairs over her inability to meet so high a standard, as lawyers "have more jilting tricks than I can hope to have after all your instructions" (62).

In the second dialogue, Mother Creswell offers the more advanced lesson of detachment: Dorothea must sacrifice both sexual pleasure and indulgence in luxuries. This approach will not only bring her financial security but will distinguish her from all other whores. This new kind of whore, Mother Creswell insists, "must strive to out-do the severest Moralist, in controlling and subjugating all your untowardly and prejudicial passions, as love, any external marks of envy, hatred, malitious anger, and such like" (179); most of all, "a universal Whore can receive but little satisfaction in point of venereal desires" (203). Dorothea resists this severity: "I never desire to arrive at that degree of mortification" (202) she insists when the bawd observes that "Ladies of large business are generally no more moved by an imbrace, than if they were made of Wood or Stone" (202). In some ways Mother Creswell tries to minimize this problem, suggesting that Dorothea's elite selectivity will rescue her from this fate. Yet Mother Creswell remains adamant on the necessity of managing desire, offering her own life of indulgence, pleasure, and subsequent poverty as a negative example to be avoided. The problem with most prostitutes, she insists, is that they immediately spend all their profits on personal indulgences (mostly sexual). Further, they tend to choose clients on the basis of their charm rather than generosity. Mother Creswell, however, declares that in Dorothea she will create a new kind of prostitute. Successful prostitutes need to develop a careful, rational core self to withhold, a dispassionate self that does not find its fullest expression in sexuality. The untrained whore does not experience this self-division because she fully expresses her core self through sexuality; the graduate of Mother Creswell's academy, however, will develop an outer self of theatrical passion and an inner accountant.[38] If she achieves this, she will not only differ from all other prostitutes, but from all other women as well. Mother Creswell, then, believes she proposes nothing short of a new form of subjectivity.

In *The Whore's Rhetorick*, prostitution satirically offers the most extreme challenge to the self-control demanded by the marketplace, for if you can train a whore to stop liking sex for the sake of business, then you can train *anyone* to relinquish what he or she understands to be the heart of his or her identity in exchange for money. Mother Creswell, after all, is not a disinterested party but rather the owner of the means of production, so to speak, training a new worker to maximize her own surplus value. The prospect of sacrificing pleasure, however, troubles the student. Dorothea wonders if a lady might now and then "divert her self with other Lovers" besides paying clients (69)—Angellica Bianca's downfall and the one Mother Creswell warns against. "Are there no other qualifications required in an amorous confident," Dorothea objects, "beside discretion, and generosity?" (70). After her first lesson, Dorothea relays an anxious dream: First she lords over an array of beasts who "lickt me from top to Toe, shewing marks of content in being thus cruelly treated" (131). But then a "stately young Buffle [Buffalo?] . . . forcibly took me on his Horns, from whence I could by no means free myself, till the Bull gave me leave to alight in the midst of a mighty Forest, and there methought I was forced to draw in a Yoak with this wild Beast: the fright of which awakened me in great confusion" (132). Mother Creswell reads this as prophetic: Dorothea will lord over many gulls until a young gentleman carries her away to his country house and shares with her the yoke of marriage. Thus the bawd promises the fantasy *Fanny Hill* will deliver: a successful prostitution career crowned by happy marriage. But Mother Creswell's reading distracts Dorothea from the ominousness that initially terrified her: the image of Dorothea yoked to a wild beast suggests both sexual threat and unpleasant drudgery. After analyzing the dream, Mother Creswell thus gives Dorothea an extended lesson on how to endure a superannuated or otherwise unappealing lover. The student wonders how it is possible "to regulate ones self" in such circumstances (149) and also worries about the opposite danger of falling in love. The bawd promises to procure for her the drug *"Misanthropia"* to keep her always in a "cool state of indifference" (154). As Dorothea listens to a range of strategies for achieving this cool state of indifference in the face of disgust, horror, pleasure or passion, she expresses dismay but eventually capitulates, accepting the yoke. To Mother Creswell's closing image of the emergent successful prostitute as emulating an ascetic in a monastery, no longer a woman, and dead before the law, Dorothea reluctantly concedes: "even so be it" (222). She thus agrees to develop a theatrical outer self for the (sexual) marketplace and a core inner self held back from it, thus glimpsing the key role the prostitute will play in eighteenth-century narratives.

Pamela/Anti-Pamela

By the end of the eighteenth century (to take a brief look ahead), the implied absurdity of the dispassionate whore had been neutralized. What began as a figure of comic incongruity had come to represent the most severe, pathetic, and fascinating form of human estrangement possible. Prostitution had become predictably contractual (although not, as we will later see, inflexibly gendered). In a late-century poem by Samuel Jackson Pratt, a prostitute confesses how

Famine, and guilt, and conscience tore my heart,
And urg'd me to pursue the wanton's part.
Take then the truth, and learn at once my shame;
Such my hard fate—I welcom'd all that came.
   But oh! no transport mingled in my stains,
No guilty pleasure ever sooth'd my pains;
No vicious hope indelicately gay,
Nor warmer passions lull'd my cares away,
The flattering compliment fatigu'd my ear,
While half-afraid, I half conceal'd a tear,
Whole nights I past insensible of bliss,
Lost to the loath'd embrace, and odious kiss;
Nor wine nor mirth the aching heart could fire,
Nor could the sprightly music aught inspire;
Alive to each reflection that oppress'd;
The more I gain'd the more I was distress'd;
Even in the moment of unblest desire,
Oft would the wretch complain I wanted fire;
Cold as a statue in his arms I lay,
Wept through the night, and blush'd along the day.[39]

While seventeenth-century prostitutes enjoy sex far too much for their own good, Pratt's fallen woman has no need for Mother Creswell's school. Reformers concurred on the prostitute's victimization rather than sexual indulgence: "If their crimes are black and their folly great," reformer Jonas Hanway argued in 1761,

their misery keeps pace with both. . . . Every other animal is obedient to his appetite, but appetite has frequently no share in the promiscuous commerce of these women.[40]

The title character in "The Suicide Prostitute" (1805) envies virtuous women because they do not know the "horrible disgust/ Of feign'd enjoyment, and affected lust."[41] While pornographers certainly kept the desiring whore alive, medical writers at the end of the century concluded that frequent dispassionate sex not only destroys "[the prostitute's] own happiness, it destroys the vigour of the genital parts."[42] This diminished sensual capacity causes sterility, and the prostitute then "loaths her body like a carrion."[43] Such women will clearly never ruin their business for the sake of pleasure, as Mother Creswell fears for her student.[44]

   The extreme capacity of the prostitute in later narratives to distance herself from her work, however, becomes grounds for sympathy and even sometimes provides the opportunity for heroism. In the "History of Ann and Mary

Woodfield," for example, two innocent sisters are tricked, drugged, and raped into prostitution. When the rakes eventually tire of them, they go "on the town" to obtain "their wretched support from any disgusting object."[45] They try to escape prostitution, but when one falls ill, the other, withholding her tears, walks the streets to support them both. Thus one woman endures prostitution not out of lust or greed but as the cruelest imaginable sacrifice she must make to support her dying sister. She becomes admirable in this narrative for her self-division into an affectionate sister at home and a dispassionate prostitute in public.

Even in some of the most virulently anti-prostitution texts, the prostitute lost to enjoyment finds leniency. In Richard King's *Frauds of London Detected* (1780?), the prostitute becomes a figure for the impersonal, dissipated, luxurious marketplace that London has, in the author's view, become.[46] But while King blames a staggering range of social ills on prostitution and elevates whoring to the ur-symptom of corruption in the marketplace, he nevertheless offers (albeit grudging and condescending) pity for the prostitutes themselves, whom he represents as victims of male desire and the greed of other women. Common prostitutes,

> lost to all shame and decency, and tho' palled with heated lust, are still, *to feed loathsome life*, devoted to every flagitious and wicked purpose for bread, and continually as it were forcing men to their disgustful embraces . . . . Compelled by necessity, they prostitute themselves for the smallest consideration . . . they become loathsome and hideous spectacles to themselves. (92)

Those who work out of houses may look more attractive, but are nevertheless oppressed and abused by bawds, "obliged to submit to their instruction, and act according to their directions, however shocking or disgraceful to their sex and humanity" (93). The most dangerous prostitutes who deserve no pity, however, are the ones who are *not* "palled with heated lust": they resemble respectable ladies overcome with passion, "But, alas! no sooner are you gone, than they jilt you, fly to some favourite paramour they are intimate with, and frequently bestow on him what you bestowed on them" (40). Unlike the pathetic, victimized prostitute, the "jilt" uses prostitution to feed her own insatiable desire and thus represents female guilt of another order. The exploited woman who deserves sympathy and becomes capable of reform has, by contrast, achieved the kind of self-division that Mother Creswell teaches: She has reserved part of her core self as separate from the marketplace and from her work; she can balance her interest against her passion, even if an initial failure to do so led to prostitution in the first place. In this respect, she (or he) serves as an intriguing paradigm for and experiment in the emerging forms of identity in the marketplace.

This becomes clear in not just the writing of reformers and social critics, but in literary texts as well. As Nancy Armstrong has influentially argued, Samuel Richardson's *Pamela* (1740) attracted so much attention because it captured not simply a servant girl's plight but something fundamental about the modern individual. This figure of modern individualism, however, becomes in the novel associated with the decision whether or not to become a prostitute, which, as Ann Kibbie observes, implicitly broadens into the novel's identification of the problem of modern individualism as the potential alienation of the self in the marketplace.[47] Prostitution clearly would have been Pamela's fate had she succumbed to her employer Mr. B——'s advances, and Richardson evokes Pamela's potential to be corrupted though details such as the inappropriately luxurious clothing she inherits.[48] That Pamela resists seduction, however, does not end the suspicion that she has resisted self-division, for those who accuse Pamela of feminine wiles find a form of prostitution (or failure to preserve the self from the marketplace) revealed in her material gain from the marriage. In the suspicious reading, Pamela does not refuse sex because of her virtue or insistence on her own inner worth, but instead holds out for the most lucrative contract. One critic has even declared the possibility of the suspicious reading as the novel's major flaw: Richardson did not take enough care to keep the readers from seeing Pamela as a hypocrite.[49]

The storm of "anti-Pamelas" that *Pamela* raised invariably associated the heroine with prostitution. They tend to accuse the novel of two related faults: first, that the narrative arouses sensuality, and second, that the heroine exploits the market value of her sexuality.[50] The anonymous author of *Pamela Censured* reportedly kept the novel from his daughter, for "no young Girl however innocent she may be . . . can possibly read several Passages in it . . . without conceiving Ideas she otherwise might never have dream'd of."[51] Pamela acts "as if she had been born and bred in Covent Garden" (22). William B. Warner has argued that *Pamela* generated this response because Richardson "overwrites" the novel of amorous intrigue, attempting to elevate his own fiction while simultaneously exploiting the success of this earlier form.[52] Warner points to striking similarities between *Pamela* and *Fantomina:* Fantomina adopts disguises to keep attracting her lover, for example, and Pamela "tricks" herself out in country clothes, a transformation that reinvigorates Mr. B's desire (194). But if much of *Pamela*'s power and durability, as Warner suggests, lies in the embedded tensions with amorous fiction, we might then think productively about *Pamela*'s difference from these novels as well. Most obviously but worth mentioning, Pamela actually resists seduction, whereas in the novels of amorous intrigue the heroines tend to succumb to their passion. Sexuality does not divide these amorous heroines; rather, they express their fullest and most profound identities *through* their sexuality. The importance (for our purposes) of Warner's insight here lies in the resulting characterization of Pamela as *resisting* sex with Mr. B, with its implication that, at some level, sex tempts her. Resistance, in fact, for contemporaries linked Pamela to prostitution (holding out for the best contract); Fantomina, by contrast, seeks no remuneration. For models of manipulative *resistance* to sex and the capacity to quell one's own desire, we must thus turn away from the novels of amorous intrigue and to prostitute narratives. Thais in *The Crafty Whore* proudly describes to Antonia how she raised her price higher and higher by setting up scenes of seduction and heroically resisting them. Whether or not texts like *The Crafty Whore* actually influenced Richardson, contemporaries recognized and parodied *Pamela*'s similarities.

Henry Fielding's *Shamela* thus satirizes the novel's claim of Pamela's escape from marketplace values through virtue. His Shamela is not an "anti-Pamela"—that is, the opposite of Pamela—but the "true" Pamela trying to get the best contract through strategic self-control. Shamela's mother, an old bawd herself, carefully advises her daughter as Mother Creswell does Dorothea: "I . . . am convinced," she declares, "it will be your own Fault if you are not married to your Master, and I would advise you now to take no less Terms,"[53] even though Shamela herself had been aiming for just a settlement (15). Mother Andrews worries that Shamela will ruin everything by sleeping with Parson Williams, for "a Married Woman injures only her Husband, but a Single Woman herself" (35). Both "Mothers" understand the whore's own sexual desire as her (and thus their) greatest enemy. Shamela, however, has absorbed the correct ethos. She rues the demand to attract and resist Squire Booby: "*Oh Parson* Williams, *how little are all the Men in the World compared to thee*" (32). Following her mother's guidance and her own good instincts, she nevertheless endures her task by fantasizing about the lover while entertaining the fool, a technique specifically recommended by Mother Creswell. By doing so, Shamela arouses the master's desire while controlling her own: Emergent bourgeois norms, Fielding suggests, find their exemplary expression in the prostitute. Pamela's resistance to prostitution, then, becomes so interesting in part because it suggests a broader problem of all selves in the marketplace. As both *Joseph Andrews* and James Parry's *The True Anti-Pamela* (1741), which places a young man in the "Pamela" position, suggest, female bodies might have come conventionally to represent marketplace tensions between desire and estrangement, but they are not the only ones able to experience them.[54]

In *Shamela*, then, Fielding satirizes Richardson by creating a heroine who exhibits Pamela's suspected mercenary qualities cloaked by the veil of virtue.

Eliza Haywood, by contrast, creates a character who *fails* to be Pamela. Like Shamela, Haywood's Syrena Tricksey likes sex; unlike the virtuous Pamela, she does not wait until marriage. Yet in Haywood, unlike in both *Pamela* and *Shamela*, the woman does not triumph. On the one hand, Haywood appears to propose this as a morally superior outcome: She subtitles the novel "Mock-Modesty Display'd and Punish'd."[55] On the other hand, the character she creates is comical and even endearing in her own vulnerable way. In episode after episode, Syrena, with the help of her bawdlike mother, carefully sets elaborate, Shamela-esque traps for wealthy men; time after time, however, her own drive toward pleasure ruins them, leaving her broke and humiliated. While Shamela also indulges in an affair, Syrena lacks Shamela's strategic discretion; further, the men in *Anti-Pamela* lack Squire Booby's gullibility. For example, Syrena at one point secures a position as an older gentleman's companion. While the relationship begins as a friendship, gradually (and painstakingly on Syrena's end) the gentleman grows more and more affectionate. He finally resolves to marry Syrena, offering the financial security to which she had long aspired. The delighted gentleman invites his son to meet his intended; upon meeting Syrena, however, the son recognizes her as the woman he had picked up in a tavern just a few nights before. He tells his father, who promptly cuts off Syrena with nothing. So although Syrena has sufficient beauty, charm, and theatricalized virtue to attract a man of means, her inability or unwillingness to forgo sexual pleasure, even for a relatively brief period of time, consistently ruins her carefully laid schemes. Syrena's mother warns against this weakness, but Syrena proves a poor student: while she allows her mother to guide her in the minutia of her social behavior, she sometimes withholds from her the strictly recreational affairs. Mother and daughter both agree that Syrena should use her sexual allure to secure wealth; Syrena, however, can never quite achieve the necessary detachment.

   Thus Haywood reveals the true opposite of Pamela not as the scheming Shamela who dupes her master into a marriage but as the strangely innocent Syrena who won't listen to her mother and follows her desires. On the one hand, Haywood calls the mother and daughter both "hypocritical" (144) and offers their story as a warning against such dangerous women. On the other hand, Syrena remains idealistic and even sympathetic in a strange way throughout: She truly believes that her beauty will bring her happiness, but at the same time places great confidence in the power of her own passion. Her mother tries to teach her the art of hypocrisy, but she never fully accepts it. Despite the novel's stated moral, then, Syrena emerges as an alternative to the relentless self-control and daughterly obedience of Pamela, Shamela, and Dorothea. Further, Haywood places her heroine's plight in the broader context of a less optimistic view of male response. Haywood condemns Syrena's indulgence, but simultaneously—and poignantly—communicates her desperation. For example, at the end of one park-walking season, Syrena finds herself without "one Conquest, which was no small Mortification to this fine Lady, especially as her Money was almost exhausted in Cloaths, luxurious Eating, and Chair-Hire" (145). She attends a masquerade, meets Lord R—, and spends the night with him, indulging in mutual dissimulation: "*Syrena* artfully mingling with her pretended Fondness certain modest Shocks to heighten his good Opinion of her, and he affecting to be possest of a more than ordinary Passion, for the more emboldning her to meet his amorous Desires with equal Warmth" (147). Nevertheless, Syrena refuses to accept this encounter as an exchange. She initially rejects his payment of ten guineas, "telling him that he injured her greatly if he imagin'd she had yielded from any motive but Love" (147). But he forces her to accept them as a token of his affection. She takes them on those terms,

> but were every Piece a Thousand I would reject them with Scorn if offer'd as the purchase of my Virtue—I am no Prostitute, continued she, and if I thought you look'd on me as such, and having accomplish'd your Desires would never see me more, I would this Instant undeceive you, by running your Sword through my too fond, too easily charm'd Heart. (147–148)

Lord R— smiles to hear her talk in such a "romantick Stile." In spite of his promises, however, she does not hear from him. Her mother advises her to let it go, but Syrena boldly and naively presents herself at his house. Shocked, Lord R— asks her to leave for the sake of "both our Reputations" (151), whereupon Syrena bursts into fake tears that don't move this experienced rake: "You were all Gaity when I saw you before," he responds, "and good Company, and if you desire to pass three or four Hours again in the same Manner, I assure you this is not the way to charm a Man of my Humour" (151). This insult, however, stirs genuine rage, hurt, and umbrage, to which Lord R— responds by suggesting she learn better manners. Syrena swoons, but Lord R— understands the swoon as fake and further humiliates her by threatening to dunk her head in a pail of water.

Haywood's narrative voice at this point intervenes to attempt to rescue Lord R— from the "Savageness and Brutality" with which the reader will surely tax him (152). But the damage has been done, for his cruelty exceeds any offense by Syrena. Syrena aspires to become a clever whore, creating a Shamela/Lord Booby or Pamela/Mr. B affair. Haywood, however, demystifies this possibility. Those who can't manage the skillful self-division of a Pamela/Shamela risk the abject humiliation that Syrena suffers: After all, wealthy men will not always be seduced into submission. Fielding and

Richardson here offer narratives of triumph, but Haywood suggests the woman's profound vulnerability. Further, while her novel officially condemns Syrena's pleasure seeking, Haywood nevertheless creates a character that ironically comes across as more sincere than Shamela and even perhaps more than Pamela for her inability to become dispassionate. *Shamela* exposes the awkward dissonance in Richardson between the intensity of Pamela's resistance and her eventual agreement to marry Mr. B—an agreement that must, at least superficially, be understood as motivated by genuine affection rather than calculation. In a less accomplished writer, this awkwardness becomes patently obvious: In the *Memoirs of the Life of Lady H—*, a narrative riding on the popularity of *Pamela* and supposedly telling the true story of the woman who provided the model for Richardson's heroine, the narrator explains this transition from resisting servant to loving wife as a detail left out earlier that must later be supplied. Pamela

> had always behaved in a very reserved Manner, and had discountenanced the Importunities and Addresses of her Fellow-Servants, and seemed entirely free from the Passion of Love. Notwithstanding which, from the Time her Master ordered her to hold the Bason whilst he washed his Hands, she felt a flutter in her Spirits, she could not account for, whenever she saw him. Her heart was then captivated, tho' she durst not even know it herself.[56]

Richardson attempts to address this problem with greater literary sophistication; nevertheless, it remains the point of vulnerability that Fielding's parody reveals. Pamela, as Catherine Gallagher suggests of women in general in the eighteenth century, must learn to regulate her desire so fully that she can avoid feelings for an inappropriate object, and yet immediately summon them when an appropriate object presents himself.[57] The accomplished Pamela has no problem with this system; the vulnerable Syrena, however, fails to manage it.

We see this in the painful incident with Lord R—. Unlike Pamela, Syrena blatantly aspires to her lord's affections and presumes a kind of human equality with him. While she does not expect marriage and seeks financial advantage, she also assumes that mutual desire would form the foundation for an ongoing relationship, even an illicit one. Thus Lord R—'s "savage and brutal" humiliation does not come across as the girl's comeuppance, as Haywood well knows. Instead, the author disturbingly exposes how Lord R— considers Syrena's sexuality a disposable commodity. Syrena, however, rebelliously refuses to accept this, even when, as her mother consistently tries to explain, it would work to her considerable advantage.

Syrena's problem, then, is not that she is too much of a whore, but rather that she is not enough of one. In this quality she joins Angelica Bianca, who undermines her own market by giving away pleasure when she might be better off selling it. Behn and Haywood both create compelling prostitute characters by showing, albeit in different ways, the prostitute's self-destructive but also compelling inability or unwillingness to sacrifice desire for advancement. We could read Haywood's "anti" in *"Anti-Pamela"* as moralistic, but we could also read it as resistance. Richardson's Pamela and Fielding's Shamela resemble prostitute figures in the way they raise male desires, but at the same time exert remarkable control over their own. Haywood, by contrast, creates a character for whom interest does not provide a successful counterbalance to passion. If Pamela and Shamela suggest the opportunities in a commercial culture for those who combine cleverness, restraint, and strategic self-division, Angellica and Syrena represent the fallout of those who ironically remain strangely unjaded and never sufficiently manage to divide themselves. In subtle ways, they and their authors—fully creatures of the marketplace themselves—suggest not the failings of individual female characters but the demands of the new economy itself and the costs to its more vulnerable subjects. If only Syrena and Angellica Bianca had studied at Mother Creswell's academy, they too might have mastered the "cool state of indifference" and earned the wealth and comfort of a Pamela.[58]

2

The "Deluge of Depravity":
Bernard Mandeville
and the Reform Societies

The Town being overstock'd with Harlots, is entirely owning
to those Numbers of Women-Servants, incessantly pouring into
it from all Corners of the Universe, and those Debaucheries
practis'd upon 'em in almost all the Families that entertain them:
Masters, Footmen, Journeymen, Lodgers, Apprentices, &c. are for
ever attempting to corrupt . . . so that a poor Wench who serves
for four or five Pounds a Year Wages, shall be liable to go through
as much Drudgery, as a Livery-Horse, that's let out to a City
'Prentice for a Sunday's Airing.

Father Poussin, *Pretty Doings in a Protestant Nation*

As Jonathan Swift's nymph Corinna prepares for bed af-
ter trolling Drury Lane, she removes her artificial hair, her crystal eye, a set
of false teeth, and eyebrows made from mouse pelt, revealing the hideousness beneath her simulated beauty. She applies plasters to her running sores
and wipes off the last of her makeup. Nightmares bring beatings in Bridewell
or transportation to Jamaica "Alone, and by no planter courted." She wakes
to discover her false body parts mangled, scattered, and infested by vermin;
she must "every morn her limbs unite" before vending her beauty again.[1] In
this poem, Corinna embodies the worst possibilities of commodification: her
body, with its lumps pressed down and hollows filled, blurs the distinction
between the human and the thing. Swift also turns to a prostitute figure to
suggest corruption in *Gulliver's Travels*, where La Puta (the whore) hovers
threateningly over the land below. In the early eighteenth century, a range of
Tory and civic humanist writers, like Swift, turned to grotesque or threaten-

ing prostitute figures to expose the consumer revolution's troubling economic, moral, and cultural dislocations.[2] Civic humanist rhetoric transformed the traditional figure of Fortuna, J. G. A. Pocock has shown, into fickle ladies embodying the new economy's corruption, unpredictability, and encouragement of dangerous desires.[3]

But it was not just traditionalists with whom the figure of the prostitute resonated as an emblem of economic modernity: Writers with considerably more ambivalence turned to this image as well. Daniel Defoe, who engaged in and supported various commercial projects, lamented that Lady Credit had become no lady.[4] Joseph Addison, Richard Steele, and the Earl of Shaftesbury attempted to extend civic humanist philosophy to the rising commercial classes through the ideal of politeness;[5] in doing so, they also invoked the prostitute to confront the pitfalls of the new economy. Addison and Steele had more patience with commercial culture than did Swift: in *The Spectator*, local and global trade could polish manners. *The Spectator* thus generated a more sentimental, less grotesque picture of prostitution, as we see in Mr. Spectator's description of his encounter with one:

> I could observe as exact Features as I had ever seen, the most agreeable Shape, the finest Neck and Bosom, in a Word, the whole Person of a Woman exquisitely beautiful. She affected to allure me with a forced Wantonness in her Look and Air; but I saw it checked with Hunger and Cold: Her Eyes were wan and eager, her Dress thin and Tawdry, her Mein genteel and childish. This strange Figure gave me much Anguish of Heart, and to avoid being seen with her I went away, but could nor forbear giving her a Crown. The poor thing sighed, curtsied, and with a Blessing, expressed with the utmost Vehemence, turned from me.[6]

Although Mr. Spectator will not risk being seen with her, this prostitute, with her combination of loveliness and despair, weary humanity and objectification ("poor thing"), affords the opportunity for an acute emotional experience that demonstrates the narrator's own refinement of feeling. The emotion, however, emerges from the tension between the prostitute's theatricalized desire ("forced Wantonness") and her desperate poverty; for a moment, Mr. Spectator glimpses the prostitute's material circumstances and the possibility that something other than salaciousness drives her. But to distinguish himself immediately from zealous (less "polite") reformers and lest he "grow too suddenly grave on this Subject," he turns to a scene from Fletcher's *Humorous Lieutenant*. Here Leucippe the court bawd "read[s] her Minutes as a Person of Business," listing the qualities and market value of each of her ladies. Steele praises this scene as having the "true Spirit of Comedy." Yet this comic scene of prostitution as ordinary business bears a strange relationship to the tragedy of a pathetically beautiful creature degraded and exploited by a Hobbesian city. Steele offers two unreconciled views of prostitution: In one, the marketplace cheerfully meets the desires of both parties; in the other, callous exploitation and human suffering lurk below the surface of an alluring exchange. Prostitution seems to summarize here *The Spectator*'s ambivalence toward emergent commercial culture itself.[7]

In formulating his ambivalence, Steele distinguishes himself from the zealous reformers who populated the Societies for the Reformation of Manners (SRMs). While polite moralists wrote poignant essays and satirists conjured grotesque images, members of the SRMs harassed living women on the streets. The SRMs launched an unprecedented and violent vigilante campaign against prostitution in the late seventeenth and early eighteenth centuries:[8] Swift may have dismembered prostitutes in verse, and Steele may have exploited their sentimental potential, but contemporary reformers hunted them down in the flesh. Streetwalking, as countless reformers complained, had become a significantly more visible part of the metropolitan landscape.[9] These activist reformers did not usually consider, except in passing, the material circumstances of suspected prostitutes; like their Restoration predecessors, they generally assumed that sexual desire drove these women into the streets. For reformers, prostitution had become a serious urban threat, encouraging disorderly practices that undermined proper business: Prostitutes drained money and male labor from industry; servant girls who became prostitutes upset the social order and diminished the available pool of household help; bawdy houses harbored criminals; streetwalkers ruined the reputation of the city in the eyes of foreigners, impeded business, destroyed families, and diminished the population through their presumed sterility. For the period's politest essayists and its rudest activists, prostitution embodied the infamous commerce that threatened to undermine legitimate trade.

The first part of this chapter explores the impact, writing, and activism of these lesser-known vigilantes rather than the period's more eloquent and better-known contenders for the crown of virtue. The SRMs had philosophical and material ties to proponents of both elite and bourgeois civic humanism, but nevertheless departed from them on certain key points. Unlike Addison and Steele (although Steele at one point declared his membership in the Societies), they upheld righteousness rather than refinement as the counterbalance to unpredictability; unlike the traditional elite civic humanists, they rejected the proposition that stability rested on the virtue of wealthy landowners. Instead, they appointed themselves guardians of middling and laboring-class virtue; they sought to purify rather than resist the newly expanded commercial economy. But while these reformers (with the notable exception of John Dunton, whom I treat separately) usually assumed that lust motivated infamous commerce on both sides, they also treated prostitution as an economic problem. For them, prostitution not only encouraged and constituted irresponsible luxury consumption but also provided the prime example of the limits of exchange a marketplace must accept in order to prosper. Prostitution dangerously represented the luxurious indulgences that would draw God's wrath upon the nation, but it also posed more earthly threats: In their presumed sterility, prostitutes failed to produce the needed workers, colonists, sailors, and soldiers; tempted by idleness, they deprived the silk, wool, and cotton industries of the cheap female labor on which they depended; as entrepreneurs, they drew capital away from proper business; as consumers, they encouraged the sale of immoral luxury goods. Swift satirized these religious vigilantes: Corinna does not fear them "because she pays them all in kind."[10] Yet reformers believed that with enough citizen action, Corinna could be stripped of her flea-bitten wig and cat-pissed plumpers and beaten into virtue for the benefit of her nation.

Bernard Mandeville scandalously dedicated his *Defence of the Publick Stews* to the reforming brethren and clearly also had them in mind in his *Fable of the Bees*.[11] Through his attacks on the SRMs, Mandeville, to whom I turn in the final part of this chapter, arrived at his notorious conclusion that "private vices" generate public benefits. Mandeville recognized the SRM critique as economic as much as moral; he recognized, but rejected, their proposition that national prosperity depended on virtue. For the SRMs, as Mandeville saw, prosperity demanded the compartmentalization of commerce into infamous and virtuous kinds, a belief at the root of their overwhelming obsession with prostitution. In answering reformers, however, Mandeville perhaps unexpectedly ended up exploring sex work as an exemplary case for not just the moral challenges posed by a commercial economy, but for the new hierarchies it was forming and new forms of fragmentation it demanded of the consumed. *The Fable of the Bees* mobilizes the popular trope of the prostitute as the embodiment of nefarious, luxurious consumption; the *Defence of the Publick Stews*, however, cannot avoid confronting Corinna's precarious status on the border between human and object. For both Mandeville and the SRMs, however, prostitution seemed to hold the secret to the ethical meaning of commercial culture itself.

"Every Tradesman and Mechanick": The Reformers

In 1709, Thomas Bray preached a sermon in memory of his fallen comrade, John Dent.[12] The one thousand people attending Dent's funeral remembered this man of modest means for his service to the SRMs, arresting "lewd and disorderly Criminals."[13] After years of "apprehending and prosecuting of several Thousands of lewd and profligate Persons," however, Dent at last fell to the swords of the miscreants who failed to appreciate his reforming and chose to defend the prostitutes instead. Just a few years earlier, Mr. John Cooper had also been killed "in the Execution of his Office" (16), and in 1712 a group of constables were badly mauled by soldiers when they tried to arrest suspected prostitutes in Covent Garden.[14] Dent's murderers were convicted, but they successfully appealed: The judge ruled that "'it was not lawful, even for a legal constable, to take up a woman upon a bare suspicion only, having been guilty of no breach of the peace, nor any unlawful act.'"[15] Thus reformers not only had no legal right to harass these women but also faced constant physical danger from those who defended themselves and their sisters, daughters, friends, and lovers.[16]

Some historians have thus considered the SRMs as failures because they met with such intense opposition from the law, from communities, and even from within the church.[17] Clearly both their goals and their methods raised controversy and generated resistance; they eventually petered out in the 1730s, giving way to new strategies of reform. Nevertheless, the SRM diagnosis of urban culture became prominent enough to draw responses from Swift and Mandeville; it gained attention in the Anglican Church; it drew praise from monarchs. The SRMs claimed responsibility for over one hundred thousand convictions in forty-four years, a figure that does not include arrests that did not lead to convictions.[18] These years also saw the formation of the Society for Promoting Christian Knowledge (SPCK), the Society for the Propagation of the Gospel in Foreign Parts (SPG), and the Religious Societies, but these groups were extensions of the Church of England; the SRMs, by contrast, acted independently and welcomed dissenters.[19] That Swift's Corinna had developed a strategy for dealing with them suggests the poet's sense of their ubiquity. Reformers claimed to have given "a great Check to the *open Lewdness* that was acted in many of our Streets"; they cleaned up not just England, but also Ireland, Scotland, North America, Holland, and Switzerland; their pamphlets were translated into Latin, French, and Dutch.[20] In their own violent, awkward, and controversial way, these reformers took the first steps toward the modern compartmentalization that arbiters of bourgeois culture would refine.[21] These reformers did not look back nostalgically to a simpler time but instead aimed to purify the public sphere for the sake of flourishing trade, solvent families, and national prosperity.

For the SRMs, the sex trade threatened the legitimate trades on which their members depended. The reform movement began with a small group of men who renounced their own libertine ways and resolved to share their moral clarity with others.[22] Although they boasted a few elite members, the Societies drew their membership mainly from carpenters, coach makers, peruke makers, bakers, butchers, drapers, grocers, haberdashers, and tailors.[23] They aimed to purge the commercial sphere on which they depended of blasphemy, profanity, drunkenness, lewdness, Sabbath breaking, and oath swearing to discourage divine wrath, but also to ensure smooth and reliable business transactions. While they thus opposed a range of vices, their records and publications suggest a particular passion for arresting prostitutes.[24] Josiah Woodward praised one Society for "root[ing] out about *Five Hundred Disorderly Houses*, and caus[ing] to be punished some *Thousands* of *Lewd Persons*."[25] Their pamphlets endlessly rail again harlots, but a few also include a "Black Roll" of those prosecuted for "*Whoring, Drunkenness, Sabbath-breaking, &c.*" An overwhelming majority of names listed are women's.[26] While women surely also drank and broke the Sabbath, if vigilantes had opposed all sins with equal zeal we might expect an arrest record with a greater gender balance. In 1718, the Societies reportedly arrested 1,253 suspects for lewd and disorderly practices, but only 202 for profane cursing, 17 for drunkenness, and 8 for keeping gaming houses.[27] In 1734 they prosecuted 395 sinners, 90 percent of those for lewd behavior.[28] Reformers prosecuted an average of 1,330 people each year between 1708 and 1724 for "lewd and disorderly practices," and "not only were the vast majority of [them] women," Robert Shoemaker has observed, "but a comparison of the societies' first 'blacklist' of offenders (for 1693) with London judicial records reveals that most were accused of 'nightwalking' and picking up men."[29] So while reformers may have held a range of pious goals, in practice they spent most of their time rounding up women thought to be whores.

Dudley Bahlman's classic explanation for reformist zeal founded on party politics—that in the eyes of its supporters, "only through a reformation of manners could the revolution [of 1688] endure"[30]—has considerable force, but does not entirely explain the focus of reformist passion. The early eighteenth century certainly inherited specific political associations with prostitution: Reformers accused Tories of whoring and Catholicism, often equating the two.[31] In the Restoration, satirists attacked Charles II by collapsing distinctions between streetwalkers and the elite mistresses of Whitehall. In the *Poor-Whores Petition* (1668), besieged prostitutes supposedly apply to Barbara Castlemaine for protection on the basis of sisterly solidarity.[32] The wit of Nell Gwynn's supposed self-identification as Charles's "Protestant whore" lies in a popular association between Tories, Catholicism, libertine indulgence, and prostitution.[33] The SRMs pitted Low Church Protestant virtue against High Church elite indulgence. High Church Tories disliked the SRM inclusion of dissenters and their Whig associations; some even feared that the SRMs would revive Puritan enthusiasm and once again threaten the monarchy. When the High Church Tory Henry Sacheverell attacked the SRMs in his sermons, Whigs accused him of undermining the Glorious Revolution and had him arrested for treason.[34] Reformers attacked Sacheverell and his Tory cohorts as whoremongers and Catholic sympathizers:[35] One writer even reported that London's whores were praying for Dr. Sacheverell.[36]

But while reformers certainly continued to condemn elite libertine indulgence well beyond the Restoration period, activists on the ground attacked women of their own class and lower. Defoe, in fact, criticized the reform movement for *ignoring* the sins of elite libertines.[37] Reformers instead policed their own class to ensure the stability of the family networks on which it depended and the lower classes to establish an orderly access to their labor. As their opponents noticed, SRM claims to moral authority did not so much criticize the elite as circumvent them by usurping their traditional prerogatives. Sacheverell decried this presumptuous self-empowerment: "every *Tradesman* and *Mechanick*," he objected, "is to take upon him the Gift of the Spirit, and to expound the difficult Passages of Scripture, and every *Justice of Peace* is allow'd to settle Its Canon, and Infallibly Decide what is Orthodox or heretical," sacrificing church authority to the "Fanaticism" and "the Senseless and Giddy Multitude."[38] Reformers, others objected, "went beyond their proper station"; they dictated "'to those by whom they are to be govern'd.'"[39] Satirists emphasized the disparity between the tradesman's right to moral authority and his social status, calling reformers "A Gang of such ill-looking Vermin, / Like Butchers some, and some like Carmen."[40] On the other side, reformers accused their High Church detractors of an un-Protestant elitism. High Churchmen, argued William Bisset,

> Are not only *High for Rituals* but for carrying all things with a very *High Hand*, and make little Conscience of the *Apostle's* Charge, *to condescend to Men of low Estate*.[41]

While traditionalists accused reformers of exceeding their class's authority, liberal writers accused them of interfering with strictly private vices.[42] For reformers, however, prostitution endangered the community more urgently than the individual soul. Miscreants possess an "Unnatural and Selfish Temper"; how "can that Nation avoid Ruin, that is overrun with Flagitious Impieties, which Naturally as well as Judicially threaten Destruction"?[43] In making the case against vice on the primary basis of public order rather than individual salvation, these reformers departed from earlier religious enthusiasts (despite their detractors' attempts to blur this distinction).[44] As Mandeville saw so clearly, in doing so they attempted to enforce a particular economic vision as much as a theological one.[45] Prostitution, as one reformist description suggests, amounted at one level for them to one business getting in the way of another:

> With what Impatience and Indignation have I walked from *Charing-Cross* to *Ludgate*, when being in full Speed upon important Business, I have every now and then been put to the Halt; sometimes by the full Encounter of an audacious Harlot, whose impudent Leer shewd she only stopp'd my Passage in order to draw my Observation on her.[46]

For reformers, prostitution undermined commercial transactions through such distractions, threatening to turn public commercial spaces into disrepute. As the whore's "impudent" leer suggests, prostitution also for them undermined traditional habits of deference and subordination among the lower classes on which new forms of industry depended.[47] Just as orderly heterosexual families provided the necessary foundation for prosperous business, so prostitution provided the seductive foundation of an alternative criminal economy. "Nests for *Thieves, Clippers* and *Coiners*,"[48] bawdy houses were "Nurseries of the most horrid Vices, and sinks of the most filthy Debaucheries." In these "Hellish Families . . . Hirelings consume their Wages . . . thereby Families are beggar'd and Parishes much impoverished."[49]

Prosperity, then, depended on purging the streets of prostitutes. Reformers argued that God would reward a virtuous nation and withdraw protection from a sinful one:[50] with virtue, one sermon explains, you see "your Stocks so Increased, your Houses Built; your Trade Revive; your Rents Advanced";[51] virtue, another summarizes, "is the way to procure Plenty."[52] But reformers also made their case in terms that did not depend on divine intervention. Whoring not only distracted from business but could lead to dangerous property violations: One reformer warned how *"Thomas Savage* frequenting the House of *Hannah Blan*, a noted Bawdy-House, spending upon her as much Money as he could get, to satisfy his own Lust and her craving Appetite, is tempted first to stealing and purloining from his Master, and at length to the murthering of a Maid," for which he was hanged.[53] Much anxiety around prostitution, as George Lillo's *The London Merchant* also suggests, pointed to concerns about orderly access to apprentice, servant, and other kinds of subordinated labor. Even when lustful men don't steal and/or murder to pay their whores, by visiting prostitutes they destroy their bodies through disease, create a climate of disorder that leaves their own wives, sisters, and daughters vulnerable to seduction, and—most saliently in reformist writing of this period—ruin themselves and their families financially by spending all their wages in brothels.[54] As John Disney asks, "how many Families have been brought to Beggary . . . by the mere *Expensiveness* of Vice! . . . '[T]is no wonder that Poverty over-runs the Nation; that Taxes are so generally complain'd of, and with so much difficulty paid; that Trade is neglected, Markets fail, our Gazettes are fill'd with Commissions of Bankrupt, and our Prisons with Debtors. This cuts the very Sinews of the Government."[55] Disney compares the British to the Roman Empire, warning against a similar fate: "For Luxury and Debauchery (as their natural Effect) debase the Genius of a People, dissolve them to *Effeminacy* and *Cowardice*, by chaining them down to their *Pleasures*, and diverting them from that generous Spirit which is necessary to the Preservation of the Public."[56] The elimination of vice, he goes so far as to claim, would eliminate poverty.

In spite of their religious principles and fear of divine retribution, then, these reformers actually warn more often against financial ruin than eternal damnation when they attack prostitution, revealing their own class investments: Prostitutes misdirect the flow of capital and encourage insubordination. They also, however, understood prostitution almost entirely as a problem of (male) consumption rather than (female) "production" or labor, except to represent whoring as idleness. The potential exploitation of women in the sex trade rarely appears in their writing, except occasionally to attack bawds. Reformers complained that prostitution deprived the nation of wives, mothers, and workers; they did not, however, show much interest in "reforming" prostitutes themselves or in claiming their victimization, as would later reformers. Even the case for female virtue constituted only a small part of their rhetoric; instead, they represented prostitution as the gateway to an illegitimate economy competing with the legitimate one. They directed their arguments to men: Whoring would drain their pockets, distract them from business, undermine property relations, cause insubordination in their underlings, enrich dangerous women, destroy their bodies, and ruin their daughters.[57] As a form of excessive male consumption, prostitution epitomized dangerous luxury; reformers demanded that men discipline themselves to focus on business and resist the temptations produced by an urbanized commercial marketplace.[58]

Since reformers identified prostitution as an economic threat, however, they therefore also implicitly acknowledged it as an economic activity, even if they continued explicitly to blame insatiable female desire. The inherent instability of difference between their own drive toward economic survival and that of the prostitutes they excoriated, then, soon became apparent. George Lillo's wildly popular *London Merchant* (1731), ritually performed each year for the benefit of apprentices and starkly comparing a "good" merchant with a "bad" one,[59] provides a telling example, with Millwood and Thorowgood competing for the profitable use of George Barnwell as either cully or apprentice. Millwood plunders, exploits, and colonizes; she practices not the virtuous English commerce, but the wicked Spanish kind: "I would have my conquests complete, like those of the Spaniards in the New World, who first plundered the natives of all the wealth they had and then condemned the wretches to the mines for life to work for more" (2.3.24–27). *The London Merchant* thus expresses the reformist strategy of compartmentalization by comparing legitimate ways of making money to illegitimate ones. Laura Mandell has suggested that Millwood's death functions as a kind of ritual sacrifice: The infamous whore must hang to secure legitimate commerce, and in her fall, Millwood absorbs the blame for the cruelest exploits of capitalism.[60] Yet the play also suggests the inherent instability of this compartmentalization, for Millwood insists on her own similarity to Thorowgood:

> What are your laws, of which you make your boast, but the fool's wisdom and the coward's valor, the instrument and screen of all your villainies by which you punish in others what you act yourselves or would have acted, had you been in their circumstances? The judge who condemns the poor man for being a thief had been a thief himself, had he been poor. (4.18.60–66)

As Lisa Freeman points out, "Deciphering Millwood results in the understanding that desire drives the balanced accounts of the merchant's ledger book as much as it supports the economy of Millwood's household."[61] It follows that everyone, and not just the vulnerable woman, is a potential Millwood. The play demonstrates this, for George Barnwell cannot resist her appeal and becomes part of the "Hellish family" that reformers warn against. Thus we have no assurance that the hanging of Millwood *has* secured the safety and purity of others; if anything, the play's ritual repetition during this period suggests otherwise.

This failure of purification (or compartmentalization) became a central theme in attacks on the SRMs. Just as Millwood's exploitation of Barnwell parallels Thorowgood's, so the activities of the reformers, not surprisingly, attracted suspicions of reformist desires for their own profits and pleasures. The paid informer, on whom the Societies heavily relied,[62] became a particular target: "[a] mischeivous *Vermin* bred out of the Corruption of the Body Politique; that feeds (like Toads) only on Poysons, and sucks the peccant Humours so long (like a Horse-leach) till he burst with Venome."[63] Not only is the informer himself a "prostituted Varlet" (3), but he spends money earned from informing in the bawdy houses.[64] Critics also accused reformers of sexually and financially exploiting the prostitutes they arrested. According to historian Edward Bristow, there was some truth in this charge: "Constables were continually being presented for either taking bribes from prostitutes or discharging them before bringing them into custody. . . . Thomas de Veil [of the Westminster bench] . . . used his position to arrange meetings with whores, allegedly fathering twenty-five children in the process."[65] The infamous commerce of reformers thus became a significant concern to their leaders, who urged them to become the "golden snuffers" of vice.[66] William Bisset cautioned his flock not to have sex with prostitutes they were arresting, lest they be mocked.[67] In one of their official publications, the Societies's first point of "seasonable advice" consisted of maintaining their own innocence, "a freedom from those Vices which they reprove in others," lest reformers hurt the very cause they advocate.[68]

These admonitions hold significance not just because they suggest the hypocrisy of reformers, but because they also point to the instability of reformist compartmentalization: Reformers cannot descend into the world of infamous commerce without falling under the suspicion of practicing it. Reformers could never quite convince the public that taking money for sex differed categorically from taking money for arresting women for taking money for sex. That the debate on both sides so commonly spoke to infamous commerce—profiting from an immoral practice—suggests that unlike critics speaking from the position of civic humanism, these Christian tradesmen wrestled not with an "Other" but with a disturbing inconsistency in their own ideology. They defended, rather than attacked, the marketplace, but sought to purify it of its chaos, its unpredictability, its Hobbesian aggression, its Rabbelasian disorder, its theatricality, and its disturbing dependence on desire and pleasure. In doing so, Mandeville would argue, they took up an inherently impossible project.

Nightwalkers

The impossibility of maintaining the distinction between infamous and legitimate commerce becomes most dramatically clear in the work of reformer John Dunton. Dunton's *The Night-Walker; or, Evening Rambles in Search after Lewd Women* (1696), uniquely records the adventures of one reformer who claimed to infiltrate prostitute life. Dunton apparently did this by posing as a client, but at a key moment would whip out his constable's staff and deliver a lecture on piety. In its resulting combination of edification and pornographic voyeurism,[69] *The Night-Walker* further suggests the profound instability of the compartmentalization so important to the reform movement. Dunton insists that

The Design then of this Undertaking is not to minister Fuel to Wanton Thoughts, or to please the prophane Pallats of the Beaus and Sparks of the Town, but to display Monthly their Abominable Practices in lively Colours, together with their dismal Consequences, in order to frighten or shame them out of them if possible.[70]

Dunton, however, profited from *The Night-Walker* by selling stories about prostitutes to curious readers, indulging both voyeuristic and sentimental pleasures.

But in uniquely (among reformers) recounting individual confrontations with prostitutes and eliciting their stories rather than just rehearsing the consequences of whoring on male bodies, businesses, and careers, Dunton evokes more explicitly the tendency of distinctions between infamous and legitimate commerce to collapse. Further, unlike other reformist writing, his anecdotal strategy could not avoid, as did his fellow reformers, some consideration of "production" in the context of condemning consumption; that is, how and why women became prostitutes, under what conditions they worked, how much they earned, and so on. Dunton's *Night-Walker* thus more explicitly associates prostitution less with other kinds of sin than with other kinds of commercial transactions. The marketplace in Dunton provides the occasion and context for prostitution. He complains of the citizens' wives,

who sit Trickt and Trim'd, and Rigg'd in their Shops as if they had more mind to expose themselves to Sale, than their Goods, or at least as if they had more Confidence that their Modish Dresses and Wanton Glances would attract more Customers than either their Signs or the Pictures and other Representations of their Merchandise could do; and being thus exposed to the Eye of the *Lascivious Sparks*, they take the thing in its natural signification, and come to *treat with them for themselves*, and not for the Goods in their Shops, except it be for a Cover. (October 1676, no. 2, p. 12)

Businesses entice the consumer not by displaying an image of bread, meat, or shoes to sell bread, meat, or shoes; rather, these beautiful female "commodities" generate desire for other commodities. Or maybe neither customer nor merchant need even worry about the bread, meat, or shoes at all except as a cover: In Dunton's depiction of commerce, merchants do not offer products to meet the needs of customers but rather generate and profit from luxurious desire. But while Dunton argues that women should confine their interests to the education of their children and leave "the Shops to their Husbands" (October 1676, no. 2, p. 12), he does not gender infamous and legitimate commerce quite so simplistically as do some of his fellow reformers. These prostitute wives, after all, do not function as the insidious alternatives to the virtuous male merchant—as Millwoods competing with Thorowgoods for the exploitation of Barnwells. Rather, they serve as *extensions* of male business, peddling their favors and drawing in customers with the full approval of their husbands. In Dunton, both men and women thus become responsible for infamous commerce.

In one anecdote, for example, a husband deliberately uses his wife to attract customers. Recognizing his wife's beauty, he dresses her in finery and lets her "expose" herself in the shop in the hope that she would improve business. Soon a spark begins to shop there regularly as an excuse to meet the wife; the spark eventually offers the husband four hundred pounds in exchange for ten days in the country with the wife. While the spark ultimately cheats the shopkeeper out of his promised compensation, he nevertheless makes several visits that end in various purchases. The husband never gets his money from this illegitimate contract; the original plan to attract business by displaying his wife, however, seems to have worked. Dunton, of course, does not seem to have been trying to make this point, but the merchant only loses ground when actually trying to sell his wife rather than continuing to use her for seductive bait. Dunton laments the "abominable shame" of the wife's vanity manifested in extravagant clothes, hair, and makeup; nevertheless, this investment in beauty not only serves to attract male admirers but also improves the business of the shop itself. Here prostitution supports rather than undermines business. The citizen shopkeeper and his whorish wife become partners in this seductive strategy for upward mobility.

In Dunton, infamous commerce and legitimate commerce are thus deeply intertwined: Shopkeepers sell their wares by displaying their seductive wives next to them; women sell their sexual services by displaying themselves in shops. The very title of the periodical captures this, for Dunton positions himself as a fellow nightwalker, prowling the streets in search of prostitutes.[71] Dunton plays the role of both eager client and moral reformer in the same night; his text equates its author with the prostitutes he pursues through their shared positions as "nightwalkers."[72] Not only does Dunton thus fail to become a "golden snuffer," but *Night-Walker* reveals the profound difficulty—perhaps even impossibility—of separating infamous commerce from the legitimate kind. Both tradesmen and reformers in Dunton emerge as inadvertently aligned with the prostitutes they pursue, mutually relying on the capacious and irrational desires of the marketplace.

In its obsession with prostitution as a destabilizing force in an emergent commercial culture, *Night-Walker* nevertheless resembles other reformist writing, even if it offers more complex and thus less convincing gestures of compartmentalization. But while *Night-Walker* exposes the fragility of the reformist ideology, it also differs from other reformist representations of prostitution in another important way: In Dunton, it becomes occasionally conceivable that a woman would become a prostitute for reasons other than lasciviousness. This insight emerges in part through the distinct structure of Dunton's narrative, for unlike other reformers, Dunton attends to the detailed personal histories of individual streetwalkers. In general, the women who walk the street in Dunton's periodical do so out of motives consistent with the bulk of prostitute discourse in this period: They seek both luxury and sensual indulgence. In one encounter, a woman even tries to pay Dunton for sex (December 1676, no. 4., p. 3). Another woman confesses that she became a prostitute because she was "unable to master her desire" (February 1697, no. 2., p. 15). Yet Dunton also includes stories of women who did not want to become prostitutes. In one, a woman's father (a parson) gave her neither a virtuous education nor a dowry, which left her unmarriageable and vulnerable to seduction by a servant. She found that she could neither get her living by her needle nor work in service after her reputation had been ruined; out of economic need rather than lasciviousness, then, she turned to "this horrid Trade" (December 1696, no. 4, p. 9). Dunton proposes to her alternative after alternative for employment: "had not you better work for a livelihood then follow this Infamous Trade which will ruin your Reputation, Soul and Body" (9). Even though in the end he finds her "wholly Unsensible and Hardened in her Impudence" (10) and insists that victimization does not release her morally, both her father and seducer seem to bear some responsibility for her fate. This prostitute comes across as more pathetic than evil, doomed "to die in Pain, Infamy, and Misery" (9).

The most striking difference here between Dunton and general SRM rhetoric lies in the whore's own description of herself as "forc'd" into this "horrid Trade" rather than enticed by sexual and material desire. Reformers Disney, Bisset, and Woodward don't concern themselves with how individual women became prostitutes, and libertine literature generally assumes that sex itself provides sufficient temptation. In Dunton, by contrast, we find a fascination with individual histories; recording (or inventing) these, the author formulates narrative templates that would be echoed throughout the eighteenth century. These stories function both morally and sociologically, revealing personal struggles as well as the complex world in which those struggles take place. For example, one prostitute arrogantly declares that "I must live by my Favours and no Man shall enjoy my Company for less than a Guiney per Night" (October 1676, no. 2, p. 22). As her story unfolds, however, it becomes clear that she entered prostitution out of calamitous circumstances. Her father died intestate, and a covetous brother would not allow her any fortune. As a result, no gentleman would marry her. So she went to London, where a bawd "delude[d]" her into "this vile Practice, which

I must confess I abhore when I have any calm or sedate thoughts, but when I think of abandoning this way of living, then my former Straits stare me in the Face and *Weakens my resolve*" (23). The terror of poverty more than the temptation of sin keeps her on the street. Dunton chastises her, insisting that had she lived virtuously, she "might in all probability have got a Good Husband"; he urges her to trust in providence for her support. He even offers her an inspirational story that suggests her potential to escape prostitution. In the story, a reformer helpfully recommends a penitent prostitute to a friend as a governess. Providentially, the mistress then dies and the master marries the ex-prostitute; the master, however, dies shortly afterward, leaving the ex-prostitute the heiress to his fortune. Meanwhile, the reformer had spiraled into poverty. The ex-prostitute and the reformer meet again by chance and she takes him for her husband, after which "they lived very Comfortably together for many years" (24). While this anecdote rather transparently suggests the erotic and even romantic fantasy associated with prostitute reform (that would become standard elements in the genre), it also, unlike in most SRM writing but like the reform movement that would follow, points to the transformation of the streetwalker as part of the goal.

While for most members of the SRMs, "reform" meant the removal of polluting whores from the commercial public sphere, in Dunton reform also means recovering individual women from prostitution for other kinds of labor or even marriage, as the anecdote suggests. Past prostitution does not disqualify women from respectable work, for the prostitute in the story above makes a smooth transition from the streets to service (and eventually into the arms of her reformer). For Dunton, reform means turning streetwalkers into "legitimate" contributors to society. Thus while prostitution clearly describes something other than work in *The Night-Walker*, prostitutes themselves are nevertheless *potential* workers. The whore's reforming potential, however, depends on her alienation from pleasure: Dunton holds out hope only for the ones who find sex work vile. But as in *The Whore's Rhetorick*, so in *The Night-Walker* is the truly alienated prostitute—the one who feels mostly disgust or at least can achieve a cool state of indifference—the exception rather than the rule. The reformer John Dunton and the bawd Mother Creswell agree on the superiority of this model, reserving their fear and contempt for the ones who remain undivided and passionate.

So while the figure of the prostitute suggests in *The Night-Walker* the seductive dangers of the new commercial culture and the shifting power relations it ushered in, Dunton also sometimes finds at its unforgiving core a nonlascivious woman who, as a result of dire circumstances, has nothing to exchange but her sexual labor. To their critics, the reformers' fascination with commercial sex and their profiting from arrests resembled too closely the activities of lascivious prostitutes; the ideal reformer, by contrast, resembled the divided whore—the rare one motivated by obligation rather than desire. All nightwalkers must descend into the sexual underworlds of the city without taking any pleasure in the experience. Thus in Dunton, the prostitute comes to evoke both the overwhelming seductions of the commercial marketplace *and* the struggle to survive within it. In different contexts, the negotiation of this predicament would become one of the most compelling narratives of the eighteenth century.

Of Bees and Stews: Bernard Mandeville

Like John Dunton and the members of the SRMs, Bernard Mandeville also found prostitution a meaningful vice. In his analysis of prostitution, E. J. Hundert observes, "Mandeville offered his fullest technical account of how vice may lead to public benefit."[73] Mandeville's defense of sexual commerce figured prominently in the Middlesex grand jury's 1723 condemnation of *The Fable*, which concluded that Mandeville "recommend[ed] Luxury, Avarice, Pride, and all kinds of Vices, as being necessary to *Publick Welfare* . . . Nay, the very *Stews* themselves have had strained Apologies and forced Encomiums made in their Favour and produced in Print, with Design, we conceive, to debauch the Nation."[74] Not one to back down from controversy, Mandeville took up the gauntlet by attempting to justify what the jury understood as his most revealing, most outrageous, and least defensible point.[75] The resulting *Defence of the Public Stews* (1724) explores in some detail an example of the disconcerting material consequences of believing in *The Fable*. For the reformers, the grand jury, and Mandeville himself, prostitution became an emblematic vice of excessive desire that commercial society had to confront. But in uniquely exploring policy implications in this pamphlet, Mandeville had to shift his perspective, accounting for not just the benefits of the luxury spending and the pleasure of the consumer but also at least glimpsing at what the vendor gains and what she must relinquish.

Mandeville's *Defence*, to which I will return, attempts to follow through with the general argument that *The Fable of the Bees* had already advanced. *The Fable* hit a raw nerve: not only did moralists publish dozens of rebuttals, but economists throughout the eighteenth century attempted to refute it (although they incorporated much of Mandeville's insight into their own work).[76] Hundert places Mandeville at the cutting edge of Enlightenment thought for his moral confrontation of commercial society; Mandeville, he demonstrates, "introduced into the heart of European social understanding a series of arguments designed to sustain the radically unsettling conclusion that the moral identities of his contemporaries had been permanently altered by a previously unacknowledged historical transformation."[77] *The Fable* held up for scrutiny the reproaches of elite civic humanists, urbane journalists, and vigilante reformers, challenging the link all three assumed between virtue and prosperity. While Dunton's *Night-Walker* suggests the fragility of the distinction between legitimate and infamous commerce, Mandeville deliberately and scandalously declared the artificiality of those boundaries. In *The Fable*, vice does not impede business; rather, vice drives business.

The Fable's rhetorical stance has been variously read as satiric, nonsatiric, moralistic, ambivalent, and contradictory.[78] Rather than cataloguing and adjudicating these arguments, however, I will suggest here that this perplexing range of reasonable interpretations of *The Fable* becomes possible because of the way that Mandeville deliberately sets literary image and philosophical argument at cross-purposes. Mandeville describes disturbing practices that appear indefensible—for example, the physician who cares more about his own profit than the survival of his patients—but then argues that while vice may ruin the individual, it benefits society overall. If reformers successfully prevented tradesmen from lying, the economy would collapse. Lawyers survey the laws "[a]s Burglars Shops and Houses do"; soldiers lose limbs in battle while others "staid at Home for double Pay"; "Sharpers, Parasites, Pimps, Players / Pick-pockets, Coiners, Quacks, South-sayers" proliferate in a strong economy, with "Millions endeavouring to supply / Each other's Lust and Vanity" (1:18–22). The commercial world, Mandeville proposes, thus functions by arousing and satisfying the most vicious desires. Vivid and disquieting cases evoke repugnance in *The Fable*, but Mandeville nevertheless insists that they benefit the hive. While defending commerce, he thus lays bare its toll, insisting that anyone who enjoys its comforts also profits from its abominations.

With this argument, Mandeville sets out to disprove the SRM position that vice undermines business. The strongest hive, *The Fable* insists, is the one in which the bees freely engage in unethical, exploitative, self-destructive, and deceptive practices.[79] For Mandeville, reformist attacks on vice were annoying for their hypocrisy, but also misguided because the new economy truly depended on practices that Christians traditionally had defined as vicious. Similarly, urbane journalists detailing elaborate rules for consumption hypocritically mystified commercial relationships. Without lust, pride, and vanity, the thriving marketplace would crumble and the bees either sink into despair or seek their fortunes elsewhere, leaving the hive vulnerable to foreign powers. Prosperous societies cannot even depend, as Francis Hutcheson had countered, on moderate, need-based forms of consumption; instead, they demand excess.[80] Fortunately, men and women will generally succumb to vain and sometimes self-destructive desires to possess more than nature demands. This irrationality and vanity for Mandeville constitutes the line between the animal and human realms: Animals seek only what they need, but human civilization consists of surpassing these basic needs. Mandeville thus characterizes the reformist accusation that luxury weakens and feminizes the population as absurd: "Clean Linen weakens a Man no more than Flannel; Tapistry, fine Painting or a good Wainscot are not more unwholesome than bare Walls; and a rich Couch, or a gilt Chariot are no more enervating than the cold Floor or a Country Cart" (1:119). Luxury goods have no inherent deleterious physical effect; in fact, in its own risky way, luxury, from bear-baiting to opera, offers evidence of human distinctiveness.

In making the case for the benefits of luxury spending, Mandeville drew on established arguments for mercantilism.[81] Nicolas Barbon celebrated fashion as:

> a great Promoter of *Trade*, because it occasions the Expence of Cloaths, before the Old ones are worn out: It is the Spirit and Life of *Trade*.[82]

Dudley North similarly argued that

> The main spur to Trade, or rather to Industry and Ingenuity, is the exorbitant Appetites of Men, which they will take pains to gratifie, and so be disposed to work, when nothing else will incline them to it; for did Men content themselves with bare Necessaries, we should have a poor World.[83]

Yet neither North nor Barbon stirred up the hive, so to speak, for neither of them systematically confronted the full implications of this position. Their choice of examples makes the difference. Barbon points out that the building trade employs bricklayers, carpenters, and tilers, but also that "a Magnificent Structure doth best represent the Majesty of the Person that lives in it, and is the most lasting and truest History of the Greatness of his Person" (67–68). Mandeville offers a different example:

> A Highwayman having met with a considerable Booty, gives a poor common Harlot, he fancies, Ten Pounds to new-rig her from Top to Toe; is there a spruce Mercer so conscientious that he will refuse to sell her a Thread Sattin, tho' he knew who she was? She must have Shoes and Stockings, Gloves, the Stay and Mantua-maker, the Sempstress, the Linen-Draper, all must get something by her, and a hundred different Tradesmen dependent on those she laid her Money out with, may touch Part of it before a Month is at an end. (1:88)

So while Mandeville and Barbon might be making the same argument—luxury spending supports vital businesses—Mandeville replaces the great man with the whore as the benefactor. Barbon assumes a certain propriety and limit that Mandeville insists does not and *could not* actually operate given the nature of the commercial system.

Mandeville's frequent recourse to prostitution to elaborate his position has led some to conclude that libertinism drives his arguments.[84] At the other end of the spectrum, others have held that moments like this reveal Mandeville's true Christianity: Mandeville charges his society with "worldliness, self-indulgence, complacency."[85] Neither extreme consistently holds: Mandeville does not simply advocate pleasurable consumption (he frequently acknowledges the dangerous consequences to individuals) but also opposes the moral regulation of the marketplace. The difference between Mandeville and both reformers and earlier mercantilists is that Mandeville insists on the impossibility of compartmentalizing nefarious and virtuous commodities; worse, he leaves readers with no escape from their own complicity with the inevitable infamy of commerce.[86] No amount of taste, morality, or reforming will prevent citizens from handling the same coins handled by prostitutes or benefiting from their consumption: The same tradesmen threatening to arrest the whore depend on her for a living. Mandeville thus positions himself primarily as an unmasker, a revealer of truth. He does not attempt (as did the reformers) to purify capitalism by scapegoating and sacrificing the whore;[87] rather, he rescues the prostitute from the sacrificial altar and insists that she both promotes and epitomizes modern commercial society. He demands that contemporaries recognize their comfort as inseparable from her trade. In *The Fable*, Mandeville claims the higher ground over reformers and civic humanists not through moral superiority, but through his own proposed anti-hypocritical willingness to stare commerce in the face with the same discerning eyes as the most hard-core reformer and accept the benefits of capitalism's amorality.[88]

In setting for himself the challenge of full demystification, Mandeville not only welcomes the luxury consumption that moralists condemn but also exposes the brutal and arbitrary division of labor on which the hive's prosperity depends. The passages that turn from consumption to production, though limited, provide *The Fable*'s most disturbing moments. While Mandeville rejects claims of superiority by the current elites and insists on the fundamental equality of all humans, he nevertheless observes that commercial society depends on large numbers of workers who toil for the comfort and luxury of a few:

> Some with vast Stocks, and little Pains,
> Jump'd into Business of great Gains;
> And some were damn'd to Sythes and Spades,
> And all those hard laborious Trades;
> Where willing Wretches daily sweat,
> And wear out Strength and Limbs to eat. (*Fable* 1:19)

These groups have no inherent or moral differences, according to Mandeville; nevertheless, one group labors for the excessive luxurious indulgence of the other. Mandeville describes the workforce as divided by the arbitrariness of class rather than the inherent difference of rank, demanding the misery of many for the pleasures of a few. This is neither a contradiction nor a demand for reform, but rather a claim to take into account what others mystify through moral self-righteousness or bourgeois rules of refinement. This combination of exposing but refusing to condemn violent injustice creates an unsettling text: without compartmentalization, Mandeville seems to leave no ethical ground at all. The driving force behind *The Fable* as a literary work, then, lies in the drama of the author's own audacity: the extent to which *The Fable* can stomach its own claims and force the reader to stomach them as well. *The Fable* demands that readers face the bitterness of the commercial revolution while they taste its sweets; its author claims to look the marketplace full in the face and not cower from its repulsiveness, amorality, exploitation, unpredictability, and pleasure founded on pain. Thus when the Middlesex jury condemned *The Fable* for defending *even the stews*, Mandeville could not resist the challenge.

In taking up the problem of prostitution as a practical example with the same relentless refusal to mystify, however, Mandeville confronted the outer limits of his position. As a practical project rather than a fable, the *Defence* demanded a more detailed consideration of labor, something raised only briefly, though disturbingly, in his poem. At first glance, the *Defence* appears frivolous at best: Mandeville exploits the ribald potential of his topic, signing himself "Phil-Porney" and elsewhere, "a Layman"; noting this, Richard I. Cook reads the *Defence* as mainly a satire on projectors and the sexual morality of reformers.[89] Cook cites as evidence not only the bawdy humor, but also the inherent absurdity of a utilitarian approach to prostitution. But Mandeville, like the reformers, recognized prostitution as an economic as well as a sexual practice; like them, he thought about its costs and benefits mainly, although not exclusively, in terms of male consumption. Public stews would benefit men by providing a safe, efficient, heterosexual, and cost-effective strategy for satisfying sexual needs. Men would become better husbands because of their sexual experience and would be less likely to fall for an inappropriate marriage partner. But public stews would also benefit non-prostitute women by protecting the virtuous ones, for women have equally strong sexual desires and hardly any ability to restrain them. Finally, they would even benefit the prostitutes by providing reliable working conditions and care for their children. Since public whores would perform such a crucial service in protecting other women from debauchery, prostitutes would even "retrieve their former Character."[90]

While individuals would benefit from this scheme, it would more impor-
tantly promote the interests of the nation by preventing infanticide, controlling disease, and keeping businessmen safe, happy, and productive. Men
of business have the greatest need: "in such Men the Passion is much stronger
than in Men of Pleasure" (24). But men of business also have neither the time
nor the money to embark on the protracted, expensive siege of a virgin. The
projected stews could generate predictable and appealing choices for a range
of budgets: "For the better Entertainment of all Ranks and Degrees of Gentlemen, we shall divide the twenty Women of each House into four Classes,
who for their Beauty, or other Qualifications may justly challenge different
Prices" (13). In grouping prostitutes by price, Mandeville disturbingly turns
human beings into commodities: Swift's Corinna is only *part* thing, but here
bodies and the service they provide become indistinguishable. But Mandeville intends to disturb: He takes the quintessential luxurious vice and attempts
to reconcile it to a model of rational business on the implied proposition that
if it works for prostitution, it could work for anything. (In this respect, *Defence* follows the comic logic of *The Whore's Rhetorick*.) A set fee could helpfully replace tiresome and potentially expensive seduction efforts. For the
businessman consumer, profit converts to money, which can be converted to
sex, which allows greater attention to business, which leads back to more
profit. For the SRMs, prostitution functioned as the consumer vice of vices;
for Mandeville, public stews offer the quintessential service of services: Men
have needs and the marketplace can meet them.

Mandeville proposes prostitution as a meaningful trope for consumption
in general not only to shock his readers but also because moralists themselves
often identified the danger of luxury as irrational, overly passionate, and
specifically erotic—an anxiety for which the whore served as the ideal mas-
cot. We have already seen Dunton's image of the tradesman's beautiful, overdressed wife who uses her body to tempt customers into the shop. Similarly,
Edward Ward describes how self-adornment expresses and incites sexual desire in a "mechanick's daughter" who is "Beyond her native Genius . . . bred,
/ Scarce knowing Hemp from Flax, or Yarn from Thread."[91] She rejects the
needle, which "would her Lilly hands Disgrace" (4); she can't even make a
Sunday pudding. Instead of producing, she consumes: "Dress is her Study,
and fine Clothes her Pride, / Patches and Paint, her true Complexion hide;
/ Her Garb so Ruffl'd from the Top, to th' Toes, / With such stupendious
Wings of *Furbuloes*" (1) that she looks like she could fly:

> Like *Narcissus*, that conceited Boy,
> Sh'Admires her pretty Self, she can't Enjoy.

> When thus she'as quill'd and pleated her Attire
> With busie Fingers, to her own Desire,
> Abroad she Rambles. . . .

This ambiguous self-stimulation leaves her unsatisfied; she seeks and easily finds male attention, eventually leading to a lonely death from venereal disease. Her clothes, however, initially seduced her. Roy Porter has attributed the success of Josiah Wedgwood in part to his comprehension of "the shopping secret": "I need not tell you that it will be our interest to amuse and divert & please & astonish, nay, even to ravish, the Ladies."[92] In the face of this widespread suspicion of the erotics of consumption, Mandeville takes up the challenge of demonstrating that marketing the (literally) sexiest commodity—sex— offers rational, practical advantage. The reformist figure for heinous luxury becomes in Mandeville support for his case of the impossibility of separating legitimate needs from illegitimate desires. Given the elaborate analogy between libidinal gratification and consumer gratification in general, Mandeville's unwavering insistence, inscribed as physiological fact, that men *must* have sex with women represents consumption itself as a caveat of nature.

Mandeville makes a relentlessly utilitarian case; at the same time, however, he observes that commercial desire itself depends on fantasy. As Porter points out, "More than 250 years ago . . . Mandeville was already arguing for what Baudrillard has felicitously termed the 'hysteria' of consumer capitalism—a system fabricated upon facades or simulations."[93] The *Defence* elaborates this point in its discussion of *virtuous* women who, Mandeville argues in a self-conscious reversal of expectations, generate desire and create business for whores:

> A vicious young Fellow, after having been any Hour or two at Church, a Ball, or any other Assembly, where there is a great parcel of handsome Women dress'd to the best Advantage, will have his Imagination more fired. . . . Who wou'd so much as surmise, that this is the Fault of the Virtuous Women? (*Fable*, 1:95).

The prostitutes take advantage of these erotic fantasies and allow clients to play them out; the virtuous women, however, generate them. Further, the very virtue of virtuous women rests on a network of signs rather than any substantial chastity, for women resist sex mainly because they "find their worldly Interest entirely depending upon the Reputation of their Chastity. This sense of Honour and Interest, is what we may call artificial Chastity; and it is upon this Compound of natural and artificial Chastity, that every

Woman's real actual Chastity depends" (42). Mandeville offers no example of natural chastity—only an occasional low sex drive coupled with women's extremely high financial stake in virtue. In the *Defence*, however, artificial chastity functions just as well as any other kind: virtuous women, like the businessmen they hope to marry, negotiate a complex erotic marketplace in which they must strike the right balance between their passions and interests. The virtuous woman's negotiation of her market value does not scandalize Mandeville in the least; he implicitly applauds any woman who barters the erotic fantasies she generates into a good income, for these fantasies give her an edge in a competitive marriage market. Since sexual virtue exists *only* as a performance, these women could presumably gratify their own desires as long as they maintained appearances. Thus Mandeville defends the theatrical manipulation of desire in commercial society epitomized by such feminine wiles.

In many ways, then, the *Defence* expands on arguments already set forth in *The Fable*, elaborating the single example of prostitution to show that frailty constitutes Jove's greatest gift to humanity and that prosperity depends on vice. But as Mandeville lays out the details of his plan for public houses of prostitution, claims apparently at odds with these central points begin to surface. While Mandeville accepts and even celebrates the fundamentally performative nature of female virtue as consistent with the theatricality of commercial society, elaborate restrictions on the prostitutes themselves in his proposed stews, utterly inconsistent with his recommended practices for the rest of the economy, would drain the theatricality out of infamous commerce itself. In Mandeville's proposal, close governmental regulation would protect these stews and their clients from the very excesses that he makes such a point of embracing in *The Fable*: prices would be set, behavior strictly regulated, and transactions constantly monitored, creating a tightly controlled miniature economy within a larger irrational marketplace. While the virtuous women share an economy of illusion with the businessmen, Mandeville's whores would live in a prison house of absolute value. Appointed administrators group them by beauty and set their prices: out of twenty women, "the first Class is to consist of eight, who may legally demand from each Visitant Half a Crown. The second Class to consist of six, whose fix'd Price may be a Crown . . ." (13). Oddly, since matrons would closely monitor all of their encounters, the whores would thus have to behave entirely differently from the lascivious "virtuous" women. Female desire, while driving commerce in *The Fable*,[94] finds little refuge in Mandeville's stews. Laura Mandell has suggested that Mandeville's *Defence* represents prostitutes as abject scapegoats for the "morally repugnant aspects of capitalist pursuits"[95]; yet Mandeville, as we have seen, prides himself on *embracing* the morally repugnant aspects of capitalism. While his whores would support local commerce by relieving the sexual desires of businessmen, they would not be permitted to function as entrepreneurs, nor would they, with their strictly limited incomes, contribute significantly to the luxury marketplace (as they do in *The Fable*) by spending their wealth on fine furniture and beautiful gowns. His projected public stews, then, would be populated by women devoid of the characteristics that made them so socially useful in *The Fable*.

In *The Fable*, Mandeville implicitly claims to stare capitalism, for all its hideousness and exploitation, full in face without any of the hypocrisy of his opponents, and both Mandeville and the Middlesex grand jury selected prostitution as the issue on which the integrity of his position would stand or fall. If Mandeville could rationalize the commodification of this most libidinal desire underpinning consumerism in general and the privileged transgression for the reformers, then he would leave his opponents without a leg to stand on. But what he uncovers through this challenge is something ultimately more troubling than anything in *The Fable*. Mandeville has no compunctions about reading the erotic performances of *virtuous* women as both a form of work with significant financial payoff and a dizzying production of signs without referents; nevertheless, he carefully removes his public stews from the free-flowing, corrupt marketplace filled with bribe-taking politicians, harmful physicians, and mendacious lawyers. His ideal brothel may share its *consumer* model with the erotic theatricality of the rest of marketplace, but its model of labor demands enforced transparency. The prostitutes in these stews must relinquish their share of Jove's gift; instead, they must become common workers in an elaborate bureaucracy designed to drain them of all the qualities that Mandeville himself designates as the fullest expression of human uniqueness. Under constant surveillance, these prostitutes

will have more Inducements to Honesty than any other Profession whatsoever. The same Money defends, as well as it corrupts a *Prime Minister:* A *Churchman* takes Sanctuary in a Gown, and who dare accuse a Mitre of *Simony*? Accuse a *Colonel* of Injustice, he is try'd by his Board of *Peers*, and your Information is false, scandalous, and malicious. A *Lawyer* cheats you according to Law; and you may thank the *Physician*, if you live to complain of him. *Over-reaching* in Trade, is *prudent Dealing*; and *Mechanick Cunning* is stiled *Handicraft*. Not so fares the poor Courtezan; if she commits but one ill Action, if for Instance, she should circumvent a Gentleman in a *Snuff-Box*, she can hardly escape Detection; and the first Discovery ruins her. (18)

Whores resemble lawyers, physicians, tradesmen, and merchants in that they all provide beneficial services. Yet unlike the attempts of the lawyers, physicians, and tradesmen to maximize their profits at the expense of customer service or honesty, such efforts by an enterprising whore would in Mandeville's projected stews be eliminated through intense control. Not only could these prostitutes (unlike everyone and everything else in commercial society) be read at their "face value," but the stews themselves function actively to *prevent* the very fetishization that drives the market elsewhere. Without the sexual demystification that public prostitutes would provide, "a Peer's Son . . . would be in danger of turning Knight-Errant, and might possibly take a Cobler's Daughter for his *Dulcinea*; and who knows but a sprightly young *Taylor* might turn an *Orlando Furioso*, and venture his Neck to carry off a Lady of Birth and Fortune" (28). Here the whorehouses would function, as J. Douglas Canfield puts it, as a "class prophylactic;"[96] they would turn the dazzling signs of romance back into the firm reality of tradesmen and peers.

This apparent exception in human possibility at the heart of Mandeville's argument—the entirely rational consumer purchase—shows up in part because while Mandeville analyzes the consumer possibilities of commercial sex in considerable bawdy detail, he only glimpses at its "production." This encourages a "libertine" reading focused on the essential amorality of consumption and the hypocrisy of reformist compartmentalization. Yet if we *do* read Mandeville's glimpse at production—if we read from the viewpoint of the producer rather than the consumer—then we find an interesting, yet disconcerting, tension. In some ways, commercial sex providers for Mandeville face the same unjust but socially beneficial limits that all laborers endure. Thus in his "Essay on Charity and Charity-Schools" Mandeville attacks these institutions not only as self-serving ideological saturation projects, but also for creating class instability. If the children of the poor learned to read and write and thus aimed for more rewarding careers, then who, he asks, would provide the menial labor? While Mandeville argues against any inherent or moral difference between the laborer and the gentleman, he nevertheless considers the division of labor a necessary element for a flourishing hive.[97] Yet Mandeville also concedes that "if here and there one of the lowest Class by uncommon Industry, and pinching his Belly, lifts himself above the Condition he was brought up in, no body ought to hinder him" (*Fable*, 1:193). In the *Defence*'s projected stews, however, prostitutes do not even enjoy this scant opportunity for mobility: state-appointed matrons oversee their every move; physicians monitor their bodies; "if there are any so foolish as to love Rambling better, or who are not qualify'd to please Gentlemen according to Law, they ought to be transported" (15). So while Mandeville boldly proposes to accept sexual service as a commodity like any other, his glimpse at "production" reveals a different cost: The prostitutes themselves must relinquish the vices that Mandeville elsewhere defines as constituting the essence of humanity and the qualities that ultimately distinguish humans from animals. Under his plan, these women wouldn't be able to cheat, to produce illusions, to deceive, to leave for a better offer, to indulge their own sexual tastes, to overspend on luxuries. They wouldn't even be allowed to go out for a walk without surveillance. They sacrifice their human idiosyncrasy in the service of someone else's profit; they become reified as their sexual labor and thus radically less apian than the other bees in the hive.

It is tempting to attribute this inconsistency to misogyny, but this offers only a partial explanation.[98] In Mandeville's project, after all, nonprostitute women could continue freely to market their illusive chastity, exploiting and enjoying irrational consumption. Selling sexual labor, not just being a woman, both initially stands as the perfect example of private vices leading to public good, but, as the details unfold, serves as an argument for active and oppressive intervention to control the human passions, ambitions, and idiosyncrasies of workers. The *Defence* thus categorizes prostitutes by their work rather than their gender alone. Sex becomes the exemplary commodity: not just one of many but the *modus operandi*, as Roy Porter argues, of the marketplace itself. The hive, Mandeville proposes, would benefit if buying sexual service became as convenient and morally neutral as buying a hat. But in prostitution, the production of the commodity resists mystification and even physical separation from the producer;[99] the prostitute's humanity—her difference from a hat—is difficult to control but even harder to disguise. The unregulated whore—the woman who sets her own price, who exploits irrational desire, creates theatrical illusions to seduce clients, doesn't stop working when she contracts a disease, charges beyond her "value"—thus becomes in the *Defence* an insidious and ominously destabilizing radical threat: She must be transported. And yet only this kind of independent whore, excoriated in the *Defence*, would retain her humanity as defined specifically by Mandeville.

By choosing a commodity inseparable from its human production, the *Defence*, then, ends up exploring the kind of labor demanded by the kind of marketplace that *The Fable* celebrates. Mandeville partially resists the implied connection between sex work and labor in general by representing prostitutes as tainted (xii); unlike the reformers who assumed the lasciviousness of the whore, however, he also considers what might motivate a woman to become a prostitute in the first place. When he does so, he represents her (unlike the reformers) as not inherently different from anyone else who needs to make a living. In contrast to men, Mandeville points out, women lose their best chance for status or economic security when they give in to sexual temptation; when this happens, they often turn to prostitution for support rather than out of lasciviousness. Mandeville thus attacks reformers for impoverishing prostitutes through imprisonment in the absurd hope that this "may put her in a Way of living Honestly, tho' the want of Money was the only Reason of her living otherwise" (x). Once working as prostitutes, women, he observes, "Can seldom or never change that Course of Life for the better":

> [T]hey themselves in Reality utterly abhor it [prostitution]: And indeed there appears nothing in it so very alluring and bewitching, especially to People who have that Inclination to Lewdness intirely extinguish'd, which is the only thing that could possibly make it supportable. (9)

As already deeply disaffected, prostitutes, more than the other bees, might be able to endure the extremely restrictive, yet economically predictable, conditions of his projected public stews. In the *Defence*, then, Mandeville exposes the glaring paradox of modern commerce in which the passionate, amoral indulgences of some depends on the regulation, control, and alienation of others. It is only *some* bees who indulge private vices to produce these public benefits; the rest labor endlessly to produce the conditions for vice with limited opportunity to indulge in it themselves. Prostitution provides the limit point and test case for this insight.

In the *Defence*, then, Mandeville confronts perhaps more directly than in *The Fable* the human trade-offs on which the thriving marketplace depends. Without a doubt, Mandeville sees sexual service as a commodity just as legitimate as any other: For Mandeville, it is an extreme version of the luxurious pleasures available in general. Yet in *The Fable*, Mandeville does not take us into the lives of silk weavers, milliners, or tailors; we know that fashion employs "many," but we see little of their working conditions or their regulation. In the *Defence*, however, the nature of the commodity of sexual service penetrates the mystifying boundary between consumption and production. The *Defence* tellingly closes with one of the most unsettling, oft-quoted moral challenges in all of Mandeville: "A Ship performing Quarantine, and known to be infected, is sunk by a Storm; some of the Crew, half drown'd, recover the Shore; but the moment they land, the *Government* orders them to be shot to Death" (68). Mandeville defends this as a moral action, but here (and throughout Mandeville) philosophical argument and literary image work at cross-purposes. With the stark description of this scenario, Mandeville does not make a convincing case: rather than describing the potential ravages of the disease contracted by the quarantined, he instead describes the survivors' struggles ashore and abrupt impending death. He demands that we see the implications of this case from both sides. Mandeville consistently chooses such examples—the most unsettling illustrations of his ostensible argument. Similarly, Mandeville shows how commodified sexual services could function just like any other object of desire on the marketplace, potentially leaving their producers without pleasure, mobility, freedom, autonomy, or, most of all, the opportunity to indulge in the tempting range of vices that for Mandeville define humanity itself. In Mandeville and elsewhere, prostitution evokes the potentially vicious, fetishized, and exotic luxuries newly available in the urban marketplace; at the same time, it also seems to hold the secret of what this marketplace demands in exchange for them. In *The Fable*, the bees who pine to transform themselves from wicked little insects to virtuous pests court their own destruction; in the *Defence*, however, we see how the luxurious commodities in which the wicked bees self-destructively over-indulge to the benefit of the hive become available only through the disciplined subjugation of hidden reserves of alienated drones.

3

Whore, Turk, and Jew: Defoe's Roxana

We [prostitutes] live like the Jews in all Societies.
The Highlanders Salivated

At the end of the nineteenth century, Jack the Ripper terrorized London, murdering and dismembering prostitutes. One postmortem description explains how a prostitute's

> body had been completely disembowelled and the entrails flung carelessly in a heap on the table. . . . Lumps of flesh, cut from the thighs and elsewhere, lay strewn about the room, so that the bones were exposed. And in some of the other cases, certain organs had been extracted, and, as they were missing, had doubtless been carried away.[1]

Police never discovered the murderer's true identity, but his public image, Sander Gilman has argued, evoked the Eastern Jew. No Christian, the public believed, could have committed such hideous crimes; only a Jew would know the habits of prostitutes so well and become so obsessed with them. In order to understand this link between prostitutes and Jews in the nineteenth century, Gilman argues, we must also take into account the image of prostitute bodies as both diseased and infectious. Prostitutes, but particularly dead ones, fascinated nineteenth-century artists and writers, for in death their previously contagious bodies returned to harmless innocence.[2] The dead prostitute's body then fell to the physician, who could plumb its inner depths without the risk of infection. Here for Gilman lies the key to the relationship between the "Jewish" Jack the Ripper and the prostitutes he murdered: unlike the pathologist, Jack touches the prostitute both before and after death.

Only a Jew would understand the world of prostitutes so well as to hunt them down so efficiently; homeopathically, only the inherently diseased Jew would dare to eviscerate equally corrupted and still-infectious prostitute bodies. In short, as Gilman puts it, the Jew "opens up" the whore.

In Daniel Defoe's *Roxana: The Fortunate Mistress* (1724), a Jew also "opens up" a whore. Early in the narrative, the Dutch merchant brings a Jew to the heroine to convert her wealth to a more mobile form. Roxana needs money because she has suddenly found herself "at Liberty" when the Prince of — turns virtuous;[3] the jewels she wants to exchange came from her first illicit lover (the landlord) who was murdered for them. This conversion of jewels to money marks the heroine's entrance into the marketplace and sets in motion her transformation from a privately kept "Lady of Pleasure" to a full-blown "Woman of Business" (131). All of Defoe's major characters, James Thompson has observed, face the problem of converting their wealth from a particular, identifiable form into anonymous coin.[4] But in *Roxana*, the heroine's first such attempt goes horribly wrong: "As soon as the *Jew* saw the Jewels, I saw my Folly; and it was ten Thousand to one but I had been ruin'd, and perhaps, put to Death in as cruel a Manner as possible; and I was put in such a Fright by it, that I was once upon the Point of flying for my Life, and leaving the Jewels and Money too" (112). The Jew has not only recognized the jewels, but has shockingly concluded that Roxana murdered the jeweler to get them. The Jew "held up his Hands, look'd at me with some Horrour . . . and put himself into a thousand Shapes, twisting his Body, and wringing up his Face this Way, and that Way" (113), glaring at her with his "Devil's Face" (115). Recovering herself, the heroine insists that the murdered jeweler had been her husband. The Dutch merchant does not question this explanation; the Jew, however, remains suspicious. The Jew's desire for legal action terrifies Roxana, for it would reveal her status as whore rather than wife, thus destroying her claim to the jeweler's wealth and abandoning her to a foreign legal system that might find her guilty of theft and even murder. The Dutch merchant further raises the anxiety that the French authorities, upon hearing the Jew's accusation, might force a murder confession out of Roxana by torturing her on the rack, a prospect that frightens the heroine "to Death almost" (118). Motivated by profit, the Jew, however, can "open her up" without implements.

The Jew becomes increasingly ominous as he ruthlessly seeks to gain from the heroine's vulnerability. Roxana escapes him and becomes fabulously wealthy in part by adopting a series of different identities;[5] the Jew, however, alone among men challenges one of her self-inventions. He unearths "by his unweary'd Enquiry" (133) her connection to the prince and persists in his investigations despite violent beatings by the prince's "Gentlemen." He accuses the Dutch merchant of protecting a known whore and assisting with the murder. But the merchant was "too-many" (134) for the Jew and accuses the Jew of plotting to get an innocent widow's jewels by offering him (the merchant) a share of the profit. The Jew bribes his way out of the imprisonment that results from these accusations and stalks the merchant. The fortunate mistress never forgets about the Jew: She has her maid Amy check his whereabouts throughout the novel before making any important move. The Jew may have some of the details wrong, but he accurately reads Roxana's guilty heart and unearths part of her complicated past.

The Jew's uncanny capacity to see through Roxana's deception, particularly at a moment when such a discovery would benefit him financially, suggests a similar kind of fraught intersection between the prostitute and the Jew as the one that Gilman identifies in the nineteenth century. But while in the case of Jack the Ripper disease and perversion link the prostitute and the Jew, in Defoe, significantly, money rather than the body becomes the key point of contact and exposure. Somatic contagion has surprisingly little to do with this scene or with Roxana's career; like Fanny Hill, Roxana escapes many of the material dangers of prostitution. The representation of the devil-faced Jew in *Roxana* draws from a wide range of contemporary anti-Semitic stereotypes (to which I will return): filth, Satanism, supernatural powers, sexual perversity, and child sacrifice. But in this scene, and in much eighteenth-century writing, the association of Jews with financial ruthlessness and financial success holds a particularly important place.[6] Defoe's Jew, nearly unique among males in this novel, appears to have no erotic interest in the heroine; instead, he pursues her wealth undistracted by the sexual interest with which Roxana manipulates others. The Jew's recognition of Roxana's guilt underscores the overlap in their transgressions: Both prostitutes and Jews in this period often represent the unbounded drive toward accumulation.

Most dramatically in this confrontation with the Jew, but also in other ways throughout the narrative, *Roxana* explores the social, moral, and economic transformations of the period through the extremity of prostitution. While Restoration texts such as *The Whore's Rhetorick* juxtaposed prostitution with other forms of exchange for bawdy, comic, and satirical effect, *Roxana*, though drawing on this context, more seriously explores the internal conflicts arising from marketing the commodity most prominently being reimagined as emblematic of the private—and thus, at least in theory, priceless—through a repentant prostitute's confessional memoir. The fortunate mistress certainly evokes Restoration stereotypes of beautiful, sexually indulgent, luxury-loving, and power-seeking whores associated with the court and theater of Charles II. At the same time, though, Roxana's story explores prostitution as an economic negotiation more immediately than as an expression of a lascivious disposition. Unlike the Restoration whores whom her character otherwise echoes, Roxana rarely seems to make decisions on the basis of sexual desire or to indulge in recreational sex. While such dispassion would later in the century mark prostitutes as eligible for redemption, in Defoe's narrative—written at a time when reformers still represented prostitution as motivated at least in part by lust and set at a time when this belief held even more force—the heroine's relative lack of motivation by sexual desire becomes one of her most disconcerting qualities. Graduating from the home-school version of Mother Creswell's academy, Roxana increasingly seems to have more in common with the profit-driven Jew than sexually adventurous wandering whores. The novel gradually builds tensions within the heroine between her self-proclaimed status as a "Protestant whore" and her potential descent into "Jewish" economic obsession, a tension sharpened by a broader cultural context that increasingly understood Jews and prostitutes as posing similar kinds of ideological problems in eighteenth-century commercial culture. Defoe's novel holds in tension the haunting specter of the Jew who could return and "open up" the whore against the equally disturbing possibility of the heroine's resemblance to, and even transformation into, one of his tribe.

While Roxana and the Jew both seek to profit from their meeting, the novel provides little context for the intensity with which the Jew pursues the heroine's money: The fact that he is a Jew seems sufficiently explanatory. In this sense the Jew serves, as Frank Felsenstein suggests of Jew figures in general in eighteenth-century writing, as a "paradigm of otherness." Yet Roxana seeks to exchange her jewels in the context of a personal crisis, limited options, and material aspirations. In this sense at least, her position comes closer to representing a normative set of possibilities rather than inexplicable alterity. Much criticism has focused on Roxana's moral and maternal failure; this chapter, however, will explore the extent to which Defoe's novel raises shared anxieties rather than dismisses as immoral the heroine's negotiation of a position between a (perhaps mythical) lost security and modern unpredictability; between wholeness and theatrical self-division; between acting like a "Jew" and becoming one; between a partial and a complete sacrifice of one's own flesh and blood. Neither the lascivious whore of the Restoration nor the tragic prostitute dead to all feeling imagined by mid-century reformers, Roxana fears the Jew—the posited cultural "other" of economic and moral practice—as a distorted mirror and limit point for her own looming trade-offs.

Roxana, Alterity, and Identity

Defoe's story of a spectacularly successful if ultimately Heaven-blasted whore has generally been read as a kind of reform narrative with the fortunate mistress as a moral, gendered, and/or exoticized "other" who deserves her fate within the narrative's logic for violating emergent domestic values.[7] But while the novel certainly evokes the reformist policing of sexuality, its greatest power and continuing fascination instead lies, I hope to show, not in any moral attack on female transgression, but in the heroine's own conflicted relationship to her potential embodiment of a new Mandevillian subjectivity represented in extreme form in the figure of the Jew. Few readers have failed to recognize this novel's fascination with the heroine's drive toward accumulation and extended financial negotiations, a subject that absorbed Defoe in a variety of contexts throughout his career. David Marshall has even described this novel as Defoe's "veiled autobiography"; extending this point, Sandra Sherman has argued for *Roxana* as Defoe's fullest exploration of his economic experience as a writer in an uncertain market.[8] Whatever Defoe's personal investment in his heroine, arguments by Marshall, Sherman, and others suggest that Roxana's adventures resonate not as entirely alien transgressions but as trials with which the writer, and by extension a reader, might find some anxious common ground.

One of the most powerful cases for Roxana's "otherness" has been the exoticism displayed in her seductive Turkish dance.[9] Her Turkish exoticism, however, while certainly linked to Orientalist impulses, nevertheless describes self-conscious theatricality rather than any explicit representation of the heroine's own alterity.[10] Roxana after all, does not *become* a Turk but self-consciously *performs* the Turk, fulfilling the Orientalist fantasies of her audience. She confesses to the reader the ordinariness of her faux-Turkish dance, silently enjoying the admirer who claims to recognize it from his travels. Another group of women perform a more authentic Turkish dance, but their disturbing foreign movements disgust rather than charm. Not only does this "Roxana" reproduce other Western literary "Roxanes," as Katie Trumpener has shown, but she even reproduces another literary prostitute's reproduction. In an anecdote told by a prostitute in Head and Kirkman's *English Rogue*, William Davenant's play *The Siege of Rhodes* so aroused one client that he wished he could have sex with the "real" Roxalana—that is, not the Turkish queen but the English actress dressed as a Turkish queen. For twenty pounds, his whore (Mary) promises to procure the actress. Instead, however, Mary herself dons the same dress, and her resulting sensual appearance so overwhelms the client that he takes her for the "real" Roxalana (that is, the actress Hester Davenport who played the queen).[11] Mary confesses her trick to the delight of the company, and the client laughs along with them; in fact, he enjoys this fantasy so much that in the morning he asks her to put on the Turkish dress again.[12] Thus in *The English Rogue* as in *Roxana*, the whore seduces not as a Turk but decidedly as a *faux* Turk; in both texts, the prostitute carefully balances the exotic with the local. Like Mary, Defoe's heroine functions not only as the embodiment of a fictionalized "other," but as a Mandevillian subject exploring the outer limits of the performances that her survival demands. When Defoe includes this scene, then, he draws on a known fetish and a series of theatrical figures—Head and Kirkman's prostitute who used this trick, the actress Hester Davenport, the character Roxalana—between the fortunate mistress and the Turkish queen.

Thus, rather than creating distance between the reader and the heroine through exoticism, this incident exposes the performance of the exotic, keeping the reader in on the deception and appraised of the heroine's motives (to the extent that she understands them herself). From the "editor's" plea for understanding in the introduction to the tragic blast from Heaven, the narrative attempts to render the heroine's choices and conflicts intelligible. However it may ultimately judge its heroine, Defoe's narrative demands that we see the world from the prostitute's perspective and at least in this limited sense identify with her predicament. Defoe's prostitute heroine functions, among other ways, as an example of the complex experience of negotiating a radically unstable financial world with only the body's labor and imagination's capacity as resources. Like other prostitute biographies or memoirs (as we will see in chapter 4), *Roxana* creates a heroine with compelling resilience; she rides the unpredictable waves of fortune and possesses a Mandevillian belief in the theatricality of the social world as well as the skills to manipulate it to her best advantage. She masters her situation, claims possession of her body, and enjoys the unprecedented mobility, both financial and geographical, of the emergent commercial culture. Roxana's opening situation of friendless abandonment to abject poverty with five hungry children provokes both sympathy and shared anxiety in a world of economic uncertainly: The "middling sort" hung on to their security by the delicate threads of family networks[13]—threads that all break in Defoe's novel, hurling the heroine into the terrors of poverty. Susan/Roxana navigates her way through a complex world of global and domestic commerce. She is not *just* the exotic whore and strange androgynous "man-woman" (as she calls herself), but in certain key ways the *every* "man-woman," at least in fantasy or dread.

Any reading that does not assume the complete alterity of the whore, however, must take into account the growing anxieties in the narrative and the truncated, though decidedly catastrophic ending: Roxana's original predicament may demand sympathy and even identification, but her story is undeniably tragic. Yet the conclusion that this tragic ending confirms the absolute moral and/or exoticized otherness of the prostitute tends to depend on an argument based on an assumption of poetic justice that does not quite match the events of the novel. As morally disturbing a figure as Roxana may appear to some readers, whoring itself does not provoke the "blast from Heaven." Instead, prostitution brings wealth, power, luxury, respect, status, flattery, and independence. With her elite circulation, Roxana never experiences the poverty, disease, imprisonment, transportation, and harassment by reformers that eighteenth-century sex workers historically endured. As Robert Hume points out (but dismisses as ironic), what brings Roxana's fortune crashing down at the end of the novel is not prostitution but rather her unaccountable desire to seek out her legitimate children[14]—her one drive in the narrative with no material or rational explanation. Had Roxana never become a whore, she clearly would have sunk, with her children, into abject poverty. But had she never gone back to find and assist these children, her daughter Susan would never have found her, haunted her, so unbearably threatened her security, and brought her narrative to its crisis. Thus, in a reading based strictly on poetic justice, we would have to conclude that Roxana falls not because she runs afoul of domestic ideology through prostitution but because she inexplicably hangs on to the hope of caring for these children rather than abandoning them to the individualistic marketplace to which she herself has been abandoned. In seeking her children, the "Queen of Whores" irrationally loses her grip on Mandevillian self-interest.

I do not, of course, read *Roxana* as a treatise warning against maternal care. Nevertheless, while Roxana becomes a relentless possessive individualist with a driving acquisitive passion that she displays for no man, she simultaneously harbors an inexplicable desire for her children and loses everything by acting on this desire. Defoe frames Roxana's story with child loss—or, as I will suggest, child *sacrifice:* She begins her career by leaving her children with resentful relatives, but ends her career with an ambiguous complicity in her child's murder. It is between these two sacrifices that we find Defoe's poignant exploration of the contradictory desires shaping the men and women of his age. Thus rather than reading *Roxana* as an apology for capitalism through the displacement of commercial violence onto an exoticized female "other"[15] *or* reading the novel as a critique of the corrupt modern world through the prostitute who receives poetic justice, I suggest instead that through Roxana, Defoe explores the experience of suspension between wholeness, represented here by the mother/daughter, Susan/Susan dyad, and the divided theatrically of the Mandevillian performer.

Here the Jew's unique ability to "open up" Roxana becomes crucial. While

Roxana performs but does not become a Turk, the possibility that she might become a Jew, or at least resemble one too closely, shapes the narrative in subtle ways. Roxana's passionate acquisitiveness and her embrace of usury connect her with stereotypes of Jews:[16] Her most insatiable desires emerge as economic rather than sexual. The "vital and absorbing . . . activity of [Roxana's] progressive accumulation," as Laura Brown points out, "supersedes any effective representation of sexual energy" in the novel.[17] The appearance of the Jew at Roxana's crucial moment of transition from pleasure to business evokes ancient stereotypes as well as recent historical developments. In Defoe's time, the small group of Jews becoming successful in Exchange Alley emerged as emblematic beyond their numbers. For this and other reasons, "the Jew," Michael Ragussis has documented, "was located centrally in the redefinition of England as a commercial nation."[18] As Felsenstein explains,

> The Jews' return to England from the second half of the seventeenth century coincided with the rapid post-Restoration development of the city of London as the center of what Peter Dickson has aptly dubbed "the Financial Revolution in England." According to Dickson, particularly during the first half of the eighteenth century, the "fear of dislocation of the social order by the rise of new economic interest, and dislike of commercial and financial manipulation of all kinds" were often reinforced by an intense anti-Jewish prejudice. Because a number of the more prominent financiers were indeed Jews but as much because of their age-old association in popular lore with usury, coin-clipping, and other such base pecuniary dealing, it was convenient to label all brokers and jobbers as Jews. The term *stock-jobbing*, used freely but largely pejoratively to denote the speculative transaction of stocks, bills of exchange, and public funds, became widely associated with Jewish dealing.[19]

In the eighteenth century, however, Jews not only became associated in key ways with the financial revolution but also featured prominently in prostitute stories. These narratives represent Jews as seeking prostitutes because they (like Mandeville's men of business) want efficiently to dispense with sex, have discretionary income, are unattractive, and, perhaps most of all, reduce all human relations to financial transactions. Jewish men, according to one prostitute, though great customers require considerable female art to arouse because of "their incessant thought of business, the rise and fall of stocks, and the like."[20] In George Granville's adaptation of Shakespeare's *Merchant of Venice* (1701), Shylock blatantly reveals his erotic impulses as directed toward money rather than women. In one scene, Bassanio, Antonio, and Gratiano propose a toast to their deal: Antonio raises his glass to his friendship with Bassanio, Bassanio to Portia, and Gratiano to "the Sex in general." Yet Shylock declares money as his true passion:

> I have a Mistress, that out-shines 'em all—
> Commanding yours—and yours tho' the whole Sex:
> O may her Charms encrease and multiply;
> My Money is my Mistress! Here's to Interest upon Interest.[21]

As an emblem of their reputed wealth and preference for commercial transactions, Jews commonly feature as a girl's first keeper in this period: Hogarth's plate 2 of *A Harlot's Progress* (1732) represents Moll Hackabout entertaining her Jewish client while her lover sneaks out of the room; a 1733 ballad opera based on *A Harlot's Progress* takes its name, *The Jew Decoy'd*, from this scene.[22] In Eliza Haywood's *Betsy Thoughtless*, Miss Foreword begins her prostitution career with a Jewish keeper; the famous bawd Mother Douglas reportedly began her career as a prostitute after selling her (fake) maidenhead to a Jew.[23] The bawd Charlotte Hayes reportedly considered Jews her best customers.[24] Mrs. Slammekin in *The Beggar's Opera* names Jews as the best kinds of keepers (2.4.104–105), and the prostitute Fanny Davies reportedly formed a business partnership with a Jew.[25] To the infamous Teresia Constantia Phillips, "Jew Merchants" reportedly "the richest in the City, / Have offered Settlements exceeding pretty."[26] The presumption of Jews as a fertile market for the sex trade was so widespread that Mr. Harris, bawd and author of guides to London prostitutes, advertised Fanny Murray as "Fit for high keeping with a Jew merchant."[27]

Other narratives find prostitutes and Jews not just as commercial sexual partners, but locked in antagonistic struggles, perhaps implicitly due to the similarity of their motives. In *The Life and Intrigues of the Late Celebrated Mrs. Mary Parrimore* (1729), a prostitute conducts her business from a milliner's shop that she sets up near Exchange Alley specifically to attract business from Jewish brokers. These Jews lose their "ill-gotten Wealth" to whores, the author points out, as quickly as they gain it through their shady financial machinations.[28] Mrs. Parrimore's trouble begins when a Jew pays for her favors, but proves impotent. This leaves the prostitute outraged, not only over the sexual disappointment but also for the incident's potential to ruin her reputation and thus her business. She concocts an elaborate plot in revenge, in which she convinces the Jew through a series of letters that a fine lady has fallen in love with him. (Parrimore, or someone impersonating her, published these letters in a separate volume entitled *Love upon Tick* [1724]). Mrs. Parrimore has her Irish stallion disguise himself as a physician and undertake to cure the Jew of his impotence so as not to lose his chance with the widow. The stallion recommends his own expensive elixir and a diet high in shellfish, from which the Jew finally begins "to look fresh and plump" (34). Mrs. Parrimore continually delays the Jew's meeting with the fine lady to torment him, but finally arranges the long-wished-for rendezvous, at which he finds no widow. Thus Mrs. Parrimore extracts her revenge and considerable profit (for the "physician's" services); she even repairs her reputation by seducing him. While the eighteenth century certainly reproduced stereotypes of Jewish lasciviousness, here and elsewhere the Jew devotes so much of his passion toward profit that he fails sexually and becomes vulnerable to the prostitute's machinations.

The prostitute's devotion to profit, sometimes at the expense of sexual pleasure, could increasingly become part of her danger in the eighteenth century and was commonly expressed through comparisons to Jews.[29] When a prostitute happens to be a Jew, her greed is overdetermined: One prostitute reportedly "inherited from her [Jewish] father, and confirmed by a strict attention to the duties of the Synagogue, an unbounded inclination to the acquisition of money."[30] The prostitute Betty Ireland lectures her aristocratic client on the value of gold, siding with the Jews on this point: "if any man shall discredit what I say, I will bring the whole tribe of Levi to justify it."[31] Her antagonistic relationship with a particular Jew forms one of her biography's central tensions and precipitates her transition from an impoverished but sensual whore to a colder, wealthy professional. As in *Roxana*, a confrontation with a Jew marks Betty's conversion from a "Lady of Pleasure" to a "Woman of Business." "Jewish" ruthlessness offers a model for prostitutes in other cases: "we live," one fictionalized prostitute declares, "like the Jews of all Societies, and if we but knew, as well as they, to improve our lawful Profits, we might have Houses and Gardens like any of the *Inns of Court.*"[32] At least one satiric poet, in fact, compared the naturalization of Jews to the toleration of bawdy houses.[33] Thomas Brown accused a prostitute with a Jewish lover of putting "in practice what your kind keeper's ancestors did formerly in the wilderness, that is, you fall down before the golden calf which, the Rabbis say, was some excuse for their idolatry."[34] Apparently this was a common analogy: The author of *The Female Fire-Ships* also suggests that whores "Like Jews they still adore the Golden Calf."[35]

When prostitutes turn into bawds, they come to resemble Jews even more closely. In Henry Fielding's *Miss Lucy in Town*, the Jew Mr. Zorobabel is outraged to learn that Mrs. Midnight has promised a new girl to Lord Bawble without first offering her to him: "'tis an affront not only to me, but to all my friends: and you deserve never to have any but Christians in your house again," he declares.[36] Mrs. Midnight, however, realizes that insulting Mr.

Zorobabel will ruin her business (whorehouses depend on Jews) and promises him the girl. "You are a sensible woman," he replies, "and I commend your care; for reputation is the very soul of a Jew" (46). Mrs. Midnight not only serves Jews but also has in a sense here *become* a "Jew." Bawds practiced a form of human usury, turning women into things and maintaining control over them through debt. The bawd Charlotte Hayes:

> [T]ook care to have the *choicest goods*, as she called them, that could be had at market . . . she knew how to fix the price upon a gown, a saque, a trollopee, a watch, a pair of buckles, or any other trinket. She charged [her prostitutes] in proportion for their board, washing and lodging; and by keeping her Nuns constantly in her debt, she secured them.[37]

Women become themselves "goods," but also elided with their dresses—a gown, a "saque," a "trollopee," the last ambiguously referring to both a loose garment and a loose woman. Moll King also kept "a great many of the poor Females under her Thumb" by lending them money at high interest.[38] In Richardson's *Pamela*, Mrs. Jewkes, the heroine's oppressive guardian and a former bawd, evokes her ethnic counterpart in her name. While some narratives thus represent prostitutes as abused victims of usurious, Jew-like bawds, others that tell stories of more independent prostitutes elide these characteristics into one figure. Moll King objectifies other women, but Roxana and other independent prostitutes must learn to understand their own sexual activity instrumentally.

Roxana not only resembles the stereotyped Jew in her threat to reduce human relations to economic ones—a resemblance shared with all prostitutes—but also evokes this parallel through her lack of permanent attachment to one nation and her ethnic origin. French Protestants and Jews shared associations in the eighteenth century as adept financiers[39] and endured similar stereotypes; both groups had the reputation for callous accumulation and were said to live "with that amalgam of unrestrained passion and self-interest which supposedly eroded a devotion to the common good."[40] The two groups later became associated in debates over naturalization. Arguing in favor of the later "Jew Bill" of 1753, "Philanthropos" cites similar objections to naturalizing "foreign Protestants," which would have been a mistake given the contributions of this group to the textile industry.[41] One "Solomon Abrabanel" characterizes both Jews and French Huguenots as usurers:

> As far as *Dirt, Avarice*, and *Extortion* can make them [French Huguenots] JEWS, they might be convicted upon any Statute against *Judaism*; and even *Circumcision* is not wanting to most of them.[42]

Thus Roxana's own origin would have linked her with Jews in an immediate political way that readers would have recognized.

Roxana's first full self-identification as a whore comes at the same moment that she self-consciously performs the role of the Old Testament figure Rachel. I refer here to the notorious scene in which Roxana puts Amy to bed with the landlord, a gesture that the fortunate mistress herself explains as a strategy for maintaining her authority over her maid.[43] Roxana certainly victimizes Amy here, but Amy had originally proposed this arrangement by positioning Roxana as Rachel: "if you won't consent [to sleeping with the landlord]," she says, "tell him you'll do as *Rachel* did to *Jacob*, when she could have no Children, put her Maid to Bed to him" (39).[44] While still far from the "Woman of Business" or even "Lady of Pleasure" she would become, this seduction by the landlord marks Roxana's first departure from virtue. Thus in the moment of her initiation into sexual transgression, Amy flatteringly casts her mistress as Jacob's beautiful second wife. Amy's naming her mistress as Rachel becomes either prophetic or supernaturally performative, for Roxana, like Rachel, at first has no children with the jeweler and lends him her maid, who gets pregnant. Roxana assures both the jeweler and Amy that she, like Rachel, will take this child as her own. While Amy casts her mistress as Rachel as a way of guiding her toward profitable sexual exchange, Roxana only fully accepts her identity as a whore when she fulfills Amy's prophecy. This reenactment of the "handmaiden's tale" transforms her identity; she calls it proof that now "I was a Whore" (45).

While in this scene Roxana first accepts her identity as a whore, the narrative associates Roxana with atavistic "Jewish" rituals even earlier in her abandonment of her children. In her poverty, Roxana finds herself on the brink of "Jewish" cannibalism: "we had eaten up almost every thing, and little remain'd, unless, like the pitiful Women of *Jerusalem*, I should eat up my very Children themselves" (18). But instead of eating them, Roxana gives up her children so that they do not all starve together, a predicament that the text spells out in excruciating detail.[45] She despairs over the misery they will endure with reluctant relatives but, prompted by Amy, leaves them nonetheless. We might think of her choice, however, as neither the consummate sign of the whore's utter heartlessness nor simply an understandable expedient in the face of poverty, but rather as a form of *sacrifice*—a possibility that embodies both her sense of their value and the significance of their loss, but also the painful cruelty of leaving them with her uncaring sister-in-law. This sacrifice associates Roxana with not just transgressive femininity, but perhaps also foreshadows her later recognition by the Jew. As Felsenstein has shown, the most virulently anti-Semitic propaganda of the eighteenth century not only blamed Jews for the murder of Christ but believed they practice a ritual reenactment of this murder through the sacrifice of children and the consumption of their blood.[46] "The sacrifice of the Passover," according to one eighteenth-century author, was in many households secretly

> changed from the typical offering of a lamb, to the real immolation of human blood, for which purpose the most beautiful children were purchased at any expence, and under any pretext, from the ignorance of necessitous parents, or the perfidious avarice of servants, if they could not be obtained by stealth, and brought from all parts of Europe, to these ceremonies: it being a long-received opinion, that the original sacrifice of a lamb was designed only for that one occasion, to conciliate the favour of heaven, to the escape of their fore-fathers out of Egypt; but that to render it propitious to their restoration to their country, and to the consummation of their promised happiness and glory, the type must be changed for the thing typified, and human blood, in the purest state of infant innocence, be offered instead of the ineffectual blood of a brute.[47]

The anonymous *Historical and Law-Treatise against Jews and Judaism* insists that throughout history Jews have rightly been persecuted for their heartless staking, crucifying, and sacrificing of children.[48] Once Jews procure a child, *The English Rogue* explains,

> at first they will cloath him in silks, ravishing him with all the delights that can be thought on, never having musick from his ears, or banquets from his taste; and thus use him, till they see he is plump, fat, and fit for their purpose, but when the poor boy least thinks of his imminent ruine, he is taken by a brace of slaves, and tyed up by the heels, so beaten by degrees to death with Cudgels.[49]

Another writer similarly relays how several Jews

> were executed for Crucifying a Child, at Lincoln, call'd Hugo . . . the Child was first fatten'd, for ten Days, with white Bread and Milk, in a secret Chamber . . . almost all the Jews in England were invited to the Crucifixion.[50]

John Toland identifies the belief in Jewish ritual sacrifice of children and consumption of their hearts as one of the most widespread unfounded accusations against Jews.[51] The belief in Jewish child sacrifice was so widespread that Menasseh Ben Israel, when arguing to Oliver Cromwell for Jewish readmission, felt obligated to point out that Jews do not really sacrifice children, and as late as 1753 Josiah Tucker, supporting Jewish naturalization, felt it necessary to lay to rest anxieties about Jewish "Levitical Sacrifices and Ceremonies."[52] Eliza Haywood's *Fair Hebrew* (1729), published just a few years after *Roxana*, offers a brutal version of the myth of Jewish child sacrifice. When the Jewish Miriam becomes pregnant outside of wedlock, her orthodox uncle imprisons her and, upon the birth of the baby

> took the poor Infant, but, instead of caressing, or cherishing it as expected, threw it immediately into a great Fire, uttering at the same Time some Words which my excessive Fright wou'd not suffer me to observe.[53]

Defoe's heroine does not literally crucify, immolate, or consume her children; nevertheless, we might productively think about her choice as a form of sacrifice that suggests her potential "Jewish" ruthlessness. Her decision to relinquish her children embodies two central aspects of sacrifice: first, she clearly understands that she is doing something harmful to them; but second, she values them and does not want to give them up. To abandon something or someone without value does not constitute a sacrifice. Roxana in one sense displays greater cruelty by sacrificing her own children; at the same time, her distress at this choice marks her difference from "Jewish" heartlessness. Amy tells the relatives that their mother has lost her reason, which begins as a lie but becomes the truth: "at parting with my poor Children, I fainted, and was like one Mad when I came to myself and found they were gone" (22). Earlier she laments that "thoughts of parting with my Children . . . sunk my very Heart within me" (19). The narrative frames Roxana's story with child sacrifice: In the beginning she sacrifices her children with profound ambivalence to their uncertain destinies; at the end, Amy presumably sacrifices young Susan, fulfilling her mistress's desire and evoking her horror. While executing the first sacrifice on her mistress's behalf, Amy calls the children "poor Lambs" (21)—a common enough word for children, but also the Passover animal that Jewish child sacrifice presumably replaces. But instead of cannibalizing her children like the women of Jerusalem, Roxana performs a less violent, incomplete sacrifice—an inconclusive partial sacrifice that will come back to haunt her. Between this ambivalent, incomplete child sacrifice and the final, mysteriously violent sacrifice lie all of Roxana's adventures as a whore.

This initial sacrifice enables the brewer's wife to reinvent herself. Rene Girard explains that sacrifice serves the double function of stemming greater violence and consolidating the identity of the community.[54] Roxana, however, sacrifices in secret and alone (except for Amy); she sacrifices her children to consolidate not a communal identity but her *own*. She sacrifices to reinvent herself as a nomadic subject of global commerce with ties neither to family or country—a position that the Jew, mythically, already inhabits. This sacrifice ultimately destroys her, however, not because of its cruelty but because of her own violation of what may be the primary rule of sacrifice: The object cannot be recovered. While Girard points out that outpourings of distress frequently become a ritualized part of the sacrifice, Roxana acts on those feelings; she doubles back and attempts to rescue her sacrificial objects. Her ability to do this reminds us that she did not truly cannibalize them as threatened. But because of the opening partial sacrifice, Susan's attempt to reclaim her mother takes on the eerie quality of a return from the dead. Susan pursues her mother beyond all reason; she "haunts" her like a ghost. Roxana violates the spirit of sacrifice by trying, for no reason consistent with her new identity as an ambitious whore, to recover her children. Nothing, Girard observes, generates so much violence as a failed sacrifice.

Roxana first reinvents herself by giving up her children to an uncertain future. As the narrative progresses, however, she begins to evoke other sinister qualities also associated with Jews in eighteenth-century anti-Semitic discourse. These disturbing qualities leave her relatively unscathed, but consistently pose serious threats to those around her. Popular culture in both the Renaissance and eighteenth century proliferated images of the knife-wielding Jew seeking to convert the unsuspecting Christian through a forced ritual of circumcision—an image that, as James Shapiro demonstrates, contemporaries unsurprisingly associated with castration.[55] Roxana never deliberately hurts any of the men in her life; nevertheless, strange, violent, disabling, and, we might say, "castrating" accidents consistently befall them. Her husband falls from his position as the wealthy businessman's heir to an impoverished vagabond. He wanders off in a daze, becomes a soldier, and eventually dies of his battle wounds. The landlord meets his bloody, violent death, foreseen by his mistress, in broad daylight. In a bizarre coincidence, a wild boar gores the Prince of — just when Roxana begins to think seriously about rejoining him. Might this tragedy echo the fate of Adonis, in love with Venus but gored in the groin by a wild boar? After the meeting with the Jew, the Dutch merchant ends up fleeing the country in fear for his life. The novel doesn't reveal his ultimate fate at the end, but it is difficult to imagine that he suffered no ill effects from the final blast from Heaven. During Lord —'s relationship with Roxana, he "grew old, and fretful, and captious . . . he grew worse and wickeder the older he grew, and that to such Degree, as is not fit to write of" (198–199). Of all her lovers, only the king (presumably Charles II) apparently survives unscathed. Nevertheless, images of impotence proliferated during Charles II's reign as a symbolic critique of the ways in which the king's sexual recreations had diminished his political authority.[56] We could even see Roxana's prostitute identity as enabled by a form of castration. When she impersonates a Turk and explicitly *becomes Roxana*, she deliberately and advantageously positions herself as the fetishized object of the male gaze. Roxana *knows* she becomes a fetish; she explicitly competes with the other women at the gathering for this honor. She knows that a faux-Turkish dance will give her a better chance to be fetishized, since fetishism depends on a level of fantasy absent in the more authentic Turkish dance. Thus her entire identity *as Roxana* is inextricably bound up with her creation of herself as a fantasy, fetishized object, which in psychoanalytic terms by definition (over)compensates for the "castrated" spectator. Roxana's performance as Roxana thus suggests at one level the castration of those who admire her.

Eighteenth-century writers further associated Jews with Satanism, mysticism, and supernatural, particularly prophetic, powers. Roxana's own impression of the Jew's devil face has its roots in widespread associations of Jews with Satanism.[57] Sometimes the Jew's reputation as a possessor of supernatural powers and as an adept financier merged in the anxiety of the fickle stock market as itself supernaturally manipulated.[58] Defoe's fortunate mistress possesses supernatural powers as well, but she cannot control them. She predicts and seems indirectly and mysteriously to bring about the death of the jeweler; she wishes for a storm at sea and it comes to pass. While the jeweler's death greatly distresses Roxana, the "strange Notices I had of it" (55) trouble her even more. She becomes convinced of her "Second-Sight" and later dismisses the first midwife that the foreign prince provides for her out of a conviction that she was "set privately to dispatch me out of the World" (77). Uncanny coincidences shape the narrative: not only does the Jew recognize the jewels, but also Roxana meets her husband the brewer in France, where he serves the king as a guard. This strange coincidence so shocks the brewer that he takes Amy, who Roxana sends to gather more information, for a supernatural being: "*I knew you when you were alive, but what you are now, whether Ghost or Substance, I know not*" (88). In the most haunting coincidence that ends Roxana's good fortune, her own daughter Susan ends up serving her as a maid at the height of her fame as a courtesan.

In the face of all the misery she inadvertently causes, Roxana cannot understand what drives her. Unforgettably, at the height of her wealth and comfort, she asks herself "*What was I a Whore for now?*" (201). Her question has generally been taken as a rhetorical statement of self-castigation, but it also seems to identify a genuine enigma in her desire.[59] Initially Roxana has a clear motive, for her wayward husband leaves her impoverished. She vehemently denies that she whores "for the sake of the Vice," which in other contexts would be the obvious answer to her question. Unlike the literary prostitutes from the Restoration that her character echoes, Roxana claims not to be driven by erotic pleasure. Critics have not consistently been convinced by her denial, and indeed Roxana appreciates her luxurious life, the attentions of wealthy men, and public displays of her body.[60] She marvels at her own beauty. Nevertheless, she differs from the Restoration whores that she otherwise recalls by her relatively limited interest in sex, even if she has not achieved the complete alienation from sexual feeling that would mark later prostitutes as ripe for reform. She never, for example, spends her wealth on stallions, the ubiquitous weakness and sure sign of lasciviousness. She remains loyal in her longer-term relationships, agreeing to hide in the country and never slipping out to enjoy more attractive men than her keepers. Desire does not pose a question for Restoration whores: Desire explains itself. Roxana's enigma of desire, however, lies less in her sexuality than in her acquisition; as in Mandeville, the marketplace carries its own libidinal compulsions. Defoe represents the fortunate mistress as caught in a compulsive desire for accumulation that seems to take her by surprise: greater wealth and prestige, not superior sexual attractions, tempt her to betray one man for another.

Naming Roxana's desire as a drive to accumulate, however, does not diminish its enigmatic quality: It has become in her case an unreasonable and excessive compulsion to acquire in potentially self-destructive ways. It does, however, put her in the company of a wide range of commercial agents, as Defoe elsewhere warns: "A tradesman drest up fine, with his long wig and sword, may go to the ball when he pleases, for he is already drest up in the habit; like a piece of counterfeit money, he is brass wash'd over with silver, and no tradesman will take him for current."[61] This warning recognizes the temptation, the infinity of desire that would lead a tradesman self-destructively to purchase expensive things that only make him ridiculous. Defoe's novel abstractly condemns the heroine's acquisitive desires while simultaneously detailing their seductiveness; in doing so, he reveals her similarity to, rather than difference from, a range of people dependent on trade.

In spite of her evocation of "Jewish" extremes of ruthless accumulating zeal, however, Defoe's "Protestant whore" still remains distinct enough from this possibility to find her own desires disturbing.[62] The narrative thus in subtle ways generates tension around the extent to which the heroine will remain "Protestant" in the face of her increasing similarity to the Jew. Just as prostitution, as we have seen, demands scrutiny of the human costs and benefits of commodification, so Jewish business practices generated anxieties not because they were completely alien but because their differences from Protestant ones were becoming increasingly unclear. Many of these arguments about Jews later came to a head in debates over the Bill for Jewish Naturalization (1753). Arguing against the bill, Jonas Hanway warned that prosperity driven by Jewish success could change the character of the nation if "a Jewish landed interest should predominate."[63] Evoking the parallel to whores, Hanway argued that reformed prostitutes could fill the nation's need for workers more effectively than naturalized Jews.[64] For other writers, however, the naturalization of Jews was consistent with the goals of a growing commercial empire. One defender of naturalization straightforwardly insisted that "the more Money and the more Inhabitants we have in *England*, the better." Besides, "go to *Lisbon*, and let ten *Jews* and ten *Portuguese* be alike drest, and I will defy you, without the Spirit of Divination, to know one from the other."[65] Josiah Tucker found Jews indistinguishable in their business practices as well, arguing that the vilification of usury has been based on a misreading of the Bible. Further, he argued, some Christians want Jews out of the way because the Jews actually charge less and thus drive down the rates of interest in general.[66] Observing London a decade after the "Jew Bill" controversy, Pierre Jean Grosley concluded that English anti-Semitism had its roots in envy: The Jews' "wealth makes part of the capital of a nation, and they contribute to its splendor."[67]

Jews and prostitutes thus posed related ideological challenges in their extremity, but not necessarily clear distinction from other economic agents. By the end of the century Patrick Colquhoun would attribute virtually all urban and commercial pathologies to the nefarious influence of these two groups.[68] Prostitutes and Jews certainly served at one level as scapegoats—as bad merchants against whom the good merchants can be defined. But the cultural *ambivalence* toward both of these figures suggests something more complicated. Some writers accused Jews of dishonest practices, but others suggest that they were only more skilled. Similarly, prostitutes in certain obvious ways (that Aphra Behn commonly pointed out in her plays) do not differ from other women in their recognition of the value of their sexual services; they are only (in some cases) better at defining it. Further, prostitutes only differ from other merchants in the nature of the commodity they vend. If prostitutes cannot be dismissed as simply lascivious, immoral, or overly desirous women, and if we can understand them, however tentatively, as making reasonable choices appropriate to a possessive market society in which anyone without an inheritance has to exchange *something*, then the reformist insistence on the compartmentalization of virtuous and vicious commodities, as well as the emerging ideological distinctions between public and private on which bourgeois morality comes to rest, threatens to collapse entirely. Defoe embodies this moral collapse in the figure of the Jew; the fortunate mistress herself, however, hovers on the brink.

Roxana opens with the same problem that most of Defoe's characters face: How does one survive, and even flourish, when left with only the body? Like other prostitutes, Roxana takes the values of the marketplace on their own terms, selling not her body but the sexual and theatrical labor she can produce with it and that, in Lockean terms, she rightfully owns. Throughout his career, Defoe embraced certain emergent commercial values. At the end of his career with *Roxana*, however, he explored the kinds of self-transformation that these values might demand and the ethical collapse they might threaten. If weakness before sexual temptation were leading Roxana down the slippery slope ending in child-murder, then virtuous readers would be able to take comfort in the whore's alterity. *Roxana*, however, takes advantage of emergent interest in the possibility that other exigencies might lead to this choice—exigencies faced not just by lascivious women but by others as well. In doing so, Defoe offers a much more disturbing tale, not of the immorality of an exoticized other, but of structural contradictions that few can escape.

Roxana's Children

The novel contextualizes Roxana's terror in meeting the Jew, then, with the possibility that she might come to resemble him too closely. In one significant way, however, the fortunate mistress still differs from the stereotyped Jew: while potentially just as heartless, she nevertheless harbors a desire to repair her self-division, to glimpse the possibility of wholeness beyond her split Mandevillian performance and ruthless, castrating acquisitiveness. Shylock misses his jewels more than his daughter; Roxana, however, cannot stop wanting both. Many critics have argued that the novel reveals Roxana's heartlessness and otherness, particularly in her maternal failure,[69] and indeed she shows little concern for the children who result from her prostitution. And while she may offer her legitimate children money instead of personal care, the failed maternity argument cannot explain her impulse to seek them out after she has abandoned them. Her child-recovery project may appear as an afterthought—an inadequate penance for a long career of whoring—since we learn of it only toward the end of the narrative. A careful reading of the plot, however, shows that Roxana begins to plan for them as soon as it becomes possible. To see this, we must return to her moment of transition from "Lady of Pleasure" to "Woman of Business." She meets the Jew in her first attempt to put her jewels—and her "jewel"—on the marketplace; before that, she had been secretively confined as a private mistress. She can complete this new kind of transaction only with the help of the Dutch merchant but notoriously refuses his offer of marriage and instead pays him back with the currency of her sexual labor. This refusal to marry has been cited as her moment of transformation from victim to predator: instead of staying with the merchant, she sets off for London and consults with Robert Clayton to create an investment portfolio.[70] Roxana decides that the commodification of her sexual labor secures both liberty and property, while marriage takes them away. The fortunate mistress may not find her own arguments delineating the superiority of whoring convincing, but she nevertheless chooses prostitution over marriage at this turning point.[71]

Her meeting with Clayton, however, suggests that another motive besides ruthless ambition might be complicating her decision. Clayton tries to convince Roxana that she should invest some of her money instead of spending it on luxuries. She objects: "I was a young Woman; that I had been us'd to live plentifully, and with a good Appearance; and that I knew not how to be a Miser" (168). Clayton visits her several times with this scheme for delayed gratification, but she continually objects that she would rather enjoy her money now rather than in her old age. Finally Clayton asks, "*Then . . . I suppose your Honour has no Children?*"

> None, Sir *Robert*, said I, *but what are provided for*; so I left him in the dark, as much as I found him: However, I consider'd his Scheme very well, tho' I said no more to him at that time, and I resolv'd, tho' I would make a very good Figure, I say, I resolv'd to abate my Expence, and draw in, live closer, and save something. (168)

While she carefully avoids revealing to Sir Robert the connection between his question and her acquiescence to fiscal conservatism, the narrative does not hide it from the reader. Men who hear of Roxana's fortune begin to court her, but she makes clear to Clayton her opinion of marriage. Clayton "own'd that my Observation was just, and that, if I valued my Liberty, as I knew my Fortune, and that it was in my own Hands, I was to blame, if I gave it away to any-one" (169). Sir Robert demonstrates to her the art of making money out of money, which fascinates her, but

> Sir *Robert* knew nothing of my Design; that I aim'd at being a kept Mistress, and to have a handsome Maintenance; and that I was still for getting Money, *and laying it up too*, as much as he cou'd desire me, only by a worse Way. (169)

Until Clayton mentions children, Roxana sees no reason to save and many reasons to spend. The most lucrative marriage could not achieve the goal of providing for them, for she needs private and exclusive control over her own funds. If she had married the Dutch merchant at her first opportunity, she would have had to give up any hope of seeking and assisting her children.[72] When she later marries the merchant, she severely compromises her ability to care for them. Only then do her greatest anxieties—the "secret Hell within" (260)—take root in earnest. She decides to become respectable so that her children might not be ashamed to meet her, and yet paradoxically this "respectable" marriage renders dangerous her support of them. She is not simply guilty about her past but torn apart by the renewed child sacrifice that this marriage demands.

Roxana begins to seek some kind of reunion with her children as soon as circumstances allow. The actual sequence of events is not immediately obvious since she first describes her full career as a whore: becoming an independent "Man-Woman"; dancing the Turkish dance and earning the name of "Roxana"; withdrawing for several years with the king; returning a bit "tarnish'd" (182). After recording these events, however, she tells us that she "must go back here," and the narrative doubles back to report that

> After my coming to *England*, I was greatly desirous to hear how things stood with [my children]; and whether they were all alive or not; and in what Manner they had been maintain'd; and yet I resolv'd not to discover myself to them, in the least; or let any of the People that had the breeding of them up, know that there was such a-body left in the world, as their Mother. (188)

This concern for her children, then, appears late in the novel but at the very beginning of her career as a "Woman of Business"—essentially, at her first possible opportunity. Becoming a "Woman of Business" rather than either a wife or a secretly kept mistress makes this possible. Her reasons for caring about *these* children and showing callous indifference to most of those born from whoring can be explained in terms of her progressive alienation from erotic desire, although it also seems possible that, having once lived with and cared for her legitimate children, she formed an attachment to them that she did not form with the illegitimate ones she immediately relinquishes. Nevertheless, she also had a different kind of attachment to their father. Roxana becomes a prostitute out of need for support and later a driving passion for acquisition rather than sexual desire; she achieves the productive Mandevillian self-division of the whore, which here seems to include emotional distance from any resulting children. She met the brewer's son, however, long before she had developed this skill. Against her father's approval, Roxana marries him out of sexual attraction rather than rational assessment of his character or future. She quickly regrets this choice:

> After I have told you that he was a Handsome Man, and a good Sportsman, I have, indeed, said all; and unhappy was I, like other young People of our

Sex, I chose him for being a handsome, jolly Fellow, as I have said; for he was otherwise a weak, empty-headed, untaught Creature, as any Woman could ever desire to be coupled with (7).

Defoe might be using "sportsman" for its double meaning here: Libertine literature often refers to sexual adventures as "sporting" and libertines themselves as "sportsmen." The husband was, in other words, good in bed. In *Conjugal Lewdness; or, Matrimonial Whoredom* (1727), Defoe lectures against women who marry out of sexual attraction and describes their fate in similar terms. Within a few years, a woman who marries for sex will

see she wedded a worthless, senseless, vain and empty shadow of a Man, in gratification of the Humour which she was at that time in for a Bedfellow; that she has the Man, and no more, and that now all the rest is wanting . . . and what bitter Reproaches does she load her self with when she sees her self in the Arms of a Fool instead of a Man of Sense . . . and all this occasioned by her following blindly and rashly that young wanton Inclination, which she knew not how to govern.[73]

As a reader of *Conjugal Lewdness* could have predicted, the man disappoints her. Yet this original passion, contrasted so sharply with her subsequent sexual distance, may have contributed to producing a lasting attachment to the products of this alliance.[74] Though legitimate, each of the original five is also in a sense a child of passion.

If we think of Defoe's fortunate mistress as *entirely* consumed by financial ambition, then, we cannot possibly understand why she seeks out these children. "Roxana" plays the "Turk" and dangerously resembles the "Jew" through much of the novel; the name "Roxana" itself signifies an exoticist, erotic fantasy that she self-consciously creates to raise her price. As "Roxana," she becomes triumphantly detached; an independent and liberated "Man-Woman." The search for these children could only threaten this glorious wealth and independence. Yet her knowledge of their existence and potential suffering haunts her: She cannot resist investing for them, seeking them out, and assisting them. She must support them in secret, for "I cou'd by no means think of ever letting the Children know what a kind of Creature they ow'd their Being to, or giving them an Occasion to upbraid their Mother with her scandalous Life" (205). The unexpressed goal of this search seems to be an attempt to heal the whore's well-practiced self-division, but, tragically, finding them only exacerbates it. This contradiction becomes almost too much to bear. She takes great satisfaction in setting up her son as an apprentice to a merchant, but cou'd not find in my Heart to let my Son know what a Mother he had and what a Life she liv'd; when at the same time that he must think himself infinitely oblig'd to me, he must be oblig'd, if he was a Man of Virtue, to hate his Mother, and abhor the Way of Living, by which all the Bounty he enjoy'd, was rais'd (204).

This contradiction inspires her to think about reforming, but this effort goes horribly wrong. This son, whom she pines to meet and earn approval from, does not show gratitude but, in a gesture that Roxana reads as contempt, rejects his mother's choice for his wife. Had she become entirely driven by profit and free from other kinds of longing—had she come to occupy the full otherness of the "Jew"—she would have seen that finding these children could only damage her. Thus, rather than punishing Roxana as an example of monstrous maternity, Defoe instead represents her feelings for her children as a kind of transcendent longing to heal the theatrical self-division she has so proudly achieved as a "Woman of Business," a desire founded in part in erotic nostalgia. This, I believe, is how Defoe near the end of his life described not an intractable, immoral "other" but predicament of commercial modernity: Roxana between the two sacrifices remains suspended between a longing to recover her sacrifices and the enigmatic drive to become fully a creature of the marketplace.

In the paragraph that follows her son's rejection of her choice for his wife, Roxana reports that her reflections on her past "made bitter every Sweet." In spite of her affluence and respectable though passionless marriage,

I grew sad, heavy, pensive, and melancholly; slept little, and eat little; dream'd continually of the most frightful and terrible things imaginable: Nothing but Apparitions of Devils and Monsters; falling into Gulphs, and off from steep and high Precipices, *and the like;* so that in the Morning, when I shou'd rise, and be refresh'd with the Blessing of Rest, I was *Hagridden* with Frights . . . (264)

These nightmarish apparitions soon grow flesh in the shape of her daughter Susan. As Lincoln Faller has argued, Susan herself appears to have no sinister motives: "Roxana's daughter loves her (poor creature!) and means her no harm. All she really seems to want is to throw herself at her mother's feet."[75] Faller concludes that the fortunate mistress's own moral bankruptcy and consequent cruelty thus brings her tumbling down. As the legitimate child of a marriage now ended by death, Susan, he argues, poses no material threat to her mother, and Roxana's horrified response appears out of proportion.

In the context of the narrative's association of Roxana with the figure of the Jew, however, her terror in the face of Susan's persistence makes sense as the catastrophe of a failed sacrifice. Roxana attempts to reinvent herself through a form of child sacrifice, but does not prove willing at first to follow through. Because she performs the role of the Jew but has not *become* fully a "Jew"—that is, a ruthless seeker of profit with no other attachments—she returns to recover her children after her sacrifice: She arranges marriages for them, she sets them up in good positions. In doing so, however, she raises a desire in one of them—the one most like herself—for a more substantial attachment. Susan's pursuit of her mother forces Roxana to choose between completing the child sacrifice in its full, violent form and overcoming the detachment that has served her so well. The drama of these scenes and the chilling sense that Susan haunts her from beyond the grave emerge from the power of Roxana's own ambivalence. This detachment enabled her survival but did not cure her of the intense longing to recapture a maternal wholeness. Maternal wholeness, however, is not simply a domestic ideal here, but also serves as a figure for an undivided selfhood that could transcend "Jewish" rituals of child sacrifice and insatiable "Jewish" material desires.

Since her original, though partial, sacrifice, Roxana successfully had been able to keep a variety of identities in play for much of the novel. To the Dutch merchant she played the rich widow, to the king she played the exquisite courtesan playing an exotic Turk, to her children she played the mysterious benefactor, to Sir Robert Clayton she played a "Woman of Business." Had Roxana truly sacrificed her children and never looked back, she would have been able to continue this Mandevillian social performance indefinitely. Susan, after all, never would have found her mother if Roxana had not gone looking for *her*. But Roxana cannot resist turning back. This longing for her children, unaccountable in any reading of Roxana as *only* a moral failure, does little to recover the fortunate mistress for domesticity as traditionally defined. Her most passionate desires never involve heterosexual love. She marries the Dutch merchant, after all, only when she finds out that the wild boar has gored her prince and after the merchant accepts her desire to keep her "ill-gotten Wealth" separate from his "honest Estate" (260). She comes to hold little but contempt for the husband who leaves her. But rather than opposing domesticity to the marketplace, Defoe instead posits the mother/daughter desire as outside of history in a way that Roxana's relationships with men never are. In doing so, Defoe does not exactly essentialize maternity, for Roxana does sacrifice her children (although in great distress). Instead, the mother/daughter desire comes to signify the longing to overcome the alienation that Roxana otherwise embraces. Susan is not just her child but also her namesake and clearly a version of herself; as much as Susan terrorizes her mother, the older Susan cannot overcome the younger Susan's loss.

At the same time that she offers the impossible possibility of wholeness, Susan also poses a similar threat to the one posed by the Jew in her capacity to expose Roxana. The Dutch merchant knows his wife to be capable of sex outside of marriage (she did it with him), but he does not know her full history. By recognizing the exotic Turkish dress, Susan connects two of Roxana's different identities. Before Susan puts these pieces of the puzzle together, *only the Jew* in this novel had ever been able to see through one of her performances. The Jew may fade into the background, but he never leaves Roxana's consciousness: Only after Amy reports his disappearance does her mistress marry the Dutch merchant. Susan appears when the Jew disappears, replacing the Jew in the task of haunting. Further, Susan's very existence demonstrates that *the Jew was right* when he suggested to the Dutch merchant that Roxana was the jeweler's whore and not his wife, which might have led the Dutch merchant to conclude that the Jew was *also* right when he reported that she was the prince's whore. Thus Susan does not threaten to expose her mother's sexual irregularity, which her husband already has accepted. Rather, like the Jew she threatens to expose Roxana's *prostitution:* Susan holds the key to exposing not her mother's sexuality but the more deeply embarrassing, enigmatic desire for relentless acquisition through the commodification of sexual labor.

Thus Roxana fears in Susan something more profound than discord in a comfortable and convenient marriage. The older Susan believes that the younger Susan has brought her "to the Brink of Destruction" (328). Daughter Susan terrifyingly reveals the depth of her mother's Mandevillian theatricality by threatening to reconnect her with both maternal and erotic passion, to mend her self-division into wholeness, and to compromise her radical individualism. Roxana suggests this when she describes their shockingly unexpected meeting on the ship:

> I have not Time here to take Notice what a Suprize it was to me, to see my Child; how it work'd upon my Affections; with what infinite Struggle I master'd a strong Inclination that I had to discover myself to her; how the Girl was the very Counterpart of myself, only much handsomer; and how sweetly and modestly she behav'd; how on that Occasion I resolv'd to do more for her, than I had appointed. (329)

This meeting with Susan fills her with horror, yet

> it was a secret inconceivable Pleasure to me when I kiss'd her, to know that I kiss'd my own Child; my own Flesh and Blood, born of my Body; and

who I had never kiss'd since I took the fatal Farewel of them all, with a Million of Tears, and a Heart almost dead with Grief. (277)

In sacrificing her children, Roxana attempted to sacrifice part of herself. She never becomes the sentimentalized, pathetic prostitute that we see later in the century, for she takes pleasure and pride in her conquests. Her detachment proves productive and immensely rewarding. Nevertheless, flourishing in this context demands a sacrifice. Robinson Crusoe in Defoe's earlier novel disobeys his father and leaves his family; Roxana, by contrast, sacrifices her own flesh and blood.

Or at least she tries to. The story of Roxana's career as a whore unfolds in the sequence of events between the first child sacrifice and the final one; between the self-dividing act of relinquishing her children and the final ambiguous murder of the child who bears her name. This, I think, is why little precedes or follows the two sacrifices, abrupt as this may be: The normal state of subjectivity under capitalism for Defoe lies in the suspension between them. Functioning in the marketplace demands some kind of self-division, a primary Mandevillian theatricality. Roxana invests much energy and derives much pleasure from the series of fantasies she creates that follow from this self-division. Tragedy strikes, however, when she tries to *resolve* her contradictions: instead of living in this suspended state of pleasure, profit, guilt, and longing, Roxana stirs up the ghosts of her primary sacrifice by seeking the flesh and blood she once dispensed with and feeding them the tainted cash of her illicit career. When her lips touch her own daughter, more emotions flood Roxana's heart than in any other scene of physical contact in the novel:

> No Pen can describe, no Words can express, *I say*, the strange Impression which this thing made upon my Spirits; I felt something shoot thro' my Blood; my Heart flutter'd; my Head flash'd, and was dizzy, and all within me, *as I thought*, turn'd about, and much ado I had, not to adandon myself to an Excess of Passion at the first Sight of her, much more when my Lips touch'd her Face; I thought I must have taken her in my Arms, and kiss'd her again a thousand times, whether I wou'd or no. (277)

Nowhere else in this story of a professional whore do we see such a fervent response from one body touching another.[76] The fortunate mistress receives many kisses in this story, but this is the only passionate one that she bestows.[77] This passion, however, destroys both mother and daughter. *Roxana* does not end with the horrific, second child sacrifice that draws the devastating blast from Heaven because the heroine is too much of a "Jew" or too much of a whore. Rather, she must confront Susan for the second time, in scenes of desire and violence, because she never managed to become enough of either. Roxana cannot resist returning for her children when, in a world driven by profit, she would have been safer without them. Cold as Roxana has appeared to so many readers, she nevertheless in the end joins Angellica Bianca and Syrena Tricksey in the period's pantheon of whores who, unlike Mandeville's stew-workers and Mother Creswell's students, never quite manage to give up their own desire.

4

Fanny's Sisters:
The Prostitute Narrative

Public curiosity has of late manifested a very considerable
gratification in Memoirs similar to those which I have now
published.

Ann Sheldon, *Authentic and Interesting Memoirs of
Ann Sheldon* (1790)

Just as Daniel Defoe's crime stories complicate a genre
familiar from popular culture,[1] so his story of *The Fortunate Mistress* also engages a recognizable kind of tale: the prostitute narrative. *Roxana*, in fact, appeared one year after the publication of two biographies of Sally Salisbury, a
prostitute launched into fame through her trial for stabbing one of her
clients. Eighteenth-century prostitute narratives range from morally instructive works, such as *The Magdalen; or, The Dying Penitent, The Life and Adventures of a Reformed Magdalen*, and *Histories of Some of the Penitents in the
Magdalen-House*; to biographies of glamorous public figures, such as Betty
Ireland, Fanny Murray, Anne Rochford, Mary Parrimore, Lavinia Beswick,
Kitty Fisher, and Fanny Davies; to memoirs of successful prostitute/bawds,
such as Moll King, Susan Wells, Margaret Leeson, and Ann Sheldon; and to
confessional accounts by Teresia Constantia Phillips, "Emma," and Phebe
Phillips.[2] It is difficult to say exactly how many prostitute narratives were
published during this period, as they overlap significantly with actress biographies, crime stories, scandal narratives, and novels; nevertheless, we can
find at least two or three dozen of these, many of which appeared in multiple editions. Several make reference to the same people, both during their
time and from past generations.[3] John Cleland's *Memoirs of a Woman of Pleasure*, to which I will return at the end of the chapter, draws from this popu-

lar genre. The proliferation of prostitute narratives provides an enlightening context for the emphasis on female virtue in the novel: If conduct books instructed readers in proper bourgeois identities, the popularity of whore stories suggests why conduct book writers believed so many people stood in such need of instruction.

Yet these narratives reveal more than the complexity of sexual values in this period. Instead, they tend to explore, either as satire or cause for alarm, the Mandevillian compatibility of "vice" with profit in a commercial marketplace. What is surprising about reading through them, in fact, is how little space they devote to sexual activity (with the dramatic exception of *Fanny Hill*) and how much they devote to class and economic concerns, whatever the moral stance. Libertine narratives generally tell the story of a woman from humble origins and/or impoverished circumstances who reaches the heights of luxury through infamous commerce; in the reform narratives, women endure prostitution as their last desperate resort to avoid starvation.[4] While the libertine narratives represent sex with bawdy humor and the reform narratives allude to its scandal, the heroine in either kind by the eighteenth century rarely turns to prostitution out of her own lasciviousness. Prostitutes in this period certainly remained scapegoats for corruption, crime, disease, and social disorder; nevertheless, most of these narratives go well beyond the negative object lesson cliché to which they all pay homage with varying degrees of qualification and/or irony. Randolph Trumbach has suggestively argued that a new hegemony of heteronormativity in this period produced not just a general tolerance of but an active cultural interest in prostitutes that depended on their visibility.[5] It would be a vast oversimplification, then, to approach these narratives as vehicles for the vilification or exploitation of their heroines.

Many of the more alarmist ones were inspired by or published to support the activities of a new reform movement that emerged in the middle of the century. This movement differed significantly from the earlier Societies for the Reformation of Manners: Instead of arresting suspected prostitutes, the new reformers hoped to assist and transform them; they established the Magdalen Hospital in 1758 as a humane alternative to imprisonment.[6] The Magdalen Hospital provided refuge, support, training, and religious instruction for prostitutes who declared that they wanted to reform, and while the limited number of women it could actually serve was too small to significantly impact the streetwalking population, the Hospital became a fashionable and popular charity (patronized by both Samuel Richardson and Henry Fielding) with a wide-reaching cultural influence. It helped usher in a new era of reform in which moralists positioned themselves as sympathizing with rather than excoriating prostitutes. Rather than blaming female lascivious nature like their predecessors, these reformers blamed an increasingly complex commercial culture for the rise in prostitution.[7] Some prostitute narratives even suggest (as does Richardson's *Clarissa*) that sex in itself does not necessarily destroy a woman's virtue.

Among those less interested in reform, Mandevillian observations of the economic benefits of prostitution persisted: "at a modest Computation," an anonymous 1746 pamphlet declares, prostitutes support half the City of London, paying the salaries of surgeons, justices, lawyers, bailiffs, watchmen, coachmen, chairmen, milliners, brokers, and chocolate-house keepers.[8] Travel writer J. W. Archenholz (1789) observed that the British had no real stake in ending prostitution.[9] While English laws "are not favourable to the fair sex," successful prostitutes enjoy independence and add glamour to London; some prostitutes "are indeed so much their own mistresses, that if a justice of the peace attempted to trouble them in their apartments, they might turn him out of doors; for as they pay the same taxes as the other parishioners, they are consequently entitled to the same privileges."[10] Kitty Fisher, he notes, charged one hundred guineas per night; when the Duke of York left her only fifty pounds, she ate the bank note in a sandwich out of contempt for such a paltry sum. For Archenholz, such enchanting possibilities enhanced the attractions of London. Theater managers seem to have reached the same conclusion: By the end of the century, they customarily admitted prostitutes at no charge as a way of sustaining business.[11] Young wealthy single men who come in from the country spend only a small portion of their fortunes on "common expenses," Archenholz observes; the greatest part of it goes "to the ladies" (2:101):

> Were this abuse, the natural consequence of luxury and superabundance, attempted to be reformed, such a reformation, in a country like England, would be attended with the most pernicious consequences to trade and commerce. If they were to establish a tribunal of chastity in London, as was formerly done at Vienna, that great city would soon be depopulated; the melancholy of the English would become intolerable; the fine arts would be frightened away; one half of the inhabitants would be deprived of subsistence, and that superb metropolis converted into a sad and frightful desert. (2:100)[12]

Rather than only describing the rise and/or fall of an abjected "other," then, prostitute narratives offer extreme versions of the period's more general exploration of material temptation and material survival in a commercial context. While reformist and libertine prostitute stories have different aims, they share a fascination with forms of self-distancing demanded by marketplace transactions. Libertine narratives marvel at the prostitute's self-ownership but at the same time suggest her ambivalence toward the instrumental use of her body; they register both anxiety over and admiration for her social mobility through this partial self-objectification. Reform narratives, by contrast, represent prostitution as economic desperation leading to tragic self-estrangement. In both cases, the prostitute emerges as an extreme version of an emergent modern selfhood in her rational distance from herself, her self-definition through manners, presentation, activity, or even work rather than natal origin, and her negotiation of public and private versions of identity.

In exploring the dangers and pleasures of an expanded commercial culture, most prostitute narratives written in this period represent the adventures of their heroines as indicative of specific historical conditions. While libertine writers implicitly represent spectacular forms of mobility available through prostitution as a recent historical development that exposes an emergent economic and political reorganization, reformist writing makes the explicit case for the "problem" of prostitution as a modern one, different from anything previously seen. By the middle of the century, reformers came to believe that British commercial prosperity and imperial expansion accounted for a dramatic increase in prostitution. Unlike the presumed sexual epicureans of the Restoration, prostitutes in midcentury reform literature attract sympathy as the pathetic fallout of a callous marketplace bereft of traditional safety nets. At the same time, because they become, according to reformist rhetoric, deadened to sexual pleasure, they deserve admiration as extreme models of self-division, enduring unpleasant work while retaining a virtuous core. In his pornographic version of the prostitute's predicament, Cleland's *Memoirs of a Woman of Pleasure*, by contrast, experiments with the possibility of Mandevillian theatricality without the sacrifice of pleasure, cultivation, or sentiment. In creating idealized conditions with self-conscious reference to the prostitute narrative genre as a whole, however, Cleland both participates in and satirizes the emergent bourgeois mystification of economic mobility and its political consequences,[13] as well as the extraordinary optimism in some quarters about the pleasures, opportunities, and forms of refinement available through an expanding commercial sphere.[14]

The Libertine Narrative

The domestic novel, Nancy Armstrong has argued, represents the formation of middle-class hegemony through the figure of a woman for the purpose of mystifying class conflict and the politics of social mobility.[15] In libertine prostitute narratives, however, the point seems to be the opposite: the satiric *exposure* of these conflicts through the heroine's embrace of Lockean self-ownership and sexual commodification despite the variety of political perspectives from which these narratives were written. Biographies of Sally Salisbury, appearing early in the century, register a sense of the marketplace's capacity to confuse not just rank, but people and objects. Hailing from humble origins, Sally Salisbury apparently worked as a cheap streetwalker, an orange vendor, and finally a very expensive courtesan.[16] While accounts of her life draw on her established celebrity, her arrest for stabbing her client John Finch and her consequent death in prison from jail fever launched her story into print; thus a sense of the whore's danger to herself and others frames these narratives. One broadside marvels at Sally's rise from her "mean extraction" to the most elite circles,[17] a climb that so endeared her to the "Populace" that they composed a song about her called "Sally in our Alley."[18] Disgusted, however, the author describes his subject as exploiting the nobility who foolishly mistook her for one of their own.

Both 1723 biographies of Sally Salisbury include disconcerting scenes of the prostitute's objectification in the marketplace. Entrance into prostitution demands this: In the more conventional anonymous narrative, her first bawd

caused her to pluck off all her Clothes, felt every Limb one by one, touch'd her to see if she was sound; as a *Jockey* handles a Horse or Mare in *Smithfield;* or as the Planters in *America,* the Feature of the *Negroes* before they purchase 'em.[19]

Here Sally learns to understand her body instrumentally and as an object separate from her being. Nevertheless, in a different biography—presumably a collection of letters about Salisbury collected by Charles Walker—her acceptance of this instrumentality becomes a satirically demystifying force. Here a nobleman "with the Design of bantering a Dignify'd Fortune-hunting Clergyman" sends the clergyman to court Sally, who pretends to be an heiress. The clergyman admires the luxury she lives in, but Sally insists that "she had nothing but a very *Small Spot* to which she had any *Hereditary Right*" (143). The suitor remains unconvinced: surely a considerable number of acres must underwrite the extravagance she enjoys and the fine company that she keeps. After going back and forth on this for a while, Sally suddenly "drew up the Curtain, *alias* her Hoop-Petticoat, &c. and clapping her Hand upon *Madge,* said, *Ecce Signum,* Doctor. This is my only Support, and I hope will continue so to my Life's End."[20] When she enters the brothel in the anonymous biography, the bawd treats Sally's body like a living object, comparable to a slave or an animal. Here, however, Sally declares full possession of her body as her own property—her "estate"—, comically deflating the difference between wealth as an expression of landed authority and wealth as a product of prostitution.[21]

If Sally partially objectifies herself by using her "estate" to produce new wealth, the men in Walker's narrative, while not becoming objects, at least in one scene substitute objects for themselves. In Walker's most pornographic moment, Salisbury poses naked and upside down, with a peer holding on to each of her legs; "thus every Admirer pleas'd with the Sight, pull'd out his Gold, and with the greatest Alacrity pursued the agreeable Diversion" of tossing his money at her "tufted Chink," in which "the Guineas shone/ And each that she receiv'd was all her own." [22] The men clearly find the naked, upside down Sally sexy, but instead of pulling out their "yards," they pull out their gold and toss it between her legs. Thus the flow of gold here replaces the flow of semen. We witness a form of prostitution, but one in which actual sexual contact does not take place. It is almost as if sex itself has become superfluous, and the more interesting erotic action consists of the direct flow of money. Salisbury, for her part, becomes a spring of wealth rather than a pond, to borrow Defoe's resonant distinction between the productive trades-man and the static aristocrat;[23] she pornographically literalizes the famous image that Defoe's Moll Flanders offers when she describes a woman as a bag of gold.[24] But while Moll uses this image to evoke the danger women face without protection, Salisbury instead insatiably draws the gold to herself. Her "estate" is not just mobile but abstracted: None of the men have any actual contact with it, replacing sexual circulation with the financial kind. For their money, the men receive only the pleasure of "spending" itself.

In the Sally Salisbury biographies, then, both men and women can become confused with objects through commercial sexual exchange. Through her partial self-objectification, however, Sally also becomes, unlike the domestic heroine who mystifies emergent ideologies, a Mandevillian heroine who ex-plicitly provokes social anxiety for her ability to disturb traditional hierar-chies in rude but spirited ways. The anonymous biography characterizes her as an Amazonian "she-Hero," sometimes "going o-Nights among the Mo-hocks, drest like a beautiful Youth."[25] If she finds herself cheated or insulted, she takes swift revenge. When a French baron threatens to beat her for pox-ing him, she wins his trust back by pleading her own poverty, posing as a Catholic, and seducing him again. Not satisfied, she tricks him into a mar-riage with another whore posing as an heiress.[26] In another anecdote, Sally so arouses the desire of a "Muscovite nobleman" that he agrees to pay fifty guineas for one night with her. He foolishly tries to cheat her, however, by filling the purse with false coins and placing a few gold ones on top. But Sal-isbury carefully checks the money first. Walker thinks she would have "split

[the Muscovite's] skull" had not the bawd and her nymphs disengaged the
"disabl'd Warrior . . . from the Paws of that unhumane Tigress."[27]

In Walker's account in particular, the prostitute exuberantly embodies anxieties over commercial opportunities for social mobility. Once at a high society ball, a fine lady who suspects Sally as her husband's lover reveals her
rival's humble origins by inviting her to join in a genteel French dance, which
Salisbury cannot execute. But Sally has her revenge:

> *I perceive your Ladyship does not approve of my Manner of Dancing: But I can
> assure you, Madam, my Lord—* (naming her own Husband) *admires my Danc-
> ing above all Things, and has often told me, that he had much rather Dance, or
> —* (speaking mighty plain English) *with me than with your Ladyship at any
> time.*[28]

A gentleman fares no better in his attempt to humble her: He compliments
Sally on her smock, which he condescendingly suggests she won in an open
dancing contest at Bath. She corrects him by noting that she had sent out that
particular smock to be washed by his mother. Because the gentleman's
mother really did work as a laundress, this comment humiliates him so deeply
that he skulks out of the assembly.[29] In the first example, Sally levels her rival by suggesting that sexual skill counts more than birth; in the second example, she makes it clear that her earnings from prostitution have put her in
a position to hire someone from a family with more genteel pretensions. Both
of these examples relish the scandal of such a low-born woman humiliating
the elite: Her prostitution enables her to circulate among them as an apparent equal, radically collapsing the difference between her estate and theirs.

In the next generation, *The Memoirs of the Celebrated Miss Fanny Murray*
(1759) offers a distinctly softer and more sympathetic portrait; here too,
however, the prostitute enjoys extraordinary upward mobility through her
partial self-objectification. Drawing from the libertine tradition, Fanny Murray's *Memoirs* satirically expose elite desires, a fickle, sometimes brutal marketplace, and bourgeois hypocrisy. Nevertheless, a compelling admiration
for Fanny's resilience and her upward mobility emerges as well: Even in the
libertine context, the midcentury prostitute figure attracts sympathy for her
economic predicament. Fanny endures deeper humiliation than Sally but
rises to a higher level of respectability, becoming a leader of London fashion
and in this narrative eventually a sentimental heroine as well. After first being seduced in Bath at a young age, Murray sets out for London imagining
"in this emporium of commerce, that something might be obtained in an
honorable way."[30] Lacking money, family, and reputation, however, Murray

resigns herself to prostitution in the face of her debt. Her biographer describes her lowest point as degrading objectification and pauses to lament this phase of Fanny's career:

> A variety of lovers succeeded each other; the last as welcome as the first. . . . What a disagreeable situation is this to a generous mind? What an unhappy circle to move in for a thinking person? To be the sink of mankind! To court alike the beastly drunkard, the nauseating rake! Dissimulating distaste for enjoyment! No balmy ease, no innocent comfort; but nocturnal incontinence and repeated debauch. (1:88)

Murray succumbs to venereal infection and sinks even lower, serving apprentices in a common bawdy house. Nevertheless, she persists, keeps working, and survives until her big break: enrollment in Mr. Harris's list as a *"new face,"* in spite of her "extensive commerce" (1:100). This listing allows her to raise her price and gives her access to the legendary "Whore's Club," in which prostitutes meet each week to "compare notes" (1:109). Through this networking, Fanny earns more and more money, attracting wealthier clients. At her height she becomes a pampered mistress, receiving visits from women of character and attracting attention for her innovative fashions. (William Dodd's reformist novel *The Sisters* [1754] describes a group of elite prostitutes as wearing *"Fanny-Murray'd* hats").[31] While Sally Salisbury's association with the elite either becomes a source of scandal or provides the opportunity for scenes of the blatant demystification of rank through the leveling power of sexuality, the author of Murray's biography represents the heroine's upward mobility as similarly demystifying, but at the same time admirable in itself. Though of modest birth, Fanny (like Pamela) fully masters the manners of gentility. The "Whore's Club," which appears in other prostitute narratives as well, hovers somewhere between the Restoration-style satire of comparing prostitution to any other career and an effective opportunity for Fanny to improve her lot. Pamela's rise through her virtue may mystify emerging class relations, but Fanny's rise through persistence, networking, and submission to the degrading conditions of the brothel suggests the instrumentality and performativity of manners rather than any natural superiority of the elite. Fanny even tries to use her celebrity to escape prostitution by opening a milliner's shop, but this venture fails through the fickleness and superficiality of her fashion-conscious clients. In Fanny Murray's *Memoirs*, prostitution proves fully compatible with the Mandevellian marketplace and the desires it satisfies.

After a spectacular career as a prostitute, however, Fanny's fortunes eventually fall: She is arrested for debt and confined to a sponging house. Debt began her prostitution career; in the end she returns to this hazardous state. Seeing no other way out, she writes a pleading letter to the son of her first seducer to rescue her, and he does so with the stipulation that she become virtuous—a bargain that the narrator assures us she kept. But as in *Fanny Hill,* this "tail-piece" of morality does not erase the clear benefits of prostitution to Murray throughout the narrative. At her height she became "the reigning toast," "the standard of female dress," and "the object of every man's desire" (1:200), exemplifying the social and economic benefits of infamous commerce that J. W. Archenholtz and Bernard Mandeville describe. The *Memoirs* take full advantage of the libertine narrative's potential for both seductive glamour and exploitative degradation, but it ends with the prostitute's sentimental redemption and a plea for sympathy. The author describes Murray as

> one whose natural disposition was not vicious, but who, having made a false step, found many obstacles to return into the path of virtue—who was neither avaricious, luxurious, or debauched, further than necessity obliged, but animated with sentiments that would have adorned a much more worthy and exalted station. Ever grateful, humane, charitable, and generous: she practiced more virtues than half her sex—and yet for a single vice, incontinence, expelled from the band of virtuous society. (2:190–191)

The author represents Fanny's prostitution as emphatically circumstantial, as driven by necessity rather than as an expression of any inherently desiring nature. Because of this, prostitution in itself does not undermine her virtuous character. Fanny's objectification as a "sink for mankind" becomes counterbalanced by her individual style and her cultivated manners. Fanny, lacking the greed of a Sally Salisbury, nevertheless takes advantage of a burgeoning Mandevillian marketplace in "vice," but without sacrificing her inherent virtue.

The *Memoirs of Mrs. Margaret Leeson* (1795–1797), though libertine in its representation of sexuality, even more explicitly pleads for redemption on the basis of the prostitute's sentimental worth; any objectification involved in prostitution, in fact, becomes barely visible for much of the narrative. These volumes offer the confessional narrative of an Irish woman who, seduced, abandoned, and rejected by her family, turns first to prostitution and then to running her own brothel. She ultimately reforms, but the total disempowerment that reform brings explicitly and disturbingly suggests the incompatibility of traditional virtue with economic survival. Written, apparently, by the prostitute herself, this narrative offers the most pessimistic view of reform and most clearly delineates the continuity between prostitution and other commercial transactions.[32] Margaret Leeson narrates the highs and lows of her fortune, from astonishing prosperity to abject humiliation. While she describes falling in love, long relationships with a few men, and enduring relationships with women, she nevertheless emerges as a highly practical businesswoman and successful navigator of the marketplace with a healthy irreverence toward the elite society from whom she gets her living. As a commodity itself, Leeson's *Memoirs* entertains readers with mildly erotic voyeurism. Its more powerful appeal, however, lies in the opportunity for voyeurism not *of* Leeson but *through* her and into Irish and English elite society. Like the earlier scandalous memoirist Teresia Constantia Phillips, Leeson constantly threatens to expose the names and offenses of her lovers if they fail to settle their accounts. Phillips and Leeson, though "fallen" women, turn confidently to the public for sympathy with their complaints of injustice.

In a genteel version of Salisbury's claims to self-ownership, Leeson reveals how her financial success, despite its origin, granted her Lockean rights of property. She complains that "Dublin was infested with a set of beings, who, however they might be deemed *gentlemen* at their birth, or connexions, yet, by their actions, deserved no other appellation than that of RUFFIANS."[33] These "Pinking-dindies," like the legendary Mohocks in London, "ran drunk through the streets, knocking down whoever they met; attacked, beat and cut the watch; and with great valour, broke open the habitations of unfortunate girls, demolished the furniture of their rooms, and treated the unhappy sufferers with a barbarity and savageness, at which, a gang of drunken coal-porters would have blushed" (69). Yet these men, as Leeson reports, made the mistake of attacking *her* house. Trauma from the attack, she reports, caused her prematurely to deliver a stillborn child and led to the death of her daughter. When she offered large rewards for apprehending these men, their "Chief," who thought his noble lineage would protect him, threatened to kill her. But "by paying high," she had this leader arrested and thrown into Newgate without bail for both property damage and murder. When the Sheriffs and "some respectable persons" begged her to drop the murder charge to save the man from hanging, she eventually agreed but refused to drop her suit for damages, which she won.[34] Here and throughout the narrative, Leeson encourages her reader to admire her survival skills, loyalty to her friends and associates, ability to stand up for herself, economic success, and power that this economic success brings. She can defend her property not in spite of her prostitution but only because her prostitution has been so successful.

While never quite making explicit arguments about the public benefits of the sex trade, Leeson's *Memoirs* nevertheless suggests that prostitutes contribute to economic prosperity and even social welfare. Descriptions of her business practices not only suggest her scrupulous credibility but also her compassion for women with no place else to turn. This emerges as a consistent theme in these narratives, especially when the prostitutes tell their own stories. Ann Sheldon, who published her memoirs in the same decade as Leeson, fills her autobiography with her own acts of charity, including well-timed donations that rescue other women. Teresia Phillips devotes long passages to her care for her impoverished sister and her sister's children. Even the notorious Sally Salisbury claimed in court that she stabbed her lover because she thought he was going to corrupt her sister, whom Salisbury was providing with a virtuous education.[35] Like the London women described by Archenholz, Leeson also does her part to keep the stakes of fashion in Dublin high. She furnishes her house extravagantly and wears the latest fashions to public events, attracting the envious gazes of all women present. She also reports spending considerable sums of money to dress women in her house in the proper degree of luxury. As a courtesan of the highest rank, Leeson details the lavishness of her entertainments and the delicacy of her comestibles. When the champion of one of her rivals takes her to court on the false charge of attempting to assault his mistress, "the Petticoat prevailed over the Sword and Gorget" because "[s]ome of the gentlemen observed to the rest, that it would be a pity not to favour a woman, who, by spending considerable sums amongst the traders of the city, was of service to it" (74).

For this reason, her eventual conversion after this life of Mandevillian public service comes abruptly and inexplicably. It begs comparison to the sudden fall of Roxana, but unlike in Defoe's novel, Leeson offers no reflections on her guilt in the pages that describe her years as a prostitute. Prompted by her desire to condemn men who fail to pay their debts (221) but confronted with the apparent weakness of her own moral position, Leeson suddenly reflects on the tragic objectification of sharing "her charms indiscriminately with every ruffian who could afford a price" (222) and the insufficiency of her attempts to compensate through charity, for "of what avail are all those virtues to a blasphemous prostitute?" (222). These thoughts become so oppressive that she attempts suicide, but the opiate fails. Some female friends suggest that she leave Dublin for England or Scotland where she might be able to marry, but she declares her disgust with all of mankind.

Instead of bringing peace, however, the author's reform sets in motion a rapid decline into loneliness, poverty, and death. The last pages are filled with grotesque sexual violence. Leeson hires a companion who had been raped by sixty men when the crew of the ship bringing her from France mutinied. After sharing poverty, humiliation, and even incarceration for debt with Leeson, the companion finally dies in her mistress's arms. Five ruffians later attack, rob, strip, and rape Leeson and a new companion. Infected with venereal disease, the cure reduces them "to skeletons, all our money exhausted, deeply involved with Mrs T—, our landlady, and our clothes in pawn" (248).

This infection, the likes of which she never contracted in all her years of prostitution, and its horrendous cure bring debilitation and eventually death, the approach of which Leeson laments not because she has any remaining attachment to life but because she was, with her last volume nearly finished, "on the eve of handsomely repaying all my friends for their trouble" (249).

Leeson's conversion thus begins and ends with the problem of debt. James Thompson has observed that in the novels of Frances Burney, debt becomes the condition of womanhood.[36] For Leeson, however, debt becomes the condition of *virtuous* womanhood, while the condition of the prostitute is solvency: not only did merchants know she could pay her bills, but she built up a large collection of IOUs from clients whose need for discretion ensured their future payment. Yet when she leaves her infamous commerce for an honest life and no longer has any hold over her clients, the credit she has built up in the demimonde evaporates.[37] Her *only* remaining hold consists of her knowledge of their sexual exploits, an advantage exploited by the publication of her *Memoirs*. Leeson comments on this contradiction: "I need not depict to my fair readers my dreadful situation; though at the same time I must premise that had I not reformed, I would not have been thus abandoned and distressed. While I led a vicious course of life I had friends in abundance, but the moment I turned my thoughts to virtue, I was deserted by all" but a few (236). Virtue transforms the heroine from a robust entrepreneur to a fragile wraith, physically incapable of work. The woman who heroically confronted aristocratic rakes by pressing her legal case and collecting full damages suddenly finds herself without any ability to enforce a contract. Reform sacrifices her property in her body, and then her body itself.

While Leeson's *Memoirs* is unusual among libertine narratives in the heroine's sudden and internally driven conversion, one suspects that many libertine heroines would have faced a similar decline without their infamous source of income. Prostitution in these narratives demands a rational distance between the self and the body, but it also brings pleasure, power, and happiness, at least for a while. Libertine narratives suggest, in bitter, satiric, demystifying, and/or dramatic ways, the Mandevillian compatibility of whoring and solvency that works on a continuum with other kinds of business. In prostitution, Sally Salisbury demands, and for the most part receives, contractarian rights that would probably remain otherwise unavailable. In her case, commercial sexual exchange levels differences between sources of wealth and renders comically explicit the political challenge of mobile property to traditional hierarchies. Similarly, Fanny Murray endures degrading objectification as "the sink to all mankind," but sex work ultimately provides not just wealth but also a kind of equality in fashionable society. The author of Fanny's *Memoirs* demands that readers, both male and female, see Fanny not as an incomprehensible "other" but as someone not so different from anyone else working their way through an unpredictable commercial world. In perhaps the most vivid case, however, Leeson's attempt at self-consistency—her desire to become morally whole in order to speak from a position of moral authority—leads to a downward spiral than ends in death. These libertine heroines, then, survive not in spite of their Mandevillian self-division but because of it. In these narratives, prostitution becomes a trope for the hazards, revelations, and disruptive consequences of social mobility.

The Reform Narrative

Reform stories not only demand sympathy, but in sentimental literature the prostitute emerges as the sentimental object *par excellence*.[38] Finding himself surrounded by prostitutes, Harley, the sentimental hero of Henry MacKenzie's novel, experiences acute pity.[39] He buys a glass of wine for one, but she faints from hunger. Miss Atkins had come to London in the hope of softening the heart of the rake who had seduced her, but to no avail. Meanwhile, she had run up considerable debt to her landlady, who turned out to be a bawd and forced her into prostitution to pay off her debts. When Harley gives her some money for food, she bursts into tears: "Your generosity, Sir, is abused; to bestow it on me is to take it from the virtuous: I have no title but misery to plead; misery of my own procuring."[40] Harley, however, insists that the tears themselves reveal her virtue, for they suggest her complete estrangement from pleasure. Indeed, Miss Atkins declares

> Oh! did the daughters of virtue know our sufferings! did they see our hearts torn with anguish amidst the affectation of gaiety which our faces are obliged to assume! our bodies tortured by disease, our minds with that consciousness which they cannot lose! (45)

Libertine prostitutes flourish through the ownership of, distance from, and instrumental use of their bodies, counterbalancing objectification with spirit and self-possession. Reform narratives, however, represent the prostitute's self-division as tragic. Their heroines struggle to appear cheerful while relinquishing the defining characteristic of their being; privately, however, they may harbor delicate feelings for a parent, a child, or a sister. But this split, as we will see, constitutes not just the prostitute's misfortune but also her deservedness. Unsurprisingly, reform narratives dwell with almost pornographic detail on the prostitute's degradation; their heroines experience victimization rather than Lockean self-ownership. Yet perhaps as a result, these narratives counter even more emphatically the prostitute's objectification by insisting on her initial innocence, sociological rather than exclusively sexual vulnerability, and sentimental capacity. Further, reform writings, unlike the libertine narratives, detail the process by which the prostitute divides herself between this sentimental capacity and objectified sexual labor, suggesting ways that this division could be reoriented for more productive social use.

Midcentury reformers generally represent the proliferation of prostitution as a disturbing symptom of commercial modernity rather than female lust. Nearly all eighteenth-century prostitute narratives, libertine and reformist, follow a geographical pattern: A girl begins in country innocence; loses her family through death, disease, poverty, ambition, or disgrace; goes to the city and falls victim to material temptations, the cosmopolitan wiles of a landlady/bawd, or the seductions of a rake. In much reformist writing, however, the "harlot's progress" explicitly parallels national progress into commercial sophistication. In his *Plan for the Establishment of Charity-Houses for Exposed or Deserted Women and Girls, and for Penitent Prostitutes* (1758), Joseph Massie attributes the rise in prostitution to the nation's transformation from a rural to a busy commercial economy. In the time of Queen Elizabeth, Massie notes, people remained in the parishes of their birth. The economy discouraged movement because each parish grew its own corn, bred its own cattle, and so on. "But of late years," he observes, "*Corn* is grown in one County, *Cattle* bred in another, *Cheese* made in a third, *Butter* in a fourth, *Woollen manufacturies* confined to a few Counties," demanding contact, exchange, and increased mobility.[41] This commercial system has also encouraged the production and consumption of luxury goods, bringing instability and sometimes poverty from succumbing to temptation. The enticing new luxuries available in urban centers and the diminishing opportunities for rural self-sufficiency have conspired to lure women into prostitution. For Massie and others, prostitution had become one of the most visible and disturbing symptoms of the new property laws, enclosure, proto-industrial developments, and the "proletarianization" of the workforce: fewer and fewer families, Massie observes, could survive without some members selling their labor.[42] In 1766 Newton Ogle similarly argued that attempts at reform

> are now become necessary, and should be made to accompany our Increase of Empire, Wealth, and Luxury; to counteract, if possible, the bad Effects, the Allurements to Vice, the actual Crimes which these encourage and introduce. Where Industry and Simplicity of Manners prevail, the Demand for these public Remedies is not so great: The Virtues and Vices of Mankind are there confined to a narrower Plan: It is in rich and polished

States that Vice and Misery are found in their greatest Extremes. . . . Many Advantages, indeed, attend the Increase of Wealth and Power; but there is a melancholy Alloy in these Advantages.[43]

Like Massie, Ogle does not nostalgically oppose commercialization; instead, he insists that the nation must find a way to manage the more troubling ingredients in the "melancholy Alloy" of widespread commodification. Similarly, in a sermon preached at the end of the century to the Magdalen charity, William Bell Williams (1794) insists that while moralists in the time of David asked *"wherewithal shall a young man cleanse his way?,"* moralists in the current age of luxury must alternatively ask "How shall a young *female* escape destruction?"[44] For Massie, Ogle, and Williams, the demand for prostitute reform emerges from the historically specific conditions of commercial prosperity, imperial expansion, and the early symptoms of industrialization.

The Magdalen Hospital quickly became a successful and fashionable charity; clearly its founders had tapped into shared concerns and anxieties. In an allegorical rescue of the nation itself, the founders of the Magdalen Hospital believed they could reverse the "harlot's progress," catching women before they had become completely hardened and returning them to virtuous simplicity. Poet Edward Jerningham describes this transformation as the recovery of nature beneath layers of commodified luxury. Calling the reader's attention to a lineup of the "Magdalens" (i.e., the penitent prostitutes benefiting from the Magdalen Hospital) regularly displayed to the public by the hospital, he asks viewers to admire the innocent beauty that the simpler garb of penance reveals:

> Unbraid the cunning tresses of the hair,
>   And each well-fancied ornament remove;
> The glowing gem, the glitt'ring solitaire—
>   The costly spoils of prostituted love![45]

Thus the Magdalen charity became popular not only because it combined virtuous self-righteousness with eroticized voyeurism (as Jerningham's poem suggests) but also because it indulged the fantasy of recovering an unalloyed purity at the heart of cosmopolitan complexity.[46] It offered penance to both its inmates and its elite and bourgeois contributors for the sins of prosperity and empire. In a sense, though, the new reformers reveal themselves as heirs to Mandeville as much as the libertine writers insofar as they similarly understood "vice" as consistent with prosperity.

While reformers saw rampant prostitution as the social cost of commercial prosperity and imperial expansion, however, they also saw prostitutes as a potential economic resource whose prior objectification could be exploited. They did not, of course, make the Mandevillian case for prostitution as a useful service to men of business; instead, they envisioned the Magdalen Hospital as a place where women could be transformed to better meet the needs of a consumer culture and emergent industrialized economy.[47] Unlike the earlier Societies for the Reformation of Manners (SRM) activists, the new reformers saw prostitutes as ordinary women tempted by luxury or love, victimized, and forced to find a way to support themselves bereft of family assistance. Some even acknowledged a relationship between the reported increase in prostitution and the limited employment opportunities for women, but stressed the unpreparedness of young women even in the lower classes for labor.[48] In the view of reformers, some prostitutes thus still had the potential to contribute to society in more "productive" ways: They could renew their virtue by becoming mothers, laborers, servants, or colonists. Unreformed, they undermined national strength even if imperial triumphs produced them. Prostitutes, wrote Saunders Welch in 1758

> are rendered barren by their infamous course of life; those who understand political arithmetic, must allow this to be no less a national than a moral evil.[49]

If these women ever do produce children, Welch explained, those children are generally too weak and diseased to become useful. Instead of increasing the labor and military forces, another writer comments, "fruitless and rotten" prostitutes become "the greatest check to population."[50]

While some reformers felt that former prostitutes could be recovered for motherhood, others felt that prostitution literally "ruined" female bodies for this possibility. Most, then, instead sought ways to transform these women into useful laborers, at home or in the colonies. But moving streetwalkers into industry presented a special challenge, for reformers understood prostitution as victimization, but born out of initial female idleness.[51] Jonas Hanway argued that these women foolishly sacrifice true domestic authority for the fleeting illusion of power over men, falling victim to those "whom they might have governed."[52] Similarly, Welch held that "proneness to idleness tempts" certain women "to prefer a life of ease and debauchery, to that of industry and virtue."[53] William Dodd blamed prostitution on parents who educated their daughters above their station, "while they absurdly expend much on boarding-schools, [they] think it beneath them to have their daughters taught a trade."[54] Several insisted that prostitutes came not from the ranks of the poor and desperate, but from middling families with inappropriate aspirations: The "wrong turn of education" provided by indulgent parents "is the plentiful source from whence the bagnios and bawdy-houses are constantly supplied."[55] Girls who go into service, according to reformers, also often end up in prostitution because their mistresses give them their own cast-off clothes, which increases their vanity and spoils them for labor. While historians record a decrease in economic opportunities for women,[56] reformers often blamed the women and their families for, in a sense, absorbing emergent ideologies of gender over more traditional divisions by rank.

In this context, reformers proposed the Magdalen Hospital as a training ground for virtuous industry, countering idleness with discipline.[57] While individual reformers differ on a number of issues, nearly all of them represent prostitutes as an untapped pool of labor, and this labor as offering both individual and national renewal: The Magdalen Hospital will welcome the "girl whom no creature upon earth will receive," but only if she is "willing *to work.*"[58] John Fielding suggested establishing a public laundry to employ reforming prostitutes; Massie argued that they should be put to work spinning.[59] Robert Dingley imagined their possible employment as

Making or mending of Linen—Scowering Pewter—Making Bon-Lace—Black Lace—Artificial Flowers—Children's Toys—Spinning fine Thread, &c. and Woollen Yarn for Clothiers, Callimanco's, and Cruels—Winding Silk—Embroidery, and all branches of Millinery, Lady's Shoes, Mantua's, &c. Coat-making, Stays—Cauls for Wigs—Knitting Hose and Mittins—Making Gloves, leathern and silken—Weaving of Hair—Making Garters—Drawing Patterns, &c. or whatever EMPLOY their several Abilities and Geniuses shall lead to.[60]

In the Magdalen Hospital, penitents will "make their own Cloaths, both Linen and Woollen; knit their Stocking from the raw Materials, spinning the Thread and making the Cloth." This institution would regulate their labor, but "Quick Sale shall be made of the Product of their Labour and Ingenuity, that they may know how their Property accumulates, as an additional Spur to Industry."[61] When penitents leave, another reformer promises, they will be "stored with good principles, and with an habit of industry."[62]

Graduates of the Magdalen Hospital might also demonstrate their new diligence by becoming colonists. In his account of the hospital's founding, Dodd assures his readers that "a due attention will be had to the demands of our colonies abroad; where such as are willing, upon the best advantages and proposals, will be transferred, at the discretion and direction of the Governors."[63] Novelists record this possibility as well: Sally Godfrey partially redeems her early transgression this way in *Pamela;* Clarissa's family wants to send her to Philadelphia; Moll Flanders finds opportunity in the new world. Welch argued categorically that prostitutes *un*willing to reform should be transported to the colonies as both punishment and as a way of making the best national use of their bodies.[64] In the French territory of Louisiana as in other British and European colonial ventures, "many of the colonists," according to John Carswell, "were recruited from prisons and brothels."[65]

Reformers characterized their project as a success, going so far as to suggest that women graduating from the Magdalen Hospital were better-than-adequate workers with unusually high levels of discipline as a result of their training. Dodd reports that

> Many [Magdalens] have been introduced into decent services, where they have conducted themselves with . . . propriety. . . . For, particular application is given, not only to the habituating them all to industry, but likewise to the teaching the uninstructed such branches of female employ, as may qualify them for different provinces, and enable them to get their livelihood with honesty and credit, when they are replaced in the world.[66]

The environment he describes in the Hospital, however, resembles Mandeville's public stews in the intensity of its regulation: Magdalens must obey the rules, comply humbly with an overseeing matron, and know that "there is an absolute necessity for much *Industry*."[67] Assistants to the house matron "attend the women constantly, and observe their tempers and dispositions; and whether they appear to be worthy objects of the charity."[68] These assistants also ensure that each Magdalen says grace at mealtime, avoids improper conversation, keeps her bed neat and clean; the matron herself ensures that they "constantly attend divine service." A steward "inspects the weights, measures, and quality" of their work, keeping an "exact account" of it.[69] Magdalens may not directly receive any letters or messages. Each woman has her own bed and a small box that fits under it for all of her possessions. Each wears a plain gray gown and may not inquire into another's history. They must offer unquestioning obedience to their superiors. In this intense level of surveillance, the Magdalen Hospital not only recalls Mandeville's public stews but also looks ahead to the Benthamite panopticon that Michel Foucault has read as a trope for modern regulation[70]—indeed, Robert Bataille names the formation of the Magdalen Hospital as a "Foulcauldian moment."[71] Magdalens perhaps make even better examples of regulated subjects than prisoners, however, for they humbly, voluntarily, and even gratefully submit themselves to the gaze of the reformer, signing a contract that declares their intent to reform and admission of past guilt.[72]

What, then, is the process through which these pampered, indulgent, luxury-loving girls become changed into regulated subjects and exemplary workers? According to reform literature, the more sensual ones can probably never change. Those capable of reform, however, pass through an intermediary stage between idleness and productivity that reformers describe in terms of a fundamental alienation from pleasure and from their bodies brought about by the labor of prostitution. While idleness might attract girls to prostitution, according to reformers, the horrific conditions of sex work will lead them to welcome the advantages of the Magdalen Hospital. Progressively self-estranged by undesired sexual encounters, these women take no pleasure in streetwalking; their pay is low and their conditions wretched: "Every other animal is obedient to his *appetite*, but appetite has frequently no share in the *promiscuous* commerce of these women."[73] After an initial temptation, they find themselves trapped in "slavery" to their bawds, forced to entertain "any disgusting object."[74] They become "Wretches, who drudge in these Houses of Vice":

> There are not perhaps on Earth greater Objects of Compassion; all Sense of Pleasure are lost to them, the whole is mere Labour and Wretchedness, they are Slaves to, and buffetted by every drunken Ruffian, they are the Tools of, and tyrannized over by the Imps of Bawds.[75]

In a way, then, the Magdalen Hospital proposed to replace one form of labor with another; prostitution may begin as a form of idleness, but it quickly becomes in reformist rhetoric the most alienating and degrading form of labor imaginable.

The reforming prostitute thus implicitly becomes an excellent candidate for the most menial forms of labor because she has already learned to distance herself from her instrumentalized body. She has

> sunk into the abhorred gulf of degradation. She has sold for pay the endearments of love. In the consciousness of indelible pollution, she becomes even to herself an object of contempt. The sensation of debasement benumbs every faculty. *She seems changed to a piece of senseless mechanism. All that gave dignity to an animated being, to a human creature, seems extinguished.* She obeys the beck and nod of the tyrant of the bagnio. She exposes herself to examination as a beast in a public market, and submits to every gross caprice of every visitor who condescends to regard her with the eye of occasional desire.[76]

Through the self-distancing demanded by the commercial sale of her sexual labor, the prostitute becomes barely recognizable as human: She becomes an animal, or even worse an inanimate object, a piece of "senseless mechanism," bereft of the capacity for pleasure. Yet the prostitute's alienation—her full sexual transformation into the block of wood that Mother Creswell's student

Dorothea dreads—at the same time makes her an object worthy of pity, for "they are most of them in sober Hours, sensible of their Misery, and wish to be free from a State in which there is neither present Pleasure, nor Prospect of Future Happiness."[77] Even in their degraded state, these prostitutes harbor residual sentimental delicacy that only increases their suffering. Dead to physical pleasure, resigned to the instrumental use of her body, and more machine than human being, the unfortunately overeducated daughter is now ready to absorb the discipline necessary for a new life as another kind of worker.

Martin Madan's enormously popular biography (1763) of the reformed prostitute Fanny Sidney—at least eight editions were published on both sides of the Atlantic—chronicles the descent of one such woman.[78] Fanny Sidney falls into poverty when her father dies, leaving her vulnerable to seduction and false promises by "one who had known her in more prosperous days."[79] This man impregnates her and for a while supports mother and child, but eventually stops contributing to their maintenance. Left destitute, Sidney first takes advantage of her "genteel person" by acting on stage and strolling with players in the country. But growing tired of the "many disagreeable things in this way of life," she then "went to work at her needle" (2). Neither job provides sufficient income, so she turns to prostitution as her best hope for survival and support of her child. Sidney's inherent virtue, however, makes this life abhorrent, and she begs for admission into the Magdalen Hospital. With the discipline she learns, she attempts the kind of physically demanding jobs that she had previously avoided. First she works as a haymaker; after the harvest she works for a tradesman. Physical drudgery supports her when sewing and acting could not; it also protects her from the moral compromise of prostitution. Sidney's body, however, proves too fragile for this "excessive hard work" (3): She falls ill and dies in four months. Madan devotes the rest of the pamphlet to the religious convictions Sidney expressed on her deathbed.

In this biography, Madan wants to demonstrate that a prostitute who repents can nevertheless enjoy a peaceful death with the hope of salvation. Yet the narrative explores the problem of a limited labor market for women. Acting and needlework prove insufficiently lucrative: She seems at first to be hanging on to genteel pretensions. Prostitution, by contrast, provides sufficient support, but horrifies Sidney. But while not desirable in itself, prostitution in this narrative provides a crucial intermediary step completed by the discipline of the Magdalen Hospital; with the training the hospital offers, Sidney becomes capable of undertaking the kind of work necessary for her own support. Madan's biography suggests but does not dwell on the limits of female employment in the eighteenth century; instead, it focuses on the necessity for Sidney to adapt to the conditions of labor available. Acting and needlework take advantage of Sidney's genteel upbringing, but only prostitution finally and irrevocably cuts her off from her earlier privileged self. Once humbled, she becomes a good candidate for the Magdalen Hospital, which retrains her for a new of life of backbreaking, unbearable work. Prostitution here functions, on the one hand, as one form of employment in a string of jobs (and in fact the *only one* that pays enough money without destroying her health) and, on the other hand, as a key transitional phase in an education in appropriate but fatal labor. Prostitution provides a crucial step between hapless orphan and productive worker: Menial work demands first the humility and the self-objectification of whoring, and then the training in self-discipline provided by the Magdalen Hospital. Sidney consequently becomes such a devoted worker that she literally works herself to death. Fanny Sidney's biography thus tells the story of class-specific subjectivities: In her commitment to supporting her child, the humbling from genteel pretensions through prostitution, and the consequent "excessive hard work" that brings her death lie Sidney's heroism.

We might wonder how such a narrative could expect to draw any prostitutes to the Magdalen Hospital if they would look forward only to learning the discipline to work themselves to death. From Madan's perspective, however, Sidney's death provides not only the opportunity for religious reflection but also the culmination of Sidney's reform. Madan emphasizes the former prostitute's happy liberation from her body. Like Clarissa, Sidney embraces her death, comforting those concerned for her. The death of the prostitute in some ways also serves as the logical extension of her initial self-division: In death, her soul departs her body, and the body becomes not just metaphorically but now literally "senseless" as well. Prostitutes in reform narratives often embrace death; their willing deaths serve as further evidence of their alienation from the body's pleasures.

For the penitent victim of "tragical circumstance," however, death does not necessarily provide a good solution, for sometimes the heroine walks the streets for the sake of another. Her sacrifice elevates her at least as much as the extreme (yet morally dubious) self-sacrifice of suicide found in other accounts.[80] *The Histories of Some of the Penitents in the Magdalen-House* (1760) tells several such stories supposedly based on actual penitents.[81] The first narrative follows the seduced and abandoned Emily Markland, who endures violence and abject poverty to avoid prostitution. Love for her illegitimate son, however, "made me desirous to preserve a life which seemed to promise me nothing but misery."[82] Trapped in a whorehouse, she repeatedly refuses to see men until the bawd threatens to send her child to the officers of the parish: "the dear babe understood something of being sent from me, and running to me, hung round my neck, crying he would not go away without me, and begging me not to let that woman take him" (1:99). Thus, "delicacy . . . gave way to maternal love," and she gives in to prostitution. The old bawd's death eventually releases Emily; she struggles to support herself and her son through honest work, but she cannot obtain enough of it, especially without references. She then turns to begging, but finds that London has already been carved into territories that cannot be violated without violence. Finally, she turns to prostitution again. One night, on the verge of starvation, she earns five shillings:

> I returned home to my famished child, as soon as possible, carrying food with me, that I might receive some reward for money so ill gotten; and I confess my recompense was great, in seeing the dear babe, almost at the gates of death, revive as he eat, and the smiles of joy by degrees take place of the anguish which the pains of hunger had imprinted on his lovely face. (1:116)

She thinks again about letting herself die, but continues to work the streets for the sake of her child: "I seldom had far to go before I met with some gentleman, who, tho' hard-hearted to my distress, would be indulgent to his own vices" (1:118). Finally, a neighbor introduces her to a man from the Magdalen Hospital, where she finds kindness, shelter, and the opportunity to reform.

In this story, we are clearly a long way from the lascivious women described by Humphrey Mill who prowl the streets to fulfill their insatiable desires for sex and money. Emily loved her original seducer. Her initial poverty left her vulnerable to his advances, but she certainly did not initially comply for gain. This narrative offers little account of the process of her reform once admitted to the Magdalen Hospital, but it dwells on the pathos of having to walk the streets to preserve her child from starvation. On her own, she can neither move forward to reform or death, given her obligation to her child: The bulk of the narrative is thus occupied with this state of suspension. The narrative explores the emotional experience of Emily's enduring devotion to her child and the admirable, though excruciating, sacrifice that she makes on his behalf. Before she finds the Magdalen Hospital, prostitution in this narrative emerges as a positive moral choice and even a heroic one, as it provides the only possibility for preserving her child. Prostitution itself offers no temptation to Emily: She resists it; she would rather die! Emily becomes heroic, however, because she endures the mechanical, instrumental use of her body for the sake of another. This kind of story is repeated throughout the century. Sometimes the prostitute tearfully gives up a child she loves because she knows the child will fare better in another situation.[83] In one tragic narrative, the mother endures infamous commerce to save her daughter from starvation, but unwittingly contracts and passes along venereal disease by nursing her.[84] In spite of the stylistic differences, the stories of these prostitute mothers recall *Roxana* by thematizing a version of a split between dubious public activity and private sentiment, between the demands of an unforgiving marketplace and maternal desire.

The person protected by the heroine's prostitution, however, is not always a child. In Dodd's *The Sisters* (1754), the daughters of Mr. and Mrs. Sanson, educated above their station, become restless with their simple country life. Mr. Sanson sends them to London in the care of a distant relative, investing in their wardrobes in the hopes that they will attract wealthy genteel husbands. But the relative (Mr. Dookalb) turns out to be a pimp and sells them each to a different man. Lucy believes she has married Captain Smith when she sleeps with him, but the marriage is a sham. Caroline, however, escapes her sister's fate by falling ill. The rest of this four-volume narrative traces their different paths: Lucy descends into common prostitution, but Caroline escapes Dookalb and defends her virtue, supporting herself with menial work. The novel rewards Caroline with a happy marriage and relieves Lucy's misery with death.

That Lucy falls and Caroline does not, however, is accidental rather than revelatory of their characters, for the charms of London appeal to both girls. Lucy quickly becomes disillusioned when her "husband" turns out to be a drunken, married brute. Developing affection for another man only reveals her tragedy: "How then she began to detest her horrid situation, how to curse the hour that ever she was thus wretchedly enslaved, and to cast on herself every stinging and opprobrious reflection!"[85] Caroline proposes that they try to escape to their parents together, but Lucy refuses because she will not burden them with the shame of acknowledging her. Her concern is only for Caroline: "I never dared to offer a prayer to Heaven for myself—I never expected to be heard—but indeed have often dared to sigh for thee, and my whole prayer to God has been, 'Preserve but my sister, and I am contented to suffer thy wrath!'" (1:97). She offers Caroline money, but Caroline cannot bring herself to touch "that money which was the price of her sister's innocence"; she instead becomes determined to earn her way "by the labour of her own hands, and by honest industry" (1:103). They each refuse to sully the other: Though destitute, Caroline heroically refuses the money from Lucy's prostitution, but Lucy heroically refuses to compromise her family through contact with them. Lucy falls lower and lower, finally dying "in a little horrid gloomy apartment, stretched on the ground, on a bed of straw . . . a wretched object, piteously groaning, and sorrowfully pouring forth her lamentation with woe" (2:250).[86] Caroline saves herself in part through work, but Lucy had endured a more deeply disaffecting form of labor:

> suffice it to say, that enjoyment, so far from a pleasure to her, from this fre-
> quent and promiscuous use of it, became the greatest pain, or rather a mat-
> ter of loathsome indifference: she, like the rest of her unhappy sisterhood,
> submitted to it, as an ass submits to the burden; but satisfaction or joy was
> never found in it; man was never preferr'd by her to man, unfeeling, cold,
> and miserable. (2:203)

While the penitent stories of Fanny Sidney and Emily Markland trace the harlot's progress from seduction, to desperation, to the objectification of prostitution, to the Magdalen Hospital, and finally to the exchange of non-sexual labor, Dodd represents prostitution and other labor as different but parallel routes for these two sisters. In spite of their divergent destinies, Lucy and Caroline both remain committed to enduring for the sake of the other. The extremity of suffering in reformist narratives, however, perhaps suggests less confidence in the prostitute's resilience. In libertine narratives, with their skepticism toward bourgeois "delicacy," the prostitute accepts more readily the instrumental use of her body, sometimes even coming to find empower-ment in this possibility. In reform narratives, however, prostitution suggests a deeper division between an unfeeling body and a persisting sentimental ca-pacity that allows the heroine to harbor delicate feelings for a child, a sister, a parent, or a friend and the dispassionate sex she miserably endures. By dwelling on the endurance of sentimental feelings in the face of objectifica-tion, however, reform narratives assure their readers that even those who live by their "commodities" do not entirely become commodities: There remains a sentimental heart buried in the mechanized body that nevertheless repeat-edly gives over its senseless labor for the pleasure and profit of others. Lib-ertine narratives anxiously expose the period's new political landscape through the whore's Mandevillian upward mobility; reform narratives, by contrast, trace the heroine's descent from middle-class comfort to various forms of wage labor in demand at the dawning of industrialization.

Memoirs of a Woman of Pleasure

At a time when libertine narratives explored the prostitute's profits from the instrumental use of her body and reform narratives suggested her alienation, John Cleland published his *Memoirs of a Woman of Pleasure* (1748–1749).[87] Cleland structures the *Memoirs* like an episodic libertine narrative, but adds an overarching romantic/mock-reformist plot: born into a poor but honest family in a small country village, Fanny Hill hopes that she will better be able to support herself in the metropolis but must turn to prostitution to pay her debts. Like the libertine heroines, Fanny finds sex work both liberating and lucrative; unlike in other narratives, however, Cleland devotes considerable detail to his heroine's pleasure. Further, while Fanny enters prostitution with reluctance, she nevertheless for the most part escapes the usual shifting tides of fortune: She never contracts venereal disease; she never walks the streets (except for fun); she never has a client who refuses to pay her; rioters never attack her house; Mrs. Cole's bawdy house provides an affectionate, all-female family; her first keeper turns out to be decent and attractive; she finds a never-ending supply of work; and she ends up married, rich, virtuous, and in love.[88] Her career follows a relatively steady trajectory of increasing wealth, refinement, and sensitivity without the sudden economic losses that other prostitute narratives record. But while thus offering a decidedly optimistic version of the libertine prostitute story, Cleland engages the reformist vision as well. After detailing Fanny's increasing sophistication, sexual connoisseurship, and astonishing accumulation of wealth, Cleland ends with a satirical "tail-piece" of morality. Prostitution for Fanny provides upward mobility from rural obscurity to fashionable retirement, rewriting reformist anxieties about the threats to integrity from commercial luxury and imperial expansion as an opportunity instead for personal growth and material advancement. Fanny endures some of the objectification that other prostitute narratives explore; nevertheless, Cleland goes to extraordinary lengths to demonstrate his heroine's enduring subjectivity through the intensity of her sentimental *and* sexual feelings.[89]

Memoirs of a Woman of Pleasure, however, differs from other prostitute narratives most dramatically in its introduction into English fiction of what has been recognized as modern pornography. Lynn Hunt usefully defines pornography as "the explicit depiction of sexual organs and sexual practices with the aim of arousing sexual feelings"; until the middle or end of the eighteenth century in Europe, "it was almost always an adjunct of something else"— most often, "a vehicle for using the shock of sex to criticize religious and political authorities."[90] Cleland's pornography functions as an end in itself, idealizing Fanny's circumstances to bolster the fantasy.[91] But by representing the actual "work" of sex work with a level of detail that other prostitute narratives during this period usually avoid, Cleland not only points to the gap at the center of these others texts but also offers a much more detailed account of the (imagined) personal transformation demanded by the commodification of sexual labor—a process that, as several critics have noticed, seems in this novel to turn people into mechanized laborers. Cleland describes the penis as a "machine" and sexual congress as "'work,' 'labor,' 'force,' 'engineering,' and other factory work ('the inverted strokes of hammer over anvil,' the 'laboratory of love,' and 'she was now as a mere machine much wrought on')."[92] While Leo Braudy has read Cleland's mechanized sexual bodies as "machines of wonder,"[93] Douglas J. Stewart argues that Cleland's depiction of sex as labor reveals "the deep lesions in our soul created by the effects of the so-called 'free market' economy in areas no one has ever wanted to admit are economically conditioned."[94] By describing sex as a "learned and highly skilled activity," Cleland represents "people as performers, or as mere organs," helping to create, in his view, capitalism's "pornographic man."[95]

Stewart rightly observes that *Fanny Hill* explores both labor and objectification in capitalist society, but by assuming that commercial sex necessarily offers an entirely negative model, he misses the complexity of Cleland's project. Andrew Elfenbein, by contrast, suggests the other extreme, arguing that the novel promotes an ideal of unalienated labor and unalienated consumption.[96] While both of these arguments insightfully trace Cleland's use of prostitution as a trope for capitalist relations, neither of them take into account the shifts between mechanized performance and the possibility of recovery that suggest the different possibilities *within* prostitution. Fanny's prostitution includes, but does not stop at, mechanization; instead, *Memoirs* also pornographically explores the possibility that a select community will be able to engage in such relations without serious threats to their individuality, as distinct from a majority condemned to accept a random sailor or a hideous merchant. Prostitutes in reform narratives greet clients with equal disgust, and prostitutes in libertine narratives rarely form attachments to men. Fanny, however, instrumentalizes her body without the excruciating conflicts faced by reforming prostitutes or the full detachment of some of the libertine ladies. She can love Charles, but also perform well with Mr. H—. Recognizing the superiority of sex with Charles does not render sex with Mr. H— tragic, disgusting, or even boring. In an unusual version of the prostitute's own sexuality, Fanny takes pleasure without becoming lascivious.[97] Sex in Cleland's *Memoirs* is, on the one hand, *more* dehumanizing than in most prostitute narratives in its detailed mechanization. At the same time, Cleland's performers display an unusual resilience: Here, people turn into things, but then, magically, turn back into people.

This double transformation happens in both specific incidents and the overarching plot, with not just women but men as well. In her first observation of sexual activity, for example, Fanny witnesses an encounter between the bawd Mrs. Brown and the man who serves as the house stallion. The services of the first "wonderful machine" (25) that Fanny ever lays eyes on, then, have already been commodified.[98] More dramatically, when Fanny arouses "Good-natur'd Dick," his huge "standard of distinction" becomes an object of fellow prostitute Louisa's desire: "like an industrious bee," she was "not above gathering the sweets of so rare a flower, tho' she found it planted on a dung-hill" (160–163). Louisa objectifies Dick, splitting him into a pile of manure and the precious flower sticking out from it. She takes Dick as an object of her pleasure, but during the encounter, to her surprise, he turns into one of Braudy's "machines of wonder." Louisa heroically meets the challenge and compensates Dick by purchasing all of his remaining flowers. In exchanging money for flowers, which Cleland has already associated with the penis in this scene, Louisa concludes her association with Dick by generously paying for his performance. Afterward, he shrinks back down to his former self and can barely remember the experience. Dick's double transformation serves as an extreme example given his mental incapacity, but in a sense the same thing happens to Fanny. She begins in country innocence, naively allows a woman to arouse her sexual desires, becomes a highly skilled, if mechanical, sexual performer, and then returns fully to her unjaded self only with all of her flowers purchased, so to speak, and the profits in her pocket.

Through these double transformations, Cleland creates not just a "pornotopia" but also an idealized vision of remunerated work.[99] Cleland underplays the dangers, such as disease and violence, that prostitutes historically faced, and removes the hazards that even legitimate workers could face, such as shortage of employment, dangerous tasks, exhaustion, poverty, insufficient food, low wages, callous treatment, long work hours, and exploitation. In the elite bawdy house of Mrs. Cole, clients cheerfully pay their bills, profits stay high, and enjoyable labor merits not just comfort but luxury. Cleland signals his self-consciousness about this idealization by calling attention to other possibilities prostitutes could face and by departing from narrative convention. In particular, *Memoirs* includes a false beginning to Fanny's career in an averted threat of unpleasant mercenary sex. Mrs. Brown, the first bawd, degradingly parades Fanny in front of her proposed first client, who horrifies and disgusts the heroine. Without naming Mr. Crofts's ethnic identity, Cleland evokes eighteenth-century stereotypes of the mercenary Jew through this client's hideousness:

Imagine to yourself, a man rather past threescore, short and ill made, with a yellow cadaverous hue, great goggling eyes, that stared as if he was strangled . . . he had a peculiar ghastliness in his grin, that made him perfectly frightful, if not dangerous to women with child. (15)

Jews in eighteenth-century anti-Semitic representations often have "goggling eyes." Mr. Crofts is a wealthy merchant who is later arrested for illicit financial dealings. Thus Cleland introduces the possibility of defloration and then keeping by a hideous, unscrupulous merchant only to allow his heroine to escape him (although not entirely unscathed). Cleland expels the illicit merchant from his narrative, liberating Fanny for only the most idealized commercial relations.

Cleland expels Mr. Crofts in order to form a different kind of prostitute figure, drawing in part on an older, courtesan tradition, in which the woman serves not so much as a sex *worker* but as a sex *professional*. In her insulation from the vulnerability of other (sex) workers, Fanny joins in this novel a sexual version of the "professional-managerial" class, a group that in its nonsexual form, according to Nancy Armstrong and Lennard Tennenhouse, shaped the politics of this period and whose increasing power marks the distinction between the premodern world and modernity.[100] For Armstrong and Tennenhouse, intellectual as opposed to physical labor distinguished the emergent professional. To describe Fanny's labor as intellectual is, I realize, counterintuitive: Prostitutes make money through the sexual labor of their bodies. Yet Cleland makes intelligence an important aspect of his heroine's character: She has acquired sophisticated literary skills and authors her own story. While *Pamela* defines bourgeois individuality through the inalienable private written expression of an inner life, *Memoirs* defines bourgeois individuality as the opposite: as the capacity to market the products of this inner life. At the end Fanny learns from her client the "rational pleasurist" what she seems to intuit all along: that "the pleasures of the mind were superior to those of the body, at the same time, that they were so far from obnoxious to, or incompatible with each other" (175). Fanny becomes able to support herself (and Charles) with her literal and metaphoric inheritance from this rational pleasurist. Like Fanny, the rational pleasurist began as an impoverished orphan but acquired an enormous fortune through his "talent and activity." Fanny's ability to express herself so eloquently in writing perhaps owes something to the "cultivation" she received under his tutelage.

Yet long before he has the heroine meet this generous benefactor, Cleland distinguishes Fanny's sexual adventures by their creativity. Each encounter in *Memoirs* explores a different sexual possibility, a phenomenon that helps break up the monotony of pornography, but that also particularizes Fanny's professional life. Cleland provides considerable comic detail, to take one example, about Fanny and Mrs. Cole's clever machinations to convince Mr. Norbert of Fanny's virginity. During sex, Fanny simulates her virginity by convincing Mr. Norbert of her fear and the pain that he inflicts on her. Sex becomes a theatrical performance, complete with props (the bloody sponge) but no less pleasing to the client for its simulation. While other encounters do not always demand this level of theatricality, they each involve some orchestration that requires creativity rather than passive endurance. Stewart reads this specialization as part of the impoverishment of pornography,[101] but Fanny behaves not like an objectified commodity or even an anonymous, alienated reproducer of the same repeated act. Instead, she acts like a fully human creature, complete with sentimental and sensual feelings, expressing her creativity through her work.

Fanny's professionalism becomes most apparent in her encounter with the sadomasochist. Mrs. Cole does not ask Fanny to take on Mr. Barvile; in fact, even though she had long been trying to find him a partner, she tries to dissuade Fanny from enduring his attentions. Fanny explains her interest: It was not the higher fee, she insists, since she was already "easy" in her circumstances, nor did she feel "the least impulse or curiosity to know more of a taste, that promis'd so much more pain than pleasure" (144). Instead, she explains her choice as "a gust of fancy for trying a new experiment, mix'd with the vanity of approving my personal courage to Mrs. Cole" (144). Each encounter, including this one, offers a new experience and broadens her range of skills. She takes on Mr. Barvile not for the sex or the money, but out of a sense of what we might describe as a pornographic version of professional pride. Fanny feels satisfied that her first time at whipping so greatly pleases her client, which gives her the courage to endure her own punishment. Fanny describes the pain they each experience as real; nevertheless, both proceed as contractarian "rational pleasurists," expressing concern for each other's comfort.

The constant, delicate contractarian negotiations Fanny engages in with Mr. Barvile only exaggerate the general contractarianism of her prostitution. Cleland's characterization of prostitution as a highly skilled activity draws, as mentioned, from earlier courtesan models, such as Pietro Aretino's famous *Dialogues*. Cleland, however, invokes this model to depart from it in certain ways, for in Aretino the prostitute learns that she should "above all study deceit and flattery .... The whore's chief rule is to flimflam Sir Credulous."[102] Prostitutes in Aretino and in many early libertine narratives do not *charge* clients so much as wheedle gifts from them, trick them out of money, and even steal from them. By contrast, even though Fanny sells her fake virginity to Mr. Norbert, in general she does not flimflam Sir Credulous. Even in the case of Mr. Norbert, she succeeds in the deception not through skillful rhetoric but through sexual techniques that he finds no reason to complain about. And in all cases, unlike for many tricky whores of the Restoration, Fanny and her clients overtly understand that they have entered a contract.

Cleland not only creates an idealized contractual relationship between prostitute and client but also imagines ideal conditions between management and professionalized work. In his later *Memoirs of a Coxcomb* (1751), by contrast, Cleland represents Mother Sulpher's brothel as hideously tawdry rather than pleasing. The prostitutes are "slaves of necessity . . . obliged to feign and forge joy, in order to give joy."[103] In his *Case of the Unfortunate Bosavern Penlez*, he calls bawds (both female and male) "Enemies to Mankind" who keep prostitutes "in a State of Slavery . . . scarce less cruel, and much more infamous, than that of a Captive in *Barbary*."[104] But Fanny is no slave. Instead, the relationship between Mrs. Cole and Fanny offers an idealized vision of affection emerging from a fundamentally commercial relationship. Cleland here transforms the practice that represents in much eighteenth-century writing (including his own) the dehumanizing threat of urbanization, capitalism, and modernity into one of affective pleasure. While *Pamela* mystifies emergent forms of class mobility and other prostitute narratives confront them in various ways, *Memoirs* proposes an erotic version of faith in the marketplace's sanguine potential to refine manners and satisfy desires.

While reformist writers, then, use prostitution as a trope for commercialism's dangers to virtue and identity, Cleland depicts in Fanny's career the reification of exchange, but also a full recovery of humanity. This becomes possible, however, only in the category of professional work, as opposed to lower-class bodily exertions to which the novel opposes Fanny's intellectual creativity. Cleland draws this contrast clearly, for example, when Fanny goes "slumming": Unsatisfied by Mr. Norbert's limited powers, Fanny accepts the attentions of a sailor partly "to see the end of an adventure so novel to me as being thus treated like a common street-plyer" (140). Fanny becomes unusually passive in this sexual act; in fact, her only controlling direction—informing him that he is trying to enter the "wrong" orifice—meets with indifference: "Pooh, says he my dear, any port in a storm" (141). This incident highlights Fanny's distinction: unlike the common street-plyer, Fanny consistently reclaims her full humanity and sutures any self-division through her intellectual labor. In Mrs. Cole's idealized brothel, transactions begin with a rational contract between two individuals. In the heat of passion, bodies become mechanized and objectified: Both Fanny and her partners lose control. Yet once these experiences end, they recover: the sadomasochist apologizes profusely for any pain; "machines of wonder" shrink back down to human size. Thus Cleland posits a full recovery from temporary instrumentality for discriminating professionals: He confronts the hazards of commodification, but imagines the full restoration of identity.

One conclusion, then, might be that Cleland fully confirms the bourgeois values that he appears to satirize by idealizing the intellectual labor that, as Armstrong and Tennenhouse argue, defines the increasing hegemony of the middle class in the eighteenth century. Rather than using the whore's life to explore the liberating or estranging effects of exposing sexuality, and thus the most private dimension of the self, to the vicissitudes of the marketplace,

Memoirs instead offers a utopian model of business in which each transaction refines, pleases, and continues to perfect both parties. At the end of her career in prostitution, Fanny fully recovers her virtue, in part by marrying the man to whom she originally lost it. To some extent, then, *Memoirs* functions as a pleasing vision of the marketplace's ability to meet human desires at the highest level.

But while *Memoirs* explores the pornographic possibilities of high-end pleasure, it does not represent Fanny's refinement as the only possibility in the marketplace. In her encounter with the sailor, Fanny recognizes that had she truly been one of those "unhappy street-errants, who devote themselves to the pleasure of the first ruffian that will stoop to pick them up" (141), then she would have had to return to him (and men like him) instead of taking refuge in Mrs. Cole's house. This could easily still have become her fate, as Mrs. Cole reminds her after the incident, had she contracted a venereal disease. To work from the street would be to place her body in constant danger and render her refined capacity for rational pleasure irrelevant. In such encounters, she might not have the luxury of recovering. Further, at the beginning of Fanny's career, undertaken with reluctance out of economic desperation, Mr. Crofts nearly rapes her, turning to violence when she refuses to comply. After his attack, Mrs. Brown finds Fanny dazed and bloody; soon after, she contracts a dangerous fever. This incident reminds us that in other circumstances and for other sex workers, the repulsive, unscrupulous, and callous Mr. Crofts might be the only choice. The experiences of her lover Charles points to yet another kind of commercial story: His relatives send him to the South Seas, "where finding the estate he was sent to recover, dwindled to a trifle, by the loss of two ships, in which the bulk of his uncle's fortune lay, he was come away with the small remainder" (176). South Sea investments, as Cleland's readers knew, sometimes turn out to be bubbles. In Lancashire, report had been given out that Fanny had met an even worse fate than this and fallen victim to imperialism's demand for exploited colonial labor, "spirited away to the Plantations" (177). These alternative possibilities, threaded throughout the *Memoirs*, suggest the narrative's self-consciousness about its pornographic idealization of the activities in Mrs. Cole's house.

The *Memoirs*, then, perhaps rather than naturalizing bourgeois ideology, replaces the virtuous Pamela with prostitute Fanny Hill as the emblem of middle-class self-cultivation. The novel exposes the precariousness of Fanny's privilege, pointing toward the disturbingly arbitrary nature of the difference between elite professionals and common street-plyers, between London cosmopolites and the labor at home and abroad that supports their epicurean luxury. While Sally Godfrey chooses her own West Indian sojourn in *Pamela* (albeit under pressure), the Lancashire rumor describes Fanny as taken against her will. Cleland elsewhere, as noted, describes prostitution as a form of slavery. If sexuality, especially for women, was becoming in this period the epitome of personal, private identity, then treating the "commodity" as a source for a commodity—alienable sexual service—comes dangerously close to turning the person into an object, as slavery attempts to do. But if other people besides prostitutes also exchange products of their bodies and their minds for remuneration, then would not a similar kind of objectification threaten them as well?

Prostitute narratives in general tend to evoke this anxiety. The eighteenth century reveals an unprecedented fascination not just with prostitutes, but with their stories: How did they come to this predicament? What other choices were open to them? How do they feel about prostitution? These narratives turn prostitutes, from impoverished streetwalkers to glamorous celebrities, into novelistic heroines with their ups and downs, twists of fate, humiliations, conflicts, upward mobility, suffering, and sometimes triumph. Libertine narratives, with their skepticism toward bourgeois ideology, often take rebellious pleasure in exploring the instrumental use of the private for commercial ambition; reform narratives, by contrast, counterbalance the prostitute's alienation with effusions of personal feelings. In *Memoirs*, Cleland creates a sensitive, intelligent metropolitan professional who, rather than being degraded by the ostensibly most humiliating kind of commercial exchange, ends with her manners polished and her pockets filled. Thus Cleland creates a pornographic fantasy version of a popular story about the eighteenth-century economy: that extensive commerce produces refinement, wealth, happiness, and even bliss. Within the fiction of *Memoirs*, we follow these fulfilling possibilities from the point of view of an unusually fortunate prostitute whose experiences contrast sharply with those of others. Cleland's ambivalent satire, then, lies in his representation of Fanny's narrative as a new kind of whore's rhetoric for the consumer revolution, a fantasy of pleasurable refinement through extensive commerce in which, for an enviable elite, "life activity," remunerated work, and the cultivation of selfhood blissfully converge. For others, however, the brutal Mr. Crofts, unselective sailors, and voyages to plantations await.

5

Clarissa among the Whores

"You owe us such a lady!"
Prostitutes to Lovelace in Samuel Richardson,
Clarissa; or, The History of a Young Lady

In Samuel Richardson's novel *Clarissa*, the absent but defining moment of the narrative—the heroine's rape—takes place in a whorehouse surrounded by observing prostitutes. As Lovelace complains, these prostitutes had been constantly urging him to this action and mocking his delays. It is the prostitutes who, disguised as ladies, trick Clarissa into going back to the bawd Mrs. Sinclair's house, where they drug her and possibly even hold her down for Lovelace. Before the rape, they can't imagine why Lovelace takes so long to act; they wonder aloud why he should "make so long a harvest of so little corn."[1] Lovelace feels trapped between Clarissa's "so *visible* a superiority" and the constant demand from these whores. With characteristic futility, Lovelace tries to resist becoming their "instrument":

> And here from below, from BELOW indeed! I am so goaded on—Yet 'tis poor too, to think myself a machine—I am *no* machine—Lovelace, thou art base to thyself, but to suppose thyself a machine. (658)

And yet after he rapes Clarissa under pressure, to his chagrin he recognizes that "I am a machine at last, and no free agent" (848).[2] The prostitutes thus become even more ominous than the mechanical Lovelace in this novel, for he becomes their victim as well.[3] He helplessly rails against their impatience; he excoriates them when they have Clarissa arrested for debt. After the rape, Lovelace recedes and the prostitutes close in.

The prostitutes, however, use Lovelace as a sexual "machine" not simply to torment Clarissa, but to recruit her into prostitution. Like many heroines of prostitute narratives, Clarissa, moving from the country to the city, takes refuge in a time of crisis in an apparently safe, welcoming, feminine space that shockingly turns out to be a commercial house of prostitution, a public space masquerading as a private space. Mrs. Sinclair's house literally consists of two houses: one in front that maintains the appearance of respectability, and another in back for infamous commerce. *Clarissa* thus not only engages the economic and philosophical questions raised by prostitution but also functions as an averted prostitute narrative itself. In the context of popular prostitute narratives, *Clarissa* becomes visible as a story less about the heroine's hymen than about her refusal to commodify and alienate her sexual labor.

In its scope, linguistic richness, and brilliant relentlessness, Richardson's *Clarissa* clearly differs from the popular narratives discussed in chapter 4. Nevertheless, the house of prostitution stands at the novel's enigmatic center and becomes a figure for the range of ethical, emotional, political, and economic problems that *Clarissa* engages. The threat of prostitution occupied Richardson in *Pamela* as well: The bawdy Mrs. Jewkes hoped to transform Pamela into a whore. Like the secret house behind Mrs. Sinclair's respectable domicile, prostitute narratives form the uneasy double of both *Pamela* and *Clarissa*. But unlike in *Pamela*, in *Clarissa* Richardson takes the reader into the sexual underworlds beneath the surface of polite society. Like his contemporaries, he found prostitution compelling not only for its violation of domesticity but also for the way it raised extreme versions of questions fundamental to selfhood in a commercial market society. As an enterprising printer and commercial author, Richardson embraced and benefited from the expanding urban marketplace; in *Clarissa*, however, he explores its costs. Clarissa's tragic virtue, I will argue, resides not in resistance to sexuality itself, but in the refusal of the commodified exchange of sexual activity that threatens abjection in both her family home and in Mrs. Sinclair's brothel. That Clarissa dies for this refusal suggests not necessarily the author's idealization of an abstract economic purity, but rather his recognition of the impossibility of survival without negotiating the vulnerable boundaries of the self.

Clarissa's Virtue

Clarissa struggles to live a virtuous life; in this endeavor, she joins a range of fictional heroines. Michael McKeon has observed that eighteenth-century culture increasingly upheld women as not just "the conduit but as the repository of an honor that had been alienated from a corrupt male aristocracy."[4]

Clarissa in some ways provides the perfect example of this phenomenon: Lovelace's rakish corruption only highlights the heroine's principled behavior. In other ways, however, Clarissa's moral stance has proven the most enigmatic aspect of this text. Most critical accounts have understood Clarissa's ethics in terms of sexuality: While Richardson describes Clarissa's charity and kindness, he defines her virtue, it is generally assumed, above all as chastity.[5] But if chastity means preserving virginity until marriage, then Clarissa is not virtuous. Clarissa loses her virginity against her will, in a semi-conscious state, and with no desire to stray from purity. Yet the fact that sex does take place, however darkly, unpleasurably, and violently, suggests that the novel does not in any simple way equate virtue with preserving virginity until marriage. In *Clarissa*, Richardson defines the heroine's virtue in more complex and interesting ways that the context of the prostitute narrative can help illuminate.

Recognizing that virtue does not equal virginity opens up the possibility that Clarissa remains virtuous because she neither wants nor enjoys this violent sexual act; thus the question of her desire, as distinct from her virginity, has also been scrutinized. But even if chastity means lack of or resistance to erotic desire rather than an unpenetrated body, then Clarissa might still fail the test. Many readers have found Clarissa's ambivalence among her most compelling qualities: The vision of Clarissa as utterly puritanical has long been laid to rest.[6] While Clarissa does not in any way invite rape, she nevertheless responds to Lovelace in ways that suggest both resistance and attraction. She opens the door just wide enough to be tricked into absconding with him: Running away with Lovelace thus endangers her chastity in ways that, strictly speaking, marriage to her unappealing suitor Solmes would not. Like the Restoration rake figures from which Richardson draws, the characterization of Lovelace depends on his dangerous attractions.[7]

This issue, I believe, has proven so difficult in reading *Clarissa* because its author captures a historical moment in which the meaning of virtue, especially for women, has become unclear, unstable, and even contradictory.[8] In particular, the erosion of a traditional patriarchal order and the emergence of a possessive market society render the obligations of a middle-class daughter less obvious. As Lois Beuler argues, Clarissa's own sense of patriarchal virtue will not permit her to obey her father's command to marry Solmes, since she cannot respect him enough to serve virtuously as his wife. The men in the novel fail her, beginning with her grandfather's disruptive subversion of patriarchal inheritance by his gift of independent property.[9] Clarissa's father abdicates his patriarchal responsibilities and passes them down to his son, who cares too much about his own petty interests to function honorably. As this traditional patriarchal world crumbles, however, another world emerges that occupies the ethical attention of the author and his heroine. The novel takes place in the midst of a social transformation from, as Slavoj Žižek puts it, the fetishism of hierarchy to the fetishism of the commodity.[10] As a property owner, Clarissa in theory holds the potential to exercise traditional civic humanist virtue, but her gender, as Joy Kyunghae Lee has argued, prevents her from gaining this opportunity. Lee also suggests, however, that gender prevents Clarissa from exercising virtue in the emergent system "based on an exchange policed by manners"[11] as well, a point that the issue of prostitution complicates. Suggesting that Clarisssa's "identity is entirely tied up in her chastity," Lee concludes that the novel thus evacuates her of agency: In the end, Clarissa's body on the marriage market "can only figure in the form of a cipher, an empty signifier that attains meaning only as it is impregnated with value and exchanged within the patriarchal economy."[12] For Lee and for others, Clarissa's gender prevents her from exercising virtue, in spite of her intentions, in either of these two conflicting systems.

Clarissa's heroic defiance in the novel, however, seems inconsistent with this conclusion. Consequently, others have, with grim optimism, found virtuous agency in the heroine's death. Terry Eagleton identifies this death as a political triumph, "a shocking, surreal act of resignation from a society whose power system she has seen in part for what it is." Margaret Doody, by contrast, reads the heroine's demise as a spiritual conquest.[13] But surely death constitutes a strange victory. Focusing on death as Clarissa's answer to the oppressions of Lovelace and the Harlowes leaves us, I think, vulnerable to the suggestion of Clarissa's lack of agency and, perhaps even more fundamentally, to Christopher Hill's classic point that Clarissa must die because a violated woman has no value in the eighteenth century's specifically capitalist version of the patriarchal marriage market.[14] In spite of Eagleton's powerful analysis of the cultural conflicts that produced *Clarissa* and Doody's compelling reading of the author's spiritual reflections, neither argument dispels the nagging possibility that in her death Clarissa executes her own sacrifice on behalf of her oppressors.[15]

All of these arguments presume that Clarissa's sexuality defines her virtue, a view that leads to reading her death as a self-willed response to rape. Even for Eagleton and Doody, who find heroism rather than defeat in the heroine's end, death constitutes at least in part the refusal of sexual submission. Yet the novel does not fully support the initial assumption. If it is rape that threatens her virtue, then what could Lovelace mean when he declares that he wants to see if she can be as virtuous after the rape as she was before it? (869). If Clarissa's chastity becomes an alienable commodity (as Lee argues) to be circulated in a capitalist patriarchal society, then why wouldn't marriage to Lovelace, which would place her squarely back in the system of patriarchal ownership, satisfy the demands of virtue and provide narrative closure? Apparently some of Richardson's female correspondents would have preferred this ending.[16] Hugh Kelley's *Memoirs of a Magdalen* (1767), which explicitly rewrites Richardson's novel, concludes with such a marriage. Here Sir Robert seduces his fiancée before marriage, but then rejects her as tainted. Cast out of her father's house, Louisa takes a room in a residence that turns out to be a brothel; she escapes, however, and after reforming at the Magdalen Hospital marries Sir Robert. For both Kelley and Richardson's female correspondents, marriage redeems violated female characters: It satisfies the demands of patriarchy by restoring the woman to the control and protection of a man. Yet this does not happen in *Clarissa*, which suggests that the novel engages other issues in addition to the patriarchal sexual economy.

The context of the prostitute narrative helps us see, I will argue, that Clarissa's death results from her concrete refusal of not simply sexual submission but of *prostitution*. She accepts death over prostitution but not over sex; she could, after all, have begun refusing food once she recognized the danger to her virginity.[17] Greatly to Lovelace's confusion, the rape does not constitute the culmination of the test of Clarissa's virtue, for the novel continues for many more pages after this event. This conflicts with Lovelace's sense of dramatic plot. In response to Sally's "reproaches" for the "slowness of my proceedings," Lovelace objects that

in a play, does not the principal entertainment lie in the first four acts? Is not all in a manner over when you come to the fifth? And what vulture of a man must he be who souses upon his prey, and in the same moment trusses and devours? (574)

Lovelace sees sexual intercourse as the "climax," but this turns out (to his surprise) to be wrong: not only does the rape fail to offer satisfaction, but it takes place in the third act and not at the end of the fourth. Lovelace's plot is not the one that shapes *Clarissa*. Clarissa's trial lies not in whether or not she will have sex with him, for Lovelace fails to seduce her and them preempts the meaning of her chastity by raping her. Rather, at least from Clarissa's (albeit traumatized) perspective, the test lies in her response to the fact of sex; specifically, in whether or not she will accept anything in exchange for it.

Clarissa's concrete, fatal, and possibly mad refusal to accept anything— money, marriage, even food—that might seem like compensation for sex is particularly meaningful in the context of eighteenth-century prostitute narratives. As mentioned, *Clarissa* evokes these: The heroine leaves the country for the city to escape oppressive conditions at home, she is tricked into a brothel, she instinctively refuses to share a bed with Miss Parringer (thus potentially avoiding the homoerotic sexual initiation that Fanny Hill enjoys with Phoebe). As Edward Copeland points out, Clarissa and Fanny Hill have "similar suitors, similar unpleasant experiences in London, shared interest in problems of 'delicacy,' outstanding beauty, not to mention noteworthy cleanliness and neatness, and most of all, heightened capacities for 'feeling' with the greatest intensity."[18] The "odious Solmes" resembles Mr. Crofts in his "Jew"-like crass materialism and sexual objectification of women; both heroines reject these greedy, hideous men. But unlike in *Memoirs* and even reform narratives, Richardson's heroine has sex but never becomes a prostitute. She chooses instead to starve to death. Herein, I believe, lies her virtue and thus the reason why the rape neither consummates nor even constitutes her trial. In prostitute narratives, a woman with nothing but her (sexual) labor to sell enters the marketplace explicitly and literally to *avoid* starvation or, more poignantly, the starvation of her child, sister, or aging parent. The seduced woman in reformist writing faces the "[d]readful alternative" of either seeing her adored child, "perish with hunger and with thirst,—or, to obtain its support by the horror of prostitution!" which "nothing could have induced them so to procure, but the cries and tears of hungry children, craving repeated supplies of food."[19] Clarissa would find herself in this very position if the rape has impregnated her; she avoids this possibility, however, by starving her own body. Before the rape, the novel may outline the tragic disintegration of a patriarchal order that would, at least in theory, have protected Clarissa from her brother's hatred and her vulnerability to Lovelace. After the rape, however, Richardson tells the protracted history of a young lady not becoming a prostitute.[20] Thus Clarissa *does* exert agency and practice a quixotic economic virtue, one connected to her sexual virtue but not defined by it alone. But rather than becoming simply a victim of patriarchy or class conflict, she does so through her refusal of all forms of material "compensation," be they gifts, loans, or marriage settlements. From her traumatized, postrape perspective, all such offers suggest prostitution contracts.

That Clarissa prefers starvation to prostitution suggests in Richardson some compartmentalization—the demonizing of some commercial relations to exculpate the market system from similar kinds of exploitation. Yet at the same time, *Clarissa* records cultural anxieties around the potential threat to selfhood that a world of increasing commodification posed. The novel's extraordinary popularity and Clarissa's own sympathetic position as both victim and moral agent support the possibility that the novel held meaning for its readers as not simply a warning about female chastity in danger, but as a reflection on the increasingly widespread experience of negotiating which goods, services, and parts of the self might become commodities and which must remain priceless.

Sexual Contracts

Prostitute narratives inevitably confront the decision contractually to commodify sexual labor. The autobiography of Teresia Constantia Phillips (1748–1749) forms an instructive contrast with *Clarissa* on this point, given the similarities in their stories. As Phillips reports, she had become estranged from her family and thus vulnerable to seduction. An aristocratic rake tempts her to his quarters on the promise of a good view of a parade, but he drugs her wine and rapes her. In her view, the rape "left her no other Resource, but to throw herself into the Arms of her Lover, and depend entirely upon his Honour for her future Well-being."[21] He supports her for a while, but then abandons her to her inevitable fate. An old woman befriends Phillips and "soon found her Credit among those Cannibals who devour young Creatures by pretended Friendship . . . and when they are got so far in Debt, that they cannot pay, seize their Persons for their own Use, or rather for the Use of the Public" (1:57–58). Desperate in her debt, Phillips then "marries" a man who already has a wife and who sets her up in a private house that turns out to be a whorehouse.

At this point, Phillips accepts prostitution as her only choice. But her autobiography, which initially seems to promise a salacious exposé of elite scandal, turns out to be mostly a story about money. Her description (in the third person) of the compiled obligations of one lover, "Tartuffe," is typical:

> In what *costly Gifts, and fashionable Presents*, this vain Votary had dressed up her Idol, has partly been already mentioned; to which we shall only add, *a small Article, almost Daily, (for near two Years)* and *Expence* of the *most elegant Meals*, that *Rarities* of all *Kinds*, or the *richest Wines* could compose *for his Entertainment*; which, we believe, will be considered as *no trifling Object*; at the End of which she went to *Flanders*; but, at her Return, with their Acquaintance the Expence was renew'd.
>
> And now, candid Reader, let us sum up this Account of Debtor and Creditor, and see how far *the trading Tartuffe* has *ballanced* it; for she has confesssed, that *all he has had* from her, *she gave him*; yet, generous Minds always think themselves in Debt for Obligations, especially *pecuniary* ones: 'Tis true, they do so; but what is this to our *Tartufe*? how is he affected by it? For will he not say, if *a silly Woman sets* a *Price* upon *what* she has *given away, let her pay herself*. (2:195)

Phillips offers little erotic revelation but considerable detail about who paid for dinner. The autobiography reads more like a bill of accounts than a sentimental journey: These former lovers *owe* her. Like a few other extant prostitute autobiographies, Phillip's *Apology* itself was an act of (presumably failed) blackmail. Throughout the three volumes, she promises to stop publishing the stories of any man willing to settle his account, a demand directed in particular to the original rapist. Occasionally she mentions lovers whose identity she withholds because they have paid up. Phillips appears to accept her own sexual labor as a commodity; she only objects to insufficient compensation. The rapist thus comes in for the harshest critique, not so much for the personal violation but for racking up the greatest unpaid debt: Since he so dramatically reduced her market value, he owes her the largest compensation. Unable through the courts to obtain reparations, Phillips took her case to the public, hoping shame and sympathy would succeed where implied individual contracts had failed.[22]

In reading rape as an implied contract and a form of debt, Phillips differs most starkly from Clarissa yet follows, though in an extreme form, the more common expectation. Sexual contractarianism, in fact, forms the assumption of an anonymous satire of Phillips, in which an all-female jury and panel of female judges put "Mr. Grimes"—the name Phillips gives to her rapist—on trial. The prosecutor decries the rape as a property crime: The accused has undermined the lady's future prospects by taking her virginity, for men "cannot be induced to give any Thing considerable for a Commodity which has been used by another, though never so little the worse for the wearing." Further, the publicity of the case has spoiled her opportunity to fool clients with a fake maidenhead.[23] Worst of all, if rape should become the fashion it would undermine the whole sex trade. Why, the prosecutor wants to know, could Grimes not simply have taken advantage of the sexual services already available: "in this Capital, this great Emporium of Pleasure, where every Lane, every Alley, every Street and Corner, could supply him with Food enough to satisfy the most voracious Appetite, what Excuse can be made for him?" (33 – 34). If all men raped rather than purchased, "half the Ladies of the Town must starve" (27), depleting the economic vitality of the whole city. Grimes has thus not just threatened prosperity, he has also violated the civilized commercial spirit: He has barbarically used force where money would have sufficed. Satirical and misogynistic in its intention, the pamphlet nevertheless describes Phillips's position and reading of her culture with some degree of accuracy. Husbands, after all, in the eighteenth century could sue rapists for damages; Phillips differs only by claiming property in her own body. Over and over, Phillips insists that various men owe her money for their failure to offer reasonable compensation for her hospitality, feeling confident enough in the rectitude of her position to bring her case to public attention.

Clarissa, by contrast, pointedly refuses any contract, be it for marriage or prostitution, which might represent rape (as do Phillips and the women in the satiric trial of her case) as creating a debt that can be compensated. Yet in her own way, she too asserts ownership of her body, if only to insist on its pricelessness. In her comfortable, virtuous, and fashionable life before leaving Harlowe Place, Clarissa seems far from Phillips: tormented by a cruel stepmother, Phillips left home at the age of thirteen. But at least one writer in the eighteenth century seems to have connected them. In another response to the Phillips case, *A Counter-Apology* proposes to tell the continuing adventures of the heroine. Like the satiric trial of her case, this pamphlet characterizes Phillips by her contractarianism. Writing about one lover she schemed against, "Constantia" notes that in spite of his generosity "he is a man, and as such must be treated; besides, this is my trade, and I must live by it. Does any person scruple to take the best price he can get for his commodity, of whatever denomination it may be, provided there is a bidder for it? Surely not. No more shall I."[24] To attract this man and win his sympathy, she invents a story that she has run away from her parents, who tried to marry her off to an unappealing suitor. For the purpose of this scam, she goes by the name of "Clarissa."

Not only does Clarissa's predicament resemble the one faced by Phillips, but her situation at the novel's beginning resembles more generally the mid-century reformist stereotype of the kind of girl most vulnerable to the machinations of an unscrupulous bawd, even if this stereotype has a limited historical basis. As we saw in chapter 4, many reformers represented sex work not as a laboring-class strategy for economic survival but as a tragic, careless, and dissolute form of downward mobility. In their accounts, formerly middle-class girls tempted by fashion, luxury, and aristocratic rakes populate the London brothels. Libertine texts reinforce this narrative: The famous bawd Mother Douglas, according to one source, began as a young lady with a genteel education but was impregnated by a peer.[25] One Lady Fanny came from a very good family, but was raped by a peer; consequently, she first became a courtesan and then a common prostitute. One writer insists that in most brothels "you will find that the ladies . . . had all the advantages of birth, fortune, and a regular education enforced by the best example of their parents or guardian" and have only themselves to blame.[26] Such publications often describe the refined education of prostitutes to make them appear more attractive; nevertheless, they agree with reformers that most prostitutes once made the mistake of thinking their beauty and accomplishments might enable them to join the elite. Many could have avoided prostitution "had they been better instructed in the great duty of *reconciling themselves to the condition in which Providence had placed them.*"[27] The Harlowes possess wealth; Lovelace, however, looks down on them and does not understand Clarissa as his social equal. Her situation parallels the young girls of reform literature who fall very low by reaching too high. After her vehement rejection of the unrefined and materialistic Solmes, some members of the Harlowe family might even have described Clarissa as, like the vulnerable girls described by reformers, unfortunately educated above her class and overly proud.

Clarissa also fits the popular profile of the woman in danger of becoming a prostitute because of her conflict with her family. According to reformers, young women forced to marry unappealing men often end up turning to prostitution. One pamphlet even insists that the phenomenon of families throwing out disobedient daughters can account for most of the prostitutes wandering the London streets.[28] Libertine narratives often trace this trajectory as well: In *The Adventures of Melinda* (1749), the heroine agrees to marry the unattractive man, but then secretly becomes a prostitute.[29] Most of the women whom Fanny Murray meets in the Whore's Club had come from good families that treated their daughters too harshly.[30] The story of the prostitute Nancy in the second part of *A Spy upon Mother Midnight*, published in the same year as Richardson's novel, resembles Clarissa's quite closely. Nancy's stepmother is about to force her into marriage with an unappealing man when a young squire sets his eyes on her in church. He slips a billet into her hands protesting his love and vows to rescue her from the hated match. The squire "prevailed on her to leave her Father's House, and go with him to *London;* where he imposed a sham Marriage upon her, and by that Means gained his base Ends." He leaves poor Nancy in a bawdy house. Nancy begs her father to take her back, but "Her Prayers, her Tears, nor the Intercession of his Neighbours, could make not the least Impression on his obdurate Resolution: He abandoned her to Want and Infamy." Unable to find work without a character reference, Nancy becomes a prostitute, which "she as much abhors as any Woman in *England;* and I believe, if she was not necessitated to do as she does, could live in as much Decorum as those who make a greater Shew of Virtue."[31] In this context, Lovelace makes the reasonable assumption that rape will put Clarissa in his power.

Lovelace's mistake, however, is failing to take seriously Clarissa's sense of her own body's pricelessness, as well as an emergent ethos in which illicit sex alone does not turn a woman into a prostitute. By the middle of the eighteenth century, "prostitution" was being redefined specifically as a remunerative sexual contract. While Jonas Hanway in 1759 suggested that reformers use the word "prostitute" simply because "prostitute is surely a politer word than whore,"[32] Samuel Johnson's *Dictionary* defined *whore* as the more general term for a woman who engages in illicit sex and *prostitute* as a woman who does so for money.[33] Even as early as 1735, a young clergyman named Daniel Maclauchlan reflected at length on the distinction between sexually active women and professional sex workers, separating women who engage "a little Time with a Gentleman in this Way" from "those jaded, tough, callous Prostitutes, uncapable [*sic*] of Procreation . . . that will ask a Six-Pence of a Gentleman for giving him a most virulent Clap."[34] Richardson similarly distinguishes between illicit sex and commercial sexual contracts: Sally Godfrey in *Pamela*, after all, partially redeems herself after an initial slip. He also supported the prostitute reform movement, suggesting his faith that sexual indiscretion did not necessarily condemn a woman to a life of prostitution.

So when Lovelace brings Clarissa to a brothel where he knows the women and has even launched the careers of several, Richardson associates his rake with not just illicit sex, but with *commercial* sex. Lovelace shares with Phillips and Mrs. Sinclair a contractarian perspective; he has adopted this aspect of "progressive ideology" in spite of his aristocratic status and libertine assumptions.[35] John Zomchick and Sandra Macpherson, in fact, have in different ways argued that in this novel Richardson launches a critique of the contract ideology that entraps the heroine. For Zomchick, "Clarissa's sentiments work against the effects of market principles"; in her proposed marriage to Solmes, she is "split between being a subject to an agreement and an object of exchange in the same agreement. Pushed in two directions, she wishes to return to her status as pre-juridical subject of affection even as she is compelled to assert her rights as a participant in the contract."[36] Macpherson argues that not only is Clarissa herself exploited by contractarian arrangements, but that the novel demonstrates the inadequate justice of laws based on consent—the key ingredient in contract—as opposed to laws based on liability.[37] While other critics have associated Lovelace with traditional mores, Macpherson points out how consistently he operates as a contractarian: He insists on Clarissa's implicit consent, arguing that he bears no responsibility for her death because he did not intend it. Richardson's exposure of Lovelace as a specifically *sexual* contractarian, however, perhaps offers an even more powerful critique, for in this instance the novel exposes the way that the logical extension of market values profoundly conflicts with the bourgeois sexual morality presumed to attend them. Lovelace does not see the ladies in Mrs. Sinclair's establishment as victims but rather as women who willingly enter into agreements that fulfill their needs and desires. He seems to suspect that, by putting herself in such a vulnerable position, Clarissa does the same.

For this reason, Clarissa's failure to fail his test surprises Lovelace: He believes that the rape puts him in Clarissa's debt, but leaves her with no choice but to attempt to call it in through marriage or other compensation.[38] He does not imagine that she would refuse to collect; instead, he anticipates his own power in negotiating the terms. Apparently, he has put several other women to this test as well, for Mrs. Sinclair has been able to populate her brothel with women "broken in" by Lovelace. Mrs. Sinclair does not initially

distinguish Clarissa from the others. In fact, Mrs. Sinclair seems puzzled by
Lovelace's elaborate drama; she tries to convince him that she and her girls
could much more readily get the job done:

> Mrs. Sinclair wishes she never had seen the face of so skittish a lady; and
> she and Sally are extremely pressing with me, to leave the perverse beauty
> to their *breaking*, as they call it, for four or five days. (906)

Mrs. Sinclair simply assumes that Lovelace's seduction or rape will usher
Clarissa into prostitution. Clarissa's first words to Lovelace after the rape accuse him of having been part of such a scheme all along:

> But tell me (for no doubt thou hast *some* scheme to pursue), tell me, since
> I am a prisoner as I find, in the vilest of houses, and have not a friend to
> protect or save me, what thou intendest shall become of the remnant of a
> life not worth the keeping? Tell me if yet there are more evils reserved for
> me; and whether thou hast entered into a compact with the grand deceiver,
> in the person of his horrid agent in this house; and if the ruin of my soul,
> that my father's curse may be fulfilled, is to complete the triumphs of so
> vile a confederacy?—Answer me!—Say, if thou hast courage to speak out
> to her whom thou hast ruined, tell me what *further* I am to suffer from thy
> barbarity? (900)

This accusation produces a rare moment of speechlessness for Lovelace.
Clarissa here interprets her father's curse as condemning her to a life of prostitution and suggests that Lovelace has made some kind of contract with Mrs.
Sinclair in which he has agreed to "break her in." Lovelace cannot answer
this charge, partly because this is where he begins to recognize that he has
been Mrs. Sinclair's "instrument." He promises Clarissa any amends she
might require, but in this context his offer only offends her more deeply. To
accept *anything* from Lovelace at this point—even marriage—would impli-
cate her in the very economy of commodification she seeks to escape.

Lovelace does not necessarily have as his conscious plan the desire to lure
Clarissa into prostitution. Nevertheless, he approaches the rape as a contract
and reasons that if he has caused no serious economic devaluation of Clarissa
(as "Mr. Grimes" did to Teresia Phillips), then he has caused only minor damage, mostly to her pride. Even if she refuses to marry him, she will eventually receive her estate, he tells himself, and at the very least could live from
its income the comfortable single life she claims to prefer. In these letters he
seems to be trying to convince himself that her family will eventually come
around or that other relatives will be able to circumvent them (869). Richardson early on demonstrates that Lovelace *does* have some scruples about se-

duction: He "spares" Rosebud, whose violation would compromise her ability to marry well. Lovelace's reflections might seem like rationalization; however, there are ways in which the rape has not "ruined" her. Richardson makes sure that we understand that her family and friends still consider Clarissa marriageable—certainly to Lovelace, but also to Wyerely—and thus not "ruined" in this respect. Loss of virginity does not automatically turn Clarissa into a prostitute: she could marry; she could retire to her estate. Taking money for sex, however, would be something else entirely.

Before the rape, Clarissa faces the tyranny of aristocrat manqué systems of property exchange. Lovelace, however, spirits her away into the brutal world of capitalist commodification: He carries her from the enclosed patriarchal world of the Harlowe estate into the metropolitan emporium of (infamous) commerce. While dramatizing this geographical distinction, the novel also points to the fragility of the difference between these worlds. Richardson shows the victimization of Clarissa in both locations, and the proposed marriage to Solmes objectifies the heroine for her ability to enhance the family estate. Solmes looms as a version of the standard Jew figure of prostitute narratives for his crass materialism and hideousness; the Harlowes themselves have only recently acquired prominence as a family. Uncle Anthony works to expand the Harlowe estate through colonial exploitation. The traditional treatment of women as tokens of exchange becomes, in the proposed marriage to Solmes, inseparable from the accumulation of capital: Any mystification of the gift has been peeled away here. Richardson thus exposes the fragility of the distinction between the Harlowe estate and the commercialized city; nevertheless, punishment for familial mismanagement in the first world consists of the daughter's descent into the second. So while Lovelace understands the rape as the culmination of Clarissa's trial that nevertheless leaves her with a few reasonable options, Clarissa sees it as only the beginning of the most rigorous test of all.

The narrative not only assumes that the rape has not "ruined" Clarissa for marriage but also insists that it has not destroyed her virtue. After outlining all of her post-rape options, Lovelace concludes that

> She may be a more eminent example to her sex; and if she yield (a *little* yield) in the trial, may be a *completer penitent.* Nor can she, but by her own wilfulness, be reduced to *low fortunes.* (869)

While Lovelace infuriatingly suggests that this rape will only feed Clarissa's virtuous pride by giving her something to repent, he nevertheless outlines her post-rape trial: to remain as virtuous *after* as *before.* Cursed by her father, civic humanist property-owning virtue no long remains available; in fact, the first half of the novel suggests that, as a woman, perhaps it never was. But what about the kind of virtue appropriate to the urban marketplace in which she has found herself, where commerce, according to its defenders, cultivates manners?[39] Clarissa possesses the feminine capacity to exercise this kind of virtue (a point to which I will return), but prostitution plots often point to the more disturbing, objectifying, and even exploitative commercial exchanges on which this veneer of cultivation depends. They suggest that while some kinds of commerce may promote refinement, other kinds have the opposite effect. Prostitution is not just *one* of those threatening exchanges: It comes in the eighteenth century to epitomize them.

From Alienation to Abjection

In his recent study of voyages to the South Seas, Jonathan Lamb argues that a clash between two radically different cultural practices of property drove Captain James Cook to madness and contributed to his death. An heir to Lockean possessive individualism, Cook expressed his greatest anger and frustration with native Hawaiians over actions that he read as petty theft but that may have been practiced as part of the necessity of object circulation in a gift economy. For Cook, Lamb argues, the removal of these objects produced not just irritation and inconvenience but actually eroded Cook's sense of self.[40] Clarissa, I believe, experiences the rape in similar terms, and it similarly brings madness. Heiress to an estate, Clarissa understands the virtuous boundaries of her bodily integrity as inalienable; dutiful daughter of an upwardly mobile family with middle-class values, she understands her body and its labor as priceless. Her confrontations with Solmes, with Lovelace, and finally with Mrs. Sinclair, however, constitute similar kinds of encounters with strange and "savage" cultures that display no respect for or even comprehension of these boundaries. Clarissa calls Lovelace a "savage" more than once.[41] Raymond R. Hilliard has described how Richardson represents the courtship of Solmes, the aggression of Lovelace, and the profiteering of Mrs. Sinclair as forms of cannibalism: Clarissa fears being consumed by each of them.[42] The savagery of the voracious Solmes resides in his utter lack of cultivation, his beastly appearance, his lack of any aesthetic sense, and his inability to write. Lovelace appears more cultivated, but reveals an even more blatant physical savagery. With the courtship of Solmes, Clarissa continually asserts her will, even if this does not convince her family. Lovelace, however, so shockingly violates her sense of self that the rape brings first madness, then a drastic shift in perception.

Clearly Clarissa still has something to protect after the rape. Prostitution not only suggests moral weakness in this novel but also holds a visceral horror related to the chaotic violation of human boundaries that the marketplace seems to threaten. Prostitution, as we have seen, constituted a social problem in part because it carried symbolic force as the predicament of the abandoned subject with no buffering resources for survival between the body and the world. Necessity threatens the body left without the protection of estates or capital, a position perhaps more immediately haunting women but available to men as well. As Margaret Hunt has shown, members of the eighteenth-century middle class led a precarious existence, always teetering on the brink of ruin. Loss of access to familial networks promised disaster.[43]

Necessity threatens not just the body but also its boundaries—a possibility that Julia Kristeva has compellingly described as "abjection."[44] For Kristeva, horror and abjection have their roots in threats that undermine the literal integrity of the body, that blur the boundaries of the self and thus the difference between self and other. To take one of her mundane but clear examples, fingernail parings disgust because they were once continuous with the body but now no longer belong to it. They become abject because they suggest the fluidity of bodily boundaries. At the other end of the spectrum, the corpse constitutes the quintessential form of abjection for reasons of degree rather than kind. In its unstable state of constant decomposition, the corpse horrifies by its literal lack of integrity, reminding viewers of the fragile boundaries of their own living bodies.

In *Clarissa*, prostitution becomes the most salient form of abjection in the urban marketplace, manifested most dramatically in the death of Mrs. Sinclair.[45] Immediately following a spate of letters issued by Clarissa from beyond the grave, we learn from the reformed libertine Belford that with uncanny poetic justice Mrs. Sinclair has fallen down the stairs. Now facing her own agonizing death, Mrs. Sinclair sends the prostitute Sally Martin to beg Clarissa's forgiveness, which of course she can no longer give (she is already dead) (1378). Unlike the cruel Harlowe family and *even Lovelace*, Mrs. Sinclair faces eternity without Clarissa's pardon. The whores remain not only unforgiven but, in Sally's confession and Lovelace's protests, ultimately responsible for the rape: "[Sally] called [Clarissa] the ornament and glory of her sex; acknowledged that her ruin was owing more to their instigations than even (savage as thou art) to thy own vileness" (1378). With her leg broken, Mrs. Sinclair lies "raving, crying, cursing, and howling"; "a mortification" beginning to show (1387). The prostitutes who surround the dying woman, however, seem to be undergoing a living mortification of their own:

[They] seemed to have been but just up . . . with faces . . . that had run, the paint lying in streaky seams not half blowzed off, discovering coarse wrinkled skins: the hair of some of them of divers colours . . . that of others plaistered with oil and powder; the oil predominating: but every one's hanging about her ears and neck in broken curls, or ragged ends. . . . They were all slipshod; stockingless some; only underpetticoated all; their gowns, made to cover straddling hoops, hanging trollopy, and tangling about their heels. . . . And half of them (unpadded, shoulder-bent, pallid-lipped, feeble-jointed wretches) appearing from a blooming nineteen or twenty perhaps overnight, haggard well-worn strumpets of thirty-eight or forty. (1387–1388)

Prostitution brings overnight physical corruption, bordering on decomposition. Prostitution hurls them toward death, aging their skin and graying their hair. The scene calls upon a wider anti-prostitute discourse that represents such decay as their inevitable end, even footnoting Jonathan Swift's vivid image of the dismembered whore in "The Lady's Dressing Room" (1388).[46] One medical treatise even argued that the prostitute's body *spontaneously generates* venereal disease, rotting before literal death.[47]

The hideous decay of the relatively young prostitutes, however, cannot compare to the abjection of Mrs. Sinclair—although their own decay suggests that they will inevitably face the same mortification sooner rather than later, given the speed at which a whore can age:

Behold her then, spreading the whole tumbled bed with her huge quaggy carcase: her mill-post arms held up, her broad hands clenched with violence; her big eyes goggling and flaming-red as we may suppose those of a salamander; her matted grizzly hair made irreverent by her wickedness (her clouted head-dress being half off) spread about her fat ears and brawny neck; her livid lips parched, and working violently; her broad chin in convulsive motion; her wide mouth by reason of the contraction of her forehead (which seemed to be half-lost in its own frightful furrows) splitting her face, as it were, into two parts; and her huge tongue hideously rolling in it; heaving, puffing as if for breath, her bellows-shaped and various-coloured breasts ascending by turns to her chin and descending out of sight with the violence of her gasping. (1388)

Richardson describes Mrs. Sinclair here as already something other than a living human: her body is a "carcase"; her arms resemble "mill-posts"; her eyes suggest the salamander; her breasts, bellows; her lips and chin move not deliberately but like animated dead flesh. Her mouth splits her face, an image of the dismemberment that the surgeons intend for her body in general: "And so the poor wretch was to be lanced and quartered, as I may say, for an experiment only! And, without any hope of benefit from the operation, was to pay the surgeons for tormenting her!" (1391). The poisonous effluvia her carcass emits further suggest decomposition before death. Richardson speaks eloquently for a host of reformist writers when he associates prostitution with such grotesque abjection.

But Mrs. Sinclair's is not the only corpse at the end of *Clarissa*. Clarissa's detailed instructions for the fate of her own dead body and her ultimate rejection of her physical self have been read as both Christian transcendence and an extreme form of sexual modesty. Mrs. Sinclair's abject death, however, suggests another possible explanation: Clarissa will have no dismemberment, no decomposing body giving off poisonous effluvia; in short, she will have no abjection. Early in the novel, in fact, she has a nightmare that Lovelace, after stabbing her in the heart, "tumbled me into a deep grave already dug, among two or three half-dissolved carcases; thowing in the dirt and earth upon me with his hands, and trampling it down with his feet" (343). Rather than inhabiting the "half-dissolved carcass" of the whore's body, Clarissa flees her corporeality. She will haunt by the abstraction of letters, not by smell. The prostitute body becomes an animated corpse, diseased and expanding, feeding first off of men and then off of other women, if it lives long enough to become a fat bawd—and they inevitably grow fat, swollen from illicit profits. Clarissa contracts rather than expands; her body gives off no odors; she leaves little physically available to blur the distinction between the self and the non-self.

While grotesque images of the decomposing whores draw from a long tradition of misogyny, they also hold meaning here specific to prostitution as the commodification of sexual labor, pricing the priceless and alienating the inalienable. Rape does not transform Clarissa into one of these animated, rotting corpses; prostitution, however, clearly would. With her father's curse upon her, Clarissa faces a similar problem faced by Roxana, Fanny Hill, Sally Salisbury, and Teresia Phillips: pared down to the body with no protective estate, capital, or family, how does one avoid starvation?[48] In civil society, a person can no longer simply transform nature into property; a civil subject must have something to exchange, be it money, credit, or labor. Before her abduction, Clarissa had mastered the kind of economic virtue appropriate to middle- and upper-class female dependents. She was an excellent consumer: "In her dress," Anna Howe elegizes, "she was elegant beyond imitation" (1466). She took good care of her money by investing rather than hoarding or squandering; she accused her sister, by contrast, of letting her money "lie rusting in [her] cabinet" (195). Thus "she was an excellent ECONOMIST and HOUSEWIFE" (1468); the early chapters describe her pleasure in the daily tasks her dairy required. She heartily disapproved of gambling, but judiciously dispensed charity to the deserving poor. All of these virtues, however, depend on the possession of, or at least access to, some kind of estate. Clarissa can shop, invest, tend, and cultivate, but what can she do when she has no access to any of those resources?

Disowned by her family but retaining these virtues, she interprets any kind of financial assistance as turning the rape into prostitution. In a recognizable strategy for forcing women into prostitution, Mrs. Sinclair's ladies have Clarissa arrested for debt, the classic intermediary step in the transition from seduction to professional sex work. While Lovelace may not have been planning to prostitute Clarissa (as she accuses him), the prostitutes seem to take their opportunity to recruit her as compensation for their part in Lovelace's elaborate maneuvers. Lovelace constantly denies this, but Mrs. Sinclair and her ladies seem to understand it as an implied contract. Why else would they have been willing to spend so much time and effort on his behalf? For Belford, it doesn't matter whether or not Lovelace explicitly agreed to a contract: "This last act [arrest for debt], however unintended by thee, yet a consequence of thy general orders, and too likely to be thought agreeable to thee by those who know thy other villainies by her, has finished thy barbarous work" (1051). Richardson leaves us to piece together at best a misunderstanding between Lovelace and the prostitutes over the arrest: Sally Martin assumes that she has carried out Lovelace's plans, but the news of Clarissa's arrest and the implied maneuvering of her into prostitution horrifies Lovelace. He sends Belford to secure her with all imaginable financial resources: "Let her have all her clothes and effects sent her instantly, as small proof of my sincerity. And force upon the dear creature, who must be moneyless, what sums you can get her to take" (1047). Ever since the news of her arrest "he has been a distracted man," "saying he was a wretch, and made so by his own inventions, and the consequences of them" (1047, 1049). Thus Lovelace, to his horror, recognizes his complicity in a whole different plot; as James Turner has for different reasons observed, as devious as Lovelace may be, he ultimately loses control of his rakish scheme.[49] He thought that he had been using the whores to further his ends, but in this moment he realizes that they had been using *him* to further *theirs*. He has released Clarissa, with practically nothing to sell, into a marketplace from which she had been insulated.

Clarissa spends the rest of the novel ensuring that she has been raped rather than prostituted. This accounts in part for the self-victimization that so many readers have heard in her voice. The prostitutes have clearly had her arrested for reasons beyond the petty jealousy, simple cruelty, or inherent evil that the other characters variously suggest, for Sally soon visits to begin the practical negotiations: Sally "offered to carry her to her former lodgings," where implicitly she could work off her debt. "But [Clarissa] declared they should carry her thither a corpse, if they did" (1053). This rejected, Sally orders the household "to let her want for nothing" (1054), attempting to confirm and compound this debt. They offer her money, but she "would contract no debts" (1055), cleverly suggesting that she *has* no debts contracted. They even suggest that a client already awaits her, "a gentleman who saw you taken, and was so much moved for you, *Miss Harlowe*, that he would gladly advance the money for you, and leave you to pay it when you can" (1057). Belford immediately recognizes this strategy: "See, Lovelace, what cursed devils these are! This is the way, we know, that many an innocent heart is thrown upon keeping, and then upon the town." Lovelace, somewhat childishly, interprets this as a plot on Sally's part "to ruin her with me" (1084), but Sally seems seriously to be recruiting with little thought to Lovelace. His work is done. Clarissa refuses food out of emotional distress, no doubt, but she also refuses to enter into any kind of contracts, explicit or implied—even one so trivial as breakfast and even when, as Sally points out, self-destruction conflicts with her Christian principles. The refusal to contract a debt speaks to an even more powerful principle for which neither traditional Christian values nor aristocratic ideology offer a solution. Whatever conflicts she faced *before* the rape, after the rape Clarissa must negotiate the bewildering morality of the marketplace. Clarissa becomes heroic in spite of her apparent defeat because she refuses to allow the rape to become prostitution; for her, there are limits to the reach of commodification important enough to die for.

Thus having lost, in an extremely narrow sense, her sexual purity, Clarissa fights in the second half of the novel to maintain the economic kind. She systematically resists monetary offers from everyone, making no distinction between benign and insidious ones. She sells what little she has immediately available: her clothes, her "trinkets." She finally accepts three guineas from Mrs. Lovick, but only to pay the apothecary and only if Mrs. Lovick would accept a diamond ring as her security (1081). Belford tries to get money to Clarissa by purchasing her clothes for twenty guineas, but she figures out his scheme and refuses the offer (1090). She goes out of her way not to receive any medical attention that she has not paid for:

> The doctor called on her this morning, it seems, and had a short debate with her about fees. She insisted that he should take one every time he came, write or not write; mistrusting that he only gave verbal directions to Mrs. Lovick, or the nurse, to avoid taking any. (1090)[50]

She refuses money from Anna Howe through Mr. Hickman (1129). She tells Mrs. Norton that she had "no occasion for money" (1168) when her friend tries to pass along a modest five guineas. Sarah Sadleir, Elizabeth Lawrance, Charlotte Montague, and Martha Montague offer her one hundred guineas per quarter for life, or "at least till you are admitted to enjoy your own estate" (1181), an offer that she respectfully declines (1186). Belford understands her resistance: He reminds her, as do Lovelace's female relatives, that she has her own estate and that he merely wants to function "as your *banker* only—I know you will not be obliged: you *need* not" (1102). He drops a bank note behind her chair, apparently to avoid the implied contract of actually handing money to her. Yet his strategy backfires. Clarissa, unwilling to participate in this fiction of money without a source and without obligation, stoops "with pain" to return it, prompting Belford to retrieve it himself.

Before the rape, Clarissa reads her relationship with Lovelace in terms of an earlier culture of obligation that her refusal to respond to his letters without explanation would violate. After the rape, however, she commits herself to the other extreme. Thrown into the world of prostitution that represents both the troubling excess and the rational extension of the emergent capitalist system, Clarissa experiences a world in which gifts disguise themselves to mask their implied contractarian obligation. She defines her wealth by her small stock of portables; she will contract no debts and accept no credit. She reduces any exchange to the immediate barter of value for value. The entire socializing network on which credit and debt depend becomes from her traumatized view profoundly sinister. So while Richardson may indeed advance bourgeois ideology in so many ways, Clarissa's struggles after the rape take her through a hellish nightmare of impending commercial abjection that she furiously resists.

In his childish self-centeredness, Lovelace finds Clarissa's refusal to accept financial support to be either a self-righteous attack on him or utterly baffling. Yet he also finds this refusal disturbing:

> As to selling her clothes, and her laces, and so forth, it has, I own, a shocking sound with it. What an implacable, as well as unjust set of wretches are those of her unkindredly kin; who have money of hers in their hands, as well as large arrears of her own estate; yet withhold both, *avowedly* to distress her! But may she not have money of that proud and saucy friend of hers, Miss Howe, more than she wants?—And should I not be overjoyed, thinkest thou, to serve her?—What then is there in the parting with her apparel but female perverseness?—And I am not sure, whether I ought not to be glad if she does this out of *spite to me*—Some disappointed fair ones would have hanged, some drowned, themselves. My beloved only revenges herself upon her clothes. (1099)

Lovelace cannot quite shake off this news and assure himself of its triviality. Although trying to explain the sale of her clothes as the spite of a spoiled girl with endless resources, this act also, he begins to realize, suggests her refusal to recognize what he understands as a contract between them. Lovelace hatches his plot to rape Clarissa at least in part out of the conviction that it will place her in his power, leaving her with no choice but to marry him; his "generous" offer of marriage would then place her under his obligation for the rest of her life. Yet he does not count on Clarissa's economic virtue—her total self-destruction and obsessive refusal to take anything, even food, that might in any way be understood as compensation for sex. Eventually Lovelace cannot even rationalize: "There's no obliging her. She'd rather sell her clothes than be beholden to anybody, although she would oblige by permitting the obligation" (1202). Indeed, in a traditional world of civic virtue or in a functioning world of mannerly, virtuous exchange, she *would* oblige by obliging. But rape destroys the illusion of either for Clarissa: There is indeed now no obliging her. Suddenly and violently reduced to a few guineas, some clothes, and her permeable body, Clarissa finds herself in a world in which exchange threatens abjection. Her response can at times seem extreme, even mad. It seems highly unlikely that the doctor, for example, wants sex in return for medical attention. But after the rape Clarissa interprets all implied contracts as sexual ones because her body is all that remains after she sells her limited stock of portables. The possibility of nonsexual labor is not seriously entertained here: In Clarissa's elite but precarious context, it remains almost beyond representation. Sex work thus stands in for the possibility of other kinds of labor that prostitute narratives explore more explicitly.

Clarissa's refusal of all gifts nevertheless holds more reason than Lovelace understands, for it remains her only hope of reconciliation with her family and thus reinsertion into the protection that access to an estate provides. In spite of her scrupulousness, her situation already looks bad to Mr. Brand, who discovers that she has received visits from Belford. The question of money figures prominently in his letter and his conclusions: "One thing I am afraid of; which is, that miss may be under *necessities:* and that this Belford (who, as Mrs. Smith owns, has *offered her money* which she, *at the time,* refused) may find an opportunity to *take advantage* of those *necessities*" (1294). Thus Belford's *offer,* regardless of her acceptance, to say nothing of actual sex, may already have prostituted her, for "*one false step* generally brings on *another*" (1292). For Mr. Brand as for Arabella, the best option would be to send Clarissa to the colonies "in some *credible* manner," which "might save not only her *own credit* and *reputation,* but the *reputation* and *credit* of all her *family*" (1294). Richardson thus raises and declines this route: Removal to the colonies would not solve Clarissa's problem but plunge her even more deeply into the world that has so horrified her. While for writers like Defoe, the colonies could offer renewal, for Tory writers such as Aphra Behn the colonies represented the most raw, unmitigated, and ungenteel forms of indiscriminate commodification and complete disregard for human boundaries. *Oroonoko,* after all, ends with the dismemberment of both the hero and heroine. Clarissa does not lack resolve or resourcefulness, but she resists the abjection that the sexual marketplace threatens.

While Clarissa's refusal of money strikes Lovelace first as manipulative and later as mad, however, others interpret it as the epitome of virtue. Lovelace, because he does not understand the full meaning for Clarissa attached to accepting money, thinks that Belford has insulted her: "But the prettiest whim of all was to drop the bank note behind her chair, instead of presenting it on thy knees to her hand!—To make such a lady as this *doubly* stoop—by the acceptance, and to take it from the ground!—What an ungraceful *benefit-conferrer* art thou! How awkward to take it into thy head that the best way of making a present to a lady was to throw the present behind her chair!" (1107). It is difficult not to agree with Lovelace about the awkwardness of this gesture. But Belford attempts, with this admittedly absurd and potentially insulting strategy, to engage in a kind of virtuous bourgeois exchange that mystifies its material aspects through a superstructure of sociability so necessary, as J. G. A. Pocock has demonstrated, to eighteenth-century commerce.[51] He literally tries to hide the money. James Harlowe's attempt to hide his own financial interest behind his hostility to Lovelace works only a little more convincingly, but then James belongs to the class of people who needed to develop those strategies.[52] Belford does not, and thus the ridiculousness of his attempt. Yet Clarissa not only declines to participate in this absurd charade of money from nowhere, she interprets (accurately or not) a mystification even behind this mystification:

> You are very kind to me, sir, said she, and very favourable in your opinion of me. But I hope that I cannot now be easily put out of my present course. My declining health will more and more confirm me in it. Those who arrested and confined me, no doubt thought they had fallen upon the ready method to distress me so as to bring me into all their measures. But I presume to hope that I have a mind that cannot be debased, in *essential instances,* by *temporary calamities:* little do those poor wretches know of the force of innate principles, forgive my own *implied* vanity was her word, who imagine that a prison, or penury, or want, can bring a right turned mind to be guilty of a wilful baseness, in order to avoid such *short-lived evils.* (1103)

Thus Clarissa here sees the true test of her virtue as whether she will endure short-lived evils (such as lack of food) in order to avoid transforming rape into a sexual contract that could lead to other sexual contracts. The meaning of the act can only be constructed retrospectively, and Clarissa will maintain her lack of prior volition in the face of death. At one point, in fact, Clarissa calls the rape a *theft,* which produces an interesting dual possibility. On the one hand, we could read this as Clarissa's recognition of and even complicity with the commodification of her virginity. On the other hand, since rape is generally not understood as theft, we can see Clarissa's naming it as such as performative: It becomes important to her to have the rape signified as theft because then she has not entered into a contract with Lovelace. Throughout the novel, she regrets only her willing disobedience of her parents, which she understands as violating a moral code whose terms become impossible to keep. In her traumatized extremity, Belford's crude attempt to mystify implied exchange does not differ to Clarissa from the whores' campaign to corner her into prostitution. Witnesses find her resistance breathtaking: "What magnanimity!" Belford declares. "No wonder a virtue so solidly based could baffle all thy arts . . . The women were extremely affected, Mrs. Lovick especially—who said whisperingly to Mrs. Smith, We have an angel, not a woman, with us, Mrs. Smith!" (1103). Thus even Belford sees the rejection of his own gift, which he knows he offers in innocence, as impressively virtuous. That she becomes "more of soul than of body" at this point and that she renounces the resources of this world evokes, of course, the rhetoric of Christian devotion. But in this context her rejection of life-supporting gifts also exposes the potential abjection of the commercial marketplace beneath the veneer of civilizing manners. Those present find her economic virtue heroic; those absent, including even Anna Howe, find it pointless, absurd, or manipulative.

Not long after the rape, Clarissa begins to prepare for her death. But for a narrative ostensibly so concerned with the next world, we get a lot of material details about this one. That Clarissa has apparently sold her clothes for less than their market value, for example, draws considerable comment. Richardson records in agonizing detail the gradual sale of her few remaining portables. Most strikingly, as she languishes before her coffin awaiting the embrace of Death, she does not neglect to write a long, complicated, and highly detailed will. First she insists that her survivors keep her body from further violation. For anyone who thinks this paranoid or prudish, she recalls that Lovelace has already once violated her "dead" body; his later desire to cut out her heart confirms the reasonable basis of this anxiety for one seeking to escape abjection. Then she turns her grandfather's estate over to her father in a final attempt to restore the patriarchy that so failed her during her lifetime. While she made this offer many times while alive, in her will she creates the fantasy of her capacity to carry it out, writing herself into an imagined wholeness. Yet not only does she transfer the entire estate to him, but she also insists that he pay himself back out of it for her clothing allowance, even if this also means collecting the money in her escritoire. Even in death, she will tolerate debt to no one. Debt to her father at this point differs little from debt to any other man.

After consolidating her capital to bolster the incompetent patriarch, Clarissa turns to petty cash and objects. This section occupies most of the will and represents Clarissa's attempt to infuse these objects with sentimental rather than market value. It makes a fitting envoy from one who recently faced the abjection of exchange. She bequests family portraits and family plate to her two uncles; her books, musical instruments, watch, head-dresses, and ruffles to Dolly Hervey; a diamond ring and miniature of herself to William Morden; a ring to Mrs. Howe; her letters and her portrait to Anna Howe; her whole-length picture to Aunt Hervey, unless her mother should want it; books from her present lodgings to Mrs. Lovick; remaining clothes to Mrs. Norton; various gifts of cash to servants; and money to buy mourning rings to several friends. She does not forget a fund for the "sober and industrious poor," supported in part by the sale of her jewels (unless this money needs to go to her father to discharge her debts). Having escaped the most brutal marketplace that Richardson can imagine, Clarissa not only imagines herself with the property rights to settle any potentially outstanding debt but also includes heart-breaking explanations as to why each item belongs with each person. She tries to ensure that these objects, like the woman who owned them, escape conversion into their exchange value. But even when things must be liquidated, she outlines the destiny of their cash equivalents. She exhibits exemplary generosity toward her inferiors: She gives the good Mrs. Norton financial security, she lavishes cash gifts on servants who helped her along the way, and she gives detailed instructions for her Poor Fund. In her will, then, she positions herself as propertied and exercises appropriate civic humanist virtue even though the events of her life allow her no practical access to either her inheritance or these luxuries.

In *Clarissa*, the heroine resists the commodification of her effects as well as the commodification of her sexual labor. Her story explores the looming terror of abjection in the marketplace for those with no protective estates, inheritances, or family networks. This does not mean, however, that Richardson nostalgically longed for a more traditional order. We see little redemptive aristocratic wisdom or kindness that would suggest uncomplicated feudal nostalgia in this novel. Nor does Richardson's choice to place a woman at the center limit the narrative's effect to the construction of properly domestic bourgeois femininity. *Clarissa* indeed participates in the attempt to displace a specifically commercial form of abjection onto female bodies; it does not, however, simply scapegoat female participation in the marketplace as the wicked kind, as has been argued:[53] Solmes and Lovelace, after all, function as the narrative's most aggressive contractarians.

Instead, the heroine's resistance and death suggest that Richardson recognized, thought about, and dramatized the complications and potential crises of the emergent system in which he found himself.[54] As Nancy Armstrong suggests, Richardson in this novel imagines a new kind of subject. Clarissa after the rape

> lives day to day, sells off her few possessions whenever out of cash, moves to smaller rooms, takes elaborate pains to avoid incurring debt, and can still be thrown out into the street, thanks to the false claims of a former landlord. In short, until she is safely laid to rest in her fully paid-off coffin, her status as a respectable private citizen is always at the mercy of her creditors.

With Clarissa, Richardson thus "create[s] the spaces that would be occupied by modern men and women."[55] Armstrong's insight, however, leaves out the way that the prostitution plot suggests the gothic alienation haunting these spaces. While Richardson participated fully and successfully in the commercial marketplace, in *Clarissa* he creates an intriguing fantasy about the suicidal virtue of refusal. Through his virtuous heroine, Richardson explores what it might feel like (or perhaps what it *did* feel like) to have nothing left to exchange without destabilizing one's core sense of self.

Clarissa, after all, is a tragedy.[56] We cannot confine the narrative to nostalgia, radical resistance, or even compartmentalization because Clarissa's death does not categorically invalidate the new subjectivity that she refuses. Once cut off from her family estate, Clarissa simply cannot survive in the London commercial world without contracting some kind of debt. No one could. All the other women in the novel accept some degree of negotiated self-alienation as necessary for survival. Mrs. Harlowe, as much as she loves her daughter, subordinates maternal compassion to the authority of her husband and her son. Bella certainly does not share her sister's idealism. Anna Howe mocks her suitor, but nevertheless agrees to marry him. In fact, Clarissa's refusal or inability to distinguish between threatening and benign contracts borders on madness: While the prostitutes clearly want to exploit her by running up her debt, Belford has no such intention. What defines Clarissa's tragedy is Richardson's fundamental observation that in the eighteenth century's emergent capitalist economy, those who refuse contracts cannot survive. Everyone has to alienate *something*. Clarissa's quixotic heroism consists of her refusal to do so. Alienation may threaten abjection, but resistance can be fatal.

6

Tom Jones *and the "New Vice"*

> If any nice, delicate-minded reader should despise me for being so ready to yield my person merely to gratify my luxury, before they blame me, or any of my sex, for these condescensions, let them look upon mankind, examine how they came by their grandeur, and I shall not be thought to hazard too much in asserting, that the males will be found to be the worst prostitutes.
>
> Phebe Phillips, *The Woman of the Town; or, Authentic Memoirs of Phebe Phillips; Otherwise Maria Maitland; Well Known in the Vicinity of Covent Garden* (1799)

Most stories about prostitution from the eighteenth century explore predicaments facing women. I have also suggested, however, that not only would a wide range of readers have found some uncomfortable common ground with prostitute figures, but that gender did not consistently form an insurmountable barrier of difference in this process.[1] Even more than the female prostitute's androgyny as a "man-woman" or the general appeal to emergent forms of subjectivity in *Clarissa*, popular stories of "stallions," "fortune hunters," and "rogues" who rely on their sexuality for survival suggest masculine vulnerability to and exploitation of sexual commodification as well. As with their female counterparts, these male prostitutes also provoke anxieties over extreme possibilities of what the marketplace demands of those abandoned to it.

One of the most prominent eighteenth-century novels—Henry Fielding's *Tom Jones*—reaches its turning point with the prostitution of its hero, an aspect of this novel yet to be fully confronted. Tom's sexual adventures become progressively more damaging to his relationship with Sophia and his appeal as a character; his seduction by Lady Bellaston, however, has long stood out to readers as particularly disturbing. For Samuel Richardson, Tom's prostitution to Lady Bellaston marked the low point in the novel's general depravity: Why, he wondered, did Fielding make Tom "a common—What shall I call it?—And a Kept Fellow, the Lowest of all Fellows . . ?"[2] More forgiving, modern critics have tended to read Tom's prostitution as an unfortunate (or intriguing) aberration from his otherwise decent character, a desperate act by a fundamentally good-hearted young man at his circumstantial and moral nadir.[3] In this chapter, however, I will argue that if we take into account the full range of sexual contracts that *Tom Jones* explores as well as the popular narratives about male sexuality that the novel engages, we can instead see Tom's prostitution as central and even overdetermined. Tom's horrified recognition of his position as a "kept fellow" prompts his reform: Other potential horrors—incest, murder—follow but dissipate.[4] He hasn't really slept with his mother or murdered Mr. Fitzpatrick; he has, however, really served as Lady Bellaston's stallion. This affair produces the greatest crisis in Tom's adventures not because it involves illicit *sex*—which Tom had already engaged in—but because of the way it involves *money*, which has long seemed to suggest more disturbing possibilities about Tom's character. Unlike in his affairs with Molly and Mrs. Waters, Tom feels no attraction or warmth for the foul-breathed Lady Bellaston. He behaves in this affair less like a sexually adventurous boy and more like the midcentury female prostitute whose work produces self-estrangement rather than pleasure. In *Tom Jones*, as Sheridan Baker has pointed out, Fielding complicates literary stereotypes in ways that defy expectations: Bridget, for example, evokes the stock type of the "spinster," Jenny Jones, the whore, but each holds surprises.[5] Fielding, I will suggest, does something along these lines with Tom's character. The novel reaches its turning point with Tom's prostitution not as an aberration, but rather as the most explicit expression of a masculine "type"—rogue, stallion, fortune hunter—that the novel recalls, revises, and confronts as one too-near possibility of the predicament of the abandoned subject in the capitalist marketplace of goods and services.

Like *Roxana*, *Clarissa*, and popular prostitute biographies, *Tom Jones* demands that readers see the world, at least briefly, from the point of view of a person left to survive on talent alone. While we might not see *Tom Jones* quite as the "veiled autobiography" of the professional author in the marketplace that some critics have seen in *Roxana*, Fielding opens with a related version of this predicament: "An Author ought to consider himself," the first line reads, "not as a Gentleman who gives a private or eleemosynary Treat, but rather as one who keeps a public Ordinary, at which all Persons are welcome for their Money" (25). While the gentleman entertains for his own pleasure, the public ordinary must not only please his clients, but remain vulnerable to their "Right to censure, to abuse, and to d—m their Dinner without Controul" (25). These opening lines launch a series of reflections throughout the novel in which the narrator continually—even excessively—defends himself against this exposure brought by the necessity of seeking an income. As we have seen, women in eighteenth-century culture, like food servers and authors here, could be categorized by their provision of remunerated or eleemosynary pleasures. In the opening, however, Fielding places *himself* (or his narrator) in the position of the one who entertains for money, a position his hero later occupies as well. Just as Fielding, then, opens by exploring the differences between commercial and noncommercial writing and cooking, so throughout the novel he explores differences between remunerated and eleemosynary sex. He does so, however, in ways that suggest the author's own identification—and potentially that of the reader—with the position of the vendor rather than the client.

Once alerted to the opening distinction between remunerated and eleemosynary pleasures, we can see that the flow of money distinguishes the three affairs that organize the novel's plot: in the first, Tom compensates Molly and her family; in his second, he sleeps with a prostitute but no money changes hands; in his third, he receives payment from Lady Bellaston. While the narrator alerts the reader to the importance of these distinctions, Tom takes most of the novel to truly understand the ramifications of their difference. He initially believes that by having sex with Lady Bellaston he provides a gentleman's treat rather than the service of a public ordinary: This affair precipitates Tom's distress only when he recognizes in a moment of shocked disgust that he has been working, as he puts it, for "Wages" rather than "Benefits" (531). Thus while Tom may have explained Lady Bellaston's original seduction to himself as a challenge fit for a rakish gentleman raised in the elite environs of Paradise Hall, the identification of his fifty pounds (the legendary exorbitant fee of both Fanny Murray and Kitty Fisher, but also for a good "stallion"[6]) as "wages" brings the disconcerting recognition that he has become something else. He escapes Lady Bellaston's grasp by "impersonating" a fortune hunter, which immediately liberates him but, disconcertingly, also fools those whom he had hoped held his character in higher estimation. But while Tom may fail to recognize the full social meaning of his sexual behavior for much of the narrative, his similarities to stereotypical "rogues" and "stallions" evoke these connections for the reader. Throughout the novel, Fielding engages recent anxieties over London's "new vice," in which exoticized male bodies seduce for various kinds of "wages"; *Tom Jones* thus touches on the possibility of male descent from security to urban anonymity with nothing but the body's labor to sell. Like Clarissa, Tom's elite upbringing keeps him from giving much thought to (nonsexual) work when he runs out of money (and refuses to spend Sophia's). Unlike Richardson, however,

Fielding does not give full quarter to the comforting displacement of this predicament onto women. To conclude that the shock of sexual "wages" and the vulnerability of writing for the "public ordinary" point to the novel's feudal nostalgia or conservative ideology, however, would neglect the novel's ambivalence toward emerging forms of mobility. In its representation of urban hazards and unsavory ambitions, this novel explores an emergent crisis in social organization and personal identity, as Maaja Stewart has argued. Some strands of the plot, as James Thompson has shown, offer nostalgic comfort through thwarted attempts at social mobility: Black George fails to convert stolen money into land and remains unforgiven; Allworthy's bank note travels through different hands, but returns to its original owner intact.[7] But in the novel's *prostitution* plots, by contrast, characters can also find liberation from oppressive situations through contractarian possibilities: Mrs. Fitzpatrick escapes imprisonment and spousal abuse through cosmopolitan keeping; Molly Seagrim, raised in humble circumstances, receives from Tom "the greatest Share" (640) of the five hundred pounds her father stole and will probably marry Partridge; Jenny Jones, who begins as a servant in Partridge's household, receives sixty pounds from Allworthy and marries Parson Supple, on whom Western "hath bestowed a considerable Living" (640). While these closing arrangements resemble patronage more than free market triumphs, none of these women would have improved their situations had they chosen the path of virtue and refused to consider the market value of their sexuality. Further, while the city harbors Lady Bellaston, it also supports the modest business of Mrs. Miller and provides opportunities for Tom, Sophia, and Partridge to escape the patriarchal limits and flawed justice of Somersetshire.[8] The upward mobility of certain women, Allworthy's blindness, and the happiness that becomes possible only by escaping him must complicate any assumption that this novel puts its full confidence in traditional patriarchal or civic humanist values. While female prostitution brings otherwise unavailable opportunities, however, *Tom's* prostitution precipitates a crisis: It suggests, but then rather quickly averts, the possibility that gender will ultimately fail to secure male bodies from marketplace abjection.

In the end, in spite of the many traditional values espoused by admirable characters in this novel, the imagined possibility that ensures male integrity in the face of heartless commerce emerges as maternal, erotic, and contractual rather than patriarchal or nostalgic. Allworthy lacks the capacity to mete out justice in a satisfying way; his simplistic moral paradigms fail in a commercial culture that depends on the ability to read individual motivations and desires. The disempowered women surrounding him prove far

more skilled at this, fortunately for Tom. The most important and enduring contract in the novel, revealed at the end, turns out to be the one between Bridget and Jenny Jones. Tom's history begins with a secret sexual
contract between a "spinster" and a "whore" in which one woman sells her
virtue to the other—a prostitution contract of sorts, but without sexual exchange. Patriarchal authority fails to ensure the correspondence between
personal and financial credit, and individual male figures—Black George,
Blifil—do their best to exploit this blindness. Allworthy may adopt Tom, but
he cannot recognize his identity (either natal or moral) without the help of
the whore Jenny Jones. The comic outcome depends on an originating,
fragile prostitution contract in which one woman becomes a prostitute without exchanging sex and the other keeps her illegitimate baby under her
brother's nose. Fielding allows his hero to be rescued from serving at the
public ordinary, but skillful contractarian women, rather than the feudal father figure, must bring this about.

Fielding, then, offers a highly ambivalent narrative about gender, casting
commercial self-division and contractarianism as essentially feminine capacities embodied in their most extreme form by prostitution. These capacities,
however, emerge as necessary for justice in the modern world. *Tom Jones* entertains the fantasy that certain men will remain uncompromised by the necessity to negotiate of the boundaries of their identity in this way, but at the
same time demonstrates otherwise.

The "New Vice"

Tom's personal crisis comes to a head with the shocked recognition that
he has been working for "wages" rather than "benefits"; Fielding, however,
foreshadows this moment by filling the novel with related forms of male sexual exchange: Captain Blifil seduces Bridget for her fortune; Square and
Thwackum try for the same prize; Mr. Fitzpatrick attracts women so skill-
fully that he gains the choice between aunt and niece; Nightingale almost
agrees to marry for an estate. While not all of these examples constitute the
outright prostitution of Tom's arrangement, they suggest that Tom's sexual
contract with Lady Bellaston takes place in a broader context of heterosexual exchanges in which male bodies and female bodies can both leverage their
attractions for profit.[9] In *Tom Jones*, we see sinister, farcical, and sympathetic
versions of stallionhood alongside other forms of desire and desperation. In
this context, Tom to his horror discovers that neither his gender nor his privileged upbringing can protect his sexuality, and thus the most intimate aspect
of his identity, from commodification.

But Tom's prostitution occurs in an even broader context. When Fielding published *Tom Jones*, a new vice was, apparently, tearing away at the social fabric of the British nation. The anonymous *Satan's Harvest Home* (1749) excoriates the plague of female prostitution in the city, but truly

> what amazes and fills all Mankind with Wonder and Surprize, is a *new Vice* started upon us, introduced and boldly led up by Women of the first Figure and Fortune as well as Fashion, worthy the Imitation of the whole Sex. These, *vice versa*, have inverted the Order of Things, turn'd the Tables upon Men, and very fairly begun openly to *Keep their Fellows:* For Ladies during the Bands of Wedlock, as well as in a State of Widowhood, to call in private *Aid, Assistance* and *Comfort*, is an Immunity they've enjoy'd time immemorial: But for the *Fair*, and such as even profess Spinsterhood, to keep Men in private Lodgings, and visit them publickly in their Equipages, are Privileges unknown to our Ancestors.[10]

Wisely not depending on the "fine Speeches and fair Promises of a capricious Woman, who perhaps in two or three Weeks after Enjoyment, or upon sight of a new Face, may take it into her head to turn a poor deluded Fellow *upon the Common*,"[11] these men have taken to demanding a settlement "before they'll venture to part with one *Inch* of their *Virtue*." This vice does not belong to the elite alone: Tradesmen's wives have learned from their betters and begun to take full advantage of apprentices.

The "new vice" was of course not new: In 1706 John Dunton noted that "the Keeping lady" had become "Rampant."[12] But while complaints and gossip about male prostitution crop up in all periods, they seem to gather momentum in the same period that attracted so much interest in female prostitution as well. In his *History of . . . Eliz. Mann*, the author informs us that London brothels procure sexual services for women as well as men with money to spend.[13] Another writer eavesdrops on a meeting of "the *Hiberian* Society of Fortune-Hunters," which resembles the "Whore's Club" in its mock-officiousness; the author insinuates that ladies of quality require so much pin money because they need to pay off their stallions.[14] *The Adulteress* "reveals" that wealthy ladies go to the theater specifically to shop for actors, most of whom make better money in bedrooms than they do on stage.[15] The poem tells the story of Widow C— "Who kill'd one Spouse, and wed the rival Swain; / Him she exhuasted—and each strong-back'd Fool / Is paid as Labourers are for work and tool. / Two sturdy Stallions now she keeps in pay, / And feeds the Rogues with dainties ev'ry day."[16] Successful prostitutes reportedly kept men to compensate for unexciting clients: Mary Parrimore supported an Irish stallion; the prostitute "Cornelia" earned so much money that she kept an entire stable.[17] The prostitute Fanny Davies recognized the demand for this service and sometime worked in disguise as a "stallion" herself.

Popular stories about male heterosexual prostitution take two related forms. As common "stallions," they differ little from their female counterparts in hiring out sexual services. According to Thomas Brown, Mother Creswell provided services for both sexes in her bawdy house.[18] The anonymous *View of London and Westminster* tells the story of Harry Hardset who was "taken into Service and Whole Pay" by an apparently pious lady whose husband discovered them only when the lady tried to slip Harry "twenty *Golden-Proofs* of her Bounty and Deservings" in church, but accidentally dropped the coins. With resonant force, the sound of money falling exposes them.[19] A writer at the end of the century tells the story of Mrs. M—ck—y, living in the East Indies with her husband, who enjoyed sexual adventures with Captain F, "so long as she had money to pay his price for them."[20] But Captain F raised his price, and she sought cheaper lovers. She sends fifty pounds to P— (the same amount that Lady Bellaston sends to Tom), who "was much too handsome a fellow not to know the value of his person." In *Memoirs of the Seraglio of the Bashaw of Merryland*, a butler named William served the ladies neglected by their keeper. This was not William's first such job: In London two ladies had helped set him up in a perfume shop so they could visit him and pay him without attracting suspicion.[21] The late-century rake George Hanger recommended that prostitutes hire handsome footmen for their private entertainment, in emulation of the fine ladies.[22]

Fortune hunters constitute a more dangerous version of the ordinary stallion. These men, unlike stallions, often intend to marry, taking advantage of their gendered ability to take full possession of a woman's property. In one story a fortune hunter manages to marry seven wealthy women for their fortunes, although in the end the women agree to live with him "in the same house in perfect harmony."[23] In John Oakman's 1765 novel, which explicitly echoes *Tom Jones*, the handsome Irishman Benjamin Brass sets out for London to make his fortune through women as so many of his countrymen, he believes, have done before him.[24] Confident of his own beauty, he seduces a richly dressed woman in the hope of a profitable marriage. She turns out to be a prostitute, however, and sneaks out of the bagnio in the morning, leaving him with the bill and empty pockets. The bawd demands payment or sexual service from him; when he cannot manage either, a fistfight ensues. Later he pursues "Sophia Wealthy," who turns out to be running a different kind of scam: She agrees to marry him, but then returns to whoring in Covent Garden and leaves him surrounded by her creditors.

Anxiety about male prostitution was not confined to comic or libertine writing: More serious narratives describe the resulting female misery and impoverishment.[25] In his sermon before the Societies for the Reformation of Manners, William Bisset complains that actors "are (as all the World knows) both *Stallions* and *Hectors* by their calling."[26] Another reformer warns women against fortune hunters, but also attacks any marriage formed through financial interest. For certain suitors,

> All their care and industry is to gain Wealth, for which they study, ride, run, and trudge about, toil, work and care, venture Limbs, Life, and all, for Money. And if you have but this itching Humour upon you, and marry *meerly* for Money, the Lord have Mercy upon you; for it is neither *Match nor Marriage, but Wh — dom all thy Life long.*[27]

In his conduct book for women, James Bland warns that such men generally use their wives' inheritance to support their whores. Women should avoid such men and not hope to reform them because "they that dwell in Aethiopia, quickly change their Skins into a black Colour; but no Aethiopian changes his Skin white, by living in another Climate."[28]

As the above example suggests, stallions, like their female counterparts, were often imagined as exotic—frequently Irish, but also Scottish, African, and even Polynesian. Satiric poems in the wake of Captain Cook's famous voyages invite young men from the Pacific Islands to come to London where they can make money serving women:

> Come, southern youths! these happy seats explore,
> New pleasures wait you on Britannia's shore. . . .
> The genial toil, no barren labour, prove,
> For kindness crowns, and wealth attends your love . . .
> Your kind invention shall our taste befriend,
> And new-born springs to jaded pleasure lend.[29]

British ladies need to import these exotic men because men of their own class have become effeminate macaronies, failing to satisfy. The poem notes in passing another prominent stereotype of the male sexual opportunists: "careful parents tall Hibernian fear."[30] *Nocturnal Revels*, the elaborate guide to "nunneries" of the age, also suggests that men from the North should attract as much suspicion as men from the South: When "Lady Loveit" visits a brothel to "be well mounted," the bawd offers her the choice of "Captain O'Thunder" or "Sawney Rawbone,"[31] charging the legendarily standard fee of fifty guineas. (Lady Loveit in this volume visits an elite house; another bawd reportedly made arrangements for the wives of citizens at presumably more reasonable prices.[32]) *Nocturnal Revels* also contributes to suspicions that Julius Soubise, a former slave educated by the Duchess of Queensbury, paid his sponsor back by serving as her stallion.[33] Wealthy women in general, according to satirists, were turning to their servants, black and white, out of sexual frustration with the inadequacy of aristocratic men:

> Behold her Footmen, what a brawny crew!
> Pamper'd to do what Nobles cannot do.
> Their liv'ries, how superb! themselves how trim!
> As if lew'd Venus had fram'd ev'ry limb:
> They're not intended now for menial use,
> As cleaning plate, or knives, or blacking shoes;
> When they are hired, whether white or black,
> The Mistress takes them by the breadth of back;
> For search this City round, and round about,
> You'll find no class so handsome, or so stout:
> It is a maxim in which Dames are clear,
> A strapping Footman to a tiny Peer.[34]

Michael McKeon has argued that this association between elite men and effeminacy—and thus sodomy—became widespread in the eighteenth century and contributed to the modern construction of gender, for the bourgeois male could thus claim the more respectable heterosexual identity.[35] But as we can see, the figure of the effeminate peer also contrasts with the potent laboring-class or immigrant, exoticized male, uprooted by an expanding commercial empire. A variety of writers represent the predicaments of such young men as the choice between sexual labor and unwilling dislocation in an expanding empire:

> *Young men* for *stallions* may be hir'd away,
> And *melt their marrow* for some *widow's* pay;—
> Others are *kidnapp'd*—Men must now be had,
> And for the *Indies* you're a likely lad.[36]

Tom faces a similar choice. Ejected from Paradise Hall, Tom thinks about going to sea before he decides to stay and fight a domestic rebellion. Eventually, though, he melts his marrow. Choosing between the two "contact zones," Tom seeks his fortune with the women of Great Britain.

Matchless Rogues and Priceless Whores: Tom Jones

The rootless male with nothing to sell but his sexual labor appears in several literary genres before *Tom Jones*. He becomes almost a stock comic figure in Restoration drama: In Aphra Behn's *Lucky Chance*, the impoverished Gayman accepts a bag of gold from a mysterious female admirer and dutifully provides sexual services in return;[37] in George Farquhar's *Love and a Bottle*, Lyric provides sexual services to his landlady in lieu of rent. Even John Gay's MacHeath in *The Beggar's Opera* draws on this type as an outlaw version of the Irish fortune hunter. Yet Fielding draws more directly on the rogue narrative tradition. Like so many of the stallions that outraged and intrigued satirists in the eighteenth century, Richard Head and Francis Kirkman's English rogue becomes rootless as the result of colonial violence, coming to England with his mother after his father's death in the Ulster rebellion.[38] Later in his travels, he comes into close and frequent contact with people from nearly every known nationality in the world, amalgamating his own identity into a composite form of exoticism. These rogues and stallions thus commonly occupy an exoticized, marginal, or laboring-class position: They are servants, footmen, and valets; they are Irish, Scottish, Polynesian, African, or "non-English" in some other way (or they impersonate such an identity); they are often bastards; they are displaced, dispossessed, homeless, and/or nomadic. Particularly in their incarnation as fortune hunters, they not only pose a profound threat to property relations but also represent changing social relations that permit such mobility. As exoticized creatures, they suggest the extent to which global commerce has permeated daily life in the metropolis. As ordinary stallions, however, they suggest that eighteenth-century commercial society could not entirely displace onto women the possibility of commodifying (what it defined as) the most intimate human property.

A brief look at one rogue narrative suggests the ways this form may have shaped *Tom Jones* and the expectations of its readers. Tom Merryman of the anonymous *Matchless Rogue* (1725) was born in Newgate, the bastard son of a prostitute named Joan Merryman.[39] Raised by the parish, Tom is adopted not by a virtuous landowner but by a "Trader several years in the *West-Indies*, *Turkey*, and the *Mediterranean*" who had "amassed much Treasure; but having no Children that he publickly owned, he made diligent Inquiry after *Tom*" (2). He provides for Tom, pays off all his charges at the parish, and "cloathed him in very genteel Apparel" (3). As with Allworthy, the merchant's generosity leads to rumors that he fathered Tom; in Merryman's case, a "Similaritude of Features" (3) further suggests this possibility. In the hopes that Tom will follow a good trade, the merchant binds him as an apprentice to a mercer. The merchant settles three thousand pounds on Tom to enable him to establish himself and leaves for the East Indies, never to return.

Like Fielding, the anonymous author of this narrative organizes the rogue's story around his sexual escapades. Tom Merryman attracts the affection of his master's daughter, whom he seduces after a masquerade on the promise of marriage. Tom soon, however, grows bored and cannot resist the advances of the Countess of — when she buys a piece of rich brocade and insists that Tom deliver it himself: "I know not whether he was a good Horseman," the narrator reports, "but I can affirm, he was well paid for *Riding*, having received an hundred Guineas for that Morning's *Exercise*" (8). After this experience, Tom refuses to marry the mercer's daughter even when the father offers to settle five thousand pounds on them. Meanwhile, Tom "indulged himself in all the Pleasures and Gaieties that he could devise; nor did he want Money to support his Extravagance, being constantly supplied by the Countess, whose Embraces he began to nauseate, but was obliged to dissemble his Uneasiness" (9). Tom becomes both objectified and exhausted by the sexual demands he must meet to support his lifestyle, a feeling he expresses in financial terms:

> If I continue this Course of Life, I shall quickly (as her Ladyship observes) become a Bankrupt; for their Bills are so large, and they draw upon me so frequently, that I must be obliged to stop Payment, not being able to answer their exorbitant Demand. (16)

While Tom Jones ends his philandering career when he recognizes that he has become the kept man of a woman of fashion, Tom Merryman begins his descent into roguery with such an arrangement. Tom Jones works his way up the social ladder from the laboring daughter of a gamekeeper to a fairly successful prostitute to a fine lady; Tom Merryman, by contrast, begins with the fine lady but sinks lower and lower, intriguing with a goldsmith's wife, a baker's daughter, and finally marrying a "common whore," with whom he finally seems to find happiness until he is caught stealing and hanged. In spite of the generosity of a wealthy and benevolent father figure, then, Tom Merryman ultimately, as the narrator points out, manifests his maternal inheritance of "*Theft* and *Whoredom*" (85).

The Matchless Rogue, however, does not represent its hero as entirely unsympathetic: Tom Merryman suffers more from a combination of weakness of will and natal destiny than from viciousness. The narrator blames his destruction on the boarding-school education that the merchant provides (Allworthy, by contrast, keeps his adopted son home), describing Tom as attractive and likeable; he was "very diligent in obliging his Master's Customers; and by his free and easy Deportment, gained the Love of the Family, and the Good will of all the Neighbours" (4). Despite his range of sexual adventures, he eventually falls in love with a woman who moves him with the (familiar) story of her life: Raised by a loving family, her mother tragically died and her father remarried, leaving her with no inheritance. She became an apprentice to a London milliner, but had to deliver goods to the home of one of her clients, where he slipped a sedative into her tea and raped her. She saw no choice but to become his kept mistress, and then later a common whore when he abandoned her and a bawd redeemed her from debtor's prison. Tom gallantly defends his wife against zealous reformers who try to arrest her for her past.

The resemblance of Tom Jones to rogues like Tom Merryman from the century's popular culture, while implicitly acknowledged by earlier work on Fielding's picaresque influences, has been overlooked by recent studies of sexuality in this novel, which tend instead to characterize Tom as a new version of the Restoration rake.[40] Tiffany Potter, for example, argues that Fielding invents a gentler version of Restoration libertinism through Tom's good heart and domestic values.[41] Similarly, Peter Carlton contends that Fielding creates a compromise in his hero between sexy cavalier masculinity and Protestant virtue.[42] Without a doubt, Fielding often raises the possibility of Tom's rakishness: Tom certainly understands his own sexuality this way and explicitly defines himself against Rochester at the novel's end. But like Tom Merryman, Tom Jones was also born to be hanged: His illegitimacy and "animal spirits" threaten the same downward mobility; he falls from the grace of an adoptive father's protection, manifesting the traits of his presumably prostituted mother. Like his namesake, Tom Jones struggles between his roguish maternal inheritance and adoptive paternal guidance. The former ultimately proves just as important for this survival as the latter.

Tom Jones's most important distinction from a Restoration or cavalier rake, however, is not good-heartedness or Christianity but the ambiguity of his class position. This, along with Tom's own failure fully to account for his position, becomes more visible in the context of the rogue narrative. Indeed, while Tom often understands his affairs as the elite misbehavior of a rake, other characters read them more ominously as the social disruption of a common rogue. The end of the novel reveals that Tom's veins run with Allworthy blood; however, until the last few pages most of the characters understand his identity as the equivalent to that of Tom Merryman: the son of a whore generously adopted into a wealthy man's house. In Restoration drama, the widely acknowledged origin of Tom's supposed libertine masculinity, the rake by contrast always clearly and unambiguously belongs to the upper class, even if he runs out of money. In the opening of George Etherege's *The Man of Mode*, the rake Dorimant and his friend Medley instruct the shoemaker not to imitate the errors of his betters, for drinking and whoring have a different meaning for men in different stations. Thus when Blifil reports on Tom's inebriation during Allworthy's illness and when he exposes him in the bushes with Molly, he suggests to Allworthy that Tom has revealed his roguish maternal origins rather than developed the genteel manipulations of the rake.

Blifil underscores this point by reminding Tom that (like most rogues but few rakes) his mother was a whore. This insistence on Tom's bastardy, which the closing revelations do not alter, provokes the fistfight with Blifil that contributes to Tom's expulsion. Rakes, by contrast, battle in appointed duels rather than spontaneously with their fists.

Not only does Tom's presumed birth suggest his dangerous potential to descend to roguery, but so do his sexual encounters. Tom never rakishly strategizes a conquest; like the rogue, he tends to blunder into sexual opportunities. Jill Campbell has shown how Tom's sexual passivity contributes to the gender fluidity in this novel; sexual passivity, however, is also a common characteristic of rogues (who also can share this gender ambiguity and who often, like Tom, prove unusually attractive to women).[43] In Restoration plays, rakes attempt to subvert power or impress their friends through sexual conquests; they express their contempt for men of business by seducing their wives. These rakes play out their stories in the parlors, parks, and malls of London; the arrival of a new heiress sends waves of gossip from one end of town to the other. But no self-respecting rake would look twice at a woman like Molly, whose filth and poverty Fielding describes in vivid detail, nor would a fashionable rake have sex in a field with a woman who reeks of the day's labor. No rake would bother with the middle-aged, unattractive, and bedraggled Mrs. Waters. What would be the point? What rival would be humiliated? The rake would not even take interest in the powerful but superannuated Lady Bellaston: Mirabell in William Congreve's *The Way of the World*, after all, sends his *servant* to court Lady Wishfort when he cannot convincingly do it himself. Yet all three ladies would have been typical lovers for rogues like Meriton Latroon or Tom Merryman.

Tom's association with rogue sexuality in part accounts for the otherwise extreme reactions of Squire Western and Squire Allworthy to his interest in Sophia. Rakes often make appropriate husbands in spite of their philandering, but a rogue's interest could only destroy an heiress. With the help of Blifil, the two patriarchs rashly conclude that Tom poses a sexual threat to their authority and their property. Fielding balances the shadiness of the rogue figure with Tom's extreme benevolence, which he makes clear to the reader but which these oblivious patriarchs fail to discern.[44] With endearing innocence produced in part by the mixed message of his upbringing, however, Tom fails fully to recognize the potentially nefarious meaning of his desire. Blifil foments anxieties over Tom's sexuality and its potential for social subversion: not only does Tom recklessly make love to Molly in a field, but, in the fears of Squire Western and the insinuations of Blifil, he thus threatens to seduce Sophia and make a claim on her fortune. Readers know that Tom's benevolence would prevent this; nevertheless, Tom's illegitimacy and his resemblance to the rogue figure suggest that he may be tempted to use his abundant charm for profit and social mobility—a suspicion that the affair with Lady Bellaston turns into crisis by confirming.

Understanding Tom as a version of the rogue rather than as a version of the rake offers a different way of reading the meaning of Tom's sexuality for the novel. As has been widely recognized, Tom's escapades structure the narrative into three parts (country, road, city) defined by three different women (Molly, Jenny Jones/Mrs. Waters, Lady Bellaston). The novel's structure also, however, maps out three roguish sexual permutations, each with its own importance: paying for sex, uncommodified sex with a whore, and getting paid for sex. In the first affair, Fielding reveals a commercial economy operating in the midst of Squire Allworthy's quasi-feudal estate in ways unbeknownst to Allworthy and initially to Tom as well. Allworthy's ignorance of this economy suggests the inadequacy of his perspective and leaves him vulnerable to manipulation; Tom, however, because of his own status ambiguity moves through a broader spectrum of Somersetshire society. Tom's seduction by a woman "in a Shift that was somewhat of the coarsest and none of the cleanest, bedewed likewise with some odoriferous Effluvia, the Produce of the Day's Labour, with a Pitchfork in her Hand" (168) recalls Tom's own presumed laboring-class birth. In this relationship, Tom hovers between the status of a lover of similar low birth who fits in with the Seagrim family and a privileged gentleman exploiting sexual opportunity with minimal obligation. Ultimately, however, the relationship transforms into a third possibility: Tom comes to see his affair with Molly as neither rural sport nor the implied privilege of elite masculinity, but rather as a contract that he can settle. Tom gives gold directly to Molly, but also takes the support of the entire family as his obligation when George, Molly's father, loses his position, which draws him further into commercial exchanges. In one stark example, Tom sells his Bible to support the Seagrims. Blifil has no trouble casting this in a bad light: Tom has not only demonstrated his lack of interest in religion, but he has treated a sacred book as a commodity. In a similar instance, Tom looks a gift-horse in the mouth when he sells this animal (a gift from Allworthy) to raise money for this family. With both the horse and the Bible, Tom must choose between honoring the semifeudal gift economy to which he does not fully belong and honoring an implied contract in which he must compensate Black George at least in part for assumed damages to Molly's value. He chooses to honor his contract and violate the older order, a choice that Fielding represents as respectable.

Tom, however, initially can't tell the difference between feudal noblesse oblige and payment for services. He understands his relationship with Black George as simply a friendship and his own offerings to George's family as a

gentleman's eleemosynary treat, although one demanded by his own per-
ceived responsibility for George's financial troubles as well as by Molly's sexual generosity. Tom offers to fulfill his gentlemanly obligation to his bastard
child and gallantly defends Molly against attacks in the graveyard. When
Tom catches Molly with Square, however, he realizes that he has been visiting a public ordinary rather than a private dinner, a recognition that liberates rather than disappoints him. Like her agricultural labor, the sexual labor
of a gamekeeper's daughter has a market value that can, in this narrative, find
reasonable accommodation. This affair ends, then, with mutual understanding rather than bitterness; Fielding, unlike Richardson, imagines a world in
which possessive and affective individualism do not necessarily conflict.
When Tom later meets Molly returning from her day's labor in the field,
then, his retirement with her to the thickest part of the grove has a different
meaning from his initial seduction. As a public ordinary rather than an
eleemosynary treat, Molly's embraces, Tom now recognizes, demand a limited obligation that from his perspective does not fatally conflict with his love
for Sophia. Blifil, however, takes full advantage of Tom's lack of restraint and
uses this incident to suggest Tom's sexual threat to Sophia because, as *The
Man of Mode* satirically confronts, drinking and whoring have a relatively benign meaning among gentleman but a subversive meaning for others.

   Unlike Tom though often paired with him—"'You may know him by the
company he keeps'" (79)—Molly's father Black George fully understands the
world of contract and seeks to exploit it. In a sense, he and his wife prostitute their daughter; Mrs. Seagrim, at least, explicitly agrees to tolerate her
daughter's sexual behavior when Molly gives her a share of the profit. Because he does not share Tom's sense of contractarian honor, George becomes
not only another deeply flawed paternal figure but also Tom's dark, more
dangerously roguish "other," absorbing the rogue's exotic alterity to define
Tom as a possibility closer to home. The two initially seem to have much in
common: Both commit minor property violations, and both become victims
to Blifil's exaggerations. They both fall from grace in Paradise Hall, beginning with comfortable positions in its semifeudal world but later forced to
seek a new kind of living in the metropolis; they both join the ranks of the
mobile, "masterless men." George's name, as John Allen Stevenson has
pointed out, recalls the famous Waltham Blacks, who would darken their skin
to avoid detection while hunting illegally at night.[45] These "Blacks," as E. P.
Thompson has shown, responded to new draconian laws about property
rights that severely limited the survival options of the lower classes.[46]
George's crimes in the agrarian world of Somersetshire, then, already suggest the breakdown of a traditional order even before he and Tom find their
different ways to London. George's color continues to mark him and associ-

ate him with the property transgressions of the "Blacks": When he reemerges at the end of the novel in London, Partridge recognizes him by his physical characteristics: "'he is a very remarkable Man, or to use a purer Phrase, he hath a most remarkable Beard, the largest and blackest I ever saw'" (538). Later Partridge confirms that the Squire's servant now dresses so well that "if it was not for his black Beard, you would hardly know him" (539). By contrast, Tom has "the most whitest [skin] that ever was seen" (134–135). Black George serves as Tom's "black" double; much later in this novel, Tom wraps himself in a black cloak and covers his face with a black mask to meet his "fairy queen" at the masque, recalling his long-standing association as a transgressive "black" and the latent threat of one in his position.

Allworthy expels Tom, however, on the suspicion raised by Blifil that Tom has been thinking about Sophia as "fair game" for "blacking" as well. Western describes Tom's interest in Sophia as "poaching": Any interest at all on his part, given the disparity of their fortunes, violates property relations. Like blacking, the stealing of an heiress became a capital crime in the eighteenth century; for Western, Tom "blackens" to the extent that he pursues Sophia. Fielding keeps Tom's "black" potential in the foreground by populating Somersetshire with a string of fortune hunters, most notoriously Blifil senior, but also Blifil junior and even Square and Thwackum, who court Bridget when she becomes a widow. Tom's bastardy, his presumed birth to a whore, his attraction to the filthy, laboring Molly, and his friendship with her "black" father, however, all associate Tom with the nomadic, exoticized males presumably responsible for the explosion of London's "new vice."

Tom had his first lesson in the difference between remunerated and eleemosynary treats with Molly; this affair, however, does not fully prepare him for the way that the cash nexus so profoundly shapes human relationships outside of Paradise Hall. The first moment he sets foot outside Allworthy's estate, Black George robs him. With his privileged upbringing Tom does not initially understand the consequences of being reduced to the cash in his pocket and the clothes on his back; he thus does not fully understand the inconsistent regard he encounters. Strangers judge Tom by his appearance as a way of assessing his capacity to pay: The soldiers love him when he buys a round of drinks; the landlady despises him when she takes him for an impoverished parson. After Northerton hits Tom over the head with a bottle, the physician refuses to continue treatment when the landlady disabuses him of the notion that he has a gentleman in his care. Partridge attaches himself to Tom out of the certainty that Allworthy will eventually reward him, a gesture that Tom takes as "Love for him, and Zeal for the Cause" (276), which he mistakes as the same as his own. Between the first inn and Upton, Tom and Partridge meet the Man of the Hill, whose story serves as an extreme alternative response to a world driven by money. Raised in the country but exposed to illicit enticements at Oxford and later in London, the Man succumbs to gambling, women, and theft. He cannot manage the temptations of the modern city and thus eventually sequesters himself in the woods, renouncing all commodities: He has no food in the house and greets Tom and Partridge "cloathed with the Skin of an Ass" (289), voluntarily reduced to a Robinson Crusoe subsistence economy. In the city without money, he warns, "a Man may be as easily starved in *Leadenhall* Market as in the Deserts of Arabia" (298). The Man experiences the full dangers of a cash economy, but responds absurdly by hiding out from them. While this scene reveals the ludicrousness of a total rejection of the market, it simultaneously serves as a warning that Tom does not absorb. He blames the Man's troubles on his poor choice of friends and consequent overgeneralization about human nature without yet fully grasping his own vulnerability.

In the midst of the anonymous world of travelers in which economic interest seems cynically to shape nearly all human relationships, Tom indulges in his only affair in which no money changes hands. While Molly greets Tom in her filthy work clothes and Lady Bellaston welcomes him in all her finery, Mrs. Waters first meets him wearing hardly anything at all, stripped of her money, jewels, and most of her clothes by Northerton. The landlady at the Upton Inn takes the half-naked Mrs. Waters for a prostitute and assumes that she and Tom have arrived for the purpose of illicit sex, which precipitates the epic battle. Illicit sex, of course, ultimately ensues, but—significantly—not prostitution. The seduction scene with Mrs. Water differs from Tom's other two seductions in that it offers an island of comic, improper but nonprofit desire in a sea of cash transactions. Mrs. Waters had lived as mistress to Captain Waters, but fallen victim to Northerton, who apparently seduced her to get her money. Yet with Tom, there is no financial motivation on either side; lust alone brings them together. Unlike in the rather elliptical descriptions of Tom's other two affairs, Fielding in this case lavishes considerable detail here on Tom's appetite and the couple's sexual fervor. In the midst of Tom's voracious consumption of three pounds of ox meat, Fielding shifts the point of view to that of Mrs. Waters, suggesting what a tender morsel Tom himself might be:

> Mr. Jones, of whose personal Accomplishments we have hitherto said very little, was in reality, one of the handsomest young Fellows in the World . . . his Face had a Delicacy in it almost inexpressible, and which might have given him an Air rather too effeminate, had it not been joined to a most masculine Person and Mein; which latter had as much in them of the Hercules, as the former had of the Adonis. He was besides active, genteel, gay

and good-humoured, and had a Flow of Animal Spirits, which enlivened every Conversation where he was present. (328)

Fielding reserves his full description of Tom's beauty for this scene, viewed through a prostitute's eyes. While in Somersetshire Tom unknowingly took advantage of the opportunity afforded by his privileged masculine position and in London he becomes the effeminate, overdressed stallion of Lady Bellaston, in this brief moment on the road he achieves the perfect balance between beauty so delicate that it borders on effeminacy but compensated by manly endowments. Unlike Lady Bellaston and Molly, Mrs. Waters makes no proprietary claim on Tom. Neither charging nor paying for this encounter, Mrs. Waters proves priceless in more ways than one: She helped bring him into the world, she provides a brief respite of nonprofit pleasure in a morass of commodification, and she will later restore his natal identity.

London sets the scene for the third and most scandalous sexual permutation, for here Tom takes the position Molly had inhabited in the first section as the compensated lover dressed beyond his or her station by a powerful patron. While no envious mob hurls mud at Tom's silk garments as they do at Molly's, each appears out of place in their new vestments. Tom does not seek to become a stallion, but by now it should be clear that his falling into this role constitutes not an inexplicable and unseemly aberration, but rather a crisis in the tensions that the novel has been building all along. Tom arrives with little money, an attractive, genteel appearance, and no training for paid employment.[47] In spite of his current shabbiness, the well-formed body beneath the clothes gains him admission to Mrs. Fitzpatrick's house. In the market for a new stallion, Lady Bellaston begins to think about Tom even before she meets him: "Then you have seen this terrible Man, Madam," she remarks to Mrs. Fitzpatrick, "pray is he so very fine a Figure as he is represented? For *Etoff* entertained me last Night almost two Hours with him. The Wench I believe is in Love with him by Reputation" (449). While Tom's beauty and gallantry overwhelm Mrs. Waters with desire, Lady Bellaston begins her calculated pursuit on the basis of secondary reports. Tom inhabits just the right position for a stallion: As Lady Bellaston knows, he has been brought up in privilege but now needs money. Thus rather than funding a man from the South Seas or engaging the services of Captain O'Thunder in a bordello, Lady Bellaston systematically seeks out this delicate object of so much female desire. When she arranges their assignation, however, she has her white stallion blacken by sending him a domino—the dark cloak and mask to be worn to the masquerade. In attending the masquerade—the eighteenth-century scene, as Terry Castle has shown, of social mixing, sensuality, and transgression[48]—Tom enters a new kind of poaching ground.

But while Tom may imagine that he follows Mr. Nightingale's instructions to "beat about for your own Game" (460), he has now become the hunted rather than the hunter. Lady Bellaston approaches him, although she lets him believe that she is Mrs. Fitzpatrick and listens to him confess his love for Sophia. Tom articulates the dilemma that Lady Bellaston has already observed: He can pursue Sophia only to her own detriment. Recognizing this, Tom concludes, "I would sacrifice every Thing to the Possession of my *Sophia*, but *Sophia* herself" (462). These "generous Sentiments made a strong Impression" on Lady Bellaston, who comes up with the most sympathetic response she can imagine:

> "She did not see his Pretensions to *Sophia* so much in the Light of Presumption, as of Imprudence. Young Fellows . . . can never have too aspiring Thoughts. I love Ambition in a young Man, and I would have you cultivate it as much as possible. Perhaps you may succeed with those who are infinitely superior in Fortune; nay, I am convinced there are Women—." (462)

Lady Bellaston stops herself, but perhaps out of self-interest rather than delicacy. Perhaps she was about to say something like: "I am convinced there are women among the finest ranks who would pay handsomely for your attention." Sex across class lines does not disrupt the social order under the appropriate circumstances. Tom desires Sophia imprudently, in Lady Bellaston's analysis, because Sophia can neither marry him nor would pay him for sex. Truly loving her, Tom also has no desire to jeopardize her future through a secret marriage. In this moment of sympathy that his true affection generates, then, Lady Bellaston wants to communicate to Tom what she sees as the reasonable and "prudent" alternative of sexual contracts of a shorter term. Given Tom's white beauty beneath his black mask, he could aim high.

For his part, Tom has no erotic interest in Lady Bellaston: "*Jones* had never less Inclination to an Amour than at present; but Gallantry to the Ladies was among his Principles of Honour; and he held it as much incumbent on his to accept a Challenge to Love, as if it had been a Challenge to Fight" (462). This moment has been widely taken to suggest Tom's commitment to a rakish code of honor; rakes, however, rarely submit to their own sexual estrangement by enduring unpleasant encounters. Tom acquiesces to Lady Bellaston's advances purely out of obligation—an obligation that he explains here as one of honor but later comes to recognize as something else. While each of Tom's affairs gets him in some kind of trouble, only following the affair with Lady Bellaston does Tom truly renounce his philandering. Lady Bellaston offers him his only experience of sexual obligation uncoupled from pleasure:

He knew the tacit Consideration upon which all her Favours were conferred; and as his Necessity obliged him to accept them, so his Honour, he
concluded, forced him to pay the Price. Thus therefore he resolved to do,
whatever Misery it cost him, and to devote himself to her, from that great
Principle of Justice, by which the Laws of some Countries oblige a Debtor
who is no otherwise capable of discharging his Debt, to become the Slave
of his Creditor. (468)

The meaning of "honor" has changed. At the initial seduction Tom describes
honor as the Cavalier obligation to fulfill any woman's request for sex; here,
however, honor has taken on a commercial contractarian meaning. Tom must
provide sex in exchange for money (and, he hopes, information about Sophia)
to fulfill the terms of his implicit contract with Lady Bellaston, however
much he despises it. Tom begins to think about trying to escape from this relationship, but he takes action only when he realizes that he has been providing commodified sexual labor. When Nightingale tells him about the
many other men on whom Lady Bellaston had "conferred Obligations of this
Kind," Tom "began to look on all the Favours he had received, *rather as Wages
than Benefits*, which depreciated not only her, but himself too in his own Con-
ceit, and put him quite out of Humour with both" (531, emphasis added).
Nightingale's information dissipates Tom's naïvely imagined explanation of
rakish obligation and forces him to recognize himself as a stallion instead.

Tom ends his philandering here not out of any renewed hope of marriage
to Sophia or acquisition of moral clarity, but because he realizes that his
arrangement has *not* been one of Cavalier honor. His gender, good humor,
and privileged upbringing have not, he recognizes with horror, protected
him from the commodification of his most private parts. He is not much like
a rake and not much different from a rogue. Nightingale's plan—to propose
marriage—works so well because with it Tom plays the role of the roguish
fortune hunter who uses his sexuality not for pleasure but for appropriation.
Several characters, such as Blifil, Aunt Western, Squire Western, and even
Allworthy had already suspected him of this strategy. In a way it works *too*
well: Sophia's willingness to take the evidence at face value suggests perhaps
that such suspicions had crossed her mind. The recognition on Tom's part
that he has served Lady Bellaston for wages rather than benefits, however, so
horrifies him that he not only immediately ends the affair but also never has
another one. Fielding includes offers from Mrs. Hunt and Mrs. Fitzpatrick
to demonstrate Tom's transformation, and Tom follows through with his reform by passionately throwing himself into Nancy Miller's cause.

It is tempting to conclude that Tom collects his rewards of love, marriage,
family, recovered masculinity, and an estate somehow as a result of this re-

form. For her part, Mrs. Miller does her best to help Tom out of gratitude for his rescue of her daughter, and Partridge stands by his friend through difficult times. Yet no one could possibly have saved him without crucial information revealed by Jenny Jones/Mrs. Waters. We might say that Providence brings these characters together or that the intrusive author/narrator calls attention to his authority through the strategic withholding of information,[49] but this still doesn't fully account for the significance of Jenny's rescue of Tom. If the hero's moral challenge lies in recovering traditional values, represented by either Allworthy or the authoritative narrator, from the mire of emergent market relations, then why does Tom's fate ultimately rest in the hands of a prostitute, the widely deployed figure for commercial encroachment on subjectivity? The virginal Sophia might be the goal, but she remains powerless to assist Tom. Jenny has no self-interested motive to reveal the truth to Allworthy. Tom's Allworthy blood may ultimately raise him above the clamor of commerce, but it takes the word of a whore to accomplish this.

Let us then turn briefly to the novel's representation of *female* prostitution as a point of comparison with the male kind that shadows the central character. In spite of the novel's endorsement, at least at one level, of the bourgeois companionate marriage, Fielding's depictions of women in *Tom Jones* draw less from reform narratives than from libertine ones. Few women in Somersetshire, it seems, can find happiness through sexual virtue. Even Sophia scandalously escapes from her father's house and undertakes a dangerous journey; on the road she is mistaken for the Pretender's reputedly Amazonian whore Jenny Cameron. Molly suffers at certain points for her relationship with Tom, but in the long run benefits. Bridget Allworthy and Jenny Jones in the end have no reason to regret their sexual choices, but their full characters and sexual identities remain veiled or misunderstood through most of the novel. We recognize the full importance of Jenny Jones only at the end; when we do, we can piece together a personal history enabled by, rather than compromised by, sexual contracts and urban possibilities of anonymous mobility. When Jenny (falsely) confesses to giving birth to Tom, Mr. Allworthy has harsh words for sexually active women:

> How base and mean must that Woman be, how void of that Dignity of Mind, and decent Pride, without which we are not worthy the Name of human Creatures, who can bear to level herself with the lowest Animal, and to sacrifice all that is great and noble in her, all her heavenly Part, to an Appetite which she hath in common with the vilest Branch of the Creation! (37)

Jenny might be a virgin at this point, for all we know. When she does become sexually active, however, she does not seem to sacrifice "all that is great and noble in her." She saves Tom twice in this novel: once by taking the blame for his birth and thus enabling his upbringing in Paradise Hall, and once again by refusing to be paid off by Blifil and Lawyer Dowling and instead revealing the truth to Allworthy. Jenny has no ulterior motive for making this revelation—in fact, she makes it at some personal risk, for in the course of identifying Tom's parentage she must also reveal her own role in the deception. At the very least, she must endure Allworthy's renewed condemnation, standing before him with no evidence outside of her word and no payoff except the hope of saving Tom and honoring his mother's wishes.

Contrary to Allworthy's declaration, then, becoming a prostitute does not, apparently, deprive Jenny Jones of her humanity. Not only does prostitution fail to dehumanize her, but sexual contracts liberate her from the stifling and even oppressive world of Somersetshire. Jenny worked as a servant for Partridge and his wife, but endured the torment of superior intelligence to her master and the vicious jealousy of his wife. Her plainness, poverty, and studiousness meant limited possibilities on the marriage market. Then one day Bridget Allworthy, attracted by Jenny's unusual intelligence, offers to buy her reputation: In Jenny's first act of prostitution, she sells her "virtue" without actually having sex.[50] Taking the blame for Tom destroys her remaining possibilities in Somersetshire; she could have accepted Bridget's offer only as her ticket out of misery.[51] The rest of the narrative offers only a few glimpses of her subsequent life, but overall she seems to have enjoyed moderate success and comfort through a series of men. As we see at Upton, she certainly endures her share of hardships. Nevertheless, she comes through them with full enthusiasm for the pleasures of the world and of the body: Prostitution does not prevent her from enjoying a night of uncommodified pleasure with Tom. Sexual commerce and the anonymity of the road liberate Jenny from Somersetshire's traditional patriarchy, and neither seems to alienate her from either enjoyment or sentiment.

But Jenny Jones is not the only lady in Somersetshire released by infamous commerce. Where, after all, would Bridget be without the ability to hire another woman to take the blame for her own pregnancy? The rogue narrative often suggests that the philandering hero gets his "animal spirits" from his whorish mother; similarly, Tom has, we come to realize, inherited his passionate nature from Bridget. Somersetshire offers few opportunities to such a woman for sexual expression; in London, however, she might have been in a position to hire a stallion. In the thicket of sexual opportunism that Fielding creates in *Tom Jones*, however, Bridget shares a moment of nonprofit passion with Summer—the moment that creates the novel's hero and that finds an echo in Tom's own affair with Jenny/Mrs. Waters. In both cases, an older, relatively unattractive woman has sex with an attractive young man and no money changes hands. These are the only two sexual encounters in the novel uncomplicated by immediate financial considerations: Square, Thwackum, and Blifil pursue Bridget for money; Blifil pursues Sophia for money; Molly seeks gold from her lovers; Tom earns wages from Lady Bellaston; Mr. Fitzpatrick marries and torments his wife for money, who in turn trades her virtue for escape; Northerton wants money from Mrs. Waters, who had relied on Captain Waters and various other men for her support; Mrs. Hunt offers her estate as her primary appeal; Nightingale must choose between Nancy and an heiress. Tom and Sophia may sincerely love each other, but the scandal of their initial attraction lies in its social and financial complications. For Bridget, the consequences of her affair render her situation precarious. As we learn early on, Bridget has no fortune of her own and thus depends on the good graces of her brother. Bridget, we are told, wished that she did not have to spend her life under his protection, but only at the end do we learn how dramatically she experienced this limit. The ability to purchase Jenny's virtue does not entirely liberate her, but it allows her to participate in raising her son without the fear of offending her brother or drawing the scorn of her community. It allows her to avoid choosing, in short, between her son's life and her own. As Jenny explains, Bridget could not imagine surviving the revelation of her sexual indiscretion; their arrangement thus allows her to avoid choosing between fatal ruin and abandoning Tom to his probable death, perhaps the more common solution to unwanted, unsupportable, and/or embarrassing babies.

Thus only at the end of the novel can we recognize how Tom's life, and thus the entire narrative, has been held together by a fragile sexual contract between a "spinster" and a "whore." This affective, maternal arrangement saves Tom from the most severe Mandevillian elements in the marketplace *and* the stark limits of patriarchal civic humanism, made flesh in Allworthy's combination of authority and insensitivity. Given Bridget's tremendous investment in her own reputation, this contract could potentially give Jenny considerable power over her patron: Jenny at any point could have exposed Bridget's sexuality. Yet Jenny takes a risk as well: although she may not have known about Allworthy's unrevealed intention to give her in "Marriage, together with a small Living, to a neighbouring Curate" (36), she sacrifices her security and opens herself up to the abuse of her neighbors and the uncertainty of the sexual marketplace. By her supposed sexual transgression, according to Allworthy, a woman is

> rendered infamous, and driven, like Lepers of old, out of Society; at least from the Society of all but wicked and reprobate Persons; for no others will associate with you . . . no Persons of Character will receive you into their

Houses. Thus you are often driven by Necessity itself into a State of Shame and Misery, which unavoidably ends in the Destruction of both Body and Soul. (37)

Jenny must have known, as Allworthy makes clear, that her acceptance of this contract with Bridget would effectively turn her into a prostitute. Hearing this speech through the keyhole could only confirm, one imagines, Bridget's resolve to keep Tom's natal identity misunderstood. And yet Jenny's later rescue of Tom and even the full context of the moment, only revealed at the end, prove Allworthy wrong. For her part, Bridget places her future in Jenny's hands in the hope of raising her own child. Initially, it seems that Tom owes his happiness to the generosity and good heart of his paternal namesake whose finger he gripped as an infant. Though flawed, Allworthy, we feel assured, like providence itself, will come to reward Tom's good nature. The end, however, suggests otherwise: Tom owes his life to a sexual contract between a spinster and a whore, each of whom sacrifice the security of the quasi-feudal world of Somersetshire for liberating alternative possibilities, for one baby, and for each other.

Perhaps surprisingly, then, we must conclude that the happy outcome of *Tom Jones* becomes possible only through women willing to recognize sexuality as an exchangeable commodity. Traditionally criticism has avoided this conclusion, blaming, sometimes by way of the novel's echoes of *Hamlet*, Tom's unhappy predicament on the sexual waywardness of his mother. This argument, however, makes limited sense, for Tom would not have existed had his mother not been sexually wayward. Further, as Eric Rothstein has demonstrated, Fielding's evocation of *Hamlet* "only serves to undermine any analogy between them."[52] For reasons Fielding never fully explains, Bridget refuses to marry Summer. Perhaps she saw him as a fortune hunter. Allworthy mentions to Bridget his observation that she might have "had some Liking to him," but Bridget, appearing to take this as an accusation of illicit sexual activity, expresses "the highest Disdain of [his] unkind Suspicion" (614). Perhaps had Summer lived, she would have married him upon discovering her pregnancy, as she later does with Blifil senior. Summer's death, however, prevents this possibility. Rather than vilifying Jenny as the agent of dispossession, then, the narrative instead reveals that, given Allworthy's view of sexually active women and Bridget's dependence on him, Jenny's agreement to protect Bridget's secret probably saves Tom's life and even allows Tom to enjoy some of the privileges of the Allworthy estate. Jenny behaves honorably by upholding her agreement with Bridget, breaking it only when revealing Tom's identity would better fulfill the spirit of her commitment to his mother.[53] Sexual contractarianism becomes necessary and advantageous for both Bridget and Jenny (and other women in Somersetshire): It allows them to circumvent the patriarchal order that not only limits their own possibilities but also would have demanded Tom's death or disappearance.

While the stories of many of the women in this novel thus in key ways resemble libertine narratives more closely than reformist ones, the reformist narrative is visible mainly in the story of the male protagonist: Born into comfort but abandoned by his family after a youthful sexual transgression, Tom seeks his fortune in the metropolis only to be plucked off the wagon by the rapacious Lady Bellaston and kept in disgraceful finery. Like the women in the *Histories of the Penitents*, Tom finds remunerated sex degrading and ultimately renounces it, but there is no Magdalen Hospital for stallions. Thus while filling the novel with women who escape intolerable situations through various forms of infamous commerce, *Tom Jones* confronts the more disturbing question (in a patriarchal context) of whether or not the most private parts of male identity might become commodified as well. Once he recognizes what he has become, Tom for the first time resists sexual opportunities: first Lady Bellaston, then Mrs. Hunt, and then Mrs. Fitzpatrick. But when he does so, the narrative's comic assurance teeters on the brink of collapse, as Tom faces the bleak consequences of an uncertain future. Like the heroines of reform narratives, he has nearly run out of money and fallen from the good graces of those who could help him. Just when Tom might have truly had to rethink his class and labor expectations, however, the ending revelations begin to unfold. The forces of coincidence combined with a contract made before his birth by two sexually suspicious women rescue Tom from economic necessity and find him a place in a comfortable family network.

In some ways, then, Fielding retains the gendered displacement apparent in Richardson: In a market economy only *women*, it seems, will regularly need to commodify their most precious parts. At the same time, Fielding's extraordinary coincidences at the end suggest some self-consciousness about the level of fantasy involved in this assurance. In scandalous satires, writers warn parents against a supposed influx of nomadic males seeking their fortunes through seduction. *Tom Jones*, however, like the prostitute narrative and the rogue narrative, tells the story at least in part from the other side, exploring the experience of displacement, dispossession, and self-commodification, suggesting, despite the hero's rescue, that gender alone cannot be trusted to maintain the body's boundary between eleemosynary treats and the public ordinary.

7

Risky Business in the
South Seas and Back

Here the sailors were suffered to make what purchases they
pleased; only women were prohibited by Capt. Cook's order, on
the severest penalties.—This created a general murmur among the
sea men, whose pleasure was centered on that kind of commerce,
in the new discovered islands wherever they went.

John Rickman, *Journal of Captain Cook's Last Voyage to the
Pacific Ocean* (1781)

Expelled from Paradise Hall, Tom Jones's first thoughts
turn to the sea, reminding us of the importance of global traffic as both an
alternative for the dispossessed and a crucial element in the eighteenth-century economy and imagination. Voyages to remote lands, like Tom's voyage
to London, commonly involved both commercial and sexual transactions.
Nowhere in eighteenth-century writing, however, do we find such interest
in the intersection of these two forms of contact than in literary representations of travel to the South Seas.[1] The British came to associate the South
Sea Islands with both disturbing and wondrous sexual possibilities, ranging
from free love liberated from intensified bourgeois constraints to a gauntlet
of mercenary seductresses who would strip a sailor down to his last shirt and
a ship down to its last nail (the currency that the sailors used to purchase sex
from Pacific women). Writers represented relations between sailors and island women as both exotic and familiar: George Robertson, who traveled
with Captain Wallis, heard that while some of the men had been trading for
food, "a new sort of trade took up most of their attention . . . but it might be
more properly called the old trade."[2] He was not sure, however, whether the
local women liked it or not: In one of his descriptions, a group of old men
line up some young girls in the makeshift marketplace for the inspection of

179

European sailors. The girls "seemd a little afraid, but soon after turnd better acqua[i]nted."[3] Just as the trade itself might be a new kind of thing or an old one, so the women themselves may nor may not have been disturbed by it.

Nearly all of the journals report on these relationships; most tend, however, toward more definitive judgments. Some resemble reformist arguments in seeing island women as tragically exploited; others represent only Mandevillian ambition. In this chapter, however, I want to look at an even more fundamental division in the ways that both travelers abroad and skeptics at home represented this sexual contact. In addition to disagreeing over the women's objectification, writers more fundamentally disagreed as to whether what was taking place could even be understood as "prostitution." Some writers describe transracial sexual contact as sensual, exoticized "free love"; for other writers, sailors engaged the same kind of infamous commerce abroad as they did in Drury Lane. This difference tends to function as an ideological marker for representing the voyages themselves as fundamentally disturbing or mutually beneficial.

As in many representations of contact zones, transracial sex in travel journals and satires functioned as a trope for contact in general, potentially suggesting a range of relationships: cooperation, pleasure, escape, conquest, scandal, danger, disease, pollution, and exploitation. Nearly all publications on the voyages try to make sense of sexual contact, invoking it out of voyeuristic fascination and for its figurative and resonant capacities. As yet uncolonized by Europeans, the South Sea Islands to some writers represented a different version of the innocence that midcentury reformers assigned to the English countryside: Voyagers described the cultures they encountered as unrepressed, unrestrained, and generally noncommercial. They lamented contact for the corruption it brought. The discovery of "prostitution" in these remote locations, however, could alternatively reveal the potential for commodification as latent in all human cultures.

This chapter examines the possibilities of both male and female South Sea Island bodies engaged in both commercial and noncommercial transracial sexual relations in British observations and imaginations. The enormously popular pantomime *Omai; or, A Trip round the World* (1785) serves as a counterpoint here: imagining a marriage between a Polynesian "prince" and a British lady, it suggests that miscegenation itself was not necessarily what the British found disturbing or controversial about these relationships. Satirists, by contrast, used rumors that Omai, who traveled back to London with Captain James Cook, learned to patronize brothels rather than read the Bible to suggest that British interest in the South Seas stemmed from commercial desires to proliferate luxury rather than the stated goals of scientific advancement. That South Sea island men would learn only whoring from contact with the British became a common satiric trope for European corruption, sometimes used to express skepticism toward imperialist ambitions.

Satirists at home spun out such scenarios from their imagination; travel writers, by contrast, assiduously recorded instances of contact between island women and British sailors, which the second half of this chapter will explore. In the journals, "free" (i.e., noncommercial) love with South Pacific women idealized the islands and the possibility of escape from bourgeois constraints; these often condescending depictions nevertheless express skepticism toward European superiority and the stated "anti-conquest" goals of the voyages.[4] Alternatively, representing these encounters as *prostitution*, as did Captain Cook when he wrote to correct John Hawkesworth's scandalous account, normalized not just foreign sexual practices but foreign economic ones as well. These narratives divide, then, on whether or not the commercial practices represented by prostitution lie outside of time and geography, and thus whether British travelers witnessed in these islands a clash between different versions of property and selfhood or the inevitable tensions between those who supply and those who demand in the (always already) global marketplace. For skeptics, the voyages spread infamous commerce; defenders, however, found accomplished merchants already working the beaches all over the world.

Representing Omai

Stories of British sailors trading a rusty nail for a night in paradise have become well known both within and outside of eighteenth-century studies. But while narratives of South Pacific women tend to describe hoards rather than individuals, many stories of male sexuality return to one man. On Captain Cook's return from his second voyage, he introduced to London society a South Pacific islander who came to be known as Omai. Unlike other displays of "noble savagery" brought to London for display, Omai not only survived but also fulfilled the hopes of his patrons beyond their expectations, becoming a celebrity in London fashionable society.[5] Accounts of his behavior, however, conflict. In some, Omai emerges as the most supremely delicate of all men of feeling, so sensitive that he refuses to eat fish once he sees the hook baited with a living worm. Joseph Banks, the elite amateur scientist who joined Cook on his first voyage, declared that Omai had "so much natural politeness I never saw in any Man;" Frances Burney wrote that Omai "appears in a new world like a man [who] had all his life studied the graces & attended with the un[re]mitting application & dilligence to form his manners."[6] Other reports, however, represent Omai as sexually transgressive and intrigued by London prostitutes, an apparent result of both his "savage" nature and rumors that his patrons brought him to whorehouses rather than churches. Representations of Omai's politeness place the voyages in a positive light by representing them as a meeting between weary overcivilization and fresh raw material, human and otherwise. With this depiction of Omai, writers helped engender the romantic appeal of the voyages and suggest their benefit to both societies. Satirists, however, cast the voyages as exploitative, frivolously elite, threatening to British identity, and part of an ever-expanding luxurious empire by repeating rumors that Omai instead spent his time in brothels. Here Omai, functioning as a representative of his culture, becomes not enlightened but infected with desires for infamous commerce.

Omai; or, A Trip round the World (1785), written by John O'Keefe, raises both possibilities, although the celebratory officially dominates. Rather than scandalizing miscegenation, the plot of *Omai* turns on transracial desire as the perfect outcome to Cook's ostensibly scientific yet covertly imperialist voyages.[7] In this play, Omai's claim to the Tahitian throne has been usurped by the "Enchantress" Oberea; Otoo, "a Descendant from the legal Kings, a Priest and a Magician" prays to his protector Towha to restore the rightful heir. Towha offers Omai a magical talisman, and Britannia descends with the maiden Londina, whom she offers as Omai's destined bride: "Still shall my sons, by *Cook*'s example taught, / The new-found world protect and humanize. / In soft alliance bound, this British maid / Be thine, and Love, a radiant throne shall fix / Firm as my rock, there sits bright *Liberty*."[8] Towha commands Omai to go to Britain, but also declares he will restore Omai to Tahiti's throne. On their way they take an elaborate trip around the world, providing ample opportunity for scene changes, elaborate costumes, dancing, and singing, evoking the different Pacific Islands described in the journals. Upon returning home they fall under the power of Oberea, but are rescued by the diplomatic Towha, who threatens to kill Oberea's lover. Oberea capitulates, and the South Sea Islands unite under Omai's rule, an event celebrated by a procession of various islanders "dressed characteristically, according to their several countries" (20). A British captain officially installs Omai as monarch by presenting "in sign of British love, this British sword" (23). This installation and wedding ends with the news of Captain Cook's death, the descent of a "Grand Painting" of the captain, and a celebration of his apotheosis.[9]

This play, which ran for fifty nights, expressed the late-century's intense Cook-worship in part through transracial erotic desire. Omai's marriage to "Londina" constitutes the most ideal symbolic outcome to the voyages; it figures British/Pacific Island relations through an erotic union in which the

British maiden embraces the "king" of the South Seas, who welcomes her influence. It also, however, functions as an anticonquest narrative: by pairing a Polynesian man with a British woman, *Omai* provides an image of global politics as domestication rather than as overt domination. In the play's narrative, Omai's installation depends on his marriage to Londina; they take place in the same ceremony. Londina, as Britannia declares, will "humanize" Omai and presumably all of the South Seas through her domestic femininity. This transracial marriage at the heart of this popular piece expresses not misogynistic contempt of female desire for exotic masculinity or shock over miscegenation, but rather the potential global power of British female domesticity.

Despite this play's notorious disregard for information brought back by travelers and embrace of fantasy, in a sense *Omai* follows Captain Cook's published journal closely, if not at the level of event then at the level of ideology. Cook's domestic version of heroism has been observed by many commentators—his humility, his unassuming country life, his simplicity, his devotion to his family, and most of all, his chastity.[10] In Cook's own *Voyage to the South Pole*, attention to domestic detail is remarkable. Cook begins and ends his *Voyage* not with grand philosophical reflections but with almost feminine details about care, cleanliness, and linen. For example, to preserve the health of his men,

> I took every necessary precaution by airing and drying the ship with fires made betwixt decks, smoking, &c. and by obliging the people to air their bedding, wash and dry their cloaths, whenever there was an opportunity. A neglect of these things causeth a disagreeable smell below, affects the air, and seldom fails to bring on sickness; but more especially in hot and wet weather.[11]

While Cook's private journals (especially of the third voyage) and other accounts indicate an authoritarian commander, in this passage we can nearly picture the captain airing out the linen himself. Stops on land include the same kind of domestic detail. At the Cape of Good Hope, "the crew of both ships were served every day with fresh beef or mutton, new baked bread, and as much greens as they could eat."[12] None of the other accounts include so much detail about the animals on board: their health, their survival on the various islands, whether they would eat local food. Cook concludes by declaring his legacy as caregiving rather than navigation, noting that while the existence of a Southern Continent may still remain controversial, he had succeeded in preserving the health of his men.[13] In Cook's highly praised *Voyage* as well as in *Omai*, domesticity becomes Britain's major export: Londina proves a happy alternative to the "enchantress" Oberea.[14] The marriage evokes not just London's infatuation with Omai but also Omai's presumed infatuation with London, his hope to "enlighten" the South Sea Islands, and his newly acquired capacity to do so. In the eyes of many British observers, however, this is precisely where Omai's patrons failed.

Rumors of Omai's sexual corruption rather than enlightenment spread rapidly, inevitably fueled by the reputations of his patrons Lord Sandwich and Joseph Banks. Upon settling in Huaneine after returning to the South Seas, Omai, according to William Ellis, "appears to have passed the remainder of his life in inglorious indolence or wanton crime."[15] John Rickman opined that Omai "out-acted the savage in every kind of sensuality"; when reporting on Omai's purchase of two boys from New Zealand, he inflects the transaction with an unmistakable hint of infamous commerce.[16] Even the pantomime *Omai*, despite its advocacy of domestic love between national representatives, includes a brothel scene with a different "Otaheitean Traveller" who had supposedly come to London with Omai. In a musical interlude, the traveler sings of going to London in a "big canoe," learning to "suck grog," powder his hair, and purchase the favors of a British lady. Within the play, the character Omai understands this song as a parody of himself and perhaps a reference to his own alleged misbehavior; he is "*driven to great Distress, and to the Exercise of his Magic Power*" (16). In the midst of the play's glorification of his domestic coupling with Londina, the performance reminds the audience of Omai's supposed alternative taste for commercial sex. Surely not by accident, this scene recalling London prostitution occurs in the Sandwich Islands, recently named after Omai's libertine patron.

By invoking the well-known rumors that Omai's patrons entertained him with visits to whorehouses, more explicit satires oppose commercial transracial sex to the imperialism-as-domesticity trope that both Omai and Cook's *Voyages* promoted. In *A Letter from Omai to the Right Honourable the Earl of *****, Late— Lord of the—* (1780), for example, "Omai" writes to thank Lord Sandwich for his London "education." Omai announces his conversion to Christianity, renouncing "the Devil and lusts of the flesh"; nevertheless, when a Methodist approaches him to talk of "Adam, and Eve, and original sin," he admits he had "never till then heard a single word of such things" and finds them unconvincing. He thanks Lord Sandwich for helping him pack up his weapons, "but in our hurry neither of us thought a syllable of putting a Bible on board."[17] When requesting that his patron send a justice of the peace to the South Seas, Omai explains that this justice should be sure to bring only one of his wives, as his own society (implicitly, unlike what he has seen in London society) does not allow polygamy (30). Through its irony, the *Letter* represents contact as a corrupting force: "Omai," for example, notes that many men of his island contracted venereal disease from their wives, "of whose courage I can say but little, who, when they went on board the European vessels, preferred their lives to their chastity, by meanly submitting to the impure embraces of the Christian crew, rather than suffer themselves to be thrown overboard, and plunged into inevitable destruction" (26). For the skeptical, then, this contact sounded more like rape. At the height of Cook's martyred popularity, this satirist appropriates the voice of Omai to offer ironic sympathy: "I cannot conclude my letter," Omai writes, "without saying how much real concern I feel for the unfortunate fate of poor Captain Cook, who was certainly very cruelly and inhumanly butchered, for nothing more than ordering his crew to fire on a banditti of naked savages, who seemed to look as if they had a right to the country in which he found them" (24).

Other satires object less explicitly to European violence but nevertheless suggest the peril of the voyages to domestic power relations when the islanders learn infamous commerce from the British. In the poem *Seventeen Hundred and Seventy-Seven; or, A Picture of the Manners and Character of the Age* (1777), supposedly written by "a Lady of Quality" but attributed to William Preston, Omai's brothel education and also his own potential (and that of his countrymen) to commodify sexual services hysterically points to the hazards of global commerce in general. Feminist critics have often observed how literary texts create parallels between imperialist and patriarchal domination.[18] This poem, however, posits commercial imperialism as the potential *demise* of patriarchy through its reduction of hierarchy to financial power. Written as a letter from a British lady to "Omiah," the narrator characterizes Omai's stay in London as a grand tour of whorehouses guided by the Earl of Sandwich.[19] The narrator celebrates the sensuality of British women through their appeal to Omai, declaring that while ladies "of old" loved their husbands and households, the modern woman delights in flirtation, seduction, and fine dressing. When women can no longer attract, they can buy their men with profits from earlier affairs and marriages. Yet the exotic ones satisfy the most: "Come then, ye sons of Nature, and restore/ The race of love, or pleasure is no more" (25), for British men remain deficient: "Rise and be MEN, ye Macaroni train!" (13), the women cry in despair. British women will start a "BANK OF LOVE," "And ev'ry woman FUND a proper man" (21) from the South Seas to compensate for the effeminacy of their husbands. According to this poem, the Cook voyages, with their importation of Omai and other exotic commodities, have begun a slippery slope of consumption that destabilizes the nation through enhanced female desire for the delights of global trade.

"Omiah: An Ode" (1786) pushes the analogy between global commerce and infamous commerce a step further, for here Omai not only visits the famous elite whorehouse of Charlotte Hayes but, according to the poet, should also consider going into business with her since he now understands the trade so well. The poet suggests that Hayes send Omai back to Tahiti where he can regale the women with stories of London entertainment.[20] Tempted by stories of rich men and their boxes of nails, the Tahitian women would follow Omai back to London where Hayes would put them to work: "For them might hermits quit the cell." In gratitude, Great Britain will "join Otaheite to the Crown, / And make OMI'—VICEROY!"[21] With the cooperation of several aristocrats mentioned along the way and even the approval of the king, Omai will become an international trafficker in women for the pleasure of British men and the profit of British whorehouses. Contact, then, instead of enlightening the benighted turns South Sea Island women into prostitutes and Omai into a sexual entrepreneur.

Of all the London bawds, the author of "Omiah" surely selected Charlotte Hayes because of a famous (reputed) performance in her brothel that used the analogy between global and infamous commerce to more ambiguous ends. *Nocturnal Revels*, an account of London brothels, reports that Hayes advertised an event in which "a dozen beautiful Nymphs, unsullied and untainted, and who breathe health and nature, will perform the celebrated rites of VENUS, as practised at *Otaheite*, under the instruction and tuition of Queen OBEREA; in which character Mrs. HAYES will appear upon this occasion."[22] The author reports that after studying John Hawkesworth's *Account of the Voyages*, which rewrote several of the journal accounts for public consumption, Hayes found inspiration in an oft-cited scene in which a young man and a young girl copulate in public "'without the least sense of its being indecent or improper.'"[23] After reading this passage, Hayes concludes that shame arises only from custom; thus she taught her "nuns" to perform this scene, but also to enhance it with postures from "Aretino." Twenty-three wealthy male patrons, barely able to wait for their turn to get into the act, watched as the women thus copulated with "a dozen of the most athletic, and best proportioned young men that could be procured" (2:25). The event earned the house "a handsome purse" (2:27).[24]

While the satire "Omiah" recommends that Hayes and Omai import women from the South Seas, in this brothel performance British prostitutes (in the tradition of Roxana) impersonate exotic women to increase business. In salient ways, Hayes's performance, as Christopher B. Balme points out, participates in the long-standing link between theatricalization and colonialism: *Nocturnal Revels* and (if we accept its report) the bawd/director both exploit the eroticized exoticism that Hawkesworth's account reproduced.[25] Moralists reviled Hawkesworth; passages from his *Account* were excerpted as soft-core pornography in *Covent Garden Magazine*, a periodical specializing in bawdy entertainment.[26] The author of *Nocturnal Revels* was not unique in exploiting the sexual suggestiveness of the iron nail "of at least twelve inches in length," ritually presented on stage to each prostitute "in imitation of the presents received by the Ladies of *Otaheite* upon these occasions, giving the preference to a long Nail before any other compliment" (2:26). Pacific women thus become both objects of an erotic, European gaze and eager seekers of the sexual pleasure that those long nails promise.

But while the sexual and Eurocentric exploitation in the *Nocturnal Revels* passage cannot be denied, some key differences between the Hawkesworth report and the Hayes performance might suggest a critical intervention, or at least irony, on the part of the British prostitute. Hayes seems to have organized the performance with a great deal of self-consciousness that distinguishes her performance text from Hawkesworth's "ethnographic" one. She makes no attempt to create the *illusion* of Pacific womanhood: In fact, just as Roxana performs a Turkish dance organized by European choreography, Hayes teaches her ladies to mitigate their exotic appearance and enhance their sexual appeal with postures already familiar to her audiences through "Aretino" and regularly performed in London by "posture girls."

Most significantly, though, Hayes seems also to have transformed Hawkesworth's account by placing the rites of commerce at the heart of the performance. Hawkesworth explicitly (and scandalously) connected the public sexual encounter witnessed in the South Seas with religious ritual rather than prostitution: Once after the British sailors had attended religious services, "our Indians thought fit to perform Vespers of a very different kind. A young man, near six feet high, performed the rites of Venus with a little girl about eleven or twelve years of age, before several of our people, and a great number of the natives."[27] Yet Hayes replaces Hawkesworth's religious analogy (the classically inflected "rites of Venus") by opening this "salacious Olympic" with the presentation of the nail, placing the commercial transaction of prostitution at the forefront.[28] There is no nail in this scene in Hawkesworth: His "rites of Venus" involve neither transracial nor commercial sex. If anything, the scene in Hawkesworth suggests its distinction from prostitution, in a sense: an extreme "innocence" that inspires reflection of the cultural construction of sexual mores. Hayes herself has clearly (as represented in *Nocturnal Revels*) taken what Hawkesworth (scandalously) represents as a religious ritual and transformed it into a highly self-conscious performance of *commercial* sex. The festivities begin with symbolic payment (the presentation of the nail on "stage"), and the show itself ends with a "collection . . . for the Votaries of VENUS" (2:27). But this does not end the evening; it only introduces the second half of the performance in which the men in the audience now may take the places of the men on stage. It is not clear, then, where performance ends and prostitution begins: Hayes first represents public sex as exotic, but then tempts her audience to transgress the line between watching and participating.

By focusing on the rites of commerce, Hayes marks her own side of the world as defined by profit. While declaring her own Mandevillian empowerment in this system—she takes the role of Oberea, interpreted by British travelers as the queen and depicted by O'Keefe as an "enchantress"—her performance simultaneously changes the element of Hawkesworth's report that some readers, including Captain Cook, found most disconcerting. Such limited information about this performance—if it even took place— makes Hayes's motives impossible to determine; the transformation of sexual contact in Hawkesworth's text from "free love" to prostitution, however, falls into a larger pattern. While the specter of Banks and Lord Sandwich leading Omai through London brothels undermined, according to critics, the lofty claims of the voyages and revealed instead their status as just another contribution to British commercial luxuriousness, the possibility that women and men in the South Seas knew only free love rather than commercial sex before European influence emerged as one of Hawkesworth's most disturbing suggestions.

"Europe's Crimes with Europe's Commerce Spread": The Journals

Satirists and dramatists imagined sexual relationships between Omai and British ladies in both scandalous and idealized ways; passionate affairs between weary sailors and sensuous island girls, however, more saliently shocked and fascinated readers for generations. Representations in travel journals of these affairs tend to fall broadly into two fundamental kinds. For some British writers—and this perspective has persisted for centuries in fiction, travel writing, and even anthropology—the apparent sexual freedom among people of the South Pacific Islands and the reported openness of the women to sexual encounters provided a foil to the increasing regulation of sexuality in their own bourgeois world.[29] Traveling Europeans thus encounter humanity in its natural, Edenic state before the fall into labor, propriety, luxury, and commerce. A contrasting kind of representation, however, "normalizes" rather than exoticizes:[30] Captain Cook and others insisted on correcting Hawkesworth's images of blissful passion between sailors and native women by reading those relationships as *prostitution*. Thus where the exoticizers romanticize cultural difference or even depict island cultures as the state of nature itself, the normalizers universalize a particular kind of distinction *within* cultures (commercial vs. noncommercial sex). In distinguishing these two ways of representing Pacific Islanders, I am not suggesting that either the normalizers or the exoticizers represent the "other" in more sensitive or accurate ways, for both versions engage in exploitative fantasies. Instead, I want to remap the terms of normalization and exoticization to argue that the presence or absence of *commercial* sex, and not sexual contact *per se*, marks the significant difference between the two. In observing this difference, we can also then see that there was more at stake than pleasure or repression, for to normalize a system of prostitution in these islands naturalized not just bourgeois sexuality but certain kinds of commercial relations as well.

The *Voyage Round the World* of Louis de Bougainville, translated from the French in 1772 by John Reinhold Forster, perhaps most dramatically romanticized Pacific women. When Bougainville's ship approached the shore in Tahiti, men in canoes approach them, apparently offering beautiful women:

> in spite of all our precautions, a young girl came on board, and placed herself upon the quarter-deck . . . . The girl carelessly dropt a cloth, which covered her, and appeared to the eyes of all beholders, such as Venus shewed herself to the Phrygian shepherd, having, indeed, the celestial form of that goddess.[31]

This turns out to be a trap, as Bougainville suspects when he forbids his men from succumbing to such temptations. One fellow sneaks off the ship, but the islanders immediately surround, strip, and inspect him, "tumultuously examining every part of his body" (219), an experience so terrifying that he loses all interest in the girl. But while Tahitians in Bougainville's *Voyage* use sex instrumentally, the women are not defined by the author as prostitutes: Seduction here is not entrepreneurial but part of a strategic, collaborative information-gathering process. In Bougainville, in fact, the Tahitians have no property at all (252), in part because they inhabit a prelapsarian world in which food simply falls from the trees: "I thought I was transported into the garden of Eden" (228), he reports. Sexual pleasure replaces not just sexual labor, but it nearly replaces labor itself: "the very air which the people breathe, their songs, their dances, almost constantly attended with indecent postures, all conspire to call to mind the sweets of love, all engage to give themselves up to them" (257). Erotic pleasure is their only luxury product (256).

Bougainville clearly exoticizes the Pacific Islanders; their supposed "free love" (in both possible senses) suggests not only a society liberated from bourgeois constraints but also a society innocent of bourgeois production, labor, and artificial luxury. In his *Supplement to Bougainville's Voyage* (1772), Denis Diderot renders manifest the latent critique embedded in this vision.

In an imagined farewell to European interlopers, an old man uses the presence or absence of sexual property to describe the key difference between Europeans and Tahitians: "We follow the pure instinct of nature, and you have tried to erase its impress from our souls. Here, everything belongs to everyone, and you have preached to us this distinction you make between *yours* and *mine*. Our daughters and our wives are common to us all."[32] Europeans, Diderot suggests, in a tragic fall from nature have turned women into property; they bring to the islands the infection of commodification along with infectious venereal diseases.

We find similar kinds of romantic self-critique, figured through "free love," in British publications as well. In a sentimental poem called *The Injured Islanders* (1779), Queen Oberea begs Captain Wallis to return to her arms and protect Tahiti from imperialist invasion. The purity of their love for each other, she suggests, may have the power to restore the land to its previous "happy State, / Ere Lux'ry taught Ambition to be great— / Ere Lust of Power to Deeds oppressive led— / Ere Europe's Crimes with Europe's Commerce spread."[33] Why should Wallis pursue worldly accumulation, Oberea asks, when natural desire provides the key to happiness: "Does Wealth superfluous prompt to wanton Spoil?" (22). In another poem, "Omiah" observes how artificial decorations in London impair desire: "The females here, whom matchless beauties bless, / Conspire to spoil them by a tasteless dress. / The hair, which simply would have flow'd with grace, / In easy ringlets sporting round the face, / Now with foul dust its glossy colour spoil'd, / With iron riveted, and grease defil'd."[34] The poem also, however, satirizes the romanticization of Pacific Islanders: Everyone at court chuckles when Omai politely requests that one of the "nymphs" engage in public sex with him.[35] "The Injured Islanders," by contrast, entirely sentimentalizes Tahiti as threatened by "the Land where Arts engender Strife," for "What Joys can there ingenuous Freedom boast, / Where fatal Fashions spread from Coast to Coast? / Where cultur'd Commerce, as it shoots on high, / But opes new Wants it never can supply" (17). In both cases, however, Tahitian "free love" marks island freedom from commodification in general.

John Hawkesworth's *Account of the Voyages Undertaken by the Order of his Present Majesty for Making Discoveries in the Southern Hemisphere* (1773) inspired these poems; it was the British publication responsible for sparking the eroticization and exoticization of the South Sea Islands in romantic, satirical, and even pornographic ways. Hawkesworth had been hired at a premium fee to celebrate the nation's navigational success by bringing literary elegance to the journals of Samuel Wallis, John Byron, Philip Carteret, and James Cook for an eager reading public; rumors, however, attributed his death to the humiliation he suffered at the hands of reviewers. His *Account* drew sharp criticism and shocked disapproval for its sensuous descriptions of erotic encounters, its resistance to an unqualified myth of British heroism, and its refusal to account for European success as divine providence.[36] By refusing to account for British domination as part of a larger divine plan, Hawkesworth implicitly, as Jonathan Lamb has argued, suggests that "discovery" "cannot be dignified by motive, conduct, or outcome; that it is an unpredictable and unheroic activity, tending inevitably to violent excesses committed in defiance of the norms of peaceful collective existence."[37] In his introduction, Hawkesworth explains this refusal (we would have to consider failures as part of a divine scheme as well); he suggests that the dangers these voyagers encountered and the violence they wrought instead demand reflection on the overall tradeoffs of commerce itself. Exploration might be justified, he argues, only "if the gratification of artificial wants, or the increase of knowledge, are justifiable causes for the risk of life." Yet at the same time, in the economy at large, he observes, all manufacture exposes individual lives to risk: "Let us examine all the multitudes that art has employed, from the refiner who sweats at the furnace to the sedentary artificer who grows pale at the loom, and perhaps none can be found in which life is not in some degree sacrificed to the artificial necessities of civil society."[38] The problem of exploration, then, parallels the problem of industrial society in general for Hawkesworth: In both cases, it is never entirely clear whether the gratification of "artificial wants" justifies the human sacrifices. Such skepticism of commercial modernity, often suggested by idealized representations of island pleasures, drew considerable negative attention to his *Account.*

While newspaper reviews excoriated Hawkesworth's neglect of the Christian principles that would have authorized this sacrifice, the representation of sexuality in the *Account,* however, attracted at least as much attention.[39] Suggestions of affairs between South Sea Island men and British ladies became a form of satire when connected to infamous commerce for the way they implied the corruption, rather than enlightenment, of the Pacific islanders by the British. The controversial seductions in Hawkesworth, however, represent free love in the South Sea Islands innocent of commodification, sharing the implication that the British taught the commercial value of sexual labor to previously pure islanders living in harmony with nature instead of striving for artificial commodities. In Hawkesworth as in Bougainville, Pacific Islanders do not commodify sexuality or divide women into prostitutes and nonprostitutes; they do, however, use sexual allure as one of their few forms of power in the face of British weaponry. In the section on Captain Wallis, Hawkesworth describes how women greeted Wallis's ship in canoes, performing suggestive dances. When Wallis refuses to allow any of his men to follow the women ashore, canoes filled with warriors approach and attack with stones. Wallis responds by instituting a reign of terror through several demonstrations of his firearms. Trade proceeds at first with similar violence, for native thefts constantly infuriate Wallis. The two groups begin to settle into a regular market only after more displays of British military power. But more insidiously than theft, sexual contact undermines British control of trade and Wallis's control of his men: "The commerce which our men had found means to establish with the women of the island, rendered them much less obedient to the orders that had been given for the regulation of their conduct on shore, than they were at first" (1:240). Speaking through Wallis, Hawkesworth represents not a distinction between virtuous women and prostitutes, but rather a cultural difference in attitudes toward sexuality. The Tahitians, Hawkesworth reports, do not place any value on chastity, yet the women and the men both quickly come to recognize female bodies as a form of leverage (1:261). This apparent recognition, Hawkesworth reports, infuriated Wallis. Sexual commerce brings runaway inflation: As the women start demanding bigger and bigger nails, other merchants begin to raise the prices of their goods as well. Wallis tries to limit the distribution of these nails, but the men secretly begin pulling them out of the ship. While the islanders' stones remain ineffective against Wallis's firearms, the island women subvert Wallis's authority and even disassemble his vessel.

In Hawkesworth's infamous account of Cook's voyage, however, sexuality deconstructs British ideologies rather than ships. Hawkesworth's account of Cook's first voyage scandalized the public for its descriptions of erotic dances, public sex, and one society within Tahitian culture reportedly devoted so fully to sexual pleasure that they used infanticide to avoid parental responsibilities. One vehement critic declared that a reader could find "stronger Excitements to vicious Indulgences [in the *Account*] than [in] the most intriguing French Novel."[40] Yet Hawkesworth does not describe these exotic, seductive women as prostitutes; even in the Wallis section, they learn their market value only from the Europeans, and even then they participate without alienation and without violating any cultural norms of chastity. Hawkesworth alters Wallis's journal to suggest this. For example, Wallis wrote that the women would "prostitute themselves for a Nail," which Hawkesworth rephrases as "they . . . readily and openly trafficked with our people for personal favours."[41] This is not merely a change in decorum but a turn of phrase that suggests, as we find throughout Hawkesworth, that sexual encounters do not entail the exchange of sexual labor as a commodity for the island women. As in Bougainville, the islanders here remain innocent of sexual labor and labor in general. "The earth," according to Hawkesworth, "produces [food] spontaneously, or with so little culture, that they seem to be exempted from the first general curse, that 'man should eat his bread in the sweat of his brow'" (2:186). The related liberation from work and sexual constraint not only exoticizes the islanders but also provides the opportunity to question the modern ambitions of global commerce. Doing so, however, challenges the value of the voyages themselves.

For this reason, the reported behavior of Joseph Banks, an aristocratic amateur scientist who accompanied Cook, became particularly disturbing, for Banks seemed to appreciate local customs not just in theory (like Diderot and Hawkesworth) but in practice. Wits and moralists took aim at a number of incidents in the Cook voyages, but considerable mockery focused on Banks himself.[42] Several cast a presumed affair between Banks and Oberea as mock-Edenic love:

> All hail! Sweet *Oberea*, queen of charms,
> Whom oft I've clasp'd within my wanton arms!
> Desire was mutual, but the fault was mine;
> For you, fond souls, who dwell beneath the line,
> In mutual dalliance hold perpetual play,
> The golden age repeated ev'ry day.[43]

In another poem, Oberea admits that she "gave my kingdom as I have my heart."[44] She insists that, implicitly unlike the women of Banks's own country, she has no profit motive: "Think not I covet what you riches call, / Your houses, land, estates—I scorn them all" (13). Banks becomes an object of satire not only because of this reputed affair but also because of his deep and inquisitive involvement in the local culture as reported by Hawkesworth. In one incident, for example, Banks strips himself almost naked and smears himself with charcoal to participate in a mourning ceremony with equally naked women. Hawkesworth describes a kind of intimacy between the British and the Tahitians for which Banks becomes the ambassador: "they seemed to be brave, open, and candid, without either suspicion or treachery, cruelty or revenge; so that we placed the same confidence in them as in our best friends, many of us, particularly Mr. Banks, sleeping frequently in their houses in the woods, without a companion, and consequently wholly in their power" (2:188). Hawkesworth aestheticizes, eroticizes, and familiarizes the women, who "always uncover themselves as low as the waist in the evening, throwing off all that they wear on the upper part of the body, with the same negligence and ease as our ladies would lay by a cardinal or double handkerchief" (2:193). Yet Bank's intimate pleasures produced hysterical satires because they implicitly (and romantically) challenged the superiority of the "civilized" world and thus of the exploration and expansion project itself. The prelapsarian sexuality Hawkesworth describes becomes, albeit condescendingly, an emblem for their freedom from the anxieties of the modern world of labor, regulation, and commerce. Islanders feel strong emotions, but they never last for very long; they have no sense of history, "having no habits of thinking which perpetually recall the past, and anticipate the future." As a result,

> they have no project which is to be pursued from day to day, the subject of unremitted anxiety and solicitude, that first rushes into the mind when they awake in the morning, and is last dismissed when they sleep at night. (2:104–105)

Through descriptions of an ongoing sensual intimacy and liberation from daily cares of bourgeois responsibility, Hawkesworth represents desertion as a seductive and disturbing fantasy.

To point this out is not by any means to suggest that Hawkesworth's *Account* offers either a protofeminist or early postcolonial critique. While Hawkesworth's report on the Wallis voyage suggests that the women use their sexual power as a weapon, we find throughout the volumes a patriarchal eroticization of the "exotic" woman. Sometimes Hawkesworth represents the islanders as possessing a distinct culture, but other times he represents them as having no culture at all—as living in not just nature but in the time before the fall. Throughout the *Account*, however, the author suggests that the constant pursuit of acquisition might be pointless and that bourgeois sexual values might be arbitrary. Consistent with his rejection of providence as an explanation for any navigational success, Hawkesworth perhaps goes even further than Diderot in his critique by not simply sentimentalizing the "primitive" or trying to adjudicate between "primitive" and civilized ways, but by wondering if all cultural values might be contingent. Reflecting on the public sex that sailors witnessed (the one reproduced in Hayes's brothel) also raises the question of sexual values in general. Hawkesworth claims not to mention the incident out of "idle curiosity" but because it raises a philosophical question:

> Whether the shame attending certain actions, which are allowed on all sides to be themselves innocent, is implanted in Nature, or superinduced by custom? If it has its origin in custom, it will, perhaps, be found difficult to trace that custom, however general, to its source; if in instinct, it will be equally difficult to discover from what cause it is subdued or at least overruled among these people, in whose manners not the least trace of it is to be found. (2:128)

In representing transracial sexual encounters, Hawkesworth also emphasizes cultural differences (lack of sexual inhibition) rather than sexual property. The scandal of Banks lies not in any purchase of miscegenous sexual favors, but rather in the intimacy he seems to have shared with his hosts, expressed through both his pleasure and his participation in various rituals, even submitting to tattooing.

While Hawkesworth suggests the profoundly mixed effects of the voyages through exotic narratives of grand passion, sensual intimacy, and prelapsarian absence of inhibitions, sex work and work in general, the normalizing publications find instead that their own distinctions between ladies and whores apply globally. In the wake of the scandal of Hawkesworth's *Account*, Captain Cook published his *Voyage towards the South Pole, and Round the World* to maintain public support for the voyages, but also to correct Hawkesworth. The *Voyage*, which Reverend John Douglas helped edit and refine, differs from Cook's private journals and thus does not necessarily represent Cook's innermost thoughts.[45] Nevertheless, poised specifically to rescue the voyages from the scandal that Hawkesworth's *Account* generated, the *Voyage* suggests the kind of revision thought necessary to restore enthusiasm for exploration. The *Voyage* attempts in particular to revise the representation of sexuality in the South Seas. "Great injustice," Cook insists,

> has been done to the women of Otaheite, and the Society Isles, by those who have represented them, without exception, as ready to grant the last favour to any man who will come up to their price. But this is by no means the case.

As Cook goes on to explain, many women in the South Seas remain virtuous. The married women can be as difficult to seduce as such ladies in any nation, and even most of the unmarried women from all classes "admit of no such familiarities." Travelers have merely mistaken a small group of women as representative of the entire population. The women who climbed on-board the ships, he explains, were *prostitutes*, no different from the infamous women in European nations. There might be more prostitutes in these islands, he admits, but this should not lead us to draw conclusions about all of the women of the South Pacific Islands, for "on the whole, a stranger who visits England might, with equal justice, draw the characters of the women there, from those which he might meet with on board the ships in one of the naval ports, or in the purlieus of Covent-Garden or Drury Lane."[46] Cook thus insists on the lack of difference between women who greet sailors anywhere in the world: Sex work is global. Cook repeats this observation even more starkly in an account of the Friendly Islands in the third voyage. Married women, he insists, remained chaste; by contrast, "such as came to our people were *Whores by profession* and brought to us in order to make the most of the present time" (emphasis added).[47] Cook warns against confusing these two types. In New Zealand, he notes with disgust, the men "were the chief promoters of a shameful traffic, and that, for a spike nail, or any other thing they value, they would oblige the women to prostitute themselves, whether they would or no; and even without regard to that privacy, which decency requires."[48] Here the women become not only whores, but, like their despondent British sisters in reform narratives, deeply alienated. Georg Forster, who also insisted that his account corrected Hawkesworth, makes a similar point: New Zealander men, he reports, "encouraged by the lucrative nature of this infamous commerce," offered "their daughters and sisters promiscuously to every person's embraces."[49] John Rickman insists on both the material greed and sophisticated skills of Tahitian prostitutes. "The ladies of pleasure in London," he reports, "have not half the winning ways that are practiced by the Otaheitean misses to allure their gallants. . . . [T]hey are incessant in their importunities, and will never cease asking while the sailor has a rag or a nail to bestow."[50] While in Hawkesworth women seduce as part of a community political strategy or for their own pleasure, those who followed to correct him paid particular attention to what they saw as a fundamental misrepresentation. For the anti-Hawkesworth party, the commodification of sexual labor is universal: Other writers only composed "marvellous histories, which would have disgusted even the romantic disposition of our ancestors."[51]

This normalizing correction shaped Cook's subsequent reputation as well. Biographer Andrew Kippis (1788) celebrates Cook for his virtuous character and the voyages for their fulfillment of the highest ideals of pure science as well as their "design of civilizing the world and meliorating its condition."[52] Rather than the confusion and suspicion reported in Hawkesworth, for Kippis in Tahiti "the traffic with the inhabitants for provisions and refreshments . . . was carried on with as much order as in any well regulated market in Europe."[53] Kippis praises Cook for "rectifying the great injustice which had been done to the women of Otaheite and the neighbouring isles" (173) in his *Voyage* by disabusing the public of Hawkesworth's representation of their sensuality. While Rickman marvels at the clever Oceanic whores who took full advantage of British sailors, Kippis instead describes Cook's refusal of native prostitution. Upon his landing at Anamocka, for example, Cook is greeted by an old woman who offers him the services of a young girl. In an attempt politely to decline the offer, the captain pleads his poverty; the old woman, however, insists that he could have the girl on credit. Captain Cook, however, "found it more easy to withstand [the girl's] allurements than the abuses of the ancient matron, and therefore hastened into his boat" (199). Kippis notes that while Cook could not prevent his men from attempting to carry on this infamous commerce, "he never encouraged it, and always was fearful of its consequences" (260). In these contact zones, Cook becomes a heroic traveling Thorowgood navigating a sea of Millwoods.

The exoticizing and normalizing accounts reveal different ideological impulses. Cook and Forster claim to defend women by clearing the reputations of the virtuous and even representing female prostitutes as the innocent victims of a trade run by men. Forster insists that the dignified treatment of women marks the distinction between civilization and savagery. This insistence on dividing women into the virtuous and the prostituted, however, globally expands emergent bourgeois values; further, Forster clearly uses these gender relations to define European racial superiority. Hawkesworth, by contrast, broadly eroticizes the "exotic," a construction arguably no less Eurocentric or patriarchal than Forster's. The normalizing account and the exoticizing account both describe copious instances of transracial sexual contact; they differ, however, on whether they represent this contact as free love or infamous commerce. One scandalized and the other comforted, then, not because of any difference in the chastity or "feminism" of their narratives, but because Hawkesworth associated sexual contact in the South Sea Islands with a seductive, "pre-commercial" intimacy that British imperial efforts could only corrupt. Those who corrected him, by contrast, comforted readers with the presence of various forms of commodification all over the globe.

In each kind of account, then, infamous commerce functions as a trope for commercial relations in general. Although Hawkesworth sometimes attempts to rationalize British commercial imperialism, his *Account* makes its ethical problems and practical difficulties abundantly clear: The British did not meet Pacific Islanders for an exchange among equals, but rather overwhelmed them with force. Even Omai, who staked his future on an alliance with the British, had been shot and wounded in Wallis's initial siege long before he met Captain Cook.[54] And even Captain Cook noted in his journal that the Europeans "interduce among [Pacific islanders] wants and perhaps diseases which they never before knew and which serves only to disturb that happy tranquillity they and their fore Fathers had injoy'd. If any one denies the truth of this assertion let him tell me what the Natives of the whole extent of America have gained by the commerce they have had with Europeans."[55] In this unguarded moment, edited out of the official version, the British rather than the Islanders become guilty of "infamous commerce," bringing their infectious desires and diseases.

The representation of pervasive prostitution in the apologists' accounts, then, becomes so important because it portrays the South Sea Islanders as always already corrupt, always already practicing at least one key form of commodification. The professional whore of the apologists' accounts welcomes the Europeans as providing new business opportunities, and in this sense becomes an ideological marker for her community. The practice of the "old trade," whether on the other side of the world or in the heart of London, erases the history and geography of capitalist expansion, also placing sex work outside of history and geography. Rather than the violent potential conquest of one people by another, contact emerges as contractual rather than exploitative. If anything, the naïve sailor must be constantly warned against unscrupulous women who will extract from him all of his possessions, down to his last shirt. Thus the infamous commerce of the South Sea Islanders occludes the possibility of British aggression, for at the heart of these tropical islands already reside the most unscrupulous merchants of all. With the passage to the South Seas opened up by the incorruptibly chaste Captain Cook, British merchants may now cautiously embark on their own risky business.

Conclusion: Usury of the Heart

Despite impulses to universalize prostitution through time and space, eighteenth-century travelers to the Pacific Islands disagreed about the meaning of the sexual contact they witnessed. Midcentury reformers, however, consistently represented streetwalking as a novel historical problem: the distressing fallout of family ambitions in an era offering new possibilities of mobility, an allegory for the transition from a rural to an urban commercial economy, the symbolic outcome of failing to maintain a middle-class identity, and, somewhat contradictorily, both an immoral avoidance of labor and simultaneously the outer limits of labor alienation. Through activism, legislation, charity, and stories of individual plights and exploits, this period in certain specific ways constructed what we now understand as "prostitution"—the contractual alienation of sexual labor—with its complex proximity to other ways of making a living. To make this claim is not to argue that no one before the eighteenth century ever thought of leveraging power through sexual service. But generally speaking and allowing for broad overlap, we can see in the eighteenth century a shift in representations of prostitutes from figures of insatiable desire to extreme embodiments of modern commercial relations that can empower or threaten the individual through the self-division of marketplace exchange. The earliest reformers excoriated the sins of both whore and cully; after the Societies for the Reformation of Manners (SRMs), however, reformers encouraged readers to sympathize with these women as victims who had been left with nothing to exchange. While some recent feminists, arguing against an older feminist tradition, have suggested that we think about sex work more seriously as *work*, the prostitute's emergent capacity in eighteenth-century ideology to alienate as a commodity the most personal form of labor imaginable (in the period's ideology) and the very emblem of the private sphere (heterosexual sex) goes a long way toward accounting for the fascination with prostitutes and prostitution in the novel, travel literature, economic writing, drama, reform rhetoric, and popular accounts of prostitute lives. Much eighteenth-century writing exposes the explosive economic meanings of prostitution that later narratives mystify.

I have argued that stories about prostitution, fictional and "true," held meaning as a strategy for confronting the emergent commercial culture, and that different writers used this to different ends. I have tried to demonstrate, in part by rereading canonical literature in the context of some less familiar texts, that while writers used prostitute stories to enforce female virtue through negative examples, they also used these stories to suggest intriguing, productive, tragic, comic, empowering, and even liberating possibilities. While prostitute figures have long been recognized as evoking an alien other, I have tried to explore another possibility as well: that by recognizing these figures as also anxious points of recognition, we can sometimes make better sense of the period's most compelling fictions. In travel journals to the South Seas, in fact, prostitution emerges as the familiar practice and noncommercial sex as the exotic one. I have tried to show the surprising ways in which whores could, beneath the irony, misogyny, moral condemnation, and condescension of various narratives, emerge as strangely sympathetic and even heroic for their intriguing capacity to alienate the apparently inalienable. A wide variety of writers seemed to believe that a reader might, if perhaps briefly and from the safe, distancing context of the whore's exoticism, have been able anxiously to see the world through the eyes of Sally, Roxana, Clarissa, Fanny, or Tom because at some level they shared, could imagine sharing, or feared finding themselves in a comparable predicament, abandoned to an unforgiving marketplace. Thus the numerous projects, real and imagined, to manage, banish, reform, export, import, and, perhaps most of all, elicit the stories of prostitutes need to be thought of in a broader context than virtue and prurience.

The copious, even obsessive, writing about prostitution in the eighteenth century did not necessarily, we can now see, have the end of infamous commerce as its goal. Literary texts rarely imagined the possibility of eliminating prostitution. Even the reform movement had minimal practical force, despite its social significance. Nevertheless, one writer—the Reverend Martin Madan—proposed a scheme that, at least in theory, would have ended prostitution. His proposal, as well as the resistance it met with, perhaps most oddly and controversially exposed the core dilemmas of sex work, offending many along the way. I will close, then, by glancing at Madan's unusual idea and the revealing controversy it provoked.

Prostitution's End

Standard reformers saw two related alternatives for ending prostitution: Prostitutes could become useful by transforming themselves into legitimate workers, or they could help populate colonial outposts. We have already looked at the regimen through which reformers believed whores could reform for industry: In this vision, prostitution itself becomes an intermediary step between unruly passion and self-regulated labor. Already alienated from their bodies, prostitutes who could embrace the discipline of the Magdalen Hospital held the potential to become model workers. Transportation, of course, served as a common punishment for disorderly women in life as well as in art for most of the century: The voyage of the *Lady Julian* in 1789, for example, brought female convicts, including accused prostitutes, to the shores of Australia.[1] The vision of prostitutes as colonists became such a widespread notion that Ann Marie Falconbridge could believably report such a transportation project that may or may not have ever taken place. At the end of the century, Henry Smeathman proposed to colonize Sierra Leone with impoverished black men from London, many of whom had fought for the British during the American Revolution.[2] The project was represented as a positive alternative to slavery, and Falconbridge traveled to Sierra Leone with her abolitionist husband. After harsh experiences in the colony, the death of her husband, and the government's failure fairly (in her view) to compensate her, Falconbridge published a sometimes-bitter account of her experiences. One of the most striking images of her *Narrative* (1791–1793) is coming across

> seven of our country women, decrepid with disease, and so disguised with filth and dirt, that I should never have supposed they were born white; add to this, almost naked from head to foot; in short their appearance was such as I think would extort compassion from the most callous heart.[3]

Falconbridge assumes at first that they are black convicts, but later is told that they were white prostitutes and that men were employed to "collect and conduct them to Wapping, where they were intoxicated with liquor, then inveigled on board ship, and married to Black men, whom they had never seen before" (65). Falconbridge quotes one of the women lamenting that "'to the disgrace of my mother country, upwards of one hundred unfortunate women, were seduced from England to practice their iniquities more brutishly in this horrid country'" (66). Their story shocks the author:

> Good heavens! How the relation of this tale made me shudder;—I questioned its veracity, and enquired of the other women who exactly corroborated what I had heard; nevertheless, I cannot altogether reconcile myself to believe it; for it is scarcely possible that the British Government, at this advanced and enlightened age, envied and admired as it is by the universe, could be capable of exercising or countenancing such a Gothic infringement on human Liberty. (66)

Even if, as some historians have suggested, Falconbridge fabricated this account out of her hostility to the British government,[4] it nevertheless interestingly combines the sympathy for fallen women cultivated by reformers with a sense that the government relied on them to assist in imperial expansion through (shocking to Falconbridge) forced miscegenous marriages. These prostitutes hover between black and white, exotic and familiar, tragic "others" and points of sympathetic identification. Exporting prostitutes, however, is not simply a punishment but a strategy for gaining a foothold in remote locations and colonizing a potentially unruly population. The goal of transportation, then, is not so much to end prostitution or to get rid of prostitutes, but rather to distribute them usefully throughout the empire. As perhaps the population with the most minimal stake in civic humanist ideals, prostitutes, who have already learned to alienate the least alienable commodity, here prove useful to the colonial project.

Both the transportation of prostitutes and the Magdalen Hospital, then, attracted attention, but neither ended prostitution or even seemed designed to do so.[5] The Reverend Martin Madan, however, offered a plan that, at least in theory (although the practical implications indeed seem insurmountable) would have worked; it attracted perhaps the most attention of any single statement on prostitution published in the eighteenth century—most of it negative.[6] In 1780–1781, Madan published his three-volume *Thelyphthora; or, A Treatise on Female Ruin, in its Causes, Effects, Consequences, Prevention, and Remedy*, proposing to solve the problem of female prostitution through legalized polygamy. Briefly, Madan argued that marriage was a sacred rather than secular institution, and in the eyes of God *every sex act constitutes a marriage*. For Madan, if a married man seduces another woman, he gains the moral (and, Madan wants to add, legal) responsibility for taking care of her and her children for life. Madan supports this point with copious evidence from the Bible, and in particular by consistently returning to the point that Old Testament Jews practiced polygamy and that God would not lay down one set of laws for his chosen people and another set of laws for their descendants.

At least as remarkable as *Thelyphthora* itself was the clamor that it produced: Numerous detractors answered Madan in not just pamphlets and
satirical poems, but in learned, book-length treatises that attempted a thor-
ough refutation of his plan. Many of these insisted that *Thelyphthora*'s popularity motivated their response; apparently it sold very well.[7] But while
many apparently bought this book and a few defended Madan's proposal—
the rake George Hanger, for example, insisted that "we should not see a fifti-
eth part of the prostitutes walking the streets" if the nation adopted Madan's
idea[8]—most published responses expressed shock and vehement disagreement. The controversy forced Madan to resign from his position as chaplain of the Lock Hospital. While polygamy had been discussed in print
already in this period—several detractors, in fact, accused Madan of plagia-
rism—the topic had never before produced this kind of sustained scandal
and print war.[9]

The level of hysteria that *Thelyphthora* generated demands an explanation.
The objections in themselves are not surprising; the level of attention to such
an apparently unlikely solution, however, points to the more fundamental issues associated with sex work in this period. Madan's high-profile position
and possible libertine history contributed to, but do not entirely account for,
the amount of attention that his treatise received. There seemed to have been
no serious possibility that the British government would legalize polygamy
and enforce this scheme. Further, Madan's treatise was in many ways conventional: *Thelyphthora* centrally condemns sodomy as the greatest sexual
transgression that his plan would help eliminate. As Randolph Trumbach
points out, a kind of unacknowledged polygamy was already widely in practice in eighteenth-century culture, with married men commonly and openly
supporting a mistress and her children.[10] While Madan's scheme would have
forced men to provide for seduced women, its author was no radical feminist: Multiple spouses should be available to men but not women because
God places the wife "under the absolute *power* of her *husband*" and because
"[s]he is not at liberty to make any *contract* whatsoever, without her husband's
consent" (1:278). Madan contextualizes his concern with the common worry
about depopulation: lack of soldiers, sailors, and workers, many feared, was
weakening the global power of the British Empire. Madan continually cal-
culates the national loss in population due to prostitution, which, he reports,
leads to child poverty, infanticide, and the eventual sterility (as was widely
believed) of prostitutes themselves. Indeed, the "Female Ruin" of his title
seems to suggest not so much a moral failure but the literal destruction of
these women as reproducers: "almost every woman, who is driven into *common* prostitution, is a loss of one *breeding-woman* to the public" (2:266). As a
result of the current limits on marriage, "our fleets want sailors, our armies

men . . . many thousands of acres lie uncultivated and uninhabited" (2:248). Madan can be very specific in his calculations:

> Let us say, that 20,000 females are, in the space of seven years, rendered barren by *prostitution*, who would otherwise, under the sobriety of matrimony, have produced *four children* each. Here is a defalcation of 80,000 people from the community. (2:250)

So with Madan's *Treatise* we have a text that supports some of the most mainstream ideals of the time—patriarchy, heteronormativity, domesticity, imperialism, extreme family values—through a modern demographic perspective.

Yet Madan's strange combination of conservatism and idiosyncrasy was clearly both plausible and threatening enough to stir up a great deal of attention. Felicity Nussbaum has argued that "England's toying with and ultimate rejection of polygamy near the end of the eighteenth century was part of a nation's defining itself both as distinct from and morally superior to the polygamous Other."[11] Much of this discussion to which Nussbaum refers consisted of responses specifically to Madan, although throughout the century, as she points out, we find reference to the depravity of polygamy as one piece of "evidence" in favor of the argument that the European slave trade benefited Africans by civilizing them. In making the case *for* polygamy, however, Madan chooses more romanticized and also more familiar others: African polygamy does not figure prominently in *Thelyphthora*. Madan instead turns to the South Seas for evidence that polygamy works very well in some cultures, especially when the women outnumber the men (1:103). Later he uses the example of Tahiti to shame his countrymen. Tahitians "pursue incontinent gratifications, where ever inclination leads them" (3:320), but as they have no formal marriage ceremony, when the woman becomes pregnant the man becomes her husband. The British share with these "savages . . . the pursuit of incontinent gratifications . . . but as to the consequences of this, with regard to the *women*, the *females* at *Otaheite* have vastly the advantage of *ours;* for the *Christian* women, on their becoming *pregnant* . . . are treated with a degree of barbarity and inhumanity, which we may suppose the *savages* would be ashamed of" (3:319). For Madan, then, British prostitution compares unfavorably to Oceanic polygamy.

Far more than either Africans or even South Sea Islanders, however, Jews in Madan figure as the most significant alternative. Madan defines the prostitution problem as historical as well as geographical. The ancient Jews, he argues, appreciated marriage as a sacred rather than a secular institution, a recognition lost in modern culture. The Marriage Act in particular offended Madan, as it put up too many roadblocks to marriage. Equally disturbing,

however, is the way that the Marriage Act defined marriage as a secular contract. In the Old Testament, Madan insists, men took on several wives because they understood that every act of sexual intercourse constituted a
sacred marriage. Sexual consummation, Madan points out, defines and com-
pletes the marriage ceremony. Polygamy worked to the advantage of the
ancient Jews, as it allowed them to become a populous and powerful community. But even more important than the practical advantages of polygamy,
the Old Testament Jews held the higher moral ground:

> When a man *took a virgin*, she became his *woman*, i.e. his *property*, not by
> any outward ceremony, but by the surrendering of *her person* into his *pos-
> session*; this, either *anticipatively* by promise or *betrothing*, or *actually* by car-
> *nal knowledge*, where not betrothing or espousal went before; this, and this
> *only*, made them *one flesh*—this did, and it *ever* must have the same effect
> in the *sight* of GOD; for He changeth not. (2:292–293)

Throughout *Thelyphthora* and in his *Letters* defending his treatise, Madan repeats the argument that the laws of God do not change. Jews have not
changed: Like the "savages" in the South Seas they "may shame us *Christians* for the little respect we pay to the *preservation* of the *female sex*, or to
those *laws of Heaven* which were made to insure it!" (2:298). The modern
world adds mercilessness to divine disobedience by condemning women to
Bridewell:

> To punish a poor deserted creature for being a *prostitute*, when it is put out
> of her power to force her *seducer* to provide for her as the *divine law* enjoins,
> is equally cruel and foolish: not very unlike the man who threw his child
> into a ditch, and then beat him for being dirty. (2:300)

Old Testament Jews, by contrast, ensured the well-being of all women by demanding that their seducers support them. This system would eliminate
prostitution because it eliminates the need for the seduced woman to seek
her living on the street. To their credit, the Jews followed God's command
to go forth and multiply, and "when we consider that there is no part of the
world where Jews are not found, we may well suppose their numbers to be
immense (2:252). Here and throughout we find an uneasy balance in Madan
between pious admiration for Jewish obedience to God's will and concern
with the ensuing results. If Christians, in other words, do not stop wasting
so many breeders through the secular insistence on monogamy as well as restrictive laws like the Marriage Act, they will find themselves overrun by
Jews, who obey the word of God most directly.

Madan's detractors varied widely, from bawdy satirists to serious theologians to fellow reformers deeply sympathetic with his motives but distressed by his solution. In general, however, we can break the arguments against him into three interlocking points. First—and this isn't really an argument—some simply attack Madan personally. For example, *A Poetical Epistle to the Reverend Mr. Madan* (1781), supposedly written by "A Nymph of King's Place," suggests that Madan only advocates polygamy because he wants to have sex with a lot of different women; she thus invites him to come visit her brothel, where men and women contract marriages every night and dissolve them in the morning. Another poetical epistle, however, warns that the whores of London will riot to defend their trade and their freedom if polygamy were instituted.[12] Connecting Madan's defense of Jews to the author's own presumed sexual history, Edward Burnaby Greene wondered "whether, that our David hath now, or formerly had, his Bathshebas, remain problematical, or not."[13] Greene finds Madan's ideas "fitter by far for a Jew than for a Christian!"(73).

That Madan's *Treatise* has revealed the author as a "Jew" as well as a rake suggests the second major point that his detractors raised: They vehemently asserted both the geographical and historical superiority of their own nation.[14] But while these writers easily dismiss African polygamy as a sign of savagery not to be imitated, the case of the Jews, as both ultra-ancients and ultramoderns, honored ancestors and predatory merchants, presents a different problem. Greene thus explains Jewish polygamy as a special circumstance permitted by God to increase the population; moderns, on the other hand, must resign to the "Jew, his blind and servile prepossession in favor of Mosaic ceremonies, done away by a newer and better covenant" (xvii). Jews who lived among pagans often fell into their wicked ways. But on Madan's point that polygamy must be lawful because Jews practiced it, Greene observes "that the guilt of the Israelites in their idolatry among the heathens is constantly pictured as an indulgence of their passions with the female sex" (48), an indulgence that Madan claims as marriage but the Bible records as "whoredom" and a form of "idolatry" (49). So while Madan reads the Jews as an example to follow, Greene reads the Old Testament as recounting an outdated covenant long since replaced by Christ. The admission of multiple heterosexual partners of the Jews was not lawful polygamy, but rather idolatry for which God *punished* them. James Cookson agreed that Jewish polygamy never had divine sanction but was instead a sinful custom picked up by Jews as a result of living among heathens. The descendants of Cain, he argues, first practiced polygamy, and Ishmael

> was rejected on account of his being the offspring of a polygamous connection. After his rejection he lived by rapine in the wilderness; and his pos-

terity, to this day, infest Arabia, and its neighbourhood, with their incursions and robberies; they live in a state of perpetual war, and their extirpation has often been unsuccessfully attempted.[15]

In short, "the Jews were addicted to vice"; they "frequently abandoned the rites of their own religion for the impure, absurd, and barbarous ones of the heathen nations about them"(381). "Idolatry," Cookson argued, "itself is frequently in scripture denominated whoredom" (17). According to another detractor, the Jews "thought whoredom for gain was only forbidden to the native Hebrew women, but that it was not forbidden to strangers that sojourned among them."[16] Jews, then, not only worshipped the golden calf, but they also worshipped heathen women: They fetishized idols and pagan women. Thus the debate that Madan provoked turned quickly into a discussion over the essential difference between Jews and Christians: As Cookson put it, "What is the revival of [polygamy], but revival of Judaism?" (20).

The split significance of the Jews at the end of the eighteenth century in anti-Semitic rhetoric as both benighted primitives and ruthless moderns suggests another underlying issue in this passionate debate. In the eyes of his detractors, Madan resembles the Jews he so admires by his refusal to separate the public from the private; specifically, both benighted ancient and corrupt, overly modern subjects fail to separate a commercial sphere from a domestic one. Madan's argument itself combines an old-fashioned Filmerian patriarchy with a modern sociological perspective: Polygamy solves the problems of depopulation, infanticide, and female poverty. Further, Madan reads prostitution as overwhelmingly an economic issue; his solution presumes that women become prostitutes as an economic necessity and for no other reason. In fact, his detractors objected that Madan did not include enough moral condemnation of women in his *Treatise:* By confining his definition of the word *harlot* to "a woman who prostitutes her body for gain," Madan implies "that none can be considered as guilty of fornication but the common prostitute."[17] Madan's economic view of sexuality—or perhaps we should say, his refusal to uphold the extremely fragile ideological division between the public sphere and the private sphere—once again links him to the atavistic yet overly modern (commercialized) Jews. In the Old Testament, Jewish men were compelled to marry women they seduced, Greene admits, but this was really just a way to protect the men financially, for "by this regulation the woman and her friends were precluded from the exercise of any sinister artifice to rifle the purse of the offender; she became his wife, and the Jewish command obliged him to maintain her" (130). Jews also practiced divorce against the will of God; but, Greene argues, "Jews are particularly experienced to hesitate little at the violation of an act of God, if they can but screen themselves by the basest duplicity from punishments attendant upon a breach of the laws of man. The usury of the heart is their familiar practice" (109). Jews, then, epitomize both financial and sentimental forms of usury. This is not simply an argument about the distant past. "Were the Jews of old time all principled?" Greene asks rhetorically. "If so, modern Jews are their antipodes." Jews, according to Greene, are ruthless seekers of money and sex, commodity and sexual fetishists, usurers of capital and usurers of the heart.

Madan's scheme, in the eyes of his detractors, would essentially turn everyone into unabashed "usurers of the heart" because they would be forced to understand all marriages as financial arrangements. Yet with this change, Madan's plan, unlike any other eighteenth-century solution, really would eliminate prostitution (in a sense) by refusing to make a distinction between sexual relationships inside and outside of economic interest. Perhaps most scandalously, Madan thus dispenses with romantic love, which associates him for some with radical libertines, but for others with extreme patriarchal conservatism. For his detractors, the love that could serve as the foundation for a domestic family can be recognized primarily by the *absence* of financial motivation, a formulation that provides in the eighteenth century endless plots for sentimental plays and novels. (The playwright Richard Brinsley Sheridan satirizes this sentimental plot in *The Rivals*, where Lydia Languish can experience romantic love only as desire for the penniless Ensign Beverly, even when he is the same person as the well-established Captain Absolute.)

Some attackers identify this dispensing with romance as the tyranny against women that polygamy would bring. In Asiatic societies, Cookson argues, "the women are treated as the most abject slaves, shut up in a seraglio, and guarded like prisoners—a common consequence of polygamy" (416). Another argues that among the polygamous Mahometans "the poor defenceless beings [women] are generally locked and barred in separate apartments."[18] "Wheresoever this custom prevails," yet another writes, "what is the state of the women? Go all over the East, particularly in China, where they have no inheritance; and in Persia they are not considered as having souls."[19] Thus a host of detractors make the "feminist" point that polygamy would degrade women into the abject inferiors of men, as they remain in supposedly less-civilized nations. Yet for others, polygamy would give women too much power and turn husbands into exhausted sex slaves. Richard Hill argues that because only the strongest women could bear seeing their husbands with others, only the most Amazonian ones would marry and wives would therefore universally become shrews.[20] Cookson worries about the health of men under this system, for "man is enervated by the use of many women, and this enervation increasing with time, weakens gradually the constitution" (335). This possibility, expanded into the social and affective realms, constitutes the joke of the farce *Chit-Chat* (1781), performed in the wake of Madan's *Treatise*. For Sir Oliver in this farce, polygamy would be its own punishment: How could he ever "please two wives, when I have been these twenty years striving in vain to please one"?[21]

Thus Madan's *Treatise* sparked the most voluminous debate of any statement about prostitution because it revealed the contradictions of modern gender formations and would have eliminated the ideological distinction between commercial and noncommercial sex on which they depended. While it is difficult to imagine an effective implementation of Madan's scheme, at least in theory he defines prostitution out of existence. This caused trouble at two levels. First, the limited scope of reform projects (such as the Magdalen Hospital), the strategy of transporting prostitutes all over the globe, and the deeply offended responses to Madan all suggest that despite reformist fervor, a world without commercial sex does not seem to have been the goal. Outside of the reform movement there was at many different levels, as I have suggested throughout, both toleration for and fascination with infamous commerce. In Madan as in Cook, prostitution represents the British, as opposed to the exotic, sexual practice. In the Madan controversy, it emerges as essential to maintain an ideological opposition between infamous commerce and romantic love, between sexuality immersed in and separated from financial concerns.

But if, as I have argued, prostitution in both literature and culture also became meaningful not only as infamous sex but specifically as infamous *commerce*, then the surprisingly extensive controversy over *Thelyphthora* might have held another meaning as well. At a more abstract level, the elimination of prostitution in this controversy undermines the self-divided theatricality necessary for operation in the public commercial sphere, leaving either ancient "Jewish" patriarchy or the modern "Jewish" reduction to economic motive. To see this we need to turn to the specific way Madan solves the problem of prostitution. Madan offers five fundamental propositions:

1. That marriage is a *divine* institution, and, as such, to be abided by as revealed to us by its holy and blessed author.
2. That those who look upon it merely as a *civil contract*, and therefore subject to the alteration and controul of men, have different views of it from those given us in the scripture.
3. That a woman's *person* cannot be separated from her *self;* wherever she bestows the *one,* the *other* is bestowed also.
4. That when she delivers her *person,* and consequently her *self,* into the possession of a man, she is (if not betrothed to another) by *that* act, inseparably united to him, so indissolubly joined, that she cannot leave him, *nor may he put her away all his days.*

5. That if these truths were received, as they are indeed the truths of GOD, millions of women (especially of the lower sort) would be saved from ruin; for, being protected, received, and provided for as GOD's law enjoins, as the *wives* of those men who first enticed them, they could not be turned out upon the wide world, with the loss of reputation, friends, and consequently all power of helping themselves, but by ways too dreadful to think of! (*Thelyphthora*, 1:40–41)

For Madan, then, marriage is not really a contract, and, strictly speaking, prostitution does not actually exist because sexual labor *cannot be alienated:* A woman's person (that would perform the sexual labor) cannot be separated from herself, defined at the core by sexuality. Thus Madan does not so much argue against the sexual alienation of prostitution as suggest its impossibility: It is not that men *should* marry women they seduce, but that they *have* married them. He strenuously objects to the secularization of marriage and the additional burden demanded by the Marriage Act when sexual union, in his view, is the literal "one flesh" that no human ceremony can create. One is no more married after a wedding, he argues, than more dead after a funeral (20–23). Thus if prostitution became so fascinating to readers and writers in the eighteenth century in part because it served as a trope for and an experiment in the experience of self-division and vulnerability in the commercial marketplace and thus provided the opportunity to work through the meaning of this condition, then Madan's proposal challenges nothing less than the foundation of this emergent form of subjectivity.

Contemporaries, then, were both so taken by and outraged over Madan because he got to the heart of what so much prostitute discourse was about in the eighteenth century: the looming possibility or pressing reality of having to exchange a precious part of the "self" in a commercial marketplace. In general, eighteenth-century reformers represent prostitution as the profoundest form of human alienation; unlike reformers in the seventeenth century, however, eighteenth-century reformers do not simply condemn prostitutes as lost to the world but rather imagined them as potential workers and colonists. Their alienation as prostitutes prepared rather than disqualified them for these possibilities. Outside of reformist writing, the prostitute's ambitious theatricality could serve as a comic trope for the vigor of the marketplace or as a satiric trope for its corruption and threat to selfhood. Yet for Madan to suggest that the sexual labor of a woman could not possibly be divided from her person was, as we have seen, disruptive and profoundly disturbing. It was either an atavistic idea or an overly modern one; it belonged to a world of traditional absolutist patriarchy or to the dystopian nightmare of universal prostitution in which prostitutes (and other workers) sell not their labor but themselves. Madan implies that men and women do not form couples as complete individuals, making fully consensual contracts in the civil sphere. Any woman who has sex with a man becomes from the moment of copulation his property: There is no such thing as (sexual) labor that can be separated from the body. For his part, the man becomes burdened with supporting the woman for life: There is no such thing as the purchase of (sexual) services in the marketplace. Thus unlike in the rest of eighteenth-century culture's emergent commercial culture and emergent capitalist forms of organization and modes of production, in Madan, despite the claims of his detractors, there can be no such thing as usury of the heart, for a "woman's person cannot be separated from her self."

Yet this potential separation of the person from the self, imagined perhaps first as a female possibility, emerges as key to eighteenth-century constructions of gender, work, class, and identity. Stories about prostitutes in the eighteenth century, then, were not *simply* stories about women or men who have many sexual encounters and compromise their virtue. Prostitution functioned as such a powerful trope because it exposed the fragility of the distinction between the public and private sphere at the moment of their tenuous formation; it proposed a fundamental model for subjectivity and at the same time challenged emergent social structures. Prostitute stories explored the alienation of the most personal kind of labor before the industrial alienation of labor had become routine; they explored the abject limits and intriguing possibilities of emergent commercial relations. Prostitute stories fascinated readers because they potentially suggested the plight of a range of modern subjects, symbolically thrown out of Paradise Hall and forced to imagine what they could bring to a marketplace of tempting luxuries and unstable values that demanded and excoriated the usury of the heart.

While writers throughout history have been intrigued with prostitute figures, nightwalkers held a particular fascination for Britain's eighteenth century, not just in the literary purlieus of Grub Street but at the center of works that critics have long identified as the period's most compelling and most characteristic texts. Criticism, however, has often stopped short of fully coming to terms with their significance, although not, at least in recent years, out of resistance to analyzing gender or sexuality. The explosive intersection of sexuality and commodification, however, remains fraught: Within a progressive context, there are good reasons both to support the rights of sex workers and to find the history of sex work disturbing. Some of the narratives I have looked at in this book have been overlooked; others, however, have long been familiar. Prostitute narratives suggest that by reading women as confined to a private sphere in this period we mistake an ideological work in progress for cultural hegemony, although the voyeuristic depiction, reform, exploitation, and demarcation of prostitutes certainly contributed to this division. Nevertheless, while for Captain Cook the global universality of the alienation of sexual labor naturalized emergent capitalist relations in the expanding British Empire, for writers as diverse politically as Aphra Behn, Bernard Mandeville, Daniel Defoe, Eliza Haywood, John Gay, Samuel Richardson, and Henry Fielding, sex work provided an explosive opportunity to hold capitalist relations up for scrutiny. For a variety of writers, feminists, and sex workers, it has done so ever since.

The heightened capacity of prostitute narratives to explore the predicament of economic desperation and enigmas of desire, however, depended on the ways in which the eighteenth century reimagined sex work in the context of contractarianism and expanding commercialization. Economic restructuring changed the meaning of the "oldest profession," demanding, it seems, more precise definitions throughout the culture between eleemosynary treats and the public ordinary. Related reconceptualizations of gender, sexuality, and the female body changed the meaning of sex work as well, expanding narrative possibilities for the prostitute's pathos and alienation. While eighteenth-century prostitute narratives represented their heroines and heroes as anxious points of recognition for a range of subjects who might find themselves with nothing else to sell, however, the century's fascination with prostitution, complaints of its ambiguity, and construction of sex work as a social problem surfaced alongside the erosion of women's traditional economic importance in the family. Only limited opportunities for "legitimate" work were available to compensate for this loss. Young women especially, then, seemed to embody a new kind of vulnerability in this world of expanding commodification. In dividing the public from the private, this period increasingly defined women by their sexuality, but at the same time rendered infamous any attempt to claim possession of its economic value. That "the commodity" could function as a commodity thus emerged as one of the period's greatest puzzles, biggest scandals, most absorbing narratives, and most revealing contradictions.

Notes

Introduction

1. John Gay, *The Beggar's Opera*, act 2, scene 4, lines 73–75. Future references cited in the text.

2. On sexuality as the emblem of the private sphere, see Michel Foucault, *The History of Sexuality*. See also Roy Porter and Leslie Hall, *The Facts of Life*. On the range of uses of the terms "public" and "private" and the instability of their gendering, see Lawrence Klein, "Gender and the Public/Private Distinction in the Eighteenth Century." I rely on these terms but hope that my work contributes to the general project of challenging their stability.

3. On these changes and the nation's redefinition of itself as commercial, see Joyce Appleby, *Economic Thought and Ideology*; Fernand Braudel, *Civilization and Capitalism, 15th to 18th Century*, esp. vol. 2, *The Wheels of Commerce*; John Brewer, *The Sinews of Power*; John Brewer and Roy Porter, eds., *Consumption and the World of Goods*; Shelley Burtt, *Virtue Transformed*; John Carswell, *The South Sea Bubble*; M. J. Daunton, *Progress and Poverty*; P. G. M. Dickson, *The Financial Revolution in England*; Peter Earle, *The Making of the English Middle Class*; Peter Linebaugh, *The London Hanged*; C. B. Macpherson, *The Political Theory of Possessive Individualism*; Neil McKendrick, John Brewer, and J. H. Plumb, *The Birth of a Consumer Society*; J. G. A. Pocock, *The Machiavellian Moment* and *Virtue, Commerce, and History*; John Sekora, *Luxury*; E. P. Thompson, *The Making of the Working Class*, *Whigs and Hunters*, and *Customs in Common*.

4. James Thompson, *Models of Value*, 3.

5. Srinivas Aravamudan, *Tropicopolitans*, 105–106, Joyce Appleby, *Liberalism and Republicanism*, 126, 135.

6. Some excellent examples include Liz Bellamy, *Commerce, Morality, and the Eighteenth-Century Novel*; Laura Brown, *Ends of Empire*; Catherine Gallagher, *Nobody's Story*; Deidre Shauna Lynch, *The Economy of Character*; Erin Mackie, *Market á La Mode*; Colin Nicholson, *Writing and the Rise of Finance*; Felicity A. Nussbaum, *Torrid Zones*; Gillian Skinner, *Sensibility and Economics*; Thompson, *Models of Value*.

7. Important exceptions, however, include Gallagher, *Nobody's Story*, chap. 1; Vivien Jones, "Eighteenth-Century Prostitution" and "Placing Jemima"; Robert Erickson, *Mother Midnight*; Alison Conway, "The Protestant Cause and a Protestant Whore"; Ruth Perry, "Good Girls and Fallen Women" and *Novel Relations*, chap. 6; John Radner, "The Youthful

Harlot's Curse"; Jennie Batchelor, "'Industry in Distress'"; Elizabeth Kowaleski-Wallace, *Consuming Subjects.*

8. Randolph Trumbach, *Sex and the Gender Revolution;* Tony Henderson, *Disorderly Women in Eighteenth-Century London;* Judith R. Walkowitz's indispensable *Prostitution and Victorian Society* begins in the eighteenth century. Ruth Mazo Karras in *Common Women: Prostitution and Sexuality in Medieval England* provides an important point of contrast with what would follow. See also Edward J. Bristow, *Vice and Vigilance;* Vern Bullough, *The History of Prostitution;* Linda Mahood, *The Magdalenes;* W. A. Speck, "The Harlot's Progress in Eighteenth-Century England"; Stanley Nash, *Prostitution in Great Britain, 1485–1901: An Annotated Bibliography.*

9. Walkowitz, however, focuses mostly on dramatic changes in the middle of the nineteenth century and thus places the emergence of modern prostitution somewhat later than Trumbach and Henderson.

10. To describe erotic literature before *Fanny Hill*—or even to describe *Fanny Hill* with this term—is admittedly anachronistic, but I use the term for convenience to refer to libertine, erotic, bawdy, and sexually explicit texts. On the history of pornography, see Lynn Hunt, ed., *The Invention of Pornography.*

11. See, e.g., James Grantham Turner, *Libertines and Radicals in Early Modern London;* Perry, *Novel Relations,* chap. 6.

12. For a defense of this separation, see Gayle Rubin, "Thinking Sex."

13. On the comparison of libertine to reformist representations, see Vivien Jones's groundbreaking "Eighteenth-Century Prostitution."

14. Male homosexual prostitution drew attention in this period as well. James Bland, for example, in *An Essay in Praise of Women* (1733) complains that "Some Women get their Bread by obliging of Men; and which is worse still, some Men live by obliging one another" (180). Responses to male homosexual prostitution are often, however, overshadowed by the scandal of sodomy rather than the scandal of sexual commodification. No form of homosexual sex was fully acceptable; eighteenth-century culture, however, divided heterosexual sex into acceptable and unacceptable forms. Because of this difference, homosexual prostitution for the most part lies beyond the scope of my project and deserves a study of its own. On male homosexual subcultures, see Rictor Norton's *Mother Clap's Molly House.*

15. On prostitution and female virtue, see, for example, Nancy Armstrong, *Desire and Domestic Fiction,* esp. 77, 182–183, 252–253; Brown, *Ends of Empire;* Jean B. Kern, "The Fallen Woman"; Michael McKeon, *The Origins of the English Novel,* esp. 158; Nussbaum, *Torrid Zones;* Thompson, *Models of Value.* On libertine literature and pornography, see David Foxon, *Libertine Literature in England 1660–1745;* Hunt, ed. *Invention of Pornography;* Bradford Mudge, *The Whore's Story;* Turner, *Libertines and Radicals;* Roger Thompson, *Unfit for Modest Ears;* Pamela Cheek, *Sexual Antipodes,* chaps. 2 and 3. Turner in particular demonstrates the centrality of prostitutes to libertine literature, but see also his "Novel Panic" on the collapsing distinctions between erotic and virtuous reading. On visiting prostitutes as part of masculine self-fashioning, see Trumbach, *Sex and the Gender Revolution.*

16. I use "empathy" in distinction from "sympathy" here: Representations may not ask the reader to feel kindly toward the prostitute, but they often point to the disturbing possibility of sharing her plight.

17. Amanda Anderson, *Tainted Souls and Painted Faces,* 18, 52.

18. Carole Pateman, *The Sexual Contract.*

19. Trumbach, *Sex and the Gender Revolution,* 136, 163.

20. Thomas Laqueur, *Making Sex.*

21. See McKeon, *Origins of the English Novel.*

22. Michael McKeon's "Historicizing Patriarchy" provides an excellent overview, synthesis, and analysis of this issue.

23. While writing mostly about contemporary prostitution, Julia O'Connell Davidson in *Prostitution, Power, and Freedom* offers one of the most useful discussions of gender and heterosexual prostitution, particularly in her cautions against overgeneralizations of all kinds.

24. Joseph Roach, *Cities of the Dead,* 75.

25. Bridget Hill, *Women, Work, and Sexual Politics*, 173.
26. On the emergence of "proletarianized" labor during this period, see John Rule, *The Experience of Labour in Eighteenth-Century English Industry*, esp. 31, 30–34, 74–94; Linebaugh, *The London Hanged*. On women's labor, see Hill, *Women, Work, and Sexual Politics*; Maxine Berg, *The Age of Manufactures: Industry, Innovation, and Work in Britain, 1700–1820*, esp. chap. 6; Alice Clark, *Working Life of Women*; Dorothy George, *London Life in the Eighteenth Century*; Katrina Honeyman, *Women, Gender and Industrialisation in England, 1700–1870*. On women's increasing economic vulnerability in the eighteenth century, see Ruth Perry's indispensable *Novel Relations*, chap. 1.
27. By contrast, as Walkowitz points out, by the nineteenth century prostitutes had been divided into a distinct class of women.
28. Father Poussin, *Pretty Doings in a Protestant Nation*, 5.
29. As James Turner observes, "Centuries before Marxism, the whore stood for the human face of the Commodity, and vice versa." *Libertines and Radicals*, 9.
30. Henderson, *Disorderly Women*, 50; Trumbach, *Sex and the Gender Revolution*, 70. On the increase in prostitution, see also Lawrence Stone, *The Family, Sex and Marriage*, 619.
31. Berg, *Age of Manufactures*, 94. On urbanization, see also Lee Davison, Tim Hitchcock, Tim Keirn, and Robert Shoemaker, *Stilling the Grumbling Hive*.
32. Margaret R. Hunt, *The Middling Sort*, 1. Future references cited in the text.
33. See ibid., 81.
34. Perry makes this point as well in the context of the transformation of kinship in this period; see her *Novel Relations*.
35. Thompson, *Models of Value*, intro.
36. Hirschman, *The Passions and the Interests*, 132, 51–52.
37. Gallagher, *Nobody's Story*, chap. 1.
38. Bertell Ollman, *Alienation*, 133. See also Karl Marx, "Estranged Labour," in Tucker, ed. *The Marx-Engels Reader*, 71–81.
39. Perry, *Novel Relations*, 283.
40. Walkowitz, *Prostitution and Victorian Society*, 4.

A "Cool State of Indifference"

1. Karras, *Common Women*, esp. 3, 6, 48.
2. The representation of the prostitute as lascivious, of course, persists even to our own time. In this chapter I am proposing not the disappearance of this possibility but the expansion of alternative ones.
3. For discussions of the prostitute's association with theatricality, see Bradford Mudge, *The Whore's Story*.
4. Many representations, of course, fall between these extremes. On the changing perception of prostitution in the eighteenth century, see Tony Henderson, *Disorderly Women*, esp. 197.
5. For a more detailed description of this debate, see Vivien Jones, "Eighteenth-Century Prostitution."
6. Gayle Rubin articulates this position in her influential essay "Thinking Sex." See also Ann McClintock, "Sex Workers and Sex Work" as well as the issue of *Social Text* (edited by McClintock) in which McClintock's introductory essay appears; Priscilla Alexander and Frédérique Delacoste, eds., *Sex Work*; Jill Nagle, *Whores and Other Feminists*; Kamala Kempadoo and Jo Doezema, eds., *Global Sex Workers*.
7. Wendy Chapkis, *Live Sex Acts*, chap. 3.
8. Jeffreys, *The Idea of Prostitution*. See also Kathleen Barry, *Female Sexual Slavery*. Jeffreys provides a good overview of the feminist case against prostitution.
9. Pateman, *The Sexual Contract*, 207.
10. For extended critiques of Pateman's formulation, see Nancy Fraser, *Justice Interruptus*, chap. 10, and McClintock, "Sex Workers and Sex Work."

11. Radin, *Contested Commodities*.

12. See Joyce Oldham Appleby, *Economic Thought*, which describes the urgent conflicts over commodification in this period.

13. "Private Property and Communism" in *The Marx-Engels Reader*, 82, n.7.

14. Chancer, "Prostitution, Feminist Theory, and Ambivalence," 146.

15. *The Rover*, act 2, scene 2, p. 188.

16. Turner, *Libertines and Radicals*, 5.

17. Turner, *Libertines and Radicals*, 239.

18. Similarly, Frances Dolan has shown how sexual slander functioned in anti-Catholic rhetoric; Jill Campbell has shown how sexual slander became a powerful weapon in Fielding's anti-Jacobite writings; Alison Conway has shown how thinking about the figure of the courtesan can help us reread the politics of Aphra Behn's *Love Letters from a Nobleman to his Sister*. See Dolan, *Whores of Babylon*; Campbell, *Natural Masques*; Conway, "The Protestant Cause and a Protestant Whore." Conway also suggests, however, how the courtesan in Behn's novel explores the possibility of a new kind of personal freedom.

19. See, e.g., Manuela Mourão, "The Representation of Female Desire in Early Modern Pornographic Texts, 1660–1745."

20. On the consistent representation of prostitution as something other than labor in this period, see Melissa M. Mowry, *The Bawdy Politic in Stuart England*, chap. 5. Mowry singles out Alexander Oldy's *The London Jilt* as an exception; nevertheless, the heroine, while sometimes motivated by need in the narrative, is also driven to prostitution by sexual desire.

21. Humphrey Mill, *A Night's Search* (1640), 27. Future references cited in the text. Mill predates most of the other examples in this chapter, but his poem shows some interesting similarities.

22. [John Garfield], *The Wandring Whore* (1660), no. 2, p. 12. Future references cited in the text.

23. *Character of a Town-Miss* (1690), 3.

24. Edward Ward, *The Insinuating Bawd and the Repenting Harlot* (1700), 2.

25. *The London-Bawd* (1711), 6. The date of first publication is unknown, but probably in the late seventeenth century. As Turner notes, *The London-Bawd* "greedily plagiarizes" from *A Night's Search*. See his "Pictorial Prostitution."

26. Turner, *Libertines and Radicals*, 155.

27. Karras, *Common Women*, 11.

28. On the seventeenth-century conflicts in Ireland, see R. F. Foster, *Modern Ireland*, part 1. On Head's Irish experience, see Christopher Wheatley, *Beneath Iërene's Banners*, chap. 1.

29. Richard Head and Francis Kirkman, *The English Rogue*. Long sections of volume 1 are mispaginated, and the chapters are misnumbered; this incident occurs in the third appearance of a page 15 in volume 1. Head seems to be the sole author of volume 1 and Kirkman of volume 2. I refer to the dual authorship throughout.

30. I wish to thank John Stevenson for suggesting this reading of the fat bawd in another context.

31. Hirschman, *The Passions and the Interests*.

32. See Ollman, *Alienation*.

33. *The Crafty Whore* (1658). Future references cited in the text. As James Turner points out, many libertine writers in this period, like the author of *The Crafty Whore*, found inspiration in Pietro Aretino's *Dialogues* (*Libertines and Radicals*, 125). Aretino's *Dialogues* also provides a strong precursor for the tensions between business and pleasure in Restoration texts. While Aretino's *Dialogues* discuss the financial motivations for prostitution, the women involved are also lascivious. When the initiate asks about the whore's own "lust and love of lewdness," her teacher replies that "the man who drinks all the time is never very thirsty, and the person who sits all day at the table is rarely hungry." (131). Good prostitutes, then, are sexually fulfilled, even glutted. She expresses contempt for whores who "just lie down and open their legs," predicting that they will inevitably fail at prostitution (194–195). Aretino, *Aretino's Dialogues*.

34. On faked virginity, see Tassie Gwilliam, "Female Fraud."

35. Gallagher, *Nobody's Story*, chap. 1. On *The Whore's Rhetorick*, see also James Grantham Turner, "*The Whore's Rhetorick*." Turner argues for the contribution of early pornography to the novel, especially in its creation of new forms of subjectivity. *The Whore's Rhetorick* is a "loose English translation" of Ferrante Pallavicino's *La retorica delle puttane;* see also Turner's discussion of this text in *Libertines and Radicals*, 3.

36. *The Whore's Rhetorick* (1683), 36. Future references cited in the text. This text spells the bawd's names as "Creswel," but I have used the more common spelling of her name here.

37. On literary connections between usury and prostitution, see Ann Louise Kibbie, "Monstrous Generation."

38. For a compelling analysis of ideas about inner and outer selves as related to the marketplace, see Deidre Shauna Lynch, *The Economy of Character.* Lynch argues that the "round" character, who attempts to resolve tensions between inner and outer identities as she or he consumes in the marketplace, only truly emerges in the second half of the eighteenth century. But while characters may not be fully "rounded" in earlier writing, texts such as *The Whore's Rhetorick* (1683) begin to explore the tensions between the possibility of a self in the marketplace and a self held back from it. Writers found the figure of the prostitute particularly revealing in regard to this problem.

39. Samuel Jackson Pratt, "Almeria; or, The Penitent," in *Life of a Lady of the Town* (1801), 11–12.

40. Jonas Hanway, *Letters Written Occasionally on the Customs of Foreign Nations in Regard to Harlots* (1761), 318.

41. *The Suicide Prostitute: A Poem* (1805), 7.

42. James Graham, *A Lecture on the Generation, Increase, and Improvement of the Human Species* (1784), 7.

43. N. D. Falck, *A Treatise on Venereal Disease* (1772), 87.

44. In his defense of divorce, Gideon Archer [Peter Annet] argues that even conjugal sex becomes prostitution when emotional engagement has dissolved. In this situation, the wife "prostitute[s]" herself to her husband because she sleeps with him without desire: "Is it not rather intrinsically whoredom in the worst sense of it?" [Peter Annet], *Social Bliss Considered* (1744), 30.

45. Pratt, *Life of a Lady of the Town*, 31.

46. King, *The Frauds of London Detected* (1780?), v. Future references cited in the text. "Richard King" is probably a pseudonym.

47. Ann Louise Kibbie, "Sentimental Properties."

48. Robert A. Erickson, *Mother Midnight*, esp. 77.

49. Mark Kinkead-Weekes, *Samuel Richardson*, 88. On this point, see also Carol Houlihan Flynn, *Samuel Richardson*, 136. Flynn argues that Richardson revealed middle-class ideology a bit too clearly, thus arousing the storm of anti-Pamelas.

50. On this controversy, see also Richard Gooding, "*Pamela, Shamela*, and the Politics of the *Pamela* Vogue"; Scarlett Bowen, "'A Sawce-Box and Boldface Indeed.'"

51. *Pamela Censured* (1741), 19.

52. William B. Warner, *Licensing Entertainment*, chaps. 1 and 5. On *Pamela* as pornography, see also Stephen Raynie, "Hayman and Gravelot's Anti-Pamela Designs for Richarson's Octavo Edition of *Pamela*."

53. Henry Fielding, *An Apology for the Life of Mrs. Shamela Andrews*, 35. Future references cited in the text.

54. On Parry's self-feminization, see Terri Nickel, "*Pamela* and Fetish."

55. Eliza Haywood, *Anti-Pamela; or, Mock-Modesty Display'd and Punish'd* (1742). A different subtitle—"Feign'd Innocence Detected"—appears on the title page. Future references cited in the text.

56. *Memoirs of the Life of Lady H* (1741), 23.

57. See her reading of *The Female Quixote* in chapter 4 of *Nobody's Story*.

58. On the cost of Pamela's upward mobility, see James Cruise, "*Pamela* and the Commerce of Authority."

The "Deluge of Depravity"

1. "A Beautiful Young Nymph Going to Bed," in *Jonathan Swift: The Complete Poems*, 453–454.

2. See John Radner, "The Youthful Harlot's Curse"; Robert Erickson, *Mother Midnight*. Laura Brown has shown how both Whig and Tory writers misogynistically used the figure of a woman in their critique or defense of capitalism. Many of the figures she looks at are not only women but also "whores." See her *Ends of Empire*. On the Tory literary critique of capitalism in this period, see Colin Nicholson, *Writing and the Rise of Finance*.

3. Pocock, *Virtue, Commerce, and History*. See also Paula Backscheider, "Defoe's Lady Credit"; Sandra Sherman, "Lady Credit No Lady"; Catherine Ingrassia, "The Pleasure of Business and the Business of Pleasure." For an interesting alternative reading, see Terry Mulcaire, "Public Credit; Or, the Feminization of Virtue in the Marketplace."

4. See Sherman, "Lady Credit No Lady."

5. Pocock, *Virtue, Commerce, and History*, 235–238; Lawrence Klein, "The Third Earl of Shaftesbury and the Progress of Politeness."

6. Joseph Addison and Richard Steele, *The Spectator*, ed. Donald F. Bond, 2:534–535; no. 266, Friday, January 4, 1712.

7. On this ambivalence, see Erin Mackie, *Market á La Mode*, intro.

8. See Shelly Burtt, *Virtue Transformed*.

9. On the economic conditions that may have increased prostitution, see Lee Davison, Tim Hitchcock, Tim Keirn, and Robert B. Shoemaker, "Introduction," in *Stilling the Grumbling Hive: The Response to Social and Economic Problems in England, 1689–1750*; Bridget Hill, *Women, Work, and Sexual Politics*. Hill argues that women's access to labor decreased during this period, a problem unacknowledged by reformers that surely contributed to the increase in urban prostitution. See also Maxine Berg, *The Age of Manufactures*; Katrina Honeyman, *Women, Gender and Industrialisation in England, 1700–1870*; John Rule, *The Experience of Labour*.

10. Swift, "A Beautiful Young Nymph Going to Bed," 454. See also Defoe, *Reformation of Manners* (1702); Jonathan Swift, "A Project for the Advancement of Religion and the Reformation of Manners" (1709).

11. Bernard Mandeville, *The Fable of the Bees; or, Private Vices, Publick Benefits*, ed. F. B. Kaye (2 vols.), and *A Modest Defence of Publick Stews* (1724). Membership in the SRMs seems to have been primarily, if not exclusively, male. I have not encountered a single reference to a female SRM member or activist.

12. On Thomas Bray, see Samuel Smith, *Publick Spirit* (1746).

13. Thomas Bray, *The Good Fight of Faith* (1709), 15.

14. Edward J. Bristow, *Vice and Vigilance*, 25.

15. Ibid., 25.

16. On prostitution and the law in the eighteenth century, see Tony Henderson, *Disorderly Women*.

17. Dudley W. R. Bahlman, *The Moral Revolution of 1688*; Shelly Burtt, "The Societies for the Reformation of Manners."

18. Bahlman, *Moral Revolution of 1688*, 62.

19. See Tina Isaacs, "The Anglican Hierarchy and the Reformation of Manners 1688–1738."

20. Josiah Woodward, *An Account of the Progress of the Reformation of Manners*, 3–5.

21. On liberal compartmentalization, see Margaret Jane Radin, *Contested Commodities*, 30.

22. Josiah Woodward, *An Account of the Rise and Progress of the Religious Societies*.

23. T. C. Curtis and W. A. Speck, "The Societies for the Reformation of Manners: A Case Study in the Theory and Practice of Moral Reform," 48.

24. See Bristow, *Vice and Vigilance*, 21; Robert B. Shoemaker, "Reforming the City: The Reformation of Manners Campaign in London, 1690–1738." As Bristow points out (25), since prostitution was not illegal, reformers generally tried to convict women of disorderly behavior. Curtis and Speck, however, point out that after 1730 the sin of Sabbath breaking began to out-

strip lewdness in the arrest records of the SRMs. Sabbath breaking also constituted a division between good and bad commerce, as their arrests were of tradesmen conducting business on the Sabbath. See Curtis and Speck, "The Societies for the Reformation of Manners."

25. Josiah Woodward, *An Account of the Societies for Reformation of Manners*, 11. Woodward's account was repeated, reprinted, quoted, and summarized for many years. See, e.g., Francis Grant Cullen, *A Brief Account of the Nature, Rise, and Progress of the Societies for the Reformation of Manners*.

26. *Proposals for a National Reformation of Manners* (1694); *A Black List of the Names, or Reputed Names, of Seven Hundred Fifty Two Lewd and Scandalous Persons . . . .* (1694).

27. James Peller Malcolm, *Anecdotes of the Manners and Customs of London during the Eighteenth Century*.

28. Ibid., 81.

29. Shoemaker, "Reforming the City," 106.

30. Bahlman, *Moral Revolution of 1688*, 40–41.

31. On the politics of prostitution and libertinism during the Restoration, see Thompson, *Unfit for Modest Ears*; Turner, *Libertines and Radicals*; Tim Harris, *London Crowds in the Reign of Charles II*, 82.

32. *Poor-Whores Petition* (1668). See also *The Citizens Reply to the Whores Petition, and Prentices Answer* (1668); *The Gracious Answer of the Most Illustrious Lady of Pleasure* (1668); *The Tryals of Such Persons under the Notion of London Apprentices Were Tumultuously Assembled in Moore-Fields, and Other Places, on Easter Holidays Last, under Colour of Pulling Down Bawdy-Houses* (1668); *The Whore's Petition to the London Prentices* (1668). On bawdy house riots, see Turner, *Libertines and Radicals*, esp. 61.

33. On associations of Catholics with illicit sexuality, see Frances E. Dolan, *Whores of Babylon*; Alison Conway, "The Protestant Cause and a Protestant Whore." For attacks in the period on Catholicism as whorish, see, for example, Francis Howgill, *Mistery Babylon the Mother of Harlots* (1659); *God's Judgments against Whoring* (1697).

34. See Geoffrey Holmes, *The Trial of Doctor Sacheverell*.

35. See John Dunton, *The Impeachment*, 15, 28.

36. *The Officers' Address to the Ladies*, cited in Holmes, *Trial of Doctor Sacheverell*, 119–120. On responses to Sacheverell's controversial sermon, *The Perils of False Brethren*, see esp. chap. 4.

37. See Defoe's *Review* no. 85, in *The Best of Defoe's Review: An Anthology* (1951), *The Poor Man's Plea* (1700), and *Reformation of Manners, a Satyr* (1702).

38. Henry Sacheverell, *The Character of a Low-Churchman*, 11.

39. Isaacs, "Anglican Hierarchy and the Reformation of Manners, 1688–1738," 402. See Matthew Hole, *The True Reformation of Manners* (1699).

40. *The Heaven-Drivers* (1701), 10.

41. William Bisset, *The Modern Fanatick* (1710), 13.

42. Burtt, "Societies for the Reformation of Manners."

43. Edmund Calamy, *A Sermon Preach'd before the Societies for Reformation of Manners* (1699), 11, 21.

44. Burtt, *Virtue Transformed*, esp. 42–61. Burtt, however, sees this line of argument as strategic, covering their spiritual motives with secular ones.

45. On the motives of a related group, the Society for Promoting Christian Knowledge (SPCK), as similarly ideological, see Tim Hitchcock, "Paupers and Preachers: The SPCK and the Parochial Workhouse Movement."

46. *Some Considerations upon Street-Walkers. With a Proposal for lessening the present number of them* (1726), 2. This pamphlet has been attributed Defoe, but its authorship remains disputed.

47. Shoemaker, "Reforming the City," 109.

48. Woodward, *Account of the Societies for the Reformation of Manners*, 22.

49. *Antimoixeia* (1691). Quoted by Henderson, *Disorderly Women*, 167–168.

50. John Spademan, *A Sermon Preach'd November 14, 1698: And Now Publish'd at the Request of the Societies for Reformation of Manners*, 35.

51. Daniel Williams, *A Sermon Preach'd before the Societies for Reformation of Manners* (1700), 21.

52. John Whitlock, *A Sermon Preached to the Society for Reformation of Manners* (1698), 31, 36.

53. George Meriton, *Immorality, Debauchery, and Profaneness, Exposed* (1698), 116. On the case of Thomas Savage, see Melissa M. Mowry, *The Bawdy Politic in Stuart England, 1660–1714*, 110.

54. See, e.g., *The Fifteen Comforts of Whoring* (1705); Josiah Woodward, *The Young Man's Monitor* (1706), 8.

55. John Disney, *An Essay upon the Execution of the Laws against Immorality and Prophaneness* (1708), ix.

56. Ibid., vii.

57. On the expectations of men in the private sphere during this time, see Shawn Lisa Maurer, *Proposing Men*.

58. On the explosion of attacks on luxury during this period, see John Sekora, *Luxury*.

59. See Laura Mandell, *Misogynous Economies*, chap. 3.

60. Ibid.

61. Lisa A. Freeman, *Character's Theater*, 121.

62. Bristow, *Vice and Vigilance*, 19.

63. *The Character of an Informer* (1675), 1.

64. Ibid., 3, 5.

65. Bristow, *Vice and Vigilance*, 26.

66. Daniel Burgess, *The Golden Snuffers* (1697).

67. Bisset, *Plain English* (1704) 15, 21.

68. *Seasonable Advice to the Societies for Reformation of Manners* (1699), 7.

69. See James Grantham Turner, "Pictorial Prostitution"; Maurer, *Proposing Men*, chap. 3.

70. John Dunton, *The Night-Walker; or, Evening Rambles in Search after Lewd Women*, preface. Future references cited in the text.

71. On the contradictions in Dunton's persona, see Turner, "Pictorial Prostitution." Turner also points out that even though Dunton claims to record his personal experience, many of his anecdotes were taken from libertine texts. On the pun on "nighwalker," see also Maurer, *Proposing Men*, 65.

72. Maurer, *Proposing Men*, 66; Turner, "Pictorial Prostitution," 58.

73. E. J. Hundert, *The Enlightenment's Fable*, 216.

74. In Mandeville, *The Fable of the Bees; or, Private Vices, Publick Benefits*, 1:385. Future references are cited in the text. Critics often quote this condemnation but, interestingly, tend to omit the last phrase in which the jury identifies the defense of the stews as Mandeville's most telling point. On the politics and timing of this condemnation, see W. A. Speck, "Bernard Mandeville and the Middlesex Grand Jury."

75. This was not the only time that Mandeville responded to his critics. See M. M. Goldsmith, "Mandeville's Pernicious System."

76. Hundert, *Enlightenment's Fable*. I am indebted to Hundert's excellent study of Mandeville. See also M. M. Goldsmith, "Regulating Anew the Moral and Political Sentiments of Mankind."

77. Hundert, *Enlightenment's Fable*, 14. See also Peter Miller, "Citizenship and Culture in Early Modern Europe."

78. For some of the major arguments on Mandeville's ethical and rhetorical stance, see Harold J. Cook, "Bernard Mandeville and the Therapy of 'the Clever Politician.'"; Stephen H. Daniel, "Myth and Rationality in Mandeville"; Timothy Dykstal, "Commerce, Conversation, and Contradiction in Mandeville's *Fable*"; Thomas R. Edwards, "Mandeville's Moral Prose"; Goldsmith, "Mandeville's Pernicious System"; M. M. Goldsmith, *Private Vices, Public Benefits*, 58; Phillip Harth, "The Satiric Purpose of *The Fable of the Bees*"; Anne Mette Hjort, "Mandeville's Ambivalence Modernity"; M. R. Jack, "Religion and Ethics in Mandeville"; Jonathan Brody Kramnick, "'Unwilling to Be Short, or Plain, in Any Thing Concerning Gain': Bernard Mandeville and the Dialectic of Charity"; D. H. Monro, *The Ambivalence of Bernard Mandeville*; W. A. Speck, "Mandeville and the Eutopia Seated in the Brain"; Gordon S. Vichert, "Bernard Mandeville's *The Virgin Unmask'd*."

79. On the debate over Mandeville as an advocate of laissez-faire economics, see Nathan Rosenberg, "Mandeville and Laissez-Faire"; Salim Rashid, "Mandeville's *Fable: Laissez-Faire* or Libertinism?"

80. Francis Hutcheson, *Thoughts on Laughter; and Observations of the Fable of the Bees* (1758).

81. See Thomas A. Horne, *The Social Thought of Bernard Mandeville*, chap. 4.

82. Barbon, *A Discourse of Trade* (1690), 65.

83. North, *Discourses upon Trade* (1691), 14.

84. Rashid, "Mandeville's *Fable*." Libertine authors made use of Mandeville's arguments; see, e.g., Gideon Archer [Peter Annet], *Social Bliss Considered*. Archer/Annet takes whole chunks of his argument for public whoring from Mandeville's *Defence*.

85. D. H. Monro, *The Ambivalence of Bernard Mandeville*, 4. Monro, however, sees the moralist as only one side of Mandeville.

86. See also Hundert, *Enlightenment's Fable*, 92.

87. For an alternative view, see Mandell, *Misogynous Economies*, chap. 3.

88. Thus Francis Hutcheson (in *Thoughts on Laughter; and Oberservations of the Fable of the Bees* [1758]) answered Mandeville not by rejecting commerce but by distinguishing (compartmentalizing) between moderate consumption that enhances life and luxurious consumption that leads to ruin.

89. Richard I. Cook, "'The Great Leviathan of Lechery': Mandeville's *Modest Defence of the Publick Stews* (1724)," 22–33. Hundert, however, calls it "wry but wholly unsatirical" (217); Samuel J. Rogal sees it as a reasonable argument against less-enlightened opponents in "The Selling of Sex: Mandeville's *Modest Defence of Publick Stews*."

90. Bernard Mandeville, *A Modest Defence of Publick Stews* (1724), 64. Future references cited in the text.

91. Ward, *The City Madam, and the Country Maid* (1702), 3–4.

92. Roy Porter, "Pre-Modernism and the Art of Shopping," 10.

93. Ibid., 12.

94. See Hundert, *Enlightenment's Fable*, 208, 217. As Hundert points out, Mandeville here repeats an ancient association between women and luxury.

95. Mandell, *Misogynous Economies*, 64. Mandell argues that there is identification between these figures as well, but the identification in her argument is mainly for the purpose of more effective scapegoating.

96. J. Douglas Canfield, "Prostitution as Class Prophylactic."

97. See Mandeville, *Fable of the Bees*, 1:19.

98. Another argument might be that Mandeville does not really advocate a free market. Thomas A. Horne argues that instead of advocating a laissez-faire economy, Mandeville, like the other mercantilists of his time, believed that the government needed to regulate international trade (66–67). Yet as Rosenberg has argued, Mandeville advocates government intervention only through the sly manipulations of clever politicians who find ways to reap social benefits out of human vice. The draconian restrictions on prostitutes here considerably exceed this model.

99. Pateman, *Sexual Contract*, 203.

Whore, Turk, and Jew

1. Quoted by Sander Gilman, *The Jew's Body*, 112.

2. Ibid., 108.

3. Daniel Defoe, *Roxana: The Fortunate Mistress*, 111. Future references cited in the text.

4. Thompson, *Models of Value*, chap. 3.

5. On Roxana's adoption of different identities, see Bradford K. Mudge, *The Whore's Story*, 180–182; David Blewett, *Defoe's Art of Fiction*, chap. 5; David Durant, "Roxana's Fictions."

6. See Frank Felsenstein, *Anti-Semitic Stereotypes: A Paradigm of Otherness in English Popular Culture, 1660–1830*.

7. Exemplary readings along these lines include *Roxana* chapters in Maximillian Novak, *Defoe and the Nature of Man;* Lincoln B. Faller, *Crime and Defoe;* Thompson, *Models of Value;* Felicity A. Nussbaum, *Torrid Zones,* 30–41; also, Ann Louise Kibbie, "Monstrous Generation: The Birth of Capital in Defoe's *Moll Flanders* and *Roxana*"; Robert Hume, "The Conclusion of Defoe's *Roxana: Fiasco* or Tour De Force?"; James H. Maddox, "On Defoe's *Roxana.*"

8. Marshall, *The Figure of Theater,* 132; Sandra Sherman, "Lady Credit No Lady." Bram Dijkstra in *Defoe and Economics: The Fortunes of "Roxana" in the History of Interpretation* argues that Defoe expresses his marketplace philosophy *most* clearly in *Roxana.* Others have seen feminist potential in Defoe's representation of Roxana's independence and his sympathetic portrayal of the heroine's predicament; see Katherine Rogers, "The Feminism of Defoe's *Roxana*"; Robyn Wiegman, "Economies of the Body"; Paula Backscheider, "Defoe's Women: Snares and Prey"; Alison Conway, "Defoe's Protestant Whore." While I agree with the insights of these critics, I also argue that the potential for anxious identification with a figure abandoned to the marketplace with the body as the only resource does not belong to women alone.

9. For recent arguments along these lines, see Nussbaum, *Torrid Zones,* 30–41; Katie Trumpener, "Rewriting Roxane."

10. On *Roxana's* exploration of theatricality, see Marshall, chap. 6.

11. Elizabeth Howe (*The First English Actresses,* 148–149) identifies Hester Davenport as having performed this role.

12. Richard Head and Francis Kirkman, *The English Rogue* (1665), 2:344.

13. See Margaret R. Hunt, *The Middling Sort.*

14. Hume, "Conclusion of Defoe's *Roxana.*" See also Ian H. Bell, *Defoe's Fiction;* Maximillian E. Novak, "Crime and Punishment in Defoe's Roxana"; John Richetti, "The Family, Sex, and Marriage in Defoe's *Moll Flanders* and *Roxana.*"

15. Laura Brown, *Ends of Empire,* chap. 4.

16. On usury in this novel, see Kibbie, "Monstrous Generation."

17. Brown, *Ends of Empire,* 150.

18. Michael Ragussis, "Jews and Other 'Outlandish Englishmen,'" 296.

19. Felsenstein, *Anti-Semitic Stereotypes,* 200.

20. *Nocturnal Revels* (1779), 1:48.

21. Granville, *The Jew of Venice* (1701), 12.

22. *The Jew Decoy'd; Or, The Progress of a Harlot* (1733). See also Theophilus Cibber, *The Harlot's Progress* (1733) *and Rake's Progress* (1778–1780).

23. *The Humours of Fleet-Street and the Strand,* 11.

24. *Nocturnal Revels,* 1:47–8.

25. *An Authentic Narrative of the Most Remarkable Adventures and Curious Intrigues Exhibited in the Life of Miss Fanny Davies, the Celebrated Modern Amazon* (1786).

26. *The Happy Courtezan; or, The Prude Demolished* (1735), 2.

27. *Memoirs of the Celebrated Miss Fanny M[urray]* (1759), 1:101.

28. *The Life and Intrigues of the Late Celebrated Mrs. Mary Parrimore* (1729), 13.

29. As we will see in greater detail in chapter 4, however, the prostitute's estrangement from pleasure could alternatively suggest her capacity to reform. In *Roxana* and other narratives, it holds a more ominous meaning.

30. *Characters of the Present Most Celebrated Courtezans* (1780), 46.

31. *The Secret History of Betty Ireland* (1750?), 11.

32. *The Highlanders Salivated* (1746), 37.

33. Humphrey Humdrum [pseud.], *Mother Midnight's Comical Pocket-Book* (1753), 46.

34. Thomas Brown, *Amusements, Serious and Comical,* 200.

35. Richard Ames, *The Female Fire-Ships* (1691), 12.

36. Henry Fielding, *Miss Lucy in Town* in *Complete Works of Henry Fielding,* 12: 44–5.

37. *Nocturnal Revels,* 1:46–47.

38. *The Life and Character of Moll King,* 9–10.

39. On this point, see also John F. O'Brien, "The Character of Credit: Defoe's 'Lady Credit,'

The Fortunate Mistress, and the Resources of Inconsistency in Early Eighteenth-Century Britain," 608–609.

40. E. J. Hundert, *The Enlightenment's Fable,* 12.

41. Philanthropos [pseud.], *A Letter to a Friend in the Country, on the Subject of the Jew Bill* (1753), 17.

42. Solomon Abrabanal [William Arnall], *The Complaint of the Children of Israel* (1736), 7.

43. For a complex reading of the power relations between the two women, see Terry Castle, "'Amy, Who Knew my Disease': A Psychosexual Pattern in Defoe's *Roxana.*"

44. This biblical story seems to have been put to bawdy use elsewhere in popular culture as well. In Charles Knipe's *A City Ramble* (1715), a woman named Rachel defends her husband against the accusation that he slept with a prostitute by declaring that he has long been impotent with her. She did, however, once catch him "trespassing with my Handmaid" (53).

45. On Roxana's dilemma for her own survival, see Toni Bowers, *The Politics of Motherhood,* 111–113.

46. See Felsenstein, *Anti-Semitic Stereotypes,* chap. 6.

47. Charles Johnstone, *Chrysal; or, The Adventures of a Guinea* (1760), 2:151.

48. *A Historical and Law-Treatise against Jews and Judaism* (1732), 4, 6, 19. Also published in 1703, 1720, 1721, 1732, 1733, 1736, 1753, and possibly earlier as well.

49. Head and Kirkman, *English Rogue,* 1:147.

50. D'Blossiers Tovey, *Anglia Judaica* (1738), 136. Tovey, however, cites this passage as an example of unjust accusations against Jews.

51. [Toland], "Reasons for Naturalizing the Jews in Great Britain and Ireland" (1714).

52. Menasseh Ben Israel, *To His Highness the Lord Protector* (1655); Josiah Tucker, *A Letter to a Friend Concerning Naturalizations* (1753), 16.

53. Eliza Haywood, *The Fair Hebrew; or, A True, but Secret History of Two Jewish Ladies, Who Lately Resided in London* (1729), 43.

54. Girard, *Violence and the Sacred.*

55. Shapiro, *Shakespeare and the Jews,* chap. 4; see also Felsenstein, *Anti-Semitic Stereotypes,* chaps. 6 and 7.

56. Harold Weber, "Carolinean Sexuality and the Restoration Stage: Reconstructing the Royal Phallus in Sodom."

57. See Felsenstein, *Anti-Semitic Stereotypes,* 43.

58. See, e.g., *Adventures under-Ground* (1750); *The Remarkable Trial of the Queen of Quavers* (1777).

59. On enigmas of desire in capitalism, I am here following Slavoj Žižek, *The Sublime Object of Ideology,* chap. 3.

60. See, e.g., Carol Houlihan Flynn, *The Body in Swift and Defoe,* 80.

61. *The Complete English Tradesman* (1726), 143.

62. On the significance of Roxana's Protestantism, see also Conway, "Defoe's Protestant Whore."

63. [Jonas Hanway], *A Review of the Proposed Naturalization of the Jews* (1753), 75.

64. Ibid., 18.

65. Philanthropos [pseud.], *Letter,* 27, 13. Nevertheless, "Philanthropos" also sees the bill as an opportunity to convert Jews and prays for their souls.

66. Tucker, *A Second Letter to a Friend Concerning Naturalizations* (1753).

67. Grosley, *A Tour to London,* 1:368.

68. Colquhoun, *A Treatise on the Police of the Metropolis* (1796).

69. See Bowers, *The Politics of Motherhood,* 111–113, which offers an excellent account and refutation of these arguments. Bowers argues that the narrative shows the severe limits of Roxana's choices.

70. See, e.g., Novak, "Crime and Punishment in Defoe's *Roxana*"; Hume, "The Conclusion of Defoe's *Roxana.*"

71. I refer here to her "wicked Arguments for Whoring" in response to Amy's suggestion

that her current wealth would qualify her for an aristocratic marriage (132), as well as her argument to the Dutch merchant.

72. This is because even though the Dutch merchant takes her for a widow, she told him that she had been married to the jeweler. He knows nothing about the brewer, who is still alive and still her husband at this point; the legitimate children, then, could never be sought or contacted.

73. *Conjugal Lewdness* (1727), 112.

74. In addition to caring for her legitimate children, Roxana also takes care of the son she had with the jeweler before she became fully a "Woman of Business."

75. Faller, *Crime and Defoe*, 235.

76. John Richetti rightly calls this scene "the emotional climax of the book" in "The Family, Sex, and Marriage in Defoe's *Moll Flanders* and *Roxana*," 33.

77. The only other kiss she even bestows is on the hand to the prince, but this is more a token of respect than passion.

Fanny's Sisters

1. See Lincoln B. Faller, *Crime and Defoe*.

2. Martin Madan, *The Magdalen: or, The Dying Penitent* (1763); *The Life and Adventures of a Reformed Magdalen in a Series of Letters to Mrs. B***, of Northampton. Written by Herself* (1763); *The Histories of Some of the Penitents in the Magdalen-House, as Supposed to Be Related by Themselves* (1760); *The Secret History of Betty Ireland* (1750? n.d.); *Memoirs of the Celebrated Miss Fanny M[urray]* (1759); *The Velvet Coffee-Woman; or, The Life, Gallantries and Amours of the late Famous Mrs. Anne Rochford* (1728); *The Life and Intrigues of the Late Celebrated Mrs. Mary Parrimore* (1729); *The Life of Lavinia Beswick, Alias Fenton, Alias Polly Peachum* (1728); *The Juvenile Adventures of Miss Kitty F[ishe]r* (1759); *An Authentic Narrative of the Most Remarkable Adventures and Curious Intrigues Exhibited in the Life of Miss Fanny Davies, the Celebrated Modern Amazon* (1786); *The Life and Character of Moll King, Late Mistress of King's Coffee-House in Covent-Garden* (1747); *The Life and Actions of that Notorious Bawd Susan Wells* (1753); Margaret Leeson, *The Memoirs of Mrs. Leeson, Madam 1727–1797*; Ann Sheldon, *Authentic and Interesting Memoirs of Miss Ann Sheldon* (1790); Teresia Constantia Phillips, *An Apology for the Conduct of Mrs. Teresia Constantia Phillips* (1748–1749); *The History of Emma; or, The Victim of Depravity* (1800); Phebe Phillips, *The Woman of the Town; or, Authentic Memoirs of Phebe Phillips; Otherwise Maria Maitland; Well Know in the Vicinity of Covent Garden. Written by Herself* (1801). This list is selective rather than comprehensive. The discussion in this chapter is, by necessity, even more selective; I have tried, however, to choose a representative sample. While nearly all of them claim to be true, I am reading them here for their representation of prostitution rather than as historical record. I cite them by the information given in the texts; nevertheless, some of those claiming to be authored by prostitutes may be either ghost-written or fabricated.

3. One biography of Kitty Fisher, for example, includes a letter supposedly from Fanny Murray; Charles Walker's narrative about Sally Salisbury opens with a litany of praise for great prostitutes from classical to modern times.

4. On differences between libertine and reformist prostitute narratives, see also Vivien Jones, "Eighteenth-Century Prostitution." On the overlap of reformist and libertine genres, see William Warner's analysis of the *Pamela* "media event" in *Licensing Entertainment*, chap. 5.

5. Trumbach, *Sex and the Gender Revolution*.

6. See H. F. B Compston, *The Magdalen Hospital: The Story of a Great Charity*, and more recently, Donna T. Andrew, *Philanthropy and Police*, 119–126. Andrew shows the significant break between this new reform movement and earlier, more physically violent ones and their interest in turning prostitutes into "useful" citizens. For an excellent discussion of the relationship between the Magdalen Hospital and "Magdalen literature," see Markman Ellis, *The Politics of Sensibility*, chap. 5.

7. In individual cases they also blame, as Ellis points out, nefarious males. A more sociological analysis, however, comes through in much of their writing, as I will show.

8. *The Highlanders Salivated* (1746), 37.

9. Many historians point out that the reform movements failed to diminish prostitution. See Trumbach, *Sex and the Gender Revolution*, 120; Edward J. Bristow, *Vice and Vigilance;* Tony Henderson, *Disorderly Women.*

10. J. W. Archenholz, *A Picture of England: Containing a Description of the Laws, Customs, and Manners,* 2:33, 2:90. Future references cited in the text.

11. Jane Moody, *Illegitimate Theatre in London, 1770–1840,* 165.

12. Consistent with Trumbach's argument that the eighteenth century tolerated prostitution because it demonstrated male heterosexuality, Archenholz follows his praises of female prostitution with brief observations of the English abhorrence of sodomy.

13. For the bourgeois mystification of economic mobility and its political consequences, see Nancy Armstrong, *Desire and Domestic Fiction.*

14. On this belief in the early part of the century see, for example, Erin Skye Mackie, *Market à la Mode.* A decade after the publication of *Memoirs,* Adam Smith would express this confidence in different ways in his *Theory of Moral Sentiments* (1759).

15. Armstrong, *Desire and Domestic Fiction,* chap. 3.

16. Most sources agree that "Sally Salisbury" was a fabricated name; nevertheless, I refer to her throughout as "Sally" or "Salisbury," the names by which she identified herself. On Sally Salisbury, see also Laura J. Rosenthal, "The Whore's Estate: Sally Salisbury, Prostitution, and Property in Eighteenth-Century London."

17. *The Effigies, Parentage, Education, Lies, Merry-Pranks and Conversation of the Celebrated Mrs. Sally Salisbury* (1722–1723).

18. Frederick T. Wood attributes "The Ballad of Sally in Our Alley" to Henry Carey, although it could have had a folk origin. Carey acknowledges but denies the popular association of this song with Salisbury: "A vulgar error having long prevail'd among many persons, who imagine Sally Salisbury the subject of this ballad, the author begs leave to undeceive and assure them it has not the least allusion to her . . . [a]s innocence and virtue were ever the boundaries of his muse." He claims that the ballad describes an apprentice's love for a young woman, and while the speaker announces his intention to marry Sally in the last stanza, other parts of the ballad suggest a commercial transaction: "When Christmas comes about again, / O, then I shall have money; / I'll hoard it up, and box and all, / I'll give it to my honey; / And would it were ten thousand pounds, / I'd give it all to Sally; / She is the darling of my heart,/ And she lives in our alley." Frederick T. Wood, ed., *The Poems of Henry Carey,* 151–153.

19. *The Genuine History of Mrs. Sarah Prydden, Usually Called Sally Salisbury* (1723), 22.

20. Captain Charles Walker, *Authentick Memoirs of the Life and Intrigues and Adventures of the Celebrated Sally Salisbury* (1723), 143–144. *The Post Boy* announced the impending publication of Walker's *Authentick Memoirs,* requesting that "Those Gentlemen who can communicate any useful Particulars towards perpetuating the Memory of this eminent Person, are desired to transmit them to the Author, directed to Jones's Coffee-House in Drury Lane." Tuesday January 8–10, 1722/3. The January 15–17 issue carries a similar request. These notices, of course, do not guarantee that the letters are authentic.

21. On eighteenth-century conflicts between landed and mobile property, see J. G. A. Pocock, *The Machiavellian Moment* and *Virtue, Commerce, and History.*

22. Walker, *Authentick Memoirs,* 68. This image of the upside-down prostitute catching money also appears in [John Garfield], *The Wandring Whore* (1660). On the popularity of this figure, see Turner, *Libertines and Radicals,* 144.

23. Defoe, *The Complete English Tradesman* (1726).

24. Sally's posture also obscenely echoes Zeus's appearance to Danae in a shower of gold, as Margaret W. Ferguson suggested to me. Sally also plays the part here of a "posture girl," an eighteenth-century form of male entertainment in which a woman would pose for the audience in various stages of undress. A short book promising the story of Elizabeth Mann, "Celebrated

Courtezan, and Posture-Mistress" appeared in 1724, but never quite gets to her posturing career. See Captain Johnson, *The History of the Life and Intrigues of That Celebrated Courtezan, and Posture-Mistress, Eliz. Mann* (1724). The hero of *The History of the Human Heart* (1749) indulges in this form entertainment and befriends a posture girl.

25. *Genuine History* (1723), 33.

26. Walker, *Authentick Memoirs*, 34–38.

27. Ibid., 121.

28. Ibid., 125.

29. According to Ruth Mazo Karras, in the Middle Ages laundresses had an unsavory reputation and were associated with prostitutes. Thus it is possible that Sally is also revealing this man's mother as a whore. See *Common Women*, 54.

30. *Memoirs of the Celebrated Miss Fanny M[urray]* (1759), 1:67. Future references from this edition and cited in the text.

31. Ibid., 2:75. A "Fanny Murray'd" hat is worn "quaintly-cock'd."

32. For other examples of narratives written by prostitutes or reputed prostitutes, or that claim to be written by such women, see *The Authentic and Interesting Memoirs of Miss Ann Sheldon* (1790); *Memoirs of Laetitia Pilkington* (1749–1754); Phillips, *Apology for the Life of Teresia Constantia Phillips* (1748–1749). On these memoirs see Lynda M. Thompson, *The 'Scandalous Memoirists.'* Neither Phillips nor Pilkington, however, were so clearly prostitutes or bawds like Margaret Leeson or Ann Sheldon. These narratives should not be read straightforwardly as historical record; nevertheless, they offer considerable insight into the period's construction of prostitution.

33. Leeson, *Memoirs of Mrs. Leeson, Madam, 1727–1797*, ed. Mary Lyons, 69. Future references are cited in the text.

34. As in the controversial case of Bosavern Penlez, on which Henry Fielding in his capacity as magistrate ruled, the law sometimes protected brothels like any other property by prosecuting those who attempted to destroy them. As a result of this case, however, Fielding was accused of being overly sympathetic to prostitutes.

35. The "Prisoner's Council" makes this argument on her behalf during her trial. See *Select Trials at the Sessions-House in the Old-Bailey* (1742), 341.

36. James Thompson, *Models of Value*, 138.

37. Leeson, intro., x–xi.

38. Nevertheless, reformers also took advantage of the erotic potential of their cause. On this point, see Sarah Lloyd, "'Pleasure's Golden Bait': Prostitution, Poverty and the Magdalen Hospital in Eighteenth-Century London." On prostitute reform and sentimentalism, see Ann Jessie Van Sant, *Eighteenth-Century Sensibility and the Novel*, 30–40; Ellis, *Politics of Sensibility*, chap. 5.

39. Henry Mackenzie, *The Man of Feeling* (1771).

40. Ibid., 34. Future references are cited in the text.

41. Joseph Massie, *A Plan for the Establishment of Charity-Houses for Exposed or Deserted Women and Girls, and for Penitent Prostitutes* (1758), 61.

42. Ibid., intro.

43. Newton Ogle, *A Sermon Preached at the Anniversary Meeting of the Governors of the Magdalen Charity* (1766), 10.

44. William Bell Williams, *Mary Magdalene. A Sermon Preached in the Chapel of Magdalen Hospital* (1794), 16.

45. Edward Jerningham, "The Magdalen," in *Poems on Various Subjects* (1767), 10–16.

46. As Edward Bristow points out (*Vice and Vigilance*, 65), attending chapel with the Magdalen inmates became a trendy source of amusement for gentlemen. Not everyone approved of this charity, however. One writer, for example, accused reformers of enabling commercial sex by essentially setting up a retirement home for old prostitutes. See *Considerations on the Fatal Effects to a Trading Nation of the Present Excess of Public Charities* (1763). Others, however, defended against such attacks; see, e.g., William Blair, *Prostitutes Reclaimed* (1809).

47. For an in-depth analysis of the relationship between gender, sexuality, and labor in the Magdalen charity, see Jennie Batchelor's excellent "'Industry in Distress': Reconfiguring Femininity and Labor in the Magdalen House." While focusing more on the reintegration of for-

mer prostitutes into domesticity, Batchelor shows the tremendous significance of labor in the prostitution debates.

48. See, e.g., William Dodd, An *Account of the Rise, Progress, and Present State of the Magdalen Hospital, for the Reception of Penitent Prostitutes,* 161.

49. Saunders Welch, *A Proposal to Render Effectual a Plan to Remove the Nuisance of Common Prostitutes from the Streets of This Metropolis* (1758), 13.

50. *The Evils of Adultery and Prostitution* (1792), 12.

51. John Fielding, who saw prostitution as an economic necessity for some women, was an exception; see his "An Account of the Origins and Effects of a Police . . . To Which Is Added a Plan for Preserving Those Deserted Girls in This Town Who Become Prostitutes from Necessity" (1758). See also Batchelor, "'Industry in Distress,'" on this point.

52. *Thoughts on the Plan for a Magdalen-House for Repentant Prostitutes,* 17.

53. Welch, *A Proposal,* 5–6.

54. *An Account of the Rise, Progress, and Present State of the Magdalen Hospital, for the Reception of Penitent Prostitutes* (1761), 162.

55. Welch, *A Proposal,* 4.

56. For an overview of this scholarship and the engagement of novelists with this change, see Ruth Perry, *Novel Relations,* chap. 1.

57. On this point, see Batchelor, "'Industry in Distress'"; Robert Bataille, "The Magdalen Charity for the Reform of Prostitutes: A Foucauldian Moment." Prostitutes sent to Bridewell had traditionally been forced to work, but the Magdalen charity differed as a private charity and voluntary institution that promised reform and training.

58. Jonas Hanway, *Reasons for an Augmentation of at Least Twelve Thousand Mariners . . . With Some Remarks on the Magdalen-House* (1759), 5.

59. John Fielding, "An Account," 49; Massie, *A Plan,* 5.

60. Robert Dingley, *Proposals for Establishing a Public Place of Reception for Penitent Prostitutes* (1758), 15–16.

61. *The Plan of the Magdalen House for the Reception of Penitent Prostitutes* (1758), 17.

62. Dodd, *An Account,* 60.

63. Ibid., 61–62.

64. Welch, *A Proposal,* 26.

65. Carswell, *The South Sea Bubble,* 86.

66. Dodd, *An Account,* 164.

67. Ibid., 234–235.

68. Ibid., 318.

69. Ibid., 317, 319.

70. Michel Foucault, *Discipline and Punish.*

71. Bataille, "The Magdalen Charity." Bataille also explores the Foucauldian regulation of sexuality implicit in this project.

72. We can see here the seeds of the kind of alibi for the regulation of working-class women that would find its full realization, as Judith Walkowitz has shown, in the nineteenth century. See her *Prostitution and Victorian Society.*

73. Jonas Hanway, *Thoughts,* 20.

74. Pratt, *Life of a Lady of the Town,* 31.

75. *The Vices of the Cities of London and Westminster* (1751), 21–22.

76. *Thoughts on Means of Alleviating the Miseries Attendant upon Common Prostitution* (1799), 17 (emphasis added).

77. *Vices of the Cities of London and Westminster,* letter 4.

78. Martin Madan was the chaplain of the Lock Hospital, which cared for people with venereal disease. His concern for the problem of prostitution ultimately resulted in the publication of an elaborate plea for legalized polygamy, which I will discuss in the conclusion.

79. Martin Madan, *The Magdalen; or, The Dying Penitent. Exemplified in the Death of F.S., Who Died April, 1763, Aged Twenty-Six Years* (1789), 2. *The Magdalen* was first published in 1763. Future references from this edition and cited in the text.

80. See, e.g., *Laura; or, The Fall of Innocence* (1787); *The Suicide Prostitute: A Poem.* (1805).
81. *The Histories* has been attributed to Sarah Fielding, Barbara Montagu, and William Dodd. A brief version appeared under Dodd's name but after his death with the title *The Magdalen; or, History of the First Penitent Prostitute Received into that Charitable Asylum* (1783).
82. *The Histories of Some of the Penitents in the Magdalen-House, as Supposed to Be Related by Themselves* (1760), 1:60. Future references are cited in the text.
83. See, e.g., Richard Cross, *The Adventures of John Le-Brun* (1739), 1:130.
84. *The History of Emma; or, The Victim of Depravity; . . . To Which Is Added the Life of the Abandoned Kitty Clark* (1800).
85. William Dodd, *The Sisters; or, The History of Lucy and Caroline Sanson, Entrusted to a False Friend* (1754), 1:94. Future references are cited in the text.
86. On *The Sisters*, see also Susan Staves, "British Seduced Maidens." Staves attributes the century's fascination with "fallen" women to changing structures of the family.
87. *Memoirs* predates the Magdalen Hospital and Magdalen literature, but not the new reform movement in general and its shift in attitudes toward prostitutes.
88. For the ways in which Fanny's experience differs from most eighteenth-century prostitutes, see Randolph Trumbach, "Modern Prostitution and Gender in *Fanny Hill*: Libertine and Domesticated Fantasy."
89. On Fanny's feelings, see Ann Kibbie, "Sentimental Properties"; Carol Houlihan Flynn, "What Fanny Felt: The Pains of Compliance in *Memoirs of a Woman of Pleasure*"; Edward W. Copeland," *Clarissa* and *Fanny Hill*: Sisters in Distress."
90. Lynn Hunt, "Introduction," in Lynn Hunt, ed., *The Invention of Pornography: Obscenity and the Origins of Modernity, 1500–1800*, 10. Bradford Mudge in *The Whore's Story* argues that the erotic novels of Aphra Behn and Eliza Haywood are pornographic, but these do not include, to invoke Hunt's distinction, the "explicit depiction of sexual organs and sexual practices."
91. For another view, see Lena Olsson, "Idealized and Realistic Portrayals of Prostitution in John Cleland's *Memoirs of a Woman of Pleasure*," in Patsy S. Fowler and Alan Jackson, ed., *Launching Fanny Hill: Essays on the Novel and Its Influences*, 81–102. Olsson makes some good points about the consistency between *Memoirs* and other descriptions of prostitution in the period; nevertheless, comparison of this novel to Cleland's other writing about prostitution, such as *Memoirs of a Coxcomb* and *The Case of the Unfortunate Bosavern Penlez*, reveals *Woman of Pleasure* as a self-consciously idealized version, especially in terms of the prostitute's pleasure.
92. Douglas J. Stewart, "Pornography, Obscenity, and Capitalism," 391. For two excellent, more recent readings that recognize the important of labor and remuneration in this novel, see Felicity Nussbaum's "One Part of Womankind"; Kate Levin, "The Meanness of Writing for a Bookseller: John Cleland's Fanny on the Market."
93. Leo Braudy, "*Fanny Hill* and Materialism."
94. Stewart, "Pornography, Obscenity, and Capitalism," 398.
95. Ibid., 395, 379. On this point, see also Nussbaum, "One Part of Womankind," 18; Gary Gautier, "Fanny Hill's Mapping of Sexuality, Female Identity, and Maternity"; "Fanny's Fantasies: Class, Gender, and the Unreliable Narrator in Cleland's *Memoirs of a Woman of Pleasure*"; Elizabeth Kubek, "The Man Machine: Horror and the Phallus in *Memoirs of a Woman of Pleasure* in Fowler and Jackson, ed., *Launching Fanny Hill*, 173–198. Gautier reads the mechanized pornography as satiric; Kubek reads it as Gothic.
96. Andrew Elfenbein, "The Management of Pleasure in *Memoirs of a Woman of Pleasure*."
97. As Elfenbein suggests, Fanny successfully manages her own pleasure.
98. John Cleland, *Memoirs of a Woman of Pleasure*, 25. Future references are cited in the text.
99. Levin interestingly argues that through his identification with Fanny, Cleland fantasizes about a positive commercial experience that contrasts sharply to his own negative one as an author.
100. Nancy Armstrong and Leonard Tennenhouse, *The Imaginary Puritan: Literature, Intellectual Labor, and the Origins of Personal Life*.
101. Stewart, "Pornography, Obscenity, and Capitalism," 393.

102. Pietro Aretino, *Aretino's Dialogues*, 186. On Aretino's influence, see Turner, *Libertines and Radicals*.
103. Cleland, *Memoirs of a Coxcomb* (1751), 158.
104. Cleland, *The Case of the Unfortunate Bosavern Penlez by Gentleman Not Concern'd* (1750), 7–8.

Clarissa among the Whores

1. Samuel Richardson, *Clarissa; or, The History of a Young Lady*, 633. Future references cited in the text. I have used the Penguin edition for its wide availability to readers. For a case for the superiority of the third edition, see Florian Stuber, "On Original and Final Intentions, or Can There Be an Authoritative *Clarissa?*"
2. As Jocelyn Harris insightfully notes, "Lovelace's moment of truth is to know he is not a Grand Signor (637) but . . . a Signor Dildo." But while Harris reads this as Lovelace being "controlled by his own excessive sexual appetites," I am arguing that he has become an instrument of the prostitutes. Harris, "Grotesque, Classical and Pornographic Bodies in *Clarissa*," 113.
3. See Judith Wilt, "He Could Go No Farther: A Modest Proposal about Lovelace and Clarissa." Wilt even suggests that the prostitutes, not Lovelace, rape Clarissa.
4. McKeon, *Origins of the English Novel*, 158.
5. This argument was perhaps first made by Dorothy Van Ghent, *The English Novel: Form and Function*, 54, but is now generally assumed rather than argued.
6. See, e.g., Terry Eagleton, *The Rape of Clarissa*, 70; Carol Houlihan Flynn, *Samuel Richardson, Man of Letters*, esp. 91–101.
7. See the discussion of *Clarissa* in Mark Kinkead-Weekes, *Samuel Richardson: Dramatic Novelist*; John Traugott, "*Clarissa's* Richardson: An Essay to Find the Reader."
8. This point is argued convincingly in different ways in Lois E. Bueler, *Clarissa's Plots*; Margaret Anne Doody, *A Natural Passion*; Eagleton, *Rape of Clarissa*; Brian McCrea, "Clarissa's Pregnancy and the Fate of Patriarchal Power." For an interesting discussion of how Clarissa is put in a "no win" situation, see Dianne Osland, "Complaisance and Complacence, and the Perils of Pleasing in *Clarissa*."
9. Bueler, *Clarissa's Plots*, 43.
10. Slavoj Žižek, *The Sublime Object of Ideology*, 25.
11. Lee, "The Commodification of Virtue: Chastity and the Virginal Body in Richardson's *Clarissa*," 40.
12. Ibid., 39.
13. Eagleton, *Rape of Clarissa*, 74; Doody, *Natural Passion*, 84.
14. Hill, "Clarissa Harlowe and Her Times."
15. See Raymond F. Hilliard, "*Clarissa* and Ritual Cannibalism."
16. See Stuber, "On Original and Final Intentions," 231. On Richardson's most famous reader, see Janice Broder, "Lady Bradshaigh Reads and Writes *Clarissa*: The Marginal Notes in Her First Edition." Lady Bradshaigh writes that "many will say, had Clar[issa] lived she might have been prevail'd upon to marry Lovelace." Bradshaigh herself, however, thought that Clarissa should have lived to prove them wrong (109).
17. I am not suggesting that Clarissa wants to be raped but that she is willing to risk her virginity by staying alive in a way that, as I will later argue, she is not willing to risk prostitution.
18. Edward W. Copeland, "Clarissa and *Fanny Hill*: Sisters in Distress," 343.
19. William Dodd, *An Account of the Rise, Progress, and Present State of the Magdalen Hospital*, 206, 162.
20. For other critical examinations of *Clarissa* and prostitution, see Elizabeth Kowaleski-Wallace, *Consuming Subjects: Women, Shopping, and Business in the Eighteenth Century*, 129–143; Jessie Anne Van Sant, *Eighteenth-Century Sensibility and the Novel: The Senses in Social Context*, 59–66. Kowaleski-Wallace reads the prostitutes in the novel as marking female participation in

business as corrupt in order to exculpate male practices. Van Sant observes the similarities between medical experiments, the display of prostitutes, and Lovelace's "experiments" with Clarissa. Terry Castle in *Clarissa's Ciphers* refutes Margaret Ann Doody's argument in *A Natural Passion* that Mrs. Sinclair is a kind of "anti-Clarissa" by showing the similarities between their positions and their fates. See also Flynn, *Samuel Richardson, Man of Letters* (especially 104); Robert A. Erickson, *Mother Midnight*; Copeland, "*Clarissa* and *Fanny Hill*." These arguments explore the importance of the prostitutes in the novel, some by showing the opposition between Clarissa and the prostitutes, others by showing their similarities. Kowaleski-Wallace's argument comes closest to my own by thinking about prostitution as not just sex but *commercial* sex, but Lovelace's contractarianism and Solmes's crass materialism in my view undermine any simple relationship between gender, commerce, and virtue. None of these critics explore in depth the threat of Clarissa's recruitment into prostitution that concerns me here, although Harris in "Grotesque, Classical and Pornographic Bodies in *Clarissa*" notes its importance.

21. Phillips [Muilman], *An Apology for the Conduct of Mrs. Teresia Constantia Phillips* (1748–1749), 1:40. Future references are cited in the text.

22. For more on the case of Phillips, see Lynda M. Thompson, *The 'Scandalous Memoirists.'* Thompson places Phillips's *Apology* in the context of female autobiography and observes that the *Apology* has less to do with sexual scandal than with "women's fraught and unequal to money, property, law, and 'priceless' reputation" (14).

23. *A Genuine Copy of the Tryal of Thomas Grimes* [1748], 27. Future references are cited in the text.

24. *Counter-Apology; or, Genuine Confession* (1749), 35.

25. *The Humours of Fleet-Street and the Strand* (1749), 6–8.

26. Ibid., 96.

27. Jonas Hanway, *Letters Written Occasionally on the Customs of Foreign Nations in Regard to Harlots* (1761), 315–316.

28. John Campbell, *A Particular but Melancholy Account* (1752), 18, 21.

29. *The Adventures of Melinda; a Lady of Distinction Now Living* (1749).

30. *Memoirs of the Celebrated Miss Fanny M[urray]*, 115.

31. *A Spy on Mother Midnight*, part 2 (1748), 18–19.

32. Hanway, *Thoughts on the Plan for a Magdalen-House for Repentant Prostitutes, with the Several Reasons for Such an Establishment* (1759), postscript.

33. Johnson, *A Dictionary of the English Language* (1756). He also gives "a prostitute" as the second definition of *whore*, but *prostitute* includes nonsexual meanings (e.g., "a mercenary"), and the first meaning of *whore* is "a woman who convenes unlawfully with men."

34. Maclauchlan, *Essay Upon Improving and Adding to the Strength of Great-Britain and Ireland by Fornication* (1735), in Leonard DeVries and Peter Fryer, eds., *Venus Unmasked*, 40–41.

35. I borrow the term "progressive ideology" from Michael McKeon, *Origins of the English Novel*.

36. John Zomchick, *Family and the Law in Eighteenth-Century Fiction*, 51, 71.

37. Sandra Macpherson, "Lovelace, Ltd."

38. On the issues of rape, contract, and consent in *Clarissa*, see Frances Ferguson, "Rape and the Rise of the Novel."

39. See J. G. A. Pocock, "The Mobility of Property and the Rise of Eighteenth-Century Sociology," in *Virtue, Commerce, and History*.

40. Lamb, *Preserving the Self in the South Seas*, 132–162.

41. See, e.g., Richardson, *Clarissa*, 699.

42. Hilliard, "*Clarissa* and Ritual Cannibalism," 1084.

43. See Margaret R. Hunt, *The Middling Sort: Commerce, Gender, and the Family in England, 1680–1780*.

44. Kristeva, *Powers of Horror: Essays on Abjection*.

45. On Clarissa's body, see also Jocelyn Harris's excellent "Grotesque, Classical and Pornographic Bodies in *Clarissa*." While not distinguishing between commercial sex and libertinism, Harris points out that "[u]nbridled sexual activity had utterly different consequences for women

in the eighteenth-century than it did for men . . . The contained body, the nonsexual body, the chaste and Platonic body is the safer paradigm, for women" (110).

46. *The Complete Poems*, 448. On differences between Swift and Richardson in representing prostitutes, see Brenda Bean, "Sight and Self-Disclosure: Richardson's Revision of Swift's 'The Lady's Dressing Room.'"

47. N. D. Falck, *A Treatise on the Venereal Disease*, 87–88.

48. Clarissa, of course, comes from a wealthy family and has connections to many wealthy people. Richardson, however, organizes the plot so as to cut her off from any of these resources. That some readers have found Clarissa's momentary poverty contrived only supports the significance of her sponging-house predicament to the narrative's meaning. In doing this, Richardson also joins other reformers in lamenting how family harshness toward daughters threatens their descent into prostitution.

49. Turner, "Lovelace and the Paradoxes of Libertinism."

50. The doctor might actually be curing her of venereal disease since her illness was "occasioned by the barbarity of the most savage of men" (1090). She could, of course, be ill due to the trauma of rape, but Belford's description seems to leave the other possibility open as well. If so, it would only underscore the danger of her descent into prostitution.

51. See Pocock, "Mobility of Property."

52. See also Mona Scheuermann (*Her Bread to Earn*, 60–95), who argues that James doesn't want Clarissa to marry Lovelace because he would thus lose money.

53. The case for this possibility is made by Kowaleski-Wallace in *Consuming Subjects*.

54. Richardson explores these problems in *Pamela* as well. On the tribulations faced by Pamela from the alienating possibilities of social mobility, see James Cruise, "*Pamela* and the Commerce of Authority"; Christopher Flint, "The Anxiety of Affluence."

55. Nancy Armstrong, "Reclassifying Clarissa: Fiction and the Making of the Modern Middle Class," 37.

56. William Park, "*Clarissa* as Tragedy"; Sheldon Sacks, "*Clarissa* and the Tragic Traditions."

Tom Jones and the "New Vice"

1. On the eighteenth-century novel's appeal to a "general reader" rather than a gender-specific reader, see William B. Warner, *Licensing Entertainment: The Elevation of Novel Reading in Britain*, 1684–1750.

2. Quoted in Henry Fielding, *Tom Jones*, ed. Sheridan Baker, 2nd ed. (New York: W. W. Norton & Co., 1995), 657. Future references to *Tom Jones* are from this edition and cited in the text. Paul-Gabriel Boucé points out that like Casanova, Tom turns into a "mechanical stud." "Sex, Amours, and Love in *Tom Jones*," 30.

3. For a discussion of the long history of critical dissatisfaction with Fielding's handling of the Lady Bellaston incident, see Gene S. Koppel, "Sexual Education and Sexual Values in *Tom Jones*." Critics as disparate as R. S. Crane ("The Plot of *Tom Jones*") and Terry Castle (*Masquerade and Civilization*) have for different reasons read Tom's prostitution as a significant aberration from his character.

4. Whether Tom changes within remains debatable, but Tom certainly changes his *behavior* after this recognition. On this point, see George A. Drake, "Historical Space in the 'History of': Between Public and Private in *Tom Jones*." Drake argues that Tom has learned manners rather than morality from his travels and experiences, which accounts for his change at the end.

5. See Sheridan Baker, "Bridget Allworthy: The Creative Pressures of Fielding's Plot."

6. In Tobias Smollett's *Peregrine Pickle* (1751), a wealthy lady offers Peregrine fifty pounds, presumably for the same reason that Lady Bellaston gives money to Tom, but Peregrine proudly rejects the offer (736). When Louisa tells Boswell that a man offered her fifty pounds, "I said I expected some night to be surprised with such an offer from some decent elderly gentlewoman" (89). These exchanges, which come after the publication of Fielding's novel, could be direct references to it or, more likely, could reflect an already-established legendary stallion fee.

7. See Maaja A. Stewart, "Ingratitude in *Tom Jones*"; James Thompson, *Models of Value*, esp. 133–134. See also John Richetti, "Ideology and Form in Fielding's *Tom Jones*."

8. Some attempts to disentangle the novel's party politics and political ideology have yielded similar complexities and ambivalences, although not necessarily gendered ones. See, e.g., Richard Braverman, "Rebellion Redux: Figuring Whig History in *Tom Jones*"; Homer Obed Brown, "Tom Jones, the 'Bastard' of History"; Peter J. Carlton, "*Tom Jones* and the '45 Once Again"; John Allen Stevenson, "Tom Jones and the Stuarts," who argues that "[w]hatever Fielding may have said about the Stuarts or the Jacobites elsewhere, in *Tom Jones* he appears to mock the black and white world of partisan debate by allowing for a more mixed version" (584).

9. On the fluidity of gender in Fielding, see Jill Campbell, *Natural Masques: Gender and Identity in Fielding's Plays and Novels*.

10. *Satan's Harvest Home; or, The Present State of Whorecraft, Adultery, Fornication, Procuring, Pimping, Sodomy, and the Game at Flatts . . .* (1749), 15. This pamphlet reproduces Father Poussin's *Pretty Doings in a Prostestant Nation*, which lifts several passages wholesale from Mandeville's *Defence of the Publick Stews*.

11. Ibid., 16.

12. John Dunton, *Dunton's Whipping Post: or, A Satyr upon Every Body . . . With the Whoring-Paquet: or, News of the St[allio]ns and Kept M[isse]s's* (1706), 114.

13. Captain Johnson, *The History of the Life and Intrigues of . . . Eliz.Mann* (1724), iv.

14. "A Trip from St James to the Royal Exchange (1744)," 205.

15. *The Adulteress* (1773), 6. On this point, see also *The Happy Courtezan* (1735), 10.

16. *The Adulteress*, 19.

17. *The Life and Intrigues of the Late Celebrated Mrs. Mary Parrimore* (1729); Richard Head, *The Miss Display'd with All Her Wheedling Arts* (1675). For the familiar representation of the whore who spends all of her earnings on stallions, see also *The Fifteen Comforts of Whoring; or, The Pleasures of A Town-Life* (1705).

18. Thomas Brown, *Amusements Serious and Comical*, 443.

19. *A View of London and Westminster* (1725), part 2, pp. 10, 11.

20. *Characters of the Present Most Celebrated Courtezans* (1780), 180.

21. Sophia Watson, *Memoirs of the Seraglio of the Bashaw of Merryland* (1768), 41–49.

22. Hanger, *Life, Adventures, and Opinions of Col. George Hanger*, 2:59.

23. *Memoirs of a Demi-Rep of Fashion; or, The Private History of Miss Amelia Gunnersbury* (1776), 1:61.

24. Oakman, *Life and Adventures of Benjamin Brass, an Irish Fortune Hunter* (1765), 6.

25. See, e.g., *The Life and Character of a Strange He-Monster, Lately Arriv'd in London from an English Colony in America* (1726).

26. William Bisset, *Plain English* (1704), 37.

27. *Reflections upon Matrimony, and the Women of This Country. In a Letter to a Young Gentleman* (1755), 28.

28. Bland, *An Essay in Praise of Women* (1733), 169.

29. [William Preston], *Seventeenth Hundred and Seventy-Seven*, 16.

30. Ibid., 5.

31. *Nocturnal Revels: or, The History of King's-Place and Other Modern Nunneries*, 1:52.

32. Ibid., 1:76.

33. Ibid., 1:216. On rumors about this relationship, see Gretchen Gerzina, *Black London*, 54–57.

34. [Edward Thompson], *The Demi-Rep* (1756), 9.

35. Michael McKeon, "Historicizing Patriarchy."

36. *The Bawd: A Poem* (1782?), 9.

37. His mysterious admirer, however, turns out to be the woman he loves, testing his loyalty.

38. On the Ulster rebellion, in which Catholics rose up against Protestant rule, see R. F. Foster, *Modern Ireland, 1600–1972*, chap. 4.

39. *The Matchless Rogue* (1725). Future references are cited in the text.

40. See, e.g., Robert Alter's classic study *The Rogue's Progress*, esp. 90–91, which outlines the generic similarities of *Tom Jones* to the rogue narrative.

41. Tiffany Potter, *Honest Sins*, chap. 5.

42. Peter Carlton, "The Mitigated Truth: Tom Jones's Double Heroism." For political readings of Tom's sexuality, see Homer Obed Brown, "Tom Jones: The 'Bastard' of History"; John Allen Stevenson, "*Tom Jones* and the Stuarts." See also Carlton, "*Tom Jones* and the '45 Once Again"; Campbell, *Natural Masques*, part 4.

43. On Tom's sexual passivity, see Campbell, *Natural Masques*, chap. 6.

44. On Allworthy's flaws, see Eric Rothstein, "Virtues of Authority in *Tom Jones*."

45. John Allen Stevenson, "Black George and the Black Act."

46. E. P. Thompson, *Whigs and Hunters: The Origin of the Black Act.*

47. He still has Sophia's money, but refuses to even think about spending it.

48. Castle, *Masquerade and Civilization.*

49. See Rothstein, "Virtues of Authority."

50. A case could be made for the erotic implications of this exchange between Jenny and Bridget, but an exploration of this possibility lies beyond the scope of this chapter.

51. Allworthy had planned to marry her off, an opportunity that her bargain with Bridget forces her to miss. But since Allworthy doesn't tell her about these plans, they have no bearing on her decision to accept Bridget's offer.

52. Rothstein, "Virtues of Authority," 121.

53. On Jenny's importance to the novel, see John Unsworth, "*Tom Jones:* The Comedy of Knowledge." Unsworth points out that Jenny Jones is the focal point of the problem of knowledge in the novel. He reads this, however, mostly as negative: "she is the primary agent of epistemological chaos in the novel, both in her interactions with other characters and in what she conceals from the reader; she is the wellspring of ignorance" (245). Jones DeRitter, however, points out that "the false accusation of incest [with Jenny] becomes the means by which [Fielding's] patriarch learns that he has been mistaken and misled. It is also the means by which the reputation of the often-vilified Jenny Waters is finally rehabilitated, and the means by which his hero is prevented from fulfilling the prophecy that he was born to be hanged." Jones DeRitter, "Blaming the Audience, Blaming the Gods: Unwitting Incest in Three Eighteenth-Century English Novels," 234–235.

Risky Business in the South Seas and Back

1. See Pamela Cheek, *Sexual Antipodes: Enlightenment Globalization and the Placing of Sex;* Rod Edmond, *Representing the South Pacific: Colonial Discourse from Cook to Gauguin;* Jonathan Lamb, *Preserving the Self in the South Seas, 1680–1840;* Roy Porter, "The Exotic as Erotic: Captain Cook in Tahiti"; Neil Rennie, *Far-Fetched Facts: The Literature of Travel and the Idea of the South Seas.* The "South Sea Islands," also referred to in this chapter as the "Pacific Islands," broadly indicate the islands of the South Pacific Ocean.

2. Robertson, *The Discovery of Tahiti*, 180.

3. Ibid., 166.

4. I borrow the idea of "anti-conquest" writing from Mary Louis Pratt, *Imperial Eyes.*

5. Several, such as the Tahitian Tupia, died along the way or soon after arrival. Others, such as the Inuit man escorted by Cartwright, appeared insufficiently impressed with British civilization to attract attention. See E. H. McCormick, *Omai: Pacific Envoy*, 23–25, 76–77, 132.

6. Quoted by McCormick, *Omai*, 103, 112, 128.

7. Cook was given both public orders and secret orders. In his third voyage, he was instructed, for example, "with the consent of the natives, to take possession, in the name of the King of Great Britain, of convenient situations in such countries as you may discover." Cook, *The Explorations of Captain James Cook in the Pacific*, 204. On transracial desire in representations of the Cook voyages, see Bridget Orr, "'Southern passions mix with northern art': Miscegena-

tion and the *Endeavour* Voyage." As Orr points out, the "pervasive and derisory satirical treatment of Banks as Pacific 'amoroso' suggests that the . . . taboo on miscegenation . . . was not yet fully in place by the 1770s but was, rather, in the process of being constructed" (213).

8. *A Short Account of the New Pantomime Called Omai; or, A Trip round the World* (1785), 4. Future references cited in the text.

9. Many of these characters have a vague relationship to Polynesians mentioned in the journals written by British travelers to the South Seas. "Oberea" refers to Purea, a Tahitian woman of rank encountered by Wallis and later Cook. Oedidee (or Odiddy), here the "pretender to the throne" and Oberea's lover, was a Boraboran named Hitihiti of chiefly birth who joined Cook on the *Resolution* as they traveled through the islands. He was generally popular with the British, apparently very attractive, and was reported to be Purea's lover by Georg Forster and others. See McCormick, *Omai*, 56. The character Otoo is named after a Tahitian ruler, but one unrelated to Omai (who was not from Tahiti, but rather the island of Raiatea). In the third voyage, however, when Cook returned Omai, he apparently tried to negotiate a marriage between a sister of Otoo and Omai, but it never came about (McCormick, *Omai*, 235). The status of Omai, whose name was really Mai or Mae, was itself a point of much controversy: While many of the journal writers locate him in the lower ranks of society, narratives of his British sojourn characterize him as sometimes a priest, sometimes the equivalent of a gentleman, sometimes an aristocrat, and sometimes as a child of nature. While initially holding him in contempt, even Captain Cook could not deny Omai's extraordinary success in London. For more details about Omai, see McCormick, *Omai*; Michael Alexander, *Omai*, *"Noble Savage"*; Thomas Blake Clark, *Omai, First Polynesian Ambassador*. McCormick confirms that "Mai . . . was, it appears, a younger son and a member of the *raatira*, the second order of Raiatean society" (1). Towha was a Tahitian warrior, probably remembered by O'Keefe as the man who apparently performed the famous human sacrifice witnessed by Cook and other officers during the third voyage. The rest of the characters (e.g., Britannia, Londina) are fictional and/or personifications. On Cook's apotheosis, see Gananath Obeyesekere, *The Apotheosis of Captain Cook: European Mythmaking in the Pacific*, esp. chap. 6.

10. See, e.g., J. C. Beaglehole's characterization of Cook in his authoritative *Life of Captain James Cook*; see also Andrew Kippis, *Captain Cook's Voyages* (1788), 357.

11. James Cook, *A Voyage towards the South Pole, and Round the World* (1777), 1:10. Benefiting from the editorial assistance of Rev. John Douglas, Canon of Windsor, Cook's *Voyage* was published to some extent to refute the scandal of John Hawkesworth's rendition of his first voyage—a point to which I will return. This book, then, was generally considered more authentically Cook's own. On Cook as a feminized hero, see also Edmond, *Representing the South Pacific*, 27.

12. Cook, *A Voyage*, 1:18.

13. Ibid., 2:292. Appended to Cook's *Voyage* is "A Discourse upon Some Late Improvements of the Means for Preserving the Health of Mariners" by John Pringle, Baronet. Obeyesekere makes the following relevant observation of Cook's manipulation of provisions on board: When the "father" (Cook) becomes angry at his "children's" rebelliousness, "he withholds grog, a powerful source of physical and psychic solace which helps one to forget the rigors of shipboard life, to dull its pains. Those who have had their fill become satiated with it; they get 'groggy' and go to sleep. Grog is the milk of the father." Obeyesekere, 45.

14. On the literary use of the "other" woman as a foil for British female virtue, see Felicity Nussbaum, *Torrid Zones*, intro.

15. Rev. William Ellis, *Polynesian Researches*, 2:369. Cited by McCormick, *Omai*, 292.

16. John Rickman, *Journal of Captain Cook's Last Voyage to the Pacific Ocean* (1781), 56, 52. See also Cook, *A Voyage*, 1:125; Lee Wallace, "Too Darn Hot: Sexual Contact in the Sandwich Islands or Cook's Third Voyage."

17. *A Letter from Omai, to the Right Honourable, The Earl of ********, Late — Lord of the —* (1780), 3, 5. Future references cited in the text.

18. See, e.g., Nussbaum, *Torrid Zones*, chap. 4; Heidi Hutner, *Colonial Women: Race and Culture in Stuart Drama*.

19. [William Preston], *Seventeen Hundred and Seventy-Seven*, 2. Future references cited in the text.

20. "Omiah: An Ode. Addressed to Charlotte Hayes," in *The New Foundling Hospital for Wit*, 2:132–137.

21. Ibid., 2:137.

22. *Nocturnal Revels*, 2:22. Future references are cited in the text.

23. This passage from Hawkesworth is quoted in *Nocturnal Revels*, 2:23. See John Hawkesworth, *An Account of the Voyages Undertaken by the Order of His Present Majesty for Making Discovering in the Southern Hemisphere* (1773), 2:128.

24. There is no way to know for sure whether this performance actually took place. On this performance, see also Christopher B. Balme, "Sexual Spectacles: Theatricality and the Performance of Sex in Early Encounters in the Pacific"; Rennie, *Far-Fetched Facts*, chap. 4.

25. Balme, "Sexual Spectacles," 68.

26. *Covent Garden Magazine*, July 1773, 251–253. The author comments that "Dr. Hawkesworth's collection of voyages, are recommended by the Editor of the Covent Garden Magazine to all parents and guardians, for the improvement of the morals of the youth of both sexes, but particularly the female, who will there find ample instructions to prepare them for the marriage-bed" (253).

27. That is, the couple had sex before an audience. Hawkesworth, *Account of the Voyages*, 2:128.

28. *Nocturnal Revels*, 2:25.

29. See Edmond, *Representing the South Pacific*; Rennie, *Far-Fetched Facts*.

30. Porter, "The Exotic as Erotic," 138.

31. Louis de Bougainville, *A Voyage Round the World* (1772), trans. John Reinhold Forster, 218–219. Future references are cited in the text.

32. Denis Diderot, "Supplement to Bougainville's *Voyage*," in *Diderot's Selected Writings*, 227.

33. Gerald Fitzgerald, *The Injured Islanders* (1779), 7. On this poem, see Shef Rogers, "Composing Conscience: *The Injured Islanders* (1779) and English Sensibility."

34. *An Historical Epistle, from Omiah, to the Queen of Otaheite; Being his Remarks on the English Nation* (1775), 30.

35. Ibid., 31.

36. John Lawrence Abbott, *John Hawkesworth, Eighteenth-Century Man of Letters*, 154. Hawkesworth undertook this project because "the Admirality wanted to issue an official, government-sanctioned account of Cook's celebrated voyage and those of Byron, Wallis, and Carteret, who preceded him into the Pacific. Such a version would replace the spurious and inaccurate texts that had already appeared, and would undoubtedly continue to appear, and would establish English claims in this part of the world" (Abbott, *John Hawkesworth*, 142).

37. Jonathan Lamb, "Circumstances Surrounding the Death of John Hawkesworth," 107.

38. Hawkesworth, *Account of the Voyages*, 1:xviii. Phillip Edwards suggests that, on balance, Hawkesworth sees this sacrifice as ultimately worthwhile in his *The Story of the Voyage*, 91. Lamb concludes the opposite. That Hawkesworth's *Account* both absorbed and disturbed readers suggests the possibility of both readings; still, Hawkesworth at the very least raised questions that unsettled any clear sense of progress in commercial modernity.

39. One anonymous contributor to *The Public Advertiser* sums up the charges as follows: "First, They say that the whole Book is written in a loose and incorrect Manner; defective in Language, and in those edifying and amusing Digressions which the Nature of the Subject furnished, and the Public had Reason to expect from the Author of so many excellent Productions on many Subjects. Secondly, That the Narrative is in some Part of it indecent and shocking to a modest Reader, particularly of the Female Sex. Thirdly, That the Property of the Book was sold to the highest Bidder, although another Bookseller was promised the Refusal of it. Fourthly, That the Preface contains one Passage truly blasphemous." Saturday, July 17, 1773.

40. "A Christian" in *Public Advertiser* August 5, 1773. Quoted by Abbott, *John Hawkesworth*, 167.

41. Passages quoted and compared in Abbot, *John Hawkesworth*, 168–169.

42. As obvious from some of the satires on Omai's stay in London, Bank's aristocratic status was meaningful here. Satirists represented his interest in traveling as a kind of dissolute, elite sex tourism.

43. *An Epistle from Mr. Banks, Voyager, Monster-Hunter, and Amoroso, to Oberea, Queen of Otaheite* (1773), 11.

44. [John Scott-Waring], *An Epistle from Oberea, Queen of Otaheite, to Joseph Banks, Esq.* (1774), 7.

45. On the differences between Cook's private journals and the expurgated version in his *Voyage*, see Edwards, *Story of the Voyage*, 118–124.

46. Cook, *Voyage towards the South Pole*, 1:187.

47. Cook, *The Journals of Captain James Cook*, 3:170.

48. Cook, *Voyage towards the South Pole*, 1:130.

49. Forster, *A Voyage Round the World* (1777), 1:211–212.

50. John Rickman, *Journal of Captain Cook's Last Voyage to the Pacific Ocean* (1781), 143–144.

51. Forster, *Voyage Round the World*, vii.

52. Kippis, *Captain Cook's Voyages*, 371. Kippis specifically hopes that his volume will correct the impressions left by Hawkesworth (20).

53. Kippis, *Captain Cook's Voyages*, 33. Future references are cited in the text.

54. McCormick, *Omai*, 11.

55. Cook, *The Journals of Captain James Cook*, 2:175; compare to the same passage in Cook's *Voyage* (1:130) in which this observation does not appear.

Conclusion

1. For an account of this project, see Siân Rees, *The Floating Brothel: The Extraordinary True Story of an Eighteenth-Century Ship and Its Cargo of Female Convicts*. Rees's account is based on John Nicol, *The Life and Adventures of John Nicol, Mariner* (1822).

2. Smeathman, *Plan of a Settlement to Be Made Near Sierra Leona* (1786).

3. Ann Marie Falconbridge, *Narrative of Two Voyages to the River Sierra Leone during the Years 1791–1793*, 64.

4. For the British colonization of Sierra Leone in the eighteenth century, see Christopher Fyfe, *A History of Sierra Leone*, chaps. 1–3.

5. Randolph Trumbach, *Sex and the Gender Revolution*, 1:286.

6. Responses included an anonymous *Poetic Epistle to the Reverend Mr. Madan* (1781); B. Walwyn, *Chit-Chat; or, The Penance of Polygamy* (London, 1781, a play in which the characters consider trying out Madan's plan after reading his book); Frederick Pilon, *Thelyphthora; or, More Wives Than One* (1781, another play); Richard Hill, *The Blessings of Polygamy Displayed* (1781); Edward Burnaby Greene, *Whispers for the Ear of the Author of Thelyphthora* (1781); James Cookson, *Thoughts on Polygamy* (1782); *An Heroic Epistle to the Rev. Martin M—d—n* (1780); *Martin's Hobby Houghed and Pounded* (1781); *The Cobler's Letter to the Author of Thelyphthora* (1781); H. W., *The Unlawfulness of Polygamy Evinced* (1780); Thomas Haweis, *A Scriptural Refutation of the Arguments for Polygamy* (1781); Henry Moore, *A Word to Mr. Madan* (1781); John Smith, *Polygamy Indefensible* (1780); John Towers, *Polygamy Unscriptural* (1781); Thomas Wills, *Remarks on Polygamy* (1781); *A Letter to the Rev. Mr. Madan, Concerning the Chapter of Polygamy* (1780); William Cowper, *Anti-Thelyphthora* (1781); James Penn, *Remarks on Thelyphthora* (1781); *Remarks Controverting Martin Madan's Thelyphthora* (1781?). Madan defended himself with his *Letters on Thelyphthora* (1782), and James Edward Hamilton supported Madan's position in *A Short Treatise on Polygamy* (1786).

7. Cookson, *Thoughts on Polygamy* (1782), 7–8.

8. Hanger, *Life, Adventures, and Opinions of Col. George Hanger*, 1:118.

9. See, e.g., Dean Patrick Delany, *Reflections on Polygamy and the Encouragement Given to that Practice in the Old Testament* (1737); Leo Miller, *John Milton among the Polygamophiles; A Dialogue*

of Polygamy (1657). Miller offers considerable information on polygamy debates in the seventeenth and eighteenth centuries.

10. Trumbach, *Sex and the Gender Revolution*, 1:188–190.
11. Nussbaum, *Torrid Zones*, 81.
12. *An Heroic Epistle to the Rev. Martin M—d—n.*
13. Greene, *Whispers*, xxviii. Future references are cited in the text.
14. See Nussbaum, *Torrid Zones*, chap. 3.
15. Cookson, *Thoughts on Polygamy* (1782), 368. Future references are cited in the text.
16. *Remarks Controverting Martin Madan's Thelyphthora* (1781?).
17. Ibid., 36–37.
18. Hill, *Blessings of Polygamy Displayed*, 41.
19. *Remarks Controverting Martin Madan's Thelyphthora*, 124.
20. Hill, *Blessings of Polygamy Displayed*, 44.
21. Walwyn, *Chit-Chat*, 15.

Bibliography

Primary Sources

Abrabanal, Solomon [William Arnall]. *The Complaint of the Children of Israel, Representing their Grievances under the Penal Laws.* London: Printed for W. Webb, 1736.

An Account of the Institution of the Lock Asylum, for the Reception of Penitent Female Patients. London: C. Watts, 1796.

Addison, Joseph, and Richard Steele. *The Spectator.* Edited by Donald F. Bond. 5 vols. Oxford: Clarendon Press, 1965.

The Adulteress. London: Printed for S. Bladen, 1773.

The Adventures of Melinda; a Lady of Distinction Now Living. Founded on Real, Authentic Facts, and Such Diverting and Suprizing Incidents as Can Scarce Be Parallell'd in History. London: Printed for H. Carpenter, 1749.

Adventures under-Ground. A Letter from a Gentleman Swallowed Up in the Late Earthquake to a Friend on His Travels. London: William Falstaff, 1750.

Ambross, Miss. *The Life and Memoirs of the Late Miss Ann Catley, the Celebrated Actress.* London: Printed for J. Bird, 1789.

Ames, Richard. *The Female Fire-Ships. A Satyr against Whoring. In a Letter to a Friend, Just Come to London.* London: E. Richardson, 1691.

Antimoixeia; or, The Honest and Joynt-Design of the Tower Hamblets for the General Suppression of Bawdy Houses, as Incouraged thereto by Publick Magistrates. London, 1691.

Archenholz, J[ohann] W[ilhelm von]. *A Picture of England: Containing a Description of the Laws, Customs, and Manners of England.* 2 vols. London: Edward Jeffrey, 1789.

Archer, Gideon [Peter Annet]. *Social Bliss Considered in Marriage and Divorce; Cohabiting Unmarried, and Publick Whoring.* London: R. Rose, 1749.

Arentine, Peter [pseud.]. *Strange & True Newes from Jack-a-Newberries Six Windmills: Or the Crafty, Impudent, Common-Whore (Turned Bawd) Anatomised, and Discovered, in the Unparralleld Practices of Miss Fotheringham.* Venus [London?]: Printed for Rodericus Castro, 1660.

Aretino, Pietro. *Aretino's Dialogues.* Translated by Raymond Rosenthal. New York: Stein and Day, 1971.

An Authentic Narrative of the Most Remarkable Adventures and Curious Intrigues Exhibited in the Life of Miss Fanny Davies, the Celebrated Modern Amazon. London: Printed for the Editor and sold by R. Jameson, 1786.

Barbon, Nicholas. *A Discourse of Trade.* London: Printed for Tho. Milbourn for the Author, 1690.

The Bawd: A Poem. Containing All the Various Practices Those Diabolical Character Make Use of to Decoy Innocent Beauty into Their Snares. By a Distinguish'd Worshipper in the Temple of Venus. London [1782?].

Behn, Aphra. *Oroonoko, The Rover, and Other Works.* Edited by Janet Todd. London, Penguin Books, 1992.

Ben Israel, Menasseh. *To His Highnesse the Lord Protector of the Common-wealth of England, Scotland, and Ireland.* London, 1655.

Billingsley, John. *A Sermon Preach'd to the Society for Reformation of Manners, in Kingston upon Hull.* London: Printed for A. and J. Churchill, and Thomas Ryals, 1700.

Bisset, William. *The Modern Fanatick. With a Large and True Account of the Life, Actions, Endowments, &c. of the Famous Dr. S——l.* London: A. Baldwin, 1710.

——. *Plain English. A Sermon Preached at St Mary-le-Bow.* London: Printed for the Author, 1704.

A Black Lists of the Names, or Reputed Names, of Seven Hundred Fifty Two Lewd and Scandalous Persons . . . . London, 1694.

Blair, William. *Prostitutes Reclaimed.* London, 1809.

Bland, James. *An Essay in Praise of Women; or, A Looking-Glass for Ladies to See Their Perfections in.* London: Printed for the Author, 1733.

Boswell, James. *Boswell's London Journal, 1762–1763.* Edited by Frederick A. Pottle. 2nd ed. New Haven: Yale University Press, 2004. This edition first published in 1950.

Bougainville, Louis-Antoine de. *A Voyage Round the World* (1772). Translated by John Reinhold Forster. Facsimile. New York: Da Capo Press, 1967.

Bray, Thomas. *The Good Fight of Faith, in the Cause of God against the Kingdom of Satan. Exemplified in a Sermon Preach'd at the Parish Church of St. Clements Danes, Westminster, on 24th of March, 1708/9. At the Funeral of Mr. John Dent, Who Was Barbarously Murder'd in the Doing His Duty, in the Execution of the Laws against Profaneness and Immorality.* London: Printed for H. Hills, 1709.

——. *A Short Account of the Several Kinds of Societies Set Up of Late Years, for Carrying on the Reformation of Manners, and for the Propagation of Christian Knowledge.* London: For J. Brudenel, 1700.

Breval, John. *Harlot's Progress. A Heroi-Comical Poem. In Six Cantos. By Mr. J. Gay. Founded upon Mr. Hogarth's Six Paintings.* Dublin: Printed for S. Powell 1739.

Brown, Thomas. *Amusement, Serious and Comical and Other Works.* Edited by Arthur L. Hayward. London: Routledge, 1927.

Burgess, Daniel. *The Golden Snuffers; or, Christian Reprovers, and Reformers, Characterized, Cautioned, and Encouraged.* London: Printed by J. Darby, 1697.

Calamy, Edmund. *A Sermon Preach'd before the Societies for Reformation of Manners in London and Middlesex.* London: Printed for John Lawrence, 1699.

Campbell, John. *A Particular but Melancholy Account of the Great Hardships, Difficulties, and Miseries, That Those Unhappy and Much-to-Be-Pitied Creatures, the Common Women of the Town, Are Plung'd into at This Juncture. By M. Lodovicus.* London: Printed for the Author, 1752.

Campbell, R. *The London Tradesman.* Facsimile. New York: A. M. Kelly, 1969.

Carey, Henry. *The Poems of Henry Carey.* Edited by Frederick T. Wood. London: Scholartis Press, 1930.

Ceremonies of the Present Jews: Being a Short and Succinct Account of the Meats That Are Clean and Unclean to Them . . . . London: J. Roberts, 1728.

The Character of an Informer, Wherein His Mischeivous Nature and Leud Practices are Detected. London, 1675.

The Character of a Town-Miss. London: Printed for Rowland Reynolds, 1680.

Characters of the Present Most Celebrated Courtezans. Interspersed with a Variety of Secret Anecdotes Never before Published. London: Printed for M. James, 1780.

Cibber, Theophilus. *The Harlot's Progress (1733) and Rake's Progress (1778–1780).* Edited by Mary F. Klinger. Los Angeles: William Andrew Clark Memorial Library, 1977.

The Citizens Reply to the Whores Petition, and Prentices Answer. London, 1668.

Cleland, John. *The Case of the Unfortunate Bosavern Penlez by a Gentleman Not Concern'd.* 2nd ed. London: Printed for T. Clement, 1750.

——. *Memoirs of a Coxcomb.* Edited by Hal Gladfelder. Ontario, Canada: Broadview Press, 2005.

——. *Memoirs of a Woman of Pleasure.* Edited by Peter Sabor. Oxford: Oxford University Press, 1999.

The Cobler's Letter to the Author of Thelyphthora. London, 1781.

Colquhoun, Patrick. *A Treatise on the Police of the Metropolis.* 3rd ed. London: Printed by H. Fry, 1796.

A Conference about Whoring. London: J. Downing, 1725.

A Congratulatory Epistle from a Reformed Rake to John F—g, Esq. London: Printed for G. Burnet, 1758.

Considerations on the Fatal Effects to a Trading Nation of the Present Excess of Public Charities. London: Printed for S. Hooper, 1763.

Cook, James. *The Explorations of Captain James Cook in the Pacific.* Edited by A. Grenfell Price. New York: Dover, 1971.

——. *The Journals of Captain James Cook on his Voyages of Discovery.* Edited by J. C. Beaglehole. 4 vols. Cambridge: Cambridge University Press, 1955.

——. *A Voyage towards the South Pole, and Round the World.* 2 vols. London: Printed for W. Strahan and T. Cadell, 1777.

Cookson, James. *Thoughts on Polygamy.* Winchester: Printed for J. Wilkes, 1782.

Counter-Apology; or, Genuine Confession. Being a Caution to the Fair Sex in General. Containing the Secret History, Amours, and Intrigues, of M—P—, a Famous British Courteszan; Who Underwent Various Scenes of Life, and Changes of Fortune, Both at Home and Abroad. London: Printed for R. Young, 1749.

Covent Garden Magazine; or, Amorous Repository: Calculated Solely for the Entertainment of the Polite World. London, July 1772–December 1774.

Cowper, William. *Anti-Thelyphthora; A Tale, in Verse.* London, 1781.

The Crafty Whore; or, The Misery and Iniquity of Bawdy-Houses, Laid Open in a Dialogue between Two Subtle Bawds. London: Printed for Henry Marsh, 1668. First published 1658.

Cross, Richard. *The Adventures of John Le-Brun.* 2 vols. London: Printed for G. Hawkins, 1739.

Cullen, Francis Grant. *A Brief Account of the Nature, Rise, and Progress of the Societies for the Reformation of Manners.* Edinburgh: Printed by George Mosman, 1700.

Defoe, Daniel. *The Best of Defoe's Review: An Anthology.* Edited by William L. Payne. New York: Columbia University Press, 1951.

——. *The Complete English Tradesman: in Familiar Letters, Directing Him in All the Several Parts and Progressions of Trade . . . .* London: Charles Rivington, 1726.

——. *Conjugal Lewdness; or, Matrimonial Whoredom (1727).* Introduction by Maximillian E. Novak. Gainesville, FL: Scholars' Facsimiles & Reprints, 1967.

——. *The Poor Man's Plea, to All the Proclamations, Declarations, Acts of Parliament, &c. Which Have Been, Or Shall Be Made, Or Published, for A Reformation of Manners.* London, 1700.

——. *Reformation of Manners, a Satyr.* London, 1702.

———. *Roxana: The Fortunate Mistress.* Edited by John Mullan. Oxford: Oxford University Press, 1996.

Delany, Patrick. *Reflections on Polygamy and the Encouragement Given to that Practice in the Old Testament. By Phileleutherus Dubliniesnsis.* London: J. Roberts, 1737.

Diderot, Denis. "Supplement to Bougainville's *Voyage.*" In *Selected Writings,* edited by Lester G. Crocker. Translated by Derek Coltman. New York: MacMillan, 1966.

Dingley, Robert. "Proposals for Establishing a Public Place of Reception for Penitent Prostitutes" (1758). In *Prostitution Reform: Four Documents,* edited by Randolph Trumbach. Facsimile. New York: Garland Publishing, Inc., 1985.

Disney, John. *An Essay Upon the Execution of the Laws against Immorality and Prophaneness.* London: Printed by Joseph Downing, 1708.

Dodd, William. *An Account of the Rise, Progress, and Present State of the Magdalen Hospital, for the Reception of Penitent Prostitutes.* 5th ed. London: Printed by W. Faden, 1776.

———. *The Sisters; or, The History of Lucy and Caroline Sanson, Entrusted to a False Friend.* 2 vols. London: Printed for T. Waller, 1754.

Dunton, John. *Dunton's Whipping Post; or, A Satyr upon Every Body . . . With the Whoring-Paquet; or, News of the St[allio]ns and Kept M[isse]s's.* London: Printed for B. Bragg, 1706.

———. *The Impeachment; or Great Britain's Charge Against the Present M—y, Sir Roger Bold, the L— C—ly, and Dr. S—ll.* London: Printer for T. Warner, 1714.

———. *The Night-Walker; or, Evening Rambles in Search after Lewd Women* (1696). Edited by Randolph Trumbach. Facsimile. New York: Garland, 1985.

The Effigies, Parentage, Education, Life, Merry-Pranks and Conversation of the Celebrated Mrs. Sally Salisbury. London: Printed by J. Wilson, 1722–1723.

Ellis, William. *An Authentic Narrative of a Voyage Performed by Captain Cook and Captain Clerke, in His Majesty's Ships Resolution and Discovery.* 2 vols. London: G. Robinson, 1782.

Ellis, Reverend William. *Polynesian Researches during a Residence of Nearly Eight Years in Society and Sandwich Islands.* New ed. 4 vols. London, 1853.

An Epistle (Moral and Philosophical) from an Officer at Otaheite. To Lady Gr*S**N*R. London, 1774.

An Epistle from Mr. Banks, Voyager, Monster-Hunter, and Amoroso, to Oberea, Queen of Otaheite. Transfused by A.B.C. Esq. Second Professor of the Otaheite, and of Every Other Unknown Tongue. London, 1773.

An Essay Towards a General History of Whoring. From the Creation of the World, to the Reign of Augustulus . . . And from Thence Down to the Present Year 1697. London: Printed for Roger Baldwin, 1697.

The Evils of Adultery and Prostitution; with An Inquiry into the Causes of the Present Alarming Increase, and Some Means for Checking Their Progress. London: Printed for T. Vernor, 1792.

Falck, N[ilolai] D[etlef]. *A Treatise on the Venereal Disease.* London, 1772.

Falconbridge, Ann Marie. *Narrative of Two Voyages to the River Sierra Leone during the Years 1791–1793.* Facsimile. London: Frank Cass & Co., 1967.

A Familiar Epistle to the Celebrated Mrs. Con. Phillips, on Her Apology. By a Gentleman of the Inner Temple. Printed for the Author, n.d. [1749?].

Faulkner, Miss [Mary Anne]. *The Genuine Memoirs of Miss Faulkner; Otherwise Mrs. D**L**N; or, Countess of H***X, in Expectancy. Containing, the Amours and Intrigues of Several Persons of High Distinction, and Remarkable Characters: With Some Curious Political Anecdotes, Never before Published.* London: Printed for William Bingley, 1770.

Fielding, Henry. *An Apology for the Life of Mrs. Shamela Andrews* (1741). Facsimile. New York: Garland, 1974.

———. *Miss Lucy in Town.* Vol. 12 of *The Complete Works of Henry Fielding.* Edited by William Earnest Henley. 16 vols. New York: Barnes and Noble, 1967.

———. *Tom Jones.* Edited by Sheridan Baker. 2nd ed. New York: W. W. Norton & Co., 1995.

Fielding, John. *An Account of the Origins and Effects of a Police . . . To Which Is Added a Plan for Preserving Those Deserted Girls in this Town Who Become Prostitutes from Necessity.* London: Printed for A. Millar, 1758.

The Fifteen Comforts of Whoring; or, The Pleasures of a Town-Life. London, 1706.

Fitzgerald, Gerald. *The Injured Islanders; or, The Influence of Art Upon the Happiness of Nature.* London: Printed for J. Murray, 1779.

Forster, Georg. *A Voyage Round the World, in His Britannic Majesty's Sloop, Resolution, Commanded by Capt. Cook.* London: Printed for B. White, J. Robertson, and P. Elmsly. 1777.

[Garfield, John]. *The Wandring Whore* (1660). Edited by Randolph Trumbach. Facsimile. New York: Garland, 1968.

Gay, John. *The Beggar's Opera.* Edited by Edgar V. Roberts. Lincoln: University of Nebraska Press, 1969.

A Genuine Copy of the Tryal of Thomas Grimes, Esq. Alias Lord S—, for a Barbarous and Inhuman Rape, Committed on the Body of Miss T.C.P. A Young Girl of Thirteen Years of Age . . . . By a Member of the Society of Antiquarians. London: Printed for E. Anderson, [1748].

The Genuine History of Mrs. Sarah Prydden, Usually Called Sally Salisbury, and Her Gallants. Regularly Containing, the Real Story of Her Life. London: Printed for Andrew Moor, 1723.

Glasse, Reverend George Henry. *A Sermon Preached before the Governors of the Magdalen-Hospital.* London: Printed for the Hospital, 1788.

God's Judgments against Whoring. London, 1697.

The Gracious Answer of the Most Illustrious Lady of Pleasure, the Countess of Castelm— To the Poor-Whores Petition. London, 1668.

Graham, James. *A Lecture on the Generation, Increase, and Improvement of the Human Species.* London, 1784.

Granville, George. *The Jew of Venice.* London, Printed for Ber. Lintott, 1701.

Greene, Edward Burnaby. *Whispers for the Ear of the Author of Thelyphthora.* London: Printed for H. Payne, 1781.

Grosley, [Pierre Jean]. *A Tour to London; or, New Observations on England, and Its Inhabitants.* Translated by Thomas Nugent. 2 vols. London: Printed for Lockyer Davis, 1772.

Hamilton, James Edward. *A Short Treatise on Polygamy; or, The Marrying and Cohabiting with More Than One Woman at The Same Time.* Dublin, 1786.

Hanger, George. *Life, Adventures, and Opinions of Col. George Hanger.* 2 vols. London: J. Debrett, 1801.

Hanway, Jonas. *A Candid Historical Account of the Hospital for the Reception of Exposed and Deserted Children; Representing the Plan of It as Productive of Many Evils.* London, 1759.

———. *Letters Written Occasionally on the Customs of Foreign Nations in Regard to Harlots: The Lawless Commerce of the Sexes: The Repentance of Prostitutes: The Great Humanity of the Magdalene Charity in London: and the Absurd Notions of the Methodists.* London: John Rivington, R. and J. Dodsely, C. Henderson, 1761.

———. *Reasons for an Augmentation of at Least Twelve Thousand Mariners . . . With Some Remarks on the Magdalen-House.* London: Sold by R. and J. Dodsley; J. Waugh, 1759.

——— [attr.]. *A Review of the Proposed Naturalization of the Jews; Being an Attempt at a Dispassionate Enquiry into the Present State of the Case.* London: Sold by J. Waugh, 1753.

———. *Thoughts on the Plan for a Magdalen-House for Repentant Prostitutes, with the Several Reasons for Such an Establishment.* London: J. and R. Dodsely, 1759.

The Happy Courtezan: or, The Prude Demolished. An Epistle from the Celebrated Mrs. C— P—, to the Angelick Signior Far—n—li. London: J. Roberts, 1735.

Harris's List of Covent Garden Ladies (1788). Edited by Randolph Trumbach. Facsimile. New York: Garland, 1986.

Haweis, Thomas. *A Scriptural Refutation of the Arguments for Polygamy, Advanced in a Treatise Entitled Thelyphthora.* London, 1781.

Hawkesworth, John. *An Account of the Voyages Undertaken by the Order of His Present Majesty for Making Discoveries in the Southern Hemisphere.* 2nd ed. 3 vols. London: Printed for W. Strahan and T. Cadell, 1773.

Haywood, Eliza. *Anti-Pamela; or, Feig'd Innocence Detected* (1742). Facsimile. New York: Garland, 1975.

———. *The Fair Hebrew; or, A True, but Secret History of Two Jewish Ladies, Who Lately Resided in London.* London, 1729.

Head, Richard. *The Miss Display'd with All Her Wheedling Arts.* London, 1675.

———. *Proteus Redivivus; or, The Art of Wheedling or Insinuations. . . . By the Author of the First Part of the English Rogue.* London, 1675.

Head, Richard, and Francis Kirkman. *The English Rogue Described in the Life of Meriton Latroon.* 4 vols. London, 1665.

The Heaven-Drivers. A Poem. London, 1701.

Heigham, Clement. *A Call to the General Reformation of Manners. And Manifesting, in Several Particulars, The Great Lets and Hindrances Thereunto.* London: Printed by John Darby, 1700.

An Heroic Epistle to the Rev. Martin M — d — n, Author of a Late Treatise on Polygamy. London: Printed for R. Faulder, 1780.

The Highlanders Salivated; or, The Loyal Association of M — ll K — ng's Midnight Club. London: Printed for M. Cooper, 1746.

Hill, Richard. *The Blessings of Polygamy Displayed, in an Affectionate Address to the Rev. Martin Madan; Occasioned by His Late Work, Entitled Thelyphthora; or, A Treatise on Female Ruin.* London, 1781.

A Historical and Law-Treatise against Jews and Judaism. London: Printed for T. Dormer, 1732.

An Historical Epistle, from Omaih, to the Queen of Otaheite; Being His Remarks on the English Nation. London: Printed for T. Evans, 1775.

The Histories of Some of the Penitents in the Magdalen-House, as Supposed to Be Related by Themselves. 2 vols. London: Printed for John Rivington and J. Dodsley, 1760.

The History of Emma; or, The Victim of Depravity; . . . To Which Is Added the Life of the Abandoned Kitty Clark. London: Printed by S. Fisher, 1800.

The History of the Human Heart; or, The Adventures of a Young Gentleman. London: Printed for J. Freeman, 1749.

Hole, Matthew. *The True Reformation of Manners; or, The Nature and Qualifications of True Zeal.* Oxford: Printed for L. Lichfield, 1699.

Howgill, Francis. *Mistery Babylon the Mother of Harlots Discovered: Her Rise, and When, with Many of Her Sorceries.* London: Printed for Thomas Simmons, 1659.

Humdrum, Humphrey [pseud.]. *Mother Midnight's Comical Pocket-Book.* London: J. Dowse, 1753.

The Humours of Fleet-Street and the Strand; Being the Lives and Adventures of the Most Noted Ladies of Pleasure; Whether in the Rank of Kept-Mistresses, or the More Humble Station of Ladies of the Town. By an Old Sportsman. London: Printed for Anthony Wright, 1749.

Hutcheson, Francis. *Thoughts on Laughter; and Oberservations of the Fable of the Bees* (1758). Bristol: Thoemmes, 1989.

Jerningham, Edward. *Poems on Various Subjects.* London: J. Robson, 1767.

The Jew Decoy'd; or, The Progress of a Harlot. London: Printed for E. Rayner, 1733.

Johnson, Captain. *The History of the Life and Intrigues of That Celebrated Courtezan, and Posture-Mistress, Eliz.Mann, alias Boyle, alias Sample, Commonly Call'd, the Royal Soveraign.* London: Printed for A. Moore, 1724.

Johnson, Samuel. *A Dictionary of the English Language.* London: Printed for J. Knapton, C. Hitch, L. Hawes, A. Millar, R. and J. Dodsely, M. and T. Longman, 1756.

Johnstone, Charles. *Chrysal; or, The Adventures of a Guinea*. 2 vols. London: T. Becket, 1760.

The Juvenile Adventures of Miss Kitty F[ishe]r. 2 vols. London: Printed for Stephen Smith, 1759.

Kelly, Hugh. *Memoirs of a Magdalen* (1767). Facsimile. New York: Garland, 1974.

King, Richard. *The Frauds of London Detected*. London: Printed for Alex. Hogg [1780?].

Kippis, Andrew. *Captain Cook's Voyages* (1788). New York: Knopf, 1924.

Knipe, Charles. *A City Ramble; or, The Humours of the Compter*. London: Printed for E. Curll and J. Pemberton, 1715.

Laura; or, The Fall of Innocence: A Poem. London: Printed for E. Macklew, 1787.

Leeson, Margaret. *The Memoirs of Mrs. Leeson, Madam, 1727–1797*. Edited by Mary Lyons. Dublin: Lilliput Press, 1995.

Legg, Thomas. *Low-Life; or, One Half of the World, Know Not How the Other Half Live*. 3rd ed. London: Printed for the Author, 1764.

A Letter from Omai, to the Right Honourable, The Earl of ********, Late — Lord of the —. London: Printed for J. Bell, 1780.

A Letter to the Rev. Mr. Madan, Concerning the Chapter of Polygamy. London: Printed for Fielding and Walker, 1780.

The Life and Actions of That Notorious Bawd Susan Wells. London: F. Clifton, 1753.

The Life and Adventures of a Reformed Magdalen in a Series of Letters to Mrs. B***, of Northampton. Written by Herself. 2 vols. London: Printed for W. Griffin, 1763.

The Life and Character of Moll King, Late Mistress of King's Coffee-House in Covent-Garden. London: Printed for W. Price, 1747.

The Life and Character of a Strange He-Monster, Lately Arriv'd in London from an English Colony in America. London, 1726.

The Life and Intrigues of the Late Celebrated Mrs. Mary Parrimore, The Tall Milliner of 'Change Alley. London: A. Moore, 1729.

The Life and Opinions of Miss Sukey Shandy (1760). Facsimile. New York: Garland, 1974.

The Life of Lavinia Beswick, Alias Fenton, Alias Polly Peachum: Containing Her Birth and Education. London: Printed for A. Moore, 1728.

Lillo, George. *The London Merchant*. Edited by William H. McBurney. Lincoln: University of Nebraska Press, 1965.

The London-Bawd: with Her Character and Life. 4th ed. (1711). Edited by Randolph Trumbach. Facsimile. New York: Garland, 1985.

Look E're You Leap; or, A History of the Lives and Intrigues of Lewd Women: with The Arraignment of Their Several Vices. London: Printed for Edw. Midwinter, [1720?].

Love upon Tick; or, Implicit Gallantry. London: Printed for J. Billingsley, W. Meadows, T. Worral, and J. Stagg, 1724.

Mackenzie, Henry. *The Man of Feeling*. Introduction by Kenneth C. Slagle. New York: W. W. Norton, 1958.

Maclauchlan, Daniel. *Essay Upon Improving and Adding to the Strength of Great-Britain and Ireland by Fornication, Justifying the same from Scripture and Reason* (1735). In Leonard De-Vries and Peter Fryer, eds., *Venus Unmasked; or, An Inquiry into the Nature and Origins of the Passion of Love*. London: Barker, 1967.

Madan, Martin. *Letters on Thelyphthora*. London: Printed for J. Dodsley, 1782.

———. *The Magdalen; or, Dying Penitent. Exemplified in the Death of F.S., Who Died April, 1763, Aged Twenty-Six Years*. Dublin, 1789. First published in 1763.

———. *Thelyphthora; or, A Treatise on Female Ruin, in Its Causes, Effects, Consequences, Prevention, and Remedy*. London: J. Dodsley, 1781. 2nd ed. 3 vols. London, 1781.

Magdalen Hospital. *By-Laws and Regulations*. London: Printed for the Charity, 1791.

———. *The Plan of the Magdalen House for the Reception of Penitent Prostitutes*. London: Printed by W. Faden, 1758.

——. *The Rules, Orders, and Regulations of the Magdalen House, for the Reception of Penitent Prostitutes.* London, 1759.

——. *A Short Account of the Magdalen Hospital.* London, 1791.

The Magdalen; or, History of the First Penitent Prostitute Received into That Charitable Asylum. With Anecdotes of Other Penitents. London: Printed for Ann Lemoine, 1799.

Malcolm, James Peller. *Anecdotes of the Manners and Customs of London during the Eighteenth Century.* London: Printed for Longman, Hurst, Rees, and Orme, 1808.

Man, Thomas. *The Benefit of Procreation.* London: Printed for T. Cooper, 1734.

Mandeville, Bernard. *An Enquiry into the Causes of the Frequent Executions at Tyburn* (1725). Introduction by Malvin R. Zirker, Jr. Facsimile. Los Angeles: William Andrews Clark Memorial Library, 1964.

——. *The Fable of the Bees; or, Private Vices, Publick Benefits.* Edited by F. B. Kaye. 2 vols. Oxford: Clarendon Press, 1924.

——. *A Modest Defence of Publick Stews* (1724). Introduction by Richard I. Cook. Facsimile. Los Angeles: William Andrews Clark Memorial Library, 1973.

——. *The Virgin Unmask'd,* London, 1709.

Martin's Hobby Houghed and Pounded; or, Letters on Thelyphthora to a Friend, on the Subjects of Marriage and Polygamy. London, 1781.

Massie, Joseph. *A Plan for the Establishment of Charity-Houses for Exposed or Deserted Women and Girls, and for Penitent Prostitutes.* London: Printed for T. Payne, 1758.

The Matchless Rogue (1725). Introduction by Josephine Grieder. Facsimile. New York: Garland, 1973.

Memoirs of a Demi-Rep of Fashion; or, The Private History of Miss Amelia Gunnersbury. 2 vols. Dublin, 1776.

Memoirs of the Celebrated Miss Fanny M[urray]. 2nd ed. 2 vols. London: Printed for J. Scott and M. Thrush, 1759.

Memoirs of the Life of Lady H (1741?). Facsimile. New York: Garland, 1975.

Meriton, George. *Immorality, Debauchery, and Profaneness, Exposed to the Reproof of Scripture and the Censure of Law.* London: Printed for John Harris and Andrew Bell, 1698.

The Midnight Rambler; or, New Nocturnal Spy, for the Present Year. London: Printed for J. Cooke, [1772?].

Mill, Humphrey. *A Night's Search, Discovering the Nature and Condition of All Sorts of Night-Walkers with their Associates . . . Digested into a Poeme by Humphrey Mill.* London: Printed for Richard Bishop, 1640.

Moore, Henry. *A Word to Mr. Madan; or, Free Thoughts on His Late Celebrated Defence of Polygamy.* Bristol: W. Pine, 1781.

Nicol, John. *The Life and Adventures of John Nicol, Mariner.* Edited by John Howell. Edinburgh: W. Blackwood, 1822.

Nocturnal Revels; or, The History of King's-Place and Other Modern Nunneries. 2 vols. London: Printed for M. Goadby, 1779.

North, Sir Dudley. *Discourses upon Trade.* London: Printed for Tho. Basset, 1691.

Oakman, John. *Life and Adventures of Benjamin Brass. An Irish Fortune Hunter.* 2 vols. London: Printed for W. Nicoll, 1765.

Ogle, Newton. *A Sermon Preached at the Anniversary Meeting of the Governors of the Magdalen Charity.* London: Printed for W. Sandby, W. Faden, and E. Easton, 1766.

Oldys, Alexander. *The London Jilt; or, The Politick Whore Shewing the Artifices and Stratagems which the Ladies of Pleasure Make Use of for the Intreaguing and Decoying Men.* Parts 1 and 2. London: Printed for Hen. Rhodes, 1683.

"Omiah: An Ode. Addressed to Charlotte Hayes." In *The New Foundling Hospital for Wit,* edited by John Almon. 6 vols. 2:102–108. London: J: Debrett, 1786.

Pamela Censured (1741). Facsimile. New York: Garland, 1974.

Parkinson, Sydney. *A Journal of a Voyage to the South Seas, in His Majesty's Ship, the Endeavour.* London: Printed for Stanfield Parkinson, the Editor, 1773.

Parry, James. *The True Anti-Pamela* (1741). Facsimile. New York: Garland, 1974.

Penn, James. *Remarks on Thelyphthora.* London: Printed for the Author, 1781.

Philanthropos [pseud.]. *A Letter to a Friend in the Country, on the Subject of the Jew Bill.* London: Printed for C. Corbett, 1753.

Phillips [Muilman], Teresia Constantia. *An Apology for the Conduct of Mrs. Teresia Constantia Phillips.* 3 vols. London: Printed for the Author, 1748–1749.

———. *A Letter Humbly Addressed to the Right Honourable the Earl of Chesterfield.* London: Printed for the Author, 1750.

Phillips, Phebe. *The Woman of the Town; or, Authentic Memoirs of Phebe Phillips; Otherwise Maria Maitland; Well Known in the Vicinity of Covent Garden. Written by Herself.* London: Printed for Ann Lemoine, 1799.

Pilkington, Laetitia. *Memoirs of Laetitia Pilkington.* Edited by A. C. Elias. 2 vols. Athens: University of Georgia Press, 1997.

Pilon, Frederick. *Thelyphthora; or, More Wives Than One.* Huntington Library manuscript, 1781.

Poetic Epistle to the Reverend Mr. Madan. London, 1781.

The Polite Road to an Estate; or, Fornication One Great Source of Wealth and Pleasure. London: J. Coote, 1759.

Poor-Whores Petition. To the Most Splendid, Illustrious, Serene, and Eminent Lady of Pleasure, the Countess of Castlemayne &c. London, 1668.

Poussin, Father. *Pretty Doings in a Prostestant Nation. Being a View of the Present State of Fornication, Whorecraft, and Adultery, in Great-Britain, and the Territories and Dependencies thereunto Belonging . . . Written Originally in French by Father Poussin.* London: J. Roberts, J. Isted, J. Jackson, W. Waring, Robert Amey, 1734.

Pratt, Samuel Jackson. *Life of a Lady of the Town, Who Afterwards Became a Penitent in the Magdalen House. In Beautiful Poetry. With the History of Ann & Mary Woodfield.* Portsea: James Williams, 1801.

The Prentices Answer to the Whores Petition. London, 1668.

[Preston, William]. *Seventeen Hundred and Seventy-Seven; or, A Picture of the Manners and Character of the Age. In a Poetical Epistle from a Lady of Quality.* London: Printed for T. Evans, 1777.

Proposals for a National Reformation of Manners. London: Printed for John Dunton, 1694.

The Public Advertiser. London: Printed by W. Egelsham, 1725–1793.

The Ramble; or, A View of Several Amorous and Diverting Intrigues Lately Pass'd between Some Ladies of Drury. London: Printed for J. Bodle, [1730?].

Reeves, Jonathan. *The Lost Sheep Found. A Sermon Preached at the Magdalen House.* London: Printed by C. Say, 1758.

Reflections Upon Matrimony, and the Women of This Country. In a Letter to a Young Gentleman. London: Printed for R. Baldwin, 1755.

The Remarkable Trial of the Queen of Quavers, and Her Associates, for Sorcery, Witchcraft, and Enchantment. London: Printed for J. Bew [1777?].

Remarks Controverting Martin Madan's Thelyphthora. N.p., n.d. [1781?].

Richardson, Samuel. *Clarissa; or, The History of a Young Lady* (1747–1748). Edited by Angus Ross. New York: Penguin, 1985.

———. *Pamela; or, Virtue Rewarded* (1740). Edited by Peter Sabor. New York: Penguin, 1980.

Rickman, John. *Journal of Captain Cook's Last Voyage to the Pacific Ocean* (1781). Facsimile. New York: Da Capo Press, 1967.

Roberts, W. H. *A Sermon Preached before the Governors of the Magdalen Hospital.* London: Printed for the Hospital, 1782.

Robertson, George. *The Discovery of Tahiti*. Edited by Hugh Carrington. London: Hakluyt Society, 1948.

Sacheverell, Henry. *The Character of a Low-Churchman*. 3rd ed. London, 1702.

——. *The Communication of Sin*. London: Printed for Henry Clements, 1709.

——. *The Perils of False Brethren, Both in Church, and State*. London: H. Hills, 1709.

Satan's Harvest Home; or, The Present State of Whorecraft, Adultery, Fornication, Procuring, Pimping, Sodomy, and the Game at Flatts . . . (1749). Edited by Randolph Trumbach. Facsimile. New York: Garland, 1985.

[Scott-Waring, John]. *An Epistle from Oberea, Queen of Otaheite, to Joseph Banks, Esq.* 2nd ed. London, 1774.

Seasonable Advice to the Societies for Reformation of Manners. London, 1699.

The Secret History of Betty Ireland. London: Published by S. Lee, [1750?].

Select Trials at the Sessions-House in the Old-Bailey (1742). 4 vols. Edited by Randolph Trumbach. Facsimile. New York: Garland, 1985.

Seymour, John. *Memoirs of the Life of Eleanor Gwinn, a Celebrated Courtezan, in the Reign of King Charles II. And Mistress to That Monarch*. London: Printed for F. Stamper, 1752.

Shakespear, Ghost of [pseud.]. *Memoirs of the Shakespear's-Head*. 2 vols. London: F. Noble and J. Noble, 1755.

Shandy, Tristram [pseud.]. *Miss L—y's Cabinet of Curiosities; or, The Green-Room Broke Open*. Utopia: William Whirlgig, 1765.

Sheldon, Ann. *Authentic and Interesting Memoirs of Miss Ann Sheldon (now Mrs. Archer)*. 4 vols. London: Printed for the Authoress, 1790.

A Short Account of the New Pantomime Called Omai; or, A Trip round the World. . . . The Pantomime, and the Whole of the Scenery, designed and invented by Mr. LOUTHERBOURG. The Words written by Mr. O'KEEFE. And the Music by Mr. Shield. London: T. Cadell, 1785.

Smeathman, Henry. *Plan of a Settlement to Be Made Near Sierra Leona, on the Grain Coast of Africa*. London: T. Stockdale, G. Kearsely, and J. Sewel, 1786.

Smith, Adam. *The Theory of Moral Sentiments*. Edited by Knud Haakonssen. Cambridge: Cambridge University Press, 2002.

Smith, John. *Polygamy Indefensible. Two sermons preached in the parish-church of Nantwich, in Cheshire, on Sunday, the 10th of December 1780. Occasioned by a late publication, entitled "Thelyphthora." To which is prefixed, a letter to the Rev. Mr. Madan*. London: Printed for the Author, 1780.

Smith, Samuel. *Publick Spirit, Illustrated in the Life and Designs of the Reverend Thomas Bray, D.D*. London: Printed for J. Brotherton, 1746.

Smollett, Tobias. *Peregine Pickle*. Edited and introduction by James L. Clifford. London: Oxford University Press, 1964.

Some Considerations upon Street-Walkers. With a Proposal for lessening the present number of them. London: A. Moore, 1726.

Some Thoughts on the Reasonableness of a General Naturalization. London, 1753.

Spademan, John. *A Sermon Preach'd November 14, 1698: And now publish'd at the request of the Societies for the Reformation of Manners*. London: Printed for Tho. Parkhurst, 1699.

A Spy on Mother Midnight; or, The Templar Metamorphos'd. Being a Lying-in Conversation. With a Curious Adventure. In a Letter from a Young Gentleman in the Country, to His Friend in Town. London: E. Penn, 1748.

Straus, Ralph, ed. *Tricks of the Town: Being Reprints of Three Eighteenth Century Tracts*. New York: Robert M. McBride & Company, 1928.

The Suicide Prostitute: A Poem. Cambridge: Printed by Mary Watson, 1805.

Swift, Jonathan. "A Beautiful Young Nymph Going to Bed." In *Jonathan Swift: The Complete Poems*, edited by Pat Rogers, 453–455. New Haven: Yale University Press, 1983.

——. "A Project for the Advancement of Religion and the Reformation of Manners (1709)." In *Selected Prose Works of Jonathan Swift*, edited by John Hayward, 439–460. London: Cresset Press, 1949.

Tanner, Anodyne. *The Life of the Late Celebrated Mrs. Elizabeth Wisebourn*. London: Printed for A. Moore, 1721.

The Temple of Prostitution: A Poem. Dedicated to the Greatest ***[Whore?] in Her Majesty's Dominions. Written by a Woman of Fashion. London, 1779.

The Temple of Venus. London: Printed for C. Moran, 1763.

[Thompson, Edward]. *The Courtesan. By the Author of the Meretriciad*. 3rd ed. London: J. Harrison, 1765.

——. *The Demi-Rep. By the Author of the Meretriciad*. 2nd ed. London: Printed for C. Moran, 1756.

——. *The Meretriciad. Second edition; Revised, and Corrected, with Large Additions*. [London]: Printed for the Author, 1761.

Thompson, Mr. *The Female Amazon; or, A Genuine Account of the Most Remarkable Adventures, Complicated Intrigues, Displayed in the Life of the Celebrated and Notorious Miss Fanny Davies*. London: Printed for R. Tread, 1786.

Thoughts on Means of Alleviating the Miseries Attendant upon Common Prostitution. London: Printed for T. Cadell Jun. and W. Davies, 1799.

[Toland, John]. *Reasons for Naturalizing the Jews in Great Britain and Ireland* (1714). In *Pamphlets Relating to the Jews in England During the 17th and 18th Centuries*, edited by P. Radin. San Francisco: California State University, 1939.

Tom King's; or, The Paphian Grove. With the Various Humours of Covent Garden, the Theatre, the Gaming Table, &C. 2nd ed. London, 1738.

Tovey, D'Blossiers. *Anglia Judaica; or, The History and Antiquities of the Jews in England*. Oxford, 1738.

Towers, John. *Polygamy Unscriptural; or, Two Dialogues between Philalethes and Monogamus*. London, 1781.

"A Trip from St. James to the Royal Exchange (1744)." In Ralph Strauss, ed. *Tricks of the Town: Being Reprints of Three Eighteenth Century Tracts*. New York: Robert M. McBride & Co., 1928.

Trusty, Simon. *An Odd Letter, on a Most Interesting Subject, to Miss K[itty] F[is]H[e]R*. London: Printed for C. B., 1760.

The Tryals of Such Persons under the Notion of London Apprentices Were Tumultuously Assembled in Moore-Fields, and Other Places, on Easter Holidays Last, under Colour of Pulling Down Bawdy-Houses. London, 1668.

Tucker, Josiah. *A Letter to a Friend Concerning Naturalizations*. London: Printed for Thomas Trye, 1753.

——. *A Second Letter to a Friend Concerning Naturalizations*. London: Printed for Thomas Trye, 1753.

Tucker, Robert C., ed. *The Marx-Engels Reader*. 2nd ed. New York: W. W. Norton & Co., 1978.

The Velvet Coffee-Woman; or, The Life, Gallantries and Amours of the Late Famous Mrs. Anne Rochford. Westminster: Printed for Simon Green, 1728.

The Vices of the Cities of London and Westminster. Dublin: Printed for G. Faulkner and R. James, 1751.

A View of London and Westminster; or, The Town Spy. In Two Parts. London, 1725.

W. H. *The Unlawfulness of Polygamy Evinced*. London: Printed for G. Kearsly, 1780.

Walker, Capt. Charles. *Authentick Memoirs of the Life, Intrigues, and Adventures of the Celebrated Sally Salisbury*. London, 1723.

Walwyn, B. *Chit-Chat; or, The Penance of Polygamy*. Dublin, 1781.

Ward, Edward. *The City Madam, and the Country Maid; or, Opposite Characters of a Virtuous Housewifely Damsel, and a Mechanick's Town-Bred Daughter*. London, 1702.

——. *The Insinuating Bawd: And the Repenting Harlot. Written by a Whore at Tunbridge, and Dedicated to a Bawd at the Bath*. London, 1700.

——. *The Miracles Perform'd by Money*. London, 1692.

——. *Rambling Rakes; or, London Libertines*. London: J. How, 1700.

Watson, Sophia. *Memoirs of the Seraglio of the Bashaw of Merryland. By a Discarded Sultana*. London: Printed for S. Bladon, 1768.

Welch, Saunders. *A Proposal to Render Effectual a Plan, to Remove the Nuisance of Common Prostitutes from the Streets of This Metropolis*. London: C. Henderson, 1758.

Whitlock, John. *A Sermon Preached to the Society for Reformation of Manners at Nottingham*. London: Printed for John Richards, 1698.

The Whore: A Poem. Written by a Whore of Quality. London: Printed for the Author, [1782?].

The Whore's Petition to the London Prentices. London, 1668.

The Whore's Rhetorick, Calculated to the Meridian of London; and Conformed to the Rules of Art: in Two Dialogues. London: Printed for George Shell, 1683.

Williams, Daniel. *A Sermon Preach'd before the Societies for Reformation of Manners, in Dublin*. Dublin: Printed by Andrew Crook, 1700.

Williams, William Bell. *Mary Magdalene. A Sermon Preached in the Chapel of Magdalen Hospital*. London: F. and C. Rivington, 1794.

Wills, Thomas. *Remarks on Polygamy*. London: T. Hughes, F. Walsh, R. Baldwin, and W. Otridge, 1781.

Woodward, Josiah. *An Account of the Progress of the Reformation of Manners in England and Ireland and Other Parts of the World*. London: J. Downing, 1701.

——. *An Account of the Rise and Progress of the Religious Societies in the City of London and of the Endeavours for the Reformation of Manners which Have Been Made Therein*. 2nd ed. London: Printed by J. D., 1698.

——. *An Account of the Societies for Reformation of Manners, in London and Westminster, and Other Parts of the Kingdom*. London, 1699.

——. *The Young Man's Monitor; Shewing the Great Happiness of Early Piety and the Dreadful Consequences of Indulging Youthful Lusts*. 11th ed. London: J. F. and C. Rivington, 1788.

Wynne, John Huddleston. *The Prostitute, a Poem*. London: Printed for J. Wheble, 1771.

Secondary Sources

Journal Abbreviations

ECS   = Eighteenth-Century Studies
ELH   = English Literary History
PMLA = Publications of the Modern Language Association
SEL   = Studies in English Literature, 1500–1900
SECC = Studies in Eighteenth-Century Culture

Abbot, John Lawrence. *John Hawkesworth: Eighteenth-Century Man of Letters*. Madison, WI: University of Wisconsin Press, 1982.

Alexander, Michael. *Omai, "Noble Savage."* London: Collins & Harvill Press, 1977.

Alexander, Priscilla, and Frédérique Delacoste, eds. *Sex Work: Writings by Women in the Sex Industry*. Pittsburgh: Cleis Press, 1987.

Alter, Robert. *Rogue's Progress: Studies in the Picaresque Novel.* Cambridge, MA: Harvard University Press, 1964.

Anderson, Amanda. *Tainted Souls and Painted Faces: The Rhetoric of Fallenness in Victorian Culture.* Ithaca: Cornell University Press, 1993.

Andersen, Hans H. "The Paradox of Trade and Morality in Defoe." *Modern Philology* 39 (1941): 23–46.

Andrew, Donna T. *Philanthropy and the Police: London Charity in the Eighteenth Century.* Princeton: Princeton University Press, 1989.

Appleby, Joyce Oldham. *Economic Thought and Ideology in Seventeenth Century England.* Princeton: Princeton University Press, 1978.

——. *Liberalism and Republicanism in the Historical Imagination.* Cambridge. MA: Harvard University Press, 1992.

Aravamudan, Srinivas. *Tropicopolitans: Colonialism and Agency, 1688–1804.* Durham, NC: Duke University Press, 1999.

Armstrong, Nancy. *Desire and Domestic Fiction: A Political History of the Novel.* Oxford: Oxford University Press, 1987.

——. "Reclassifying Clarissa: Fiction and the Making of the Modern Middle Class." In *Clarissa and Her Readers: New Essays for the Clarissa Project,* edited by Carol Houlihan Flynn and Edward Copeland, 19–43. New York: AMS Press, 1999.

Armstrong, Nancy, and Leonard Tennenhouse. *The Imaginary Puritan: Literature, Intellectual Labor, and the Origins of Personal Life.* Berkeley: University of California Press, 1992.

Backscheider, Paula. "Defoe's Lady Credit." *Huntington Library Quarterly* 44, no. 2 (1981): 89–100.

——. "Defoe's Women: Snares and Prey." *SECC* 5 (1976): 103–120.

Bahlman, Dudley W. R. *The Moral Revolution of 1688.* New Haven: Yale University Press, 1957.

Baker, Sheridan. "Bridget Allworthy: The Creative Pressures of Fielding's Plot." In *Tom Jones,* ed. Sheridan Baker, 778–786. 2nd ed. New York: W. W. Norton & Co., 1995.

Balme, Christopher B. "Sexual Spectacles: Theatricality and the Performance of Sex in Early Encounters in the Pacific." *TDR: The Drama Review* 44, no. 4 (2000): 67–85.

Barker-Benfield, G. J. *The Culture of Sensibility: Sex and Society in Eighteenth-Century Britain.* Chicago: University of Chicago Press, 1992.

Barry, Kathleen. *Female Sexual Slavery.* Englewood Cliffs, NJ: Prentice-Hall, 1979.

Bartky, Sandra Lee. *Femininity and Domination: Studies in the Phenomenology of Oppression.* New York: Routledge, 1990.

Bataille, Robert. "The Magdalen Charity for the Reform of Prostitutes: A Foucauldian Moment." In *Illicit Sex: Identity Politics in Early Modern Culture,* edited by Thomas DiPiero and Pat Gill, 109–122. Athens: University of Georgia Press, 1997.

Batchelor, Jenny. "'Industry in Distress': Reconfiguring Femininity and Labor in the Magdalen House." *ECL* 28, no. 1 (2004): 1–20.

Beaglehole, J. C. *The Life of Captain James Cook.* Stanford: Stanford University Press, 1974.

Bean, Brenda. "Sight and Self-Disclosure: Richardson's Revision of Swift's 'The Lady's Dressing Room'." *ECL* 14, no. 1 (1990): 1–23.

Bell, Ian A. *Defoe's Fiction.* London: Croom Helm, 1985.

Bellamy, Liz. *Commerce, Morality, and the Eighteenth-Century Novel.* Cambridge: Cambridge University Press, 1998.

Berg, Maxine. *The Age of Manufactures: Industry, Innovation, and Work in Britain, 1700–1820.* Totowa, NJ: Barnes & Noble, 1985.

Blewett, David. *Defoe's Art of Fiction.* Toronto: University of Toronto Press, 1979.

Boucé, Paul-Gabriel. "Sex, Amours, and Love in Tom Jones." *Studies on Voltaire and the Eighteenth Century* 228 (1984): 25–38.

Bowen, Scarlett. "'A Sawce-Box and Boldface Indeed': Refiguring the Female Servant in the Pamela-Antipamela Debate." *SECC* 28 (1999): 257–285.

Bowers, Toni. *The Politics of Motherhood: British Writing and Culture, 1680–1760.* Cambridge: Cambridge University Press, 1996.

Braudel, Fernand. *Civilization and Capitalism, 15th to 18th Century.* 3 vols. Translated by Siân Reynold. Berkeley: University of California Press, 1992. (Published in France in 1979).

Braudy, Leo. "Fanny Hill and Materialism." *ECS* 4, no. 1 (1970): 21–40.

Braverman, Richard. "Rebellion Redux: Figuring Whig History in Tom Jones." *CLIO: A Journal of Literature, History, and Philosophy of History* 24, no. 3 (1995): 251–268.

Brewer, John. *The Sinews of Power: War, Money, and the English State, 1688–1783.* Cambridge, MA: Harvard University Press, 1988.

Brewer, John, and Roy Porter, eds. *Consumption and the World of Goods.* New York: Routledge, 1993.

Bristow, Edward J. *Vice and Vigilance: Purity Movements in Britain since 1700.* Totowa, NJ: Rowman and Littlefield, 1977.

Broder, Janice. "Lady Bradshaigh Reads and Writes Clarissa: The Marginal Notes in Her First Edition." In *Clarissa and Her Readers: New Essays for the Clarissa Project*, edited by Carol Houlihan Flynn and Edward Copeland, 97–118. New York: AMS Press, 1999.

Brown, Homer Obed. "Tom Jones: the 'Bastard' of History." *Boundary II* 7, no. 2 (1979): 201–234.

Brown, Laura. *Ends of Empire: Women and Ideology in Early Eighteenth-Century English Literature.* Ithaca: Cornell University Press, 1993.

Brown, Murray L. "Authorship and Generic Exploitation: Why Lovelace Must Fear Clarissa." *Studies in the Novel* 30, no. 2 (1998): 246–259.

Bueler, Lois E. *Clarissa's Plots.* Newark: University of Delaware Press, 1994.

Bullough, Vern L. *The History of Prostitution.* New Hyde Park, New York: University Books, 1964.

———. "Prostitution and Reform in Eighteenth-Century England." *ECL* 9, no. 3 (1985): 61–74.

Burke, Helen. "*Roxana*, Corruption, and the Progressive Myth." *Genre* 23, no. 2 (1990): 103–120.

Burtt, Shelley. "The Societies for the Reformation of Manners: Between John Locke and the Devil in Augustan England." In *The Margins of Orthodoxy: Heterodox Writing and Cultural Response, 1660–1750*, edited by Roger D. Lund, 149–169. Cambridge: Cambridge University Press, 1995.

———. *Virtue Transformed: Political Argument in England, 1688–1740.* Cambridge: Cambridge University Press, 1992.

Campbell, Jill. *Natural Masques: Gender and Identity in Fielding's Plays and Novels.* Stanford: Stanford University Press, 1995.

Canfield, J. Douglas. "Prostitution as Class Prophylactic in George Lillo's Adaptation of Shakespeare's *Pericles* as *Marina*." *Restoration and 18th Century Theatre Research* 13, no. 2 (1998): 35–42.

Carlton, Peter J. "The Mitigated Truth: Tom Jones's Double Heroism." *Studies in the Novel* 19, no. 4 (1987): 397–409.

———. "*Tom Jones* and the '45 Once Again." *Studies in the Novel* 20, no. 4 (1988): 361–373.

Carswell, John. *The South Sea Bubble.* Stanford: Stanford University Press, 1960.

Castle, Terry. "'Amy, Who Knew my Disease': A Psychosexual Pattern in Defoe's *Roxana*." In *The Female Thermometer: Eighteenth-Century Culture and the Invention of the Uncanny*, 44–55. Oxford: Oxford University Press, 1995.

——. *Clarissa's Ciphers: Meaning and Disruption in Richardson's "Clarissa".* Ithaca: Cornell University Press, 1982.

——. *Masquerade and Civilization: The Carnivalesque in Eighteenth-Century English Culture and Fiction.* Stanford: Stanford University Press, 1986.

Chaber, Lois. "Matriarchal Mirror: Women and Capital in *Moll Flanders*." *PMLA* 97, no. 2 (1982): 212–226.

Chancer, Lynn Sharon. "Prostitution, Feminist Theory, and Ambivalence: Notes from the Sociological Underground." *Social Text* 37 (1993): 143–171.

Chapkis, Wendy. *Live Sex Acts: Women Performing Erotic Labor.* New York: Routledge, 1997.

Cheek, Pamela. *Sexual Antipodes: Enlightenment Globalization and the Placing of Sex.* Stanford: Stanford University Press, 2003.

Clark, Alice. *Working Life of Women in the Seventeenth Century.* New York: E.P. Dutton & Co., 1919.

Clark, Thomas Blake. *Omai, First Polynesian Ambassador to England.* San Francisco: Colt Press, 1940.

Compston, H. F. B. *The Magdalen Hospital: The Story of a Great Charity.* London: Society for Promoting Christian Knowledge, 1917.

Conway, Alison. "Defoe's Protestant Whore." *ECS* 35, no. 2 (2002): 215–233.

——. "The Protestant Cause and a Protestant Whore: Aphra Behn's Love Letters." *ECL* 25, no. 3 (2001): 1–19.

Cook, Harold J. "Bernard Mandeville and the Therapy of 'The Clever Politician'." *Journal of the History of Ideas* 60, no. 1 (1999): 101–124.

Cook, Richard I. "'The Great Leviathan of Lechery': Mandeville's *Modest Defence of the Publick Stews* (1724)." In *Mandeville Studies: New Explorations in the Art and Thought of Dr. Bernard Mandeville,* edited by Irwin Primer, 22–33. The Hague: Nijhoff, 1975.

Copeland, Edward W. "Clarissa and Fanny Hill: Sisters in Distress." *Studies in the Novel* 4, no. 3 (1972): 343–352.

Craft-Fairchild, Catherine. "The Politics of 'Passing': The Scandalous Memoir and the Novel." In *Illicit Sex: Identity Politics in Early Modern Culture,* edited by Thomas DiPiero and Pat Gill, 45–67. Athens: University of Georgia Press, 1997.

Crane, R. S. "The Plot of *Tom Jones*." Reprinted in *Tom Jones,* ed. Sheridan Baker, 677–698. 2nd ed. New York: W.W. Norton & Co., 1995.

Cruise, James. "Fielding, Authority, and the New Commercialism in Joseph Andrews." *ELH* 54, no. 2 (1987): 253–276.

——. "Pamela and the Commerce of Authority." *Journal of English and Germanic Philology* 87 (1988): 342–358.

Curtis, T. C., and W. A. Speck. "The Societies for the Reformation of Manners: A Case Study in the Theory and Practice of Moral Reform." *Literature and History* 3 (1976): 45–64.

Daniel, Stephen H. "Myth and Rationality in Mandeville." *Journal of the History of Ideas* 47, no.4 (1986): 595–609.

Daunton, M. J. *Progress and Poverty: An Economic and Social History of Britain, 1700–1850.* Oxford: Oxford University Press, 1995.

Davidson, Julia O'Connell. *Prostitution, Power, and Freedom.* Ann Arbor: University of Michigan Press, 1998.

Davison, Lee, Tim Hitchcock, Tim Keirn, and Robert B. Shoemaker, eds. *Stilling the Grumbling Hive: The Response to Social and Economic Problems in England, 1689–1750.* New York: St. Martin's Press, 1992.

Delacoste, Frédérique, and Priscilla Alexander, eds. *Sex Work: Writings by Women in the Sex Industry.* Pittsburgh: Cleis Press, 1987.

DeRitter, Jones. "Blaming the Audience, Blaming the Gods: Unwitting Incest in Three

Eighteenth-Century English Novels." In *Illicit Sex: Identity Politics in Early Modern Culture*, edited by Tom DiPiero and Pat Gill, 221–238. Athens: University of Georgia Press, 1997.

Dickson, P. G. M. *The Financial Revolution in England: A Study in the Development of Public Credit, 1688–1756*. New York: St. Martin's Press, 1967.

Dijkstra, Bram. *Defoe and Economics: The Fortunes of "Roxana" in the History of Interpretation*. New York: St. Martin's Press, 1987.

Dolan, Frances E. *Whores of Babylon: Catholicism, Gender, and Seventeenth-Century Print Culture*. Ithaca: Cornell University Press, 1999.

Doody, Margaret Anne. *A Natural Passion: A Study of the Novels of Samuel Richardson*. Oxford: Clarendon Press, 1974.

Doody, Margaret Anne, and Peter Sabor, eds. *Samuel Richardson: Tercentenary Essays*. Cambridge: Cambridge University Press, 1989.

Drake, George A. "Historical Space in the 'History of': Between Public and Private in *Tom Jones*." *ELH* 66, no. 3 (1999): 707–737.

Durant, David. "Roxana's Fictions." *Studies in the Novel* 13, no. 3 (1981): 225–236.

Dykstal, Timothy. "Commerce, Conversation, and Contradiction in Mandeville's Fable." *SECC* 23 (1994): 93–110.

Eagleton, Terry. *The Rape of Clarissa: Writing, Sexuality, and Class Struggle in Samuel Richardson*. Oxford: Blackwell, 1982.

Earle, Peter. *The Making of the English Middle Class: Business, Society and Family Life in London, 1660–1730*. Berkeley: University of California Press, 1989.

Edmond, Rod. *Representing the South Pacific: Colonial Discourse from Cook to Gauguin*. Cambridge: Cambridge University Press, 1997.

Edwards, Philip. *The Story of the Voyage: Sea-Narratives in Eighteenth-Century England*. Cambridge: Cambridge University Press, 1994.

Edwards, Thomas R. "Mandeville's Moral Prose." *ELH* 31, no.2 (1964): 195–212.

Ek, Grete. "Glory, Jest, and Riddle: The Masque of Tom Jones in London." *English Studies* 60 (1979): 148–158.

Elfenbein, Andrew. "The Management of Desire in *Memoirs of a Woman of Pleasure*." In *Launching Fanny Hill: Essays on the Novel and Its Influences*, edited by Patsy S. Fowler and Alan Jackson, 27–48. New York: AMS Press, 2003.

Ellis, Markman. *The Politics of Sensibility: Race, Gender, and Commerce in the Sentimental Novel*. Cambridge: Cambridge University Press, 1995.

Erickson, Robert A. *Mother Midnight: Birth, Sex, and Fate in Eighteenth-Century Fiction (Defoe, Richardson, and Sterne)*. New York: AMS Press, 1986.

Faller, Lincoln B. *Crime and Defoe: A New Kind of Writing*. Cambridge: Cambridge University Press, 1993.

Farrell, William J. "The Role of Mandeville's Bee Analogy in 'The Grumbling Hive'." *SEL* 25, no. 3 (1985): 511–527.

Felsenstein, Frank. *Anti-Semitic Stereotypes: A Paradigm of Otherness in English Popular Culture, 1660–1830*. Baltimore: Johns Hopkins University Press, 1995.

Ferguson, Frances. "Rape and the Rise of the Novel." *Representations* 20 (1987): 88–112.

Fissell, Mary. "Charity Universal? Institutions and Moral Reform in Eighteenth-Century Bristol." In *Stilling the Grumbling Hive: The Response to Social and Economic Problems in England, 1689–1750*, edited by Lee Davison, Tim Hitchcock, Tim Keirn, and Robert B. Shoemaker, 121–144. New York: St. Martin's, 1992.

Flint, Christopher. "The Anxiety of Affluence: Family and Class (Dis)Order in *Pamela; Or, Virtue Rewarded*." *SEL* 29, no. 3 (1989): 489–513.

Flynn, Carol Houlihan. *The Body in Swift and Defoe*. Cambridge: Cambridge University Press, 1990.

———. *Samuel Richardson, Man of Letters.* Princeton: Princeton University Press, 1982.
———. "What Fanny Felt: The Pains of Compliance in *Memoirs of a Woman of Pleasure.*" *Studies in the Novel* 19, no. 3 (1987): 284–295.
Fraser, Nancy. *Justice Interruptus: Critical Reflections on the "Postsocialist" Condition.* New York: Routledge, 1997.
Freeman, Lisa A. *Character's Theater: Genre and Identity on the Eighteenth-Century English Stage.* Philadelphia: University of Pennsylvania Press, 2002.
Foster, R. F. *Modern Ireland, 1600–1972.* London: Penguin Press, 1988.
Foucault, Michel. *Discipline and Punish: The Birth of the Prison.* Translated by Alan Sheridan. New York: Pantheon Books, 1977.
———. *The History of Sexuality.* Vol. 1. Translated by Robert Hurley. New York: Pantheon Books, 1978.
Foxon, David F. *Libertine Literature in England, 1660–1745.* New Hyde Park, NY: University Books, 1965.
Fyfe, Christopher. *A History of Sierra Leone.* Oxford: Oxford University Press, 1962.
Gallagher, Catherine. *Nobody's Story: The Vanishing Acts of Women Writers in the Marketplace, 1670–1820.* Berkeley: University of California Press, 1994.
Gautier, Gary. "Fanny's Fantasies: Class, Gender, and the Unreliable Narrator in Cleland's *Memoirs of a Woman of Pleasure.*" *Style* 28, no. 2 (1994): 133–145.
———. "Fanny Hill's Mapping of Sexuality, Female Identity, and Maternity." *SEL* 35, no. 3 (1995): 473–491.
George, Dorothy. *London Life in the XVIIIth Century.* London: K. Paul, Trench, Trubner, 1925.
Gerzina, Gretchen. *Black London: Life before Emancipation.* New Brunswick, NJ: Rutgers University Press, 1995.
Gilman, Sander. *The Jew's Body.* New York: Routledge, 1991.
Girard, Rene. *Violence and the Sacred.* Translated by Patrick Gregory. Baltimore: Johns Hopkins University Press, 1977.
Goldgar, Bertrand A. "Fielding and the Whores of London." *Philological Quarterly* 64, no. 2 (1985): 265–272.
Goldsmith, M. M. "Mandeville and the Spirit of Capitalism." *Journal of British Studies* 17, no. 1 (1977): 63–81.
———. "Mandeville's Pernicious System." In *Mandeville and Augustan Ideas,* edited by Charles W. A. Prior, 71–84. Victoria, BC: University of Victoria, 2000.
———. *Private Vices, Public Benefits: Bernard Mandeville's Social and Political Thought.* Cambridge: Cambridge University Press, 1985.
———. "Regulating Anew the Moral and Political Sentiments of Mankind: Bernard Mandeville and the Scottish Enlightenment." *Journal of the History of Ideas* 49, no. 4 (1988): 587–606.
Gooding, Richard. "*Pamela, Shamela,* and the Politics of the *Pamela* Vogue." *Eighteenth-Century Fiction* 7, no. 2 (1995): 109–130.
Gregg, Stephen H. "'A Truly Christian Hero': Religion, Effeminacy, and Nation in the Writings of the Societies for Reformation of Manners." *ECL* 25, no. 1 (2001): 17–28.
Gunn, J. "'State Hypochondriacks' Dispraised: Mandeville Versus the Active Citizen." In *Mandeville and Augustan Ideas,* edited by Charles W. A. Prior, 16–34. Victoria: University of Victoria, 2000.
Gwilliam, Tassie. "Female Fraud: Counterfeit Maidenheads in the Eighteenth Century." *Journal of the History of Sexuality* 6, no. 4 (1996): 518–548.
———. *Samuel Richardson's Fictions of Gender.* Stanford: Stanford University Press, 1993.
Harris, Jocelyn. "Grotesque, Classical and Pornographic Bodies in *Clarissa.*" In *New Essays on Samuel Richardson,* edited by Albert J. Rivero, 101–116. New York: St. Martin's, 1996.

Harris, Tim. *London Crowds in the Reign of Charles II: Propaganda and Politics from the Restoration until the Exclusion Crisis*. Cambridge: Cambridge University Press, 1987.

Harth, Philip. "The Satiric Purpose of *The Fable of the Bees*," *ECS* 2, no. 4 (1969): 321–340.

Haselkorn, Anne M. *Prostitution in Elizabethan and Jacobean Comedy*. Troy, NY: Whitston Publishing Company, 1983.

Henderson, Tony. *Disorderly Women in Eighteenth-Century London: Prostitution and Control in the Metropolis, 1730–1830*. New York: Longman, 1999.

Hill, Bridget. *Women, Work, and Sexual Politics in Eighteenth-Century England*. New York: Basil Blackwell, 1989.

Hill, Christopher. "Clarissa Harlowe and Her Times." *Essays in Criticism* 5, no. 4 (1955): 315–340.

Hilliard, Raymond F. "Clarissa and Ritual Cannibalism." *PMLA* 105, no. 5 (1990): 1083–1097.

Hirschman, Albert O. *The Passions and the Interests: Political Arguments for Capitalism before Its Triumph*. Princeton: Princeton University Press, 1977.

Hitchcock, Tim. "Paupers and Preachers: The SPCK and the Parochial Workhouse Movement." In *Stilling the Grumbling Hive: The Response to Social and Economic Problems in England, 1689–1750*, edited by Tim Hitchcock, Lee Davison, Tim Keirn, and Robert B. Shoemaker, 145–166. New York: St. Martin's, 1992.

Hjort, Anne Mette. "Mandeville's Ambivalent Modernity." *Modern Language Notes* 106, no. 5 (1991): 951–966.

Holmes, Geoffrey. *The Trial of Doctor Sacheverell*. London: Eyre Methuen, 1973.

Honeyman, Katrina. *Women, Gender and Industrialisation in England, 1700–1870*. New York: St. Martin's Press, 2000.

Horne, Thomas A. *The Social Thought of Bernard Mandeville: Virtue and Commerce in Early Eighteenth-Century England*. New York: Columbia University Press, 1978.

Howe, Elizabeth. *The First English Actresses: Women and Drama 1660–1700*. Cambridge: Cambridge University Press, 1992.

Hume, Robert. "The Conclusion of Defoe's *Roxana*: Fiasco or Tour de Force?" *ECS* 3, no. 4 (1970): 475–490.

Hundert, E. J. "Bernard Mandeville and the Enlightenment's Maxims of Modernity." *Journal of the History of Ideas* 56, no. 4 (1995): 577–593.

——. *The Enlightenment's Fable: Bernard Mandeville and the Discovery of Society*. Cambridge: Cambridge University Press, 1994.

——. "The European Enlightenment and the History of the Self." In *Rewriting the Self: Histories from the Renaissance to the Present*, edited by Roy Porter, 72–83. London: Routledge, 1977.

Hunt, Lynn, ed. *The Invention of Pornography: Obscenity and the Origins of Modernity, 1500–1800*. New York: Zone Books, 1993.

Hunt, Margaret R. *The Middling Sort: Commerce, Gender, and the Family in England, 1680–1780*. Berkeley: University of California Press, 1996.

Hutner, Heidi. *Colonial Women: Race and Culture in Stuart Drama*. Oxford: Oxford University Press, 2001.

Ingrassia, Catherine. "The Pleasure of Business and the Business of Pleasure: Gender, Credit, and the South Sea Bubble." *SECC* 24 (1995): 191–210.

Isaacs, Tina. "The Anglican Hierarchy and the Reformation of Manners, 1688–1738." *Journal of Ecclesiastical History* 33, no. 3 (1982): 391–411.

Jack, M.R. "Religion and Ethics in Mandeville." In *Mandeville Studies: New Explorations in the Art and Thought of Dr. Bernard Mandeville*, edited by Irwin Primer, 34–42. The Hague: Martinus Nijhoff, 1975.

Jeffreys, Sheila. *The Idea of Prostitution*. North Melbourne, Australia: Spinifex, 1997.

Johnson, Hershel. "Tom Jones and the Picaresque Tradition." *SEL* 26, no. 1–2 (1985): 9–17.

Jones, Vivien. "Eighteenth-Century Prostitution: Feminist Debates and the Writing of Histories." In *Body Matters: Feminism, Textuality, Corporeality*, edited by Avril Horner and Angela Keane, 127–169. Manchester: Manchester University Press, 2000.

———. "Placing Jemima: Women Writers of the 1790s and the Eighteenth-Century Prostitution Narrative." *Women's Writing* 4, no. 2 (1997): 201–220.

Karras, Ruth Mazo. *Common Women: Prostitution and Sexuality in Medieval England.* Oxford: Oxford University Press, 1996.

Kempadoo, Kamala, and Jo Doezema, eds. *Global Sex Workers: Rights, Resistance, and Redefinition.* New York: Routledge, 1998.

Kern, Jean B. "The Fallen Women, from the Perspective of Five Early Eighteenth-Century Women Novelists." *SECC* 10 (1981): 457–468.

Kibbie, Ann Louise. "Sentimental Properties: *Pamela* and *Memoirs of a Woman of Pleasure.*" *ELH* 58, no. 3 (1991): 561–577.

———. "Monstrous Generation: The Birth of Capital in Defoe's *Moll Flanders* and *Roxana.*" *PMLA* 110, no. 5 (1995): 1023–1034.

Kinkead-Weekes, Mark. *Samuel Richardson: Dramatic Novelist.* Ithaca: Cornell University Press, 1973.

Klein, Lawrence E. "Gender and the Public/Private Distinction in the Eighteenth Century: Some Questions about Evidence and Analytic Procedure." *ECS* 29, no. 1 (1995): 97–109.

———. "The Third Earl of Shaftesbury and the Progress of Politeness." *ECS* 18, no. 2 (1984): 186–214.

Koppel, Gene S. "Sexual Education and Sexual Values in *Tom Jones:* Confusion at the Core?" *Studies in the Novel* 12, no. 1 (1980): 1–11.

Kowaleski-Wallace, Elizabeth. *Consuming Subjects: Women, Shopping, and Business in the Eighteenth Century.* New York: Columbia University Press, 1997.

Kramnick, Jonathan Brody. "'Unwilling to Be Short, or Plain, in Any Thing Concerning Gain': Bernard Mandeville and the Dialectic on Charity." *The Eighteenth Century: Theory and Interpretation* 33, no. 2 (1992): 148–175.

Kristeva, Julia. *Powers of Horror: An Essay on Abjection.* Translated by Leon S. Roudiez. New York: Columbia University Press, 1982.

Kubek, Elizabeth. "The Man Machine: Horror and the Phallus in *Memoirs of a Woman of Pleasure.*" In *Launching Fanny Hill: Essays on the Novel and Its Influences*, edited by Patsy S. Fowler and Alan Jackson, 173–197. New York: AMS Press, 2003.

Laqueur, Thomas. *Making Sex: Body and Gender from the Greeks to Freud.* Cambridge, MA: Harvard University Press, 1990.

Lamb, Jonathan. "Circumstances Surrounding the Death of John Hawkesworth." *ECL* 18, no. 3 (1994): 97–113.

———. *Preserving the Self in the South Seas, 1680–1840.* Chicago: University of Chicago Press, 2001.

Lee, Joy Kyunghae. "The Commodification of Virtue: Chastity and the Virginal Body in Richardson's *Clarissa.*" *The Eighteenth Century: Theory and Interpretation* 36, no. 1 (1995): 38–54.

Levin, Kate. "The Meanness of Writing for a Bookseller: John Cleland's Fanny on the Market." *Journal of Narrative Technique* 28, no. 3 (1998): 329–349.

Linebaugh, Peter. *The London Hanged: Crime and Civil Society in the Eighteenth Century.* Cambridge: Cambridge University Press, 1992.

Lloyd, Sarah. "'Pleasure's Golden Bait': Prostitution, Poverty, and the Magdalen Hospital in Eighteenth-Century London." *History Workshop Journal* 41 (1996): 50–70.

Lynch, Deidre Shauna. *The Economy of Character: Novels, Market Culture, and the Business of Inner Meaning*. Chicago: University of Chicago Press, 1998.

Mackie, Erin Skye. *Market à la Mode: Fashion, Commodity, and Gender in the Tatler and the Spectator*. Baltimore: Johns Hopkins University Press, 1997.

Macpherson, C. B. *The Political Theory of Possessive Individualism: Hobbes to Locke*. Oxford: Clarendon Press, 1962.

Macpherson, Sandra. "Lovelace, Ltd." *ELH* 65, no. 1 (1998): 99–121.

Maddox, James H. "On Defoe's *Roxana*." *ELH* 51, no. 4 (1984): 669–691.

Mahood, Linda. *The Magdalenes: Prostitution in the Nineteenth Century*. New York: Routledge, 1990.

Mandell, Laura. *Misogynous Economies: The Business of Literature in Eighteenth-Century Britain*. Lexington: University of Kentucky Press, 1999.

Markley, Robert. "Language, Power, and Sexuality in Cleland's *Fanny Hill*." *Philological Quarterly* 63, no. 3 (1984): 343–356.

Marshall, David. *The Figure of Theater: Shaftesbury, Defoe, Adam Smith, and George Eliot*. New York: Columbia University Press, 1986.

Massai, Sonia. "From *Pericles* to *Marina:* 'While Women Are to Be Had for Money, Love, or Importunity,'" *Shakespeare Survey* 51 (1998): 67–77.

Maurer, Shawn Lisa. *Proposing Men: Dialectics of Gender and Class in the Eighteenth-Century English Periodical*. Stanford: Stanford University Press, 1998.

McAllister, Marie E. "Stories of the Origin of Syphilis in Eighteenth-Century England: Science, Myth, and Prejudice." *ECL* 24, no. 1 (2000): 22–44.

McClintock, Anne. "Sex Workers and Sex Work." *Social Text* 37 (1993): 1–10.

McCormick, E. H. *Omai: Pacific Envoy*. Auckland: Auckland University Press, 1977.

McCrea, Brian. "Clarissa's Pregnancy and the Fate of Patriarchal Power." *Eighteenth-Century Fiction* 9, no. 2 (1997): 125–148.

McKendrick, Neil, John Brewer, and J. H. Plumb, *The Birth of a Consumer Society: The Commercialization of Eighteenth-Century England*. Bloomington: Indiana University Press, 1982.

McKeon, Michael. "Historicizing Patriarchy: The Emergence of Gender Difference in England, 1660–1760." *ECS* 28, no. 3 (1995): 295–322.

———. *The Origins of the English Novel, 1600–1740*. Baltimore: Johns Hopkins University Press, 1987.

Miller, Leo. *John Milton among the Polygamophiles*. New York: Loewenthal Press, 1974.

Miller, Peter. "Citizenship and Culture in Early Modern Europe." *Journal of the History of Ideas* 57, no. 4 (1996): 725–742.

Monro, D. H. *The Ambivalence of Bernard Mandeville*. Oxford: Clarendon Press, 1975.

Moody, Jane. *Illegitimate Theatre in London, 1770–1840*. Cambridge: Cambridge University Press, 2000.

Mourão, Manuela. "The Representation of Female Desire in Early Modern Pornographic Texts, 1660–1745." *Signs* 24, no. 3 (1999): 573–602.

Mowry, Melissa M. *The Bawdy Politic in Stuart England, 1660–1714*. Burlington, VT: Ashgate, 2004.

Mudge, Bradford K. *The Whore's Story: Women, Pornography, and the British Novel, 1684–1830*. Oxford: Oxford University Press, 2000.

Mulcaire, Terry. "Public Credit; Or, The Feminization of Virtue in the Marketplace." *PMLA* 114, no. 4 (1999): 1029–1042.

Nagle, Jill, ed. *Whores and Other Feminists*. New York: Routledge, 1997.

Nash, Stanley. "Prostitution and Charity: The Magdalen Hospital, a Case Study." *Journal of Social History* 17, no. 4 (1984): 617–628.

———. *Prostitution in Great Britain 1485–1901: An Annotated Bibliography.* Metuchen, NJ: Scarecrow Press, 1994.

New, Peter. "Why Roxana Can Never Find Herself." *The Modern Language Review* 91, no. 2 (1996): 317–329.

Nicholson, Colin. *Writing and the Rise of Finance: Capital Satires of the Early Eighteenth Century.* Cambridge: Cambridge University Press, 1994.

Nickel, Terri. "*Pamela* and Fetish: Masculine Anxiety in Henry Fielding's *Shamela* and James Parry's *The True Anti-Pamela,*" *SECC* 22 (1992): 37–49.

Norton, Rictor. *Mother Clap's Molly House: The Gay Subculture in England, 1700–1830.* London: GPM, 1992.

Novak, Maximillian E. "Crime and Punishment in Defoe's *Roxana*." *Journal of English and Germanic Philology* 65 (1966): 445–465.

———. *Defoe and the Nature of Man.* Oxford: Oxford University Press, 1963.

———. *Economics and the Fiction of Daniel Defoe.* Berkeley: University of California Press, 1962.

Nussbaum, Felicity. *Torrid Zones: Maternity, Sexuality, and Empire in Eighteenth-Century English Narratives.* Baltimore: Johns Hopkins University Press, 1995.

———. "One Part of Womankind: Prostitution and Sexual Geography in *Memoirs of a Woman of Pleasure*." *Differences* 7, no. 2 (1995): 17–40.

Obeyesekere, Gananath. *The Apotheosis of Captain Cook: European Mythmaking in the Pacific.* Princeton: Princeton University Press, 1992.

O'Brien, John F. "The Character of Credit: Defoe's 'Lady Credit,' *The Fortunate Mistress,* and the Resources of Inconsistency in Early Eighteenth-Century Britain." *ELH* 63, no. 3 (1996): 603–631.

Ollman, Bertell. *Alienation: Marx's Conception of Man in Capitalist Society.* Cambridge: Cambridge University Press, 1971.

Olsson, Lena. "Idealized and Realistic Portrayals of Prostitution in John Cleland's *Memoirs of a Woman of Pleasure*." In *Launching Fanny Hill: Essays on the Novel and Its Influences,* edited by Patsy S. Fowler and Alan Jackson, 81–101. New York: AMS Press, 2003.

Orr, Bridget. "'Southern Passions Mix with Northern Art': Miscegenation and the *Endeavour* Voyage." *ECL* 18, no. 3 (1994): 212–231.

Osland, Dianne. "Complaisance and Complacence, and the Perils of Pleasing in Clarissa." *SEL* 40, no. 3 (2000): 491–509.

Park, William. "Clarissa as Tragedy." *SEL* 16, no. 3 (1976): 461–471.

Pateman, Carole. *The Sexual Contract.* Stanford: Stanford University Press, 1988.

Perry, Ruth. "Clarissa's Daughters; or, The History of Innocence Betrayed: How Women Writers Rewrote Richardson." In *Clarissa and Her Readers: New Essays for the Clarissa Project,* edited by Carol Houlihan Flynn and Edward Copeland, 119–141. New York: AMS Press, 1999.

———. "Good Girls and Fallen Women: Representations of Prostitutes in Eighteenth-Century English Fiction." In *Narrating Transgression: Representations of the Criminal in Early Modern England,* edited by Rosamaria Loretelli and Roberto De Romanis, 91–101. Frankfurt, Peter Lang, 1999.

———. *Novel Relations: The Transformation of Kinship in English Literature and Culture, 1748–1818.* Cambridge: Cambridge University Press, 2004.

Pocock, J. G. A. *The Machiavellian Moment: Florentine Political Thought and the Atlantic Republican Tradition.* Princeton: Princeton University Press, 1975.

———. *Virtue, Commerce, and History: Essays on Political Thought and History, Chiefly in the Eighteenth Century.* Cambridge: Cambridge University Press, 1985.

Porter, Roy. "The Exotic as Erotic: Captain Cook at Tahiti." In *Exoticism in the Enlighten-*

ment, edited by G. S. Rousseau and Roy Porter, 117–144. Manchester: Manchester University Press, 1990.

———. "Pre-Modernism and the Art of Shopping." *Critical Quarterly* 34, no. 4 (1992): 3–14.

Porter, Roy, and Lesley Hall. *The Facts of Life: The Creation of Sexual Knowledge in Britain, 1650–1950*. New Haven: Yale University Press, 1995.

Potter, Tiffany. *Honest Sins: Georgian Libertinism and the Plays and Novels of Henry Fielding.* Montreal: McGill-Queen's University Press, 1999.

———. "'A Certain Sign That He Is One of Us': Clarissa's Other Libertines." *Eighteenth-Century Fiction* 11, no. 4 (1999): 403–420.

Pratt, Mary Louise. *Imperial Eyes: Travel Writing and Transculturation.* New York: Routledge, 1992.

Radin, Margaret Jane. *Contested Commodities: The Trouble with Trade in Sex, Children, Body Parts, and Other Things.* Cambridge, MA: Harvard University Press, 1996.

Radner, John B. "The Youthful Harlot's Curse: The Prostitute as Symbol of the City in 18th-Century English Literature." *ECL* 2 (1976): 59–64.

Ragussis, Michael. "Jews and Other 'Outlandish Englishmen': Ethnic Performance and the Invention of British Identity under the Georges," *Critical Inquiry* 26, no. 4 (2000): 773–797.

Rashid, Salim. "Mandeville's *Fable: Laissez-faire* or Libertinism?" *ECS* 18, no. 3 (1985): 313–330.

Raynie, Stephen. "Hayman and Gravelot's Anti-Pamela Designs for Richarson's Octavo Edition of *Pamela*." *ECL* 23, no. 3 (1999): 77–93.

Rees, Christine. "Gay, Swift, and the Nymphs of Drury-Lane." *Essays in Criticism* 23 (1973): 1–21.

Rees, Siân. *The Floating Brothel: The Extraordinary True Story of an Eighteenth-Century Ship and Its Cargo of Female Convicts.* New York: Hyperion, 2002.

Rennie, Neil. *Far-Fetched Facts: The Literature of Travel and the Idea of the South Seas.* Oxford: Clarendon Press, 1995.

Richetti, John J. "The Family, Sex, and Marriage in Defoe's *Moll Flanders* and *Roxana*." *Studies in the Literary Imagination* 15 (1982): 19–35.

———. "Ideology and Literary Form in Fielding's *Tom Jones*." In *Ideology and Form in Eighteenth-Century Literature*, edited by David H. Richter, 31–46. Lubbock: Texas Tech University Press, 1999.

———. *Popular Fiction before Richardson: Narrative Patterns 1700–1739.* Oxford: Clarendon Press, 1969.

Roach, Joseph. *Cities of the Dead: Circum-Atlantic Performance.* New York: Columbia University Press, 1996.

Rogal, Samuel J. "The Selling of Sex: Mandeville's Modest Defence of Publick Stews." *SECC* 5 (1976): 141–150.

Rogers, Katharine. "The Feminism of Daniel Defoe." In *Woman in the 18th Century and Other Essays*, edited by Paul Fritz and Richard Morton, 3–24. Toronto: Hakkert, 1976.

Rogers, Shef. "Composing Conscience: *The Injured Islanders* (1779) and English Sensibility." *The Eighteenth Century: Theory and Interpretation* 38, no. 3 (1997): 259–265.

Rosenberg, Nathan. "Mandeville and Laissez-Faire." *Journal of the History of Ideas* 24 (1963): 183–196.

Rosenthal, Laura J. "The Whore's Estate: Sally Salisbury, Prostitution, and Property in Eighteenth-Century London." In *Women, Property, and the Letters of the Law in Early Modern England*, edited by Margaret W. Ferguson, A. R. Buck, and Nancy Wright, 95–120. Toronto: University of Toronto Press, 2004.

Rothstein, Eric. "Virtues of Authority in Tom Jones." *The Eighteenth Century: Theory and Interpretation* 28, no. 2 (1987): 99–126.

Rubin, Gayle. "Thinking Sex: Notes for a Radical Theory of the Politics of Sexuality." In *Pleasure and Danger: Exploring Female Sexuality*, edited by Carole S. Vance, 267–319. Boston: Routledge & Kegan Paul, 1984.

Rule, John. *The Experience of Labour in Eighteenth Century English Industry.* New York: St. Martin's Press, 1981.

Sabor, Peter. "From Sexual Liberation to Gender Trouble." *ECS* 33, no. 4 (2000): 561–578.

Sacks, Sheldon. "Clarissa and the Tragic Traditions." In *Irrationalism in the Eighteenth Century*, edited by Harold E. Pagliaro, 195–221. Cleveland: Case Western Reserve University Press, 1972.

Scheuermann, Mona. *Her Bread to Earn: Women, Money, and Society from Defoe to Austen.* Lexington: University Press of Kentucky, 1993.

Sekora, John. *Luxury: The Concept in Western Thought, Eden to Smollett.* Baltimore: Johns Hopkins University Press, 1977.

Shapiro, James. *Shakespeare and the Jews.* New York: Columbia University Press, 1996.

Sherman, Sandra. *Finance and Fictionality in the Early Eighteenth Century: Accounting for Defoe.* Cambridge: Cambridge University Press, 1996.

———. "Lady Credit No Lady; or, the Case of Defoe's 'Coy Mistress,' Truly Stat'd." *Texas Studies in Literature and Language* 37, no. 2 (1995): 185–214.

Shoemaker, Robert B. "Reforming the City: The Reformation of Manners Campaign in London, 1690–1738." In *Stilling the Grumbling Hive: The Response to Social and Economic Problems in England, 1689–1750*, edited by Tim Hitchcock, Lee Davison, Tim Keirn, and Robert B. Shoemaker, 99–120. New York: St. Martin's, 1992.

Shrage, Laurie. *Moral Dilemmas of Feminism: Prostitution, Adultery, and Abortion.* New York: Routledge, 1994.

Skinner, Gillian. *Sensibility and Economics in the Novel, 1740–1800: The Price of a Tear.* New York: St. Martin's, 1999.

Snow, Malinda. "Arguments to the Self in Defoe's *Roxana*." *SEL* 34, no. 3 (1994): 523–536.

Speck, W. A. "Bernard Mandeville and the Middlesex Grand Jury." *ECS* 11, no. 3 (1978): 362–374.

———. "The Harlot's Progress in Eighteenth-Century England." *The British Journal for Eighteenth-Century Studies* 3 (1980): 127–139.

———. "Mandeville and the Eutopia Seated in the Brain." In *Mandeville Studies: New Explorations in the Art and Thought of Dr. Bernard Mandeville*, edited by Irwin Primer, 66–79. The Hague: Martinus Nijhoff, 1975.

Staves, Susan. "British Seduced Maidens." In *The Past as Prologue: Essays to Celebrate the Twenty-Fifth Anniversary of ASECS*, edited by Carla Hay with Syndy M. Conger, 91–113. New York: AMS Press, 1995.

Stevenson, John Allen. "Black George and the Black Act." *Eighteenth-Century Fiction* 8, no. 3 (1996): 355–382.

———. "'Never in a Vile House': Knowledge and Experience in Richardson." *Literature and Psychology* 34, no. 1 (1988): 4–16.

———. "Tom Jones and the Stuarts." *ELH* 61, no. 3 (1994): 571–595.

Stewart, Douglas J. "Pornography, Obscenity, and Capitalism." *Antioch Review* 35 (1977): 389–398.

Stewart, Maaja A. "Ingratitude in Tom Jones," *Journal of English and Germanic Philology* 89, no. 4 (1990): 512–532.

Stone, Lawrence. *The Family, Sex, and Marriage in England 1500–1800.* New York: Harper & Row, 1979.

Stuber, Florian. "On Original and Final Intentions, or Can There Be an Authoritative *Clarissa?" Text: Transactions of the Society for Textual Scholarship* 2 (1985): 229–244.

Thompson, E. P. *Customs in Common.* New York: W. W. Norton, 1991.

———. *The Making of the English Working Class.* New York: Pantheon Book, 1964.

———. *Whigs and Hunters: The Origin of the Black Act.* New York: Pantheon Books, 1975.

Thompson, James. *Models of Value: Eighteenth-Century Political Economy and the Novel.* Durham: Duke University Press, 1996.

Thompson, Lynda M. *The 'Scandalous Memoirists': Constantia Phillips and Laetitia Pilkington and the Shame of 'Public Fame'.* Manchester: Manchester University Press, 2000.

Thompson, Peggy. "Abuse and Atonement: The Passion of Clarissa Harlowe." *Eighteenth-Century Fiction* 11, no. 3 (1999): 255–270.

Thompson, Roger. *Unfit for Modest Ears.* Totowa, NJ: Rowman and Littlefield, 1979.

Traugott, John. "*Clarissa's* Richardson: An Essay to Find the Reader." In *English Literature in the Age of Disguise,* edited by Max Novak, 157–202. Berkeley: University of California Press, 1977.

Trumbach, Randolph. "Modern Prostitution and Gender in *Fanny Hill:* Libertine and Domesticated Fantasy." In *Sexual Underworlds of the Enlightenment,* edited by G. S. Rousseau and Roy Porter, 69–85. Manchester: Manchester University Press, 1987.

———. *Sex and the Gender Revolution.* Vol. 1, *Heterosexuality and the Third Gender in Enlightenment London.* Chicago: University of Chicago Press, 1998.

Trumpener, Katie. "Rewriting Roxanne: Orientalism and Intertextuality in Montesquieu's *Lettres Persanes* and Defoe's *The Fortunate Mistress." Stanford French Review* 11, no. 2 (1987): 177–191.

Turner, James Grantham. *Libertines and Radicals in Early Modern London: Sexuality, Politics, and Literary Culture, 1630–1685.* Cambridge: Cambridge University Press, 2002.

———. "Lovelace and the Paradoxes of Libertinism." In *Samuel Richardson Tercentenary Essays,* edited by Margaret Anne Doody and Peter Sabor, 70–88. Cambridge: Cambridge University Press, 1989.

———. "'News from the New Exchange': Commodity, Erotic Fantasy, and the Female Entrepreneur." In *The Consumption of Culture, 1600–1800,* edited by Ann Bermingham and John Brewer, 419–439. New York: Routledge, 1995.

———. "Novel Panic: Picture and Performance in the Reception of Richardson's *Pamela." Representations* 48 (1994): 70–96.

———. "Pictorial Prostitution: Visual Culture, Vigilantism, and Pornography in Dunton's *Night-Walker." SECC* 28 (1999): 55–84.

———. "*The Whore's Rhetorick:* Narrative, Pornography, and the Origins of the Novel." *SECC* 24 (1995): 297–306.

Unsworth, John. "*Tom Jones:* The Comedy of Knowledge." *MLQ* 48, no. 3 (1987): 242–253.

Van Ghent, Dorothy. *The English Novel: Form and Function.* New York: Harper and Row, 1953.

Van Sant, Ann Jessie. *Eighteenth-Century Sensibility and the Novel: The Senses in Social Context.* Cambridge: Cambridge University Press, 1993.

Vichert, Gordon S. "Bernard Mandeville's *The Virgin Unmask'd.*" In *Mandeville Studies: New Explorations in the Art and Thought of Dr. Bernard Mandeville (1670–1733),* edited by Irwin Primer, 1–10. The Hague: Martinus Nijhoff, 1975.

Walkowitz, Judith R. *Prostitution and Victorian Society: Women, Class, and the State.* Cambridge: Cambridge University Press, 1980.

Wallace, Lee. "Too Darn Hot: Sexual Contact in the Sandwich Islands on Cook's Third Voyage." *ECL* 18, no. 3 (1994): 232–242.

Warner, William B. *Licensing Entertainment: The Elevation of Novel Reading in Britain, 1684–1750*. Berkeley: University of California Press, 1998.

Weber, Harold. "Carolinean Sexuality and the Restoration Stage: Reconstructing the Royal Phallus in Sodom." In *Cultural Readings of Restoration and Eighteenth-Century English Theatre*, edited by J. Douglas Canfield and Deborah Payne Fiske, 67–88. Athens: University of Georgia Press, 1995.

Wiegman, Robyn. "Economies of the Body: Gendered Sites in *Robinson Crusoe* and *Roxana*." *Criticism* 31, no. 1 (1989): 33–51.

Westfall, Marilyn. "A Sermon by the 'Queen of Whores'." *SEL* 41, no. 3 (2001): 483–497.

Wheatley, Christopher J. *Beneath Ierne's Banners: Irish Protestant Drama of the Restoration and Eighteenth Century*. Notre Dame, IN: University of Notre Dame Press, 1999.

Wilt, Judith. "He Could Go No Farther: A Modest Proposal about Lovelace and Clarissa." *PMLA* 92, no. 1 (1977): 19–32.

Zhang, John Z. "Defoe's 'Man-Woman' Roxana: Gender, Reversal, and Androgyny." *Etudes Anglaises* 46, no. 3 (1993): 271–288.

Žižek, Slavoj. *The Sublime Object of Ideology*. New York: Verso, 1989.

Zomchick, John P. *Family and the Law in Eighteenth-Century Fiction: The Public Conscience in the Private Sphere*. Cambridge: Cambridge University Press, 1993.

Index

Abbott, John Lawrence, 235 n36
abjection, 27–28, 64–65, 99, 130; in *Clarissa*; 142–153, 157, 208
accumulation, 8, 9, 28, 72, 74, 77, 80, 86, 121, 141, 190
Addison, Joseph, 43, 44
Adventures of Melinda, The, 138
alienation, 8, 14–15, 16, 18, 20, 28–29, 33, 68, 93, 100, 128, 153; from the body, 9, 56, 86, 90, 109, 115–116, 117, 155, 172; prostitution as the alienation of labor, 19, 30, 36, 199, 210–212
Anderson, Amanda, 7
Andrews, Donna, 224 n6
androgyny, 10, 91, 154
Annet, Peter, 217 n44
anti-*Pamela* controversy, 36–41
anti-semitism, 70–73, 74–88, 202–208
Appleby, Joyce, 3, 216 n12
Aravamuden, Srinivas, 3
Archenholz, J. W., 99, 107
Aretino, Pietro, 125, 186, 187, 216 n33
Armstrong, Nancy, 6, 36, 100, 153
Armstrong, Nancy and Lennard Tennen-house, 124, 126
Asia, supposed treatment of women in, 208

Bahlman, Dudley, 47
Balme, Christopher B., 186
Banks, Joseph, 181, 184, 188, 193–194
Barbon, Nicolas, 59

Batchelor, Jennie, 226–227 n47
bawds, 23–25, 27–28, 30–32, 37, 38, 43–44, 55–56, 78, 79–80, 97, 101, 115, 117–118, 121–123, 126, 137, 165; Mother Cresswell in *The Whore's Rhetorick*, 30–33, 34, 35, 37, 41, 56, 73, 96, 115–116, 160; Mrs. Sinclair in *Clarissa*, 143–145
bawdy house riots, 21, 219 n32
bawdy houses, 18, 49, 51, 104, 109, 110, 113, 129
Behn, Aphra, 212; *The Feigned Courtesans*, 22; *The Lucky Chance*, 162–163; *Oroonoko*, 26, 149–150; *The Rover* 17–18, 21–22, 28, 32, 41, 96
Beswick, Lavinia, 97
Bisset, William, 48, 52, 55, 161
Bland, James, 161, 214 n14
body: alienation from the, *see* alienation; boundaries of the, 143–145, 149, 151, 178; destruction of the, 101, 116; dismember-ment of the, 70–71; eighteenth-century reconceptualization of the female, 9, 212; eroticized, 62, 86, 171; objectification and/or instrumental use of the, 28, 34, 42, 101, 108, 115–116, 118–119, 120, 122, 211; ownership of the, 20, 75, 101, 136–137; pleasures of the, 171; sale of the, 19, 20, 138
Boswell, James, 231 n6
Bougainville, Louis de, *Voyage round the World*, 189, 191, 192